THE
PARINAMA
METHOD

THE PARINAMA METHOD

Transform Everything

A PRACTICAL AND PHILOSOPHICAL GUIDE

KATIE BICKFORD

Sometimes we have the absolute certainty there's something inside us that's so hideous and monstrous that if we ever search it out we won't be able to stand looking at it. But it's when we're willing to come face to face with that demon that we face the angel.

—Hubert Selby, Jr.

Contact information for Parinama LLC

Email: hello@parinama.info
Website: www.theparinamamethod.com
LinkedIn: www.linkedin.com/company/parinama-llc
Instagram: @theparinamamethod

Cover and text design by Sheila Parr
Cover images © Shutterstock

Library of Congress Control Number: 2022946700
Paperback ISBN: 979-8-9861439-0-3
eBook ISBN: 979-8-9861439

CONTENTS

PREFACE

IT'S HARD TO PIN down exactly when it all started because in a sense, I've been developing *The Parinama Method: Transform Everything—A Practical and Philosophical Guide* for most of my life. I can say that it began with my knowing there was a question I had to answer—I just didn't know what the question was. I had been straddling the business world and an ongoing quest to understand myself through all manner of esoteric practices, and I knew I needed something to help me form my inquiry.

Thankfully, I found Anodea Judith's *Eastern Body, Western Mind: Psychology and the Chakra System as a Path to the Self,* and it fit the bill in several ways. The Parinama Method's framework is in the main due to Judith's impressive work. But what I needed was a book that was more applicable to my life—one grounded in the practicalities I faced daily as a business leader and city dweller. I came to realize that Toni Morrison was, of course, right: "If there's a book you want to read, but it hasn't been written yet, then you must write it." The problem was, I didn't know how to write a book. And then I did it. It took over three years.

Among myriad other considerations, the process involved many hundreds of hours of research and interviews with over 100 people (in addition to the thousands from throughout my career who also inspired insights and inspiration). I also spoke with numerous professionals in the fields of psychology and development; ran both in-person and virtual Parinama Method practice groups; and used the Method as a consultant with professional teams in technology companies (to great result).

The Parinama Method begins with the notion that whatever calls to you is (very) real—and that what holds you back from it is both the practicality of physical survival and the falsehoods you've been told about who and what you are, passed down by people who were also lied to. Your extraordinary existence is a miracle—just as it is for everyone else you know—and the trick is to come to understand this so you can simultaneously hold compassion, boundary, hope, ambition, conviction, and a radical level of acceptance as you bravely proceed forward.

In these pages, you'll find a step-by-step, level-by-level, practical process for how to access and activate everything that's already within you. You'll understand how to excavate the unexplored, unknown, yet significant depths of your constitution. With curiosity, wonder, and awe, you'll be able to observe the marvel of *you* as the intrepid explorer who dares to touch the depths of the ocean, travel into subterranean earth and the periphery of the known cosmos, and revel in the lushest and wildest wildernesses. This is it, and it's where you'll go with *The Parinama Method.*

We grow and develop in a synchronized chronology, and there's a sequence of biological, neurological, and psychological development that progress in concert. We're raised within environmental conditions and circumstances that shape us when we're most malleable. It's through conscious reclamation that we can both see and travel within ourselves to play an active role in shaping how we experience our life by reconciling layer after layer of reflexes passed down (unknowingly) from one generation to the next.

Each stage of our development has a corresponding physicality, and by turning to your subconscious and speaking the language of the body-mind, which is sensation and movement, you extend a hand back to yourself and become either the hero you've been waiting for or the ideal family member and mentor through profound acts of presence, receiving, and generosity for yourself. We can't talk to the earliest layers within us because they're preverbal—they didn't learn through words, but through feeling. However, we *can* understand these layers and facets by using our mature, advanced cognitive functions that are capable of translating what we learn and know into the language of the body. You will communicate with the deepest, sweetest layers of who and what you are, both divine and mundane, practical and philosophical—the evolution of life itself, consciousness trying to know itself through an embodied experience.

This consciousness is hard work because it pushes on the outer limits of our nervous system's capability; the efficiency of reflexes dominates our lives, but consciousness is the leading edge of our biological technology. To be here, right now, is a chance to sign up for the work of advancing the evolution of humanity that's happening within our acts of awareness.

The Parinama Method illuminates the repeating patterns and blind spots that keep affecting our lives. It was my work with people from different backgrounds, cultures, and experiences all around the world that revealed these similar patterns to me, all working within the same very human themes. The Method also incorporates decades of working with and seeing the same struggles I was facing reflected in the experiences of so many others. I didn't know where the repeating patterns came from, yet they kept showing up for me no matter how many superficial changes I made in my life. So, I started a process of going deep into my inner recesses to explore the subterranean aspects of myself that had sometimes led to some perplexing behavior. The bottom line is that we all survive, and depending on the conditions of our circumstances, we can do things that are against what we know is at the core of our integrity—I certainly did.

There are a few things I now know, and one of them is that although our reflexes and repetitive thoughts will have us believe otherwise, there's something much grander and marvelous going on, and that your life is a part of it. There's nothing wrong with you and you don't need fixing—you may just need some focused consciousness and somatic practices to get under the surface.

While I was writing this, I imagined you reading it and was lifted and encouraged by the thought. And although it was only in my imagination, it's this moment I'm so grateful for—that you're here now, reading these words. It's my hope that you will feel the love and care that's here for you in *The Parinama Method*.

—Katie Bickford
April 2022

Part 1

THE PARINAMA METHOD

Chapter 1

THE METHOD—AN INTRODUCTION

Finally I am coming to the conclusion that my highest ambition is to be what I already am. That I will never fulfill my obligation to surpass myself unless I first accept myself, and if I accept myself fully in the right way, I will already have surpassed myself.
—Thomas Merton

YOU AND YOUR LIFE are not a series of problems to be solved. You are not a math test, a sequence of equations that need to be resolved using the correct calculations. Your life is a poem, a walk in the woods through valleys and over mountaintops with dark parts, lush areas, the tang of rot and musk blending with the air, the sun on your skin or in the rain, and muscles burning. Your life is to be lived and experienced with all these elements—sunlight, darkness, musk, verdancy, rot, and fresh air.

Our life path, like the walk in the woods, leads us through all sorts of experiences that are affected by preference for pleasure, comfort, and challenge. Buddha taught his followers that obstacles are the path, and that discomfort and hurdles are essential to our experience—think of how, when we feel lost, discomfort can act as our inner trail guide, steering and pointing out the correct course through life's swampy undergrowth and around its slippery rocks—a diviner that tells us to pay attention or that we're going the wrong way.

The Sanskrit word *parinama* refers to transformation that's both practical and philosophical—it can be both contemplative and applied. Perhaps you can remember seeing water pooled in a gutter with an iridescent rainbow floating on it. The colors shift, combine, then shift again, and every new arrangement is complex and beautiful, an ever-changing puddle of water and pollution demonstrating perspective, paradox, and ambiguity. It's showing you infinite ways to see the same phenomenon arising from the same matter, and all you have to do is look. Similar to life, things that feel final and absolute in one moment will change, revealing more layers and complexities. Insights can show themselves over and over in infinite manifestations—all magnificent, all different, yet somehow all the same. This is *being in the parinama*: staying with it, waiting for clarity to emerge, a next revelation—a new perspective, a new insight. The same shifting matter reveals something new again and again. The parinama of it all is the field of curiosity between the practicality of direct experience and the mysteries at the edge of comprehension. This is where you reconnect with the spark that started everything, the spark of life that contains all that you are and the infinite potential of all that you can become.

The reflexive will to survive begins at birth, and the functions for reasoning and judgment slowly emerge throughout childhood but don't fully develop until our mid-20s. Because they came first, our safety and survival reflexes have seniority, and their rip-current force continues to pull us toward security and away from the uncertainty of trying and creating new things.

Physical safety (a condition) and security (a state) are essential and often misunderstood and maligned as a lack of bravery instead of being respected for what they are: the required foundation for the survival of all human life. You live because you're programmed to survive, and your nervous system sees change as a risk to your safety, creating inner tension that activates the deep, biological reflexes of survival. Two common apprehensions about having an enlivened, energized, and peaceful life of purpose are that it demands a drastic change (a radical transformation) and that you must become a different person from the one you are now—yet change can happen gradually, and you will always be who you are. Further adding to this tension is the unknown—when we make a change, we know the past we're giving up, but we can only speculate about what the future holds.

The Parinama Method is a how-to manual for showing up for yourself. It provides you with a framework and a method for balancing the stability of what feels safe while accessing, activating, and optimizing joy, creativity, love, and accomplishment.

DĄBROWSKI'S THEORY OF POSITIVE DISINTEGRATION

Everyone has a unique essence and a unique destiny, both of which are bigger and broader than your safety-survival reflexes want you to know. Essence and destiny can reveal themselves in dreams or in feelings, such as envy and longing when seeing others who have what you want for yourself. Our safety reflexes are very powerful, and if you attempt to override or ignore them without considering the value they provide by keeping us alive, they fight harder. But if you work *with* the need for physical safety, it provides the grounding, boundaries, and consistency necessary for the transformation process.

Whatever it is that burns inside you—a creative longing (writing a book), a professional goal (starting a business), any type of calling (becoming a teacher) or personal objective (more free time to enjoy life)—is a message that's unique to you. How you imagine this desire may change, but the underlying nature of the impulse doesn't. If feelings of fear, anxiety, worthlessness, low energy, or pain are getting in your way, consider psychologist Kazimierz Dąbrowski's Theory of Positive Disintegration.

Dąbrowski developed the theory to explain how a person's difficult experiences can result in important personal development. The disintegration he referred to is a forcing function for surrender and the abandoning of behaviors, patterns, and attitudes that are blocking us from our true self. The resulting shift is regarded as positive because we increase our capacity to contain such experiences, gaining greater perspective, insight, and wisdom. This disintegration can be the falling away of defenses and survival adaptations—those behavior patterns formed early in life that once protected you, but no longer serve you. It's a difficult process to endure in the short term, but holding on to these stockpiled experiences ultimately hurts worse in the long term.

Dąbrowski believed in Plato's idea of essence—an individual's essence is a critical determinant of the person's course in life. One's essence sometimes needs to be realized through turbulent life experiences. Dąbrowski viewed psychological tension and anxiety as necessary for growth: disintegrative processes that are ultimately positive. He also agreed with Socrates' statement that an unexamined life is not worth living and believed that people who fail to go through positive disintegration may spend their entire lives in a state that he called "primary integration," that is, lacking true individuality, stuck in a life taken only at face value. So, take comfort in knowing there's potential for growth and personal evolution available in any situation.

THE BODY-MIND

Our brain is a first-come, first-served organ. Even if the so-called higher functions of logic, planning, contemplation, and memory believe they're running the show, the parts of our brain that do the thinking are chronologically the last to develop. Our first conscious memory is formed after many years of the so-called lower brain simultaneously growing and running the complex suite of functions that keep us alive. These reflexes and automatically regulating functions responsible for maintaining life since before birth have seniority and get served first because they're reflexive—they're fast and act without hesitation. Ask your higher executive (thinking) brain to get involved with operating your kidney and it doesn't know how, or ask it how to respond to a surprise attack and it's too slow. But ask the executive-thinking functions to consciously evaluate and reshape behavior you wish to change, and transformation becomes possible. This is the body-mind: reflexes and conscious action working together.

When we begin to unlock, restore, and develop greater functioning of the body-mind working in concert, it's important to respect all levels of our brain to achieve greater harmony and coherence within ourselves. Psychologist Mihaly Csikszentmihalyi used the term "flow states," that is, "optimal experiences," to describe people in highly focused mental states conducive to productivity as being "so involved in an activity that nothing else seems to matter." It's the feeling we have of great absorption, engagement, fulfillment, and skill, often when ignoring concerns for time, food, and other common preoccupations. But without a sense of safety and security, we cannot relax, so when we respect and understand the parts of our brain responsible for survival, we can consciously work toward growing our capacity to feel secure and invite flow states to become possible and more frequent.

Our first memory is a clue to when higher brain function began to develop. In our early years, the advanced functions exist on our developmental road map as potential, while other areas of our brain are present and active—the preverbal, ancient technology of reflex, automatic regulation, reaction, and response operates with little to no conscious effort. Neuroscientist Paul MacLean developed a simplified model of the brain—the triune brain—which is divided by development, function, and evolutionary history in three groups: reflex, emotion, and logic (see Figure 1.1). This is both the sequence in which the brain evolved and the sequence of its chronological development throughout life. And while our adult brain is always thinking, our reflexes take keeping us alive very seriously and attempt to override anything that puts us in uncertainty or danger—such as any type of change, large or small.

Survival State
BRAIN STEM

The Survival State represents the primal brain and asks the question, *"Am I safe?"* The only way to soothe the Survival State is through the creation of *Safety*.

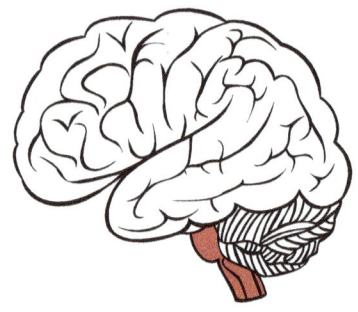

Emotional State
LIMBIC SYSTEM

This Brain State represents mid-level functionality and asks the question, *"Am I loved?"* The only way to soothe an upset emotional state is through *Connection*.

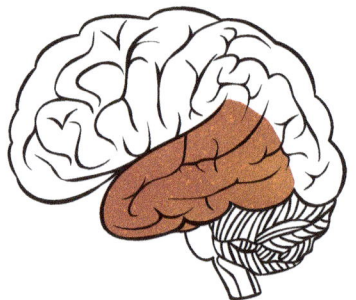

Executive State
PREFRONTAL LOBES

The Executive State represents the optimal state for problem-solving and learning. This Brain State asks the question, *"What can I learn from this?"*

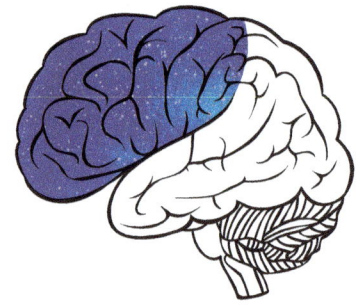

Figure 1.1: The Triune Brain: Reflex, Emotion, and Thinking

Source: Arizona Department of Education, at https://www.azed.gov/improvement/conscious-discipline.

THE TRIUNE BRAIN

A human brain is the most advanced three pounds of technology on the planet. We share many brain functions with other animals, but it's the executive function of our prefrontal lobe that provides the unique capability for innovation and change, separating us from all other living beings. The brain stem and limbic system have powerful reflexes and responses that are activated to automatically protect us when they detect lack of familiarity or change, including the associated danger in taking the risk of doing things differently (innovation). Of course, there are exceptions to this reflexive avoidance, such as when we need to innovate and change to survive or if we're so physically safe (usually meaning financially) that the cost of taking risks can be managed without significant consequences.

The brain stem regulates the body's complex automatic functions, such as temperature, hunger, and the integrated activities of all organ systems. It has the reflexive synchronization with nature we see in a lizard (hence the term "lizard brain") but, contrary to the implication of its lower position, it's an intelligence of a higher order. It doesn't require conscious management and it only understands the present moment, existing in the unified field of presence without effort. Metaphorically, it's the large, unblinking eye of a salamander staring back at you before the amphibian darts away if startled—a fear reflex and survival response. Your brain stem is a savant that can't speak or read, yet it can oversee the complexity of operating a human body. It's the part of your brain that holds deep knowledge, has a direct relationship with your body, and access to its buried truths. Your secrets are safe there, and they only get revealed when conscious inquiry occurs and trust is established.

The limbic system, also known as the mammalian brain (or emotional state), functions through connection to others and the world around us. This is the part of your brain that feels and responds with emotional and physical movement. Pleasure and pain are felt and processed, usually followed by responsive action. If the brain were a house, the stem would manage utilities—water, electricity, and heat—while the limbic system would cook, comfort, and make the house a home. These areas of your brain contain much of your unique profile of preferences and aversions, and although this can be reflexive, it can also be managed and moderated by the higher functions found in the prefrontal lobes, also called the prefrontal cortex (PFC).

The prefrontal lobes and executive function are the source of language, contemplation, creation, thinking, learning, memory, and a suite of other remarkable functions. There are two prefrontal lobes: the left and the right hemispheres. The left hemisphere performs a fascinating crossover because it controls the right side of the body and is responsible for logic, language, analytics, and order—activities like reading, writing, computation, and telling time. The right hemisphere controls the left side of the body and is responsible for visual awareness, imagination, spatial abilities, facial recognition, music awareness, and interpreting social cues. Trauma researcher Bessel van der Kolk writes in *The Body Keeps the Score* about brain-imaging studies revealing that patients with posttraumatic stress disorder (PTSD) have reduced activity in their left hemispheres—the logical brain matter that performs and processes time and chronology. This accounts for these patients' sense that traumatic events continue to happen long after they've passed, causing the distressing inability to view them with a historical perspective.

CONSCIOUS, SUBCONSCIOUS, AND UNCONSCIOUS

The frontal lobes are not only the last to fully develop, they're also the first to degenerate with memory loss. Most of what's considered consciousness is the functioning of the prefrontal lobes. But if (or when) we drop into deeper states of feeling and presence, the conscious mind reveals itself as the tip of the iceberg. The experiences of pleasure and peace reveal layers of ourselves beneath thought. The conscious mind (what we know) is primarily related to the frontal lobes of our brain. The subconscious mind (what we sort of know) is primarily the limbic system and the body. The unconscious mind (what we definitely don't know) is inaccessible information deeply coded in the brain stem, such as how to operate and manage organ function and how to breathe. We can use our conscious mind to understand and respect the reflexes of the brain stem and the even deeper knowledge of what Carl Jung believed is stored and transferred between generations—a notion that has been modernized with epigenetics, the study of inherited patterns of gene expression.

The conflict between the conscious, innovative, thinking brain that wants change and the unwavering survival programming of its unconscious functions that keeps us safe and alive can hold us in the same patterns throughout our lives. Like a shopping cart with a wonky wheel, many of us can relate to wanting to change and then getting pulled back into old patterns even when we try to steer away from them. The conscious mind is like our hands on the cart, and the subconscious self is the programming stored in the body that pulls away. This dissonance is part of the human experience, and the conscious mind gets blamed for self-sabotaging behaviors and chastised as moral or ethical weakness. The unconscious and subconscious programing deep within our body-mind follows the directions from its earliest programming while the conscious mind gets shamed and punished. The Parinama Method seeks to understand the role of subconscious information stored in our body (linked to the limbic system and brain stem) with our conscious mind (frontal lobes) and helps us work through coherent and concerted action to unify the conscious, subconscious, and unconscious through the process of conscious reclamation.

AUTONOMIC AND SOMATIC

The nervous system is organized by involuntary (autonomic) and voluntary (somatic) functioning. The reflexive functions, often referred to as involuntary, are part of the autonomic nervous system—autonomic is automatic. Conversely, our voluntary movements are the actions of the somatic nervous system. The involuntary functions are mostly governed below the subconscious by the unconscious. The voluntary functions are affected by everything—conscious, subconscious, and unconscious. There are bridges for transformation between all levels of the triune brain made accessible by conscious, voluntary action.

The autonomic nervous system regulates reflexes and responses for both excitation and relaxation: for excitation, functions like increased heart rate and breathing, and for relaxation, functions like sleep and healing. The excitation responses are labeled "sympathetic," and the rest and repair are labeled "parasympathetic." Both sympathetic and parasympathetic are automatic functions operating primarily out of the reflexive lizard brain: neither activation nor relaxation understand abstract thinking, so they don't understand time (recall the left frontal lobe relationship with trauma) or the difference between a memory and anticipation. These responses to anything seen in the mind's eye are experienced as if they're happening in the present moment. Perhaps this is why worry and fixation on a stressful memory create stress in the body, whether or not there's an active threat. Chronic stress is a uniquely human experience—most biological organisms use stress as an acute mechanism for reflexive action to support survival. If you remain activated in a low-grade stress response for long periods of time, your nervous system doesn't do parasympathetic functions to support your long-term health like good rest, good digestion, healing, sex, and reproduction because the sense of immediate threat takes precedence. The difference between a pleasantly activating stimulation versus a distressing and overwhelming stress response is an important one that I discuss in *The Parinama Method* (see Chapter 2).

Actions based on conscious decisions, such as trying a new recipe, choosing to go for a walk, or trying a new route for your work commute, are voluntary functions of the somatic nervous system. The ratio of voluntary-to-involuntary and conscious-to-unconscious functioning is humbling. Different estimates have most humans consciously operating their lives between 5 and 10 percent of the time, which means our life is between 90 and 95 percent subconscious and unconscious—most of our life is governed by the early programming of our reflexes.

So, how do you access more of your nervous system? By finding the somatic bridges between the conscious, subconscious, and unconscious: one significant bridge is breath, an automatic function linked to the stress response of elevated heart rate and respiration, which can be slowed down with conscious control. An inhale is biochemically linked to the activating, sympathetic response, and an exhale is linked to the relaxation of the parasympathetic response. Yogic breathwork, called "pranayama," uses breath to balance, relax, and stimulate the nervous system. When the inhalation is emphasized, we tend to become more alert. If you want to encourage a relaxation response, elongate the exhale.

TAMAS, RAJAS, AND SATTVA

Thousands of years ago, human consciousness was mapped and organized by Vedic scholars in India. Vedics thought chakras were like energetic wheels or vortices that were the physical headquarters for each facet of our psyche and self—hubs in which experiences and information are received, incorporated, stored, and expressed. This profound exploration by ancient scholars and mystics happened a long time before human dissection and surgery would reveal bundles of specialized nerves and neuropeptide enrichment centers located near the spinal column corresponding with each hub's unique function. The Vedics, in the tradition of Ayurveda, used the framework of *doshas*, three states of a body: *kapha* (earth), *pita* (fire), and *vatta* (air), considered to be qualities that need to be actively balanced for health and fulfillment. These qualities are also known as *tamas* (earth), *rajas* (fire), and *sattva* (ether), which correspond to rest, work, and contemplation.

In our Western lives, we tend to place highest value on the fiery, rajasic state of activity and action and to resist the heavy, earthy tamasic states of rest, digestion, healing, and repair, which often carry a stigma of laziness. And often there can be a limited tendency, if there is one at all, to cultivate the ethereal, sattvic state of contemplation, meditation, and peace—we experience sattva in moments of grace. The time spent in study or in dedication to spiritual practices is sattvic—when practical considerations are not emphasized, and energy is primarily focused on knowledge and transcendence. There are seasons in life for all these states, but the denial of our tamasic needs of rest, relaxation, and recovery creates a compounding effect on our health, leading to burnout and other health-related problems.

When we're chronically activating the nervous system with stimulation and stress, it's only a matter of time before the body will find a way to restore itself through illness or incapacitation.

NEUROPEPTIDES: THE EMOTION MOLECULES

René Descartes launched centuries of dissociation between the body and mind (*I think therefore I am,* known as Cartesian dualism), a separation so preposterous that it would require centuries of indoctrination to believe it's possible. This philosophical position states that the (conscious) mind exerts absolute control over the body, although this insistence on humans having a central position in the Universe has never landed on the right side of history (I discuss Galileo in Chapter 9). Comedian Emo Philips says, "I used to think that the brain was the most wonderful organ in my body. Then I realized who was telling me this." The Earth circles the Sun, and the body exerts more than a passing influence on the brain; science has shown us through the actions of hormones and neuropeptides how the brain takes direction from the body, and the body from the brain.

Neuropharmacology professor Candace Pert, who discovered the opioid receptor and the HIV treatment Peptide T, asserted that our body *is* our subconscious—meaning that to unlock deeper truths (those deeper than episodic memories), we should look to our physical body. Pert's *Molecules of Emotion: The Science Behind Mind-Body Medicine* chronicles her career and discovery of the biological chemicals that form bridges between the body and the mind. Her clinical explorations found that neuropeptides shift emotional pain into physical tension and physical rigidity triggered by environmental and emotional stressors by signaling tissues to cut off oxygen. Pert observed that the mind will wall off unpalatable emotions and made the fascinating revelation that the heart has the same neurotransmitter receptors as the brain. According to Pert, a healthy body is "changing, not stuck" and "flexible, not rigid."

The nervous system and the body are an ecosystem containing many functions working in concert. Communication within the body is carried out by neuropeptides, hormones, and electrical signals. The emotion molecules are part of the nervous system and are found communicating and responding throughout the body on a wide variety of cell surfaces, forming a connective bridge between our biology and our lived experience by storing it in the tissues of our body.

Another class of molecules playing a significant role in our body's relationship with its environment is glucocorticoids—stress hormones. These hormones respond to various environmental stimulations; for example, they initiate the fight, flight, or freeze response in the body used by the autonomic nervous system when it's in (sympathetic) activation. These hormones increase blood pressure and redirect energy away from growing, healing, and long-term projects like reproduction. Again, a body under chronic stress exposure gets overstimulation via glucocorticoids, so it will not be able to feel safe enough to truly sleep, digest, or relax. Keep in mind that these stress-response mechanisms existed long before the evolution of abstract thinking (and imagination) and conceptual, contemporary threats like rent, job performance, and traffic. When we concern ourselves with future threats or past hurts, the older brain structures function without time and language, and it senses everything as happening in the present moment and responds using reflexes shaped by experience.

THE HUBS

In the Parinama Method, the seven facets of a human life are organized as hubs that consolidate and organize your unique dispositions and natural inclinations in the following order: HAVE (physical safety and security); FEEL (feeling and emotion); DO (power and individuality); CONNECT (relationship and belonging); SPEAK (communication and self-expression); SEE (vision and imagination); and KNOW (knowledge and wisdom). This method helps build awareness of these hubs as organizing principles and provides you with a guide to support change. Each hub relates to a specific category of experiences and responses in our lives. These seven levels are like specialized vortices stacked from the base of your spine to the top of your head and are connected as a central axis on which your entire life turns (see Figure 1.2). It's where your body, mind, and spirit intersect and become the unified complex of life you're experiencing. Changing your patterns can't only be done with intellect—remember, your body and its nonverbal, deep intelligence has a kill switch for anything threatening what it knows to be familiar.

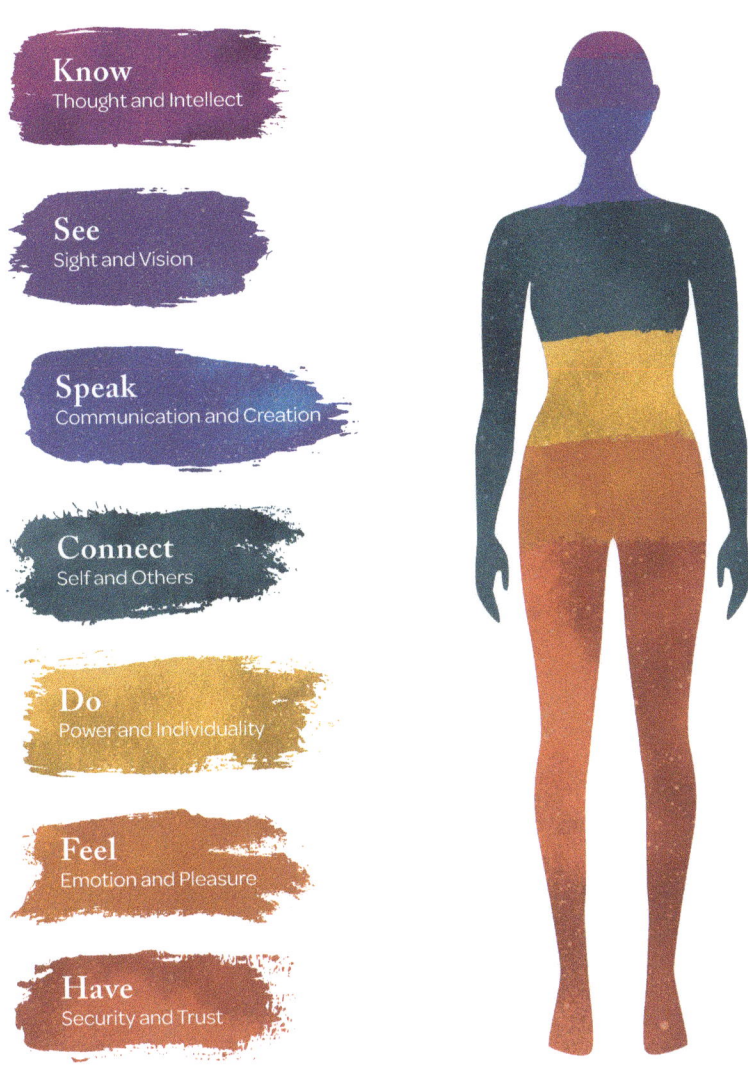

Know
Thought and Intellect

See
Sight and Vision

Speak
Communication and Creation

Connect
Self and Others

Do
Power and Individuality

Feel
Emotion and Pleasure

Have
Security and Trust

Figure 1.2: Locations of the Seven Hubs

Years ago, I was on a panel at a professional women's event and an attendee asked a question that got the audience buzzing: *How can I be more confident?* There were wise and insightful answers from my fellow panelists about how to think about confidence, but I felt compelled to give my hot take on the topic. I was nervous about departing from the other panelists' answers and knew I'd have to do a physical demonstration (at an event where sitting and talking is a professional standard); when we're protecting ourselves from vulnerability, the resistance to moving is strong—protective physical walls can keep us feeling safe.

I said to the audience, "Find your confidence physically by unapologetically taking up space and activating your core." It was a departure from the norm, but I gave a demonstration of standing up and powerfully activating the torso by extending it up and out (like a lighthouse). I explained some of the supporting theory and asked everyone to try it themselves. After the panel, I was surrounded by women excited to tell me about what they had just experienced and how they were going to use it in their upcoming meetings. The hope and excitement I observed in a room full of folks who were having a direct experience with their personal power is one of many early inspirations for writing *The Parinama Method*. But keep in mind, this practice is not a quick fix like the feelings generated in the room that night. To truly grow your capacity in a hub, the practice requires consistency. Holding power for a minute is one thing, but having the strength to sustain it requires ongoing development. As the potential grows, the direct experience becomes richer and larger.

WHAT IS A HUB?

The seven hubs organize, assimilate, integrate, and express the experience of a human life. Before we work with hubs that make you more effective in love, power, communication, and vision, we start with physical safety and security. Psychologist Abraham Maslow's popular hierarchy of needs teaches that before we can transcend to heights of actualization, we must first meet our basic needs, including food, water, warmth, and rest. Safety and security are the foundation for psychological needs of esteem and belonging. Once our physical and psychological needs have been established, achieving our full potential becomes possible. The hubs support this notion, offering a granular inspection and exploration of each hub (complete with practices for development and restoration). Before he died, Maslow added a final stage—self-transcendence—to the top of the hierarchy of needs (see Table 1.1). Above the well-known self-actualization stage, which has long been considered the hierarchy's pinnacle, Maslow came to believe that connecting to something larger than oneself, such as a relationship with God or a life purpose benefiting humanity, was the true top of his pyramid. This development was published in a little-known journal, and because it came close to the end of his life, Maslow didn't get the chance to evangelize this addition to his wildly popular model. The initial hubs correspond to this notion: a solid foundation of our individual physical reality is the platform needed to achieve the fulfillment possible in our lives.

The first recorded history of the exploration of the hubs can be found in the 4,000-year-old framework of the chakras, used as a map of the human experience with seven predominant centers connected to over 100 other minor energetic concentrations. Vedic scholars explained that after death, there's a 49-day journey during which the soul is guided through the exploration of the seven centers. This audit determines if the soul will be reincarnated into another life to do the remaining work within the chakra(s) or if the necessary work has been done and the soul can be released to a higher plane of existence.

The seven Parinama hubs are consolidations of modern developmental psychology, biochemistry, biology, and ancient traditions and practices. They are unique to this method and inspired by the work of therapist Anodea Judith in her book *Eastern Body, Western Mind: Psychology and the Chakra System as a Path to the Self*. Each hub houses specific aspects of the human experience, existing at the intersection of human development, the physical body, and the unique expression of what I call our *embloom* (sometimes referred to as "the witness"): the emblem of our uniqueness that wants to blossom (see Chapter 3).

Many traditions of Asian medicine across many cultures and millennia have studied and documented thousands of energy pathways and centers of concentration. *Nadis*, or energetic pathways, are believed to move like rivers of energy through meridians, which are energetic regions of the body. In Chinese medicine there are over 400 *jingmai* (energy channels) that run along 12 primary routes of energy (qi) that flow within the body. Vedic practitioners and scholars mapped 72,000 Nadis in a human body, counting 114 chakras that involve seven predominant centers. These seven centers are universal and can be found reflected and repeated throughout psychology, the Universe, and the body-mind (see Table 1.1).

All the hubs are present at birth, but each one requires time for its sequential growth to be synchronized with age-appropriate biological development, ultimately leading to adult maturation. Each of your hubs bears a fingerprint of your uniqueness that gets shaped through early family and social programming. Through the process of bringing intentional awareness to them, it's possible to broaden their capacity—forming a more dynamic experience within yourself that fully expresses your talents, inclinations, and personality that can come through when hubs are unobstructed.

In Chapter 2: The Method—A Map of the Hubs, I discuss each hub and provide a high-level overview of its initial development, basics, themes, interruptions and stressors, and adaptations and holding patterns, along with the Parinama Method techniques and exercises. This is preparation for Part 2, in which each chapter is an in-depth exploration of the individual hubs.

Maslow	Universal	Planet	Body	Mind	Hub
Self-transcendence	Consciousness	Space	Thought: crown of head	Contemplation	KNOW
Self-transcendence	Light waves	Light	Vision: eyes	Insight	SEE
Self-actualization	Vibration	Sound	Expression: shoulders, neck, hands, mouth, ears	Communication	SPEAK
Love/belonging	Equilibrium	Air	Balance: heart, lungs, chest, arms	Love and relationships	CONNECT
Esteem needs	Combustion	Fire	Will and power: abdomen, posture	Self-worth	DO
Safety needs	Polarity	Water	Flow: hips, pelvis	Feeling/emotion	FEEL
Physical needs	Gravity	Earth	Ground: feet, legs, bum	Survival	HAVE

Table 1.1: The Parinama Hubs Corresponding with the Body-Mind, Psychology Theory, and the Cosmos

Chapter 2

THE METHOD—A MAP OF THE HUBS

New beginnings are often disguised as painful endings.
—*Lao Tzu*

ALL SEVEN HUBS CONTRIBUTE to the full expression of your life. No hub (nor its adaptations) is superior to another, yet most people have at least one hub of primary identification (and some have several). To expand the richness of life, we extend into the full spectrum of all hubs, which are influenced by both biological and psychological development. The hubs affect the entire body, each serving as a layer of our physiology and consciousness. In Part 2 of *The Parinama Method*, each hub is given a chapter—this chapter provides an in-depth explanation of each section contained in Part 2's chapters. Each hub chapter elaborates on a hub's initial development, its basic principles, its themes, the stressors that interrupt its development, and the adaptations and holding patterns that can occur in response to stressors and concludes with techniques and exercises for practicing the method.

INITIAL DEVELOPMENT

The initial development section presents the biological and psychological theory associated with the approximate initial age range of the hub's development. This includes exploration of key events that ultimately influence and inform the development of the hub (see Figure 2.1).

The First Hub: The Infant—Initial age of development is second trimester to approximately one year of age. An infant should begin developing awareness of its physical body by feeling wanted and safe. In utero, everything is provided. As the spark of life begins to take root in the physical world, the growing fetus is still merged with the body of its mother. A shift occurs when transitioning into the outside world where physical separation from the mother takes place, and suddenly there's a need to cry and fuss to signal hunger or discomfort. When we're in this helpless state, we're given an indication of how responsive the world is—if it's safe, and if we can trust that our needs will be met.

The Second Hub: The Baby—Initial age of development is six months to approximately two years of age. The baby begins to sense both its separateness from others and the mystery of feelings arising within it.

Nerve Center	Basics	Initial Development Stage	Rights	Shadow
Cerebral Cortex	Intelligence, information processing, belief systems, connection to higher power	Late Adolescence/ Young Adult	Right to know and learn	Absolute Certainty
Carotid Plexus	Focus, insight, vision	Early Adolescence	Right to see, Right to be seen and validated	Denial, Delusion, Bias
Pharyngeal Plexus	Communication, creativity, expression, listening	Late Childhood	Right to speak and hear the truth	Lies and Deception
Cardiac Plexus	Relationships, connection with others and self	Early Childhood	Right to be loved and to love	Grief, Envy, Jealousy
Solar Plexus	Individualism, power, will, autonomy	Toddler	Right to freedom, Right to act	Anger and Shame
Sacral Plexus	Pleasure, movement, emotions, nurture	Baby	Right to feel, Right to want	Guilt
Coccygeal Plexus into sciatic nerves	Survival, trust, nourishment, safety	Infant	Right to be here, Right to have	Fear

Figure 2.1: Overview of the Seven Hubs: The First 21 Years

Adapted from *Wheels of Life*, original art created by MaryAnn Zapalac. Used with permission.

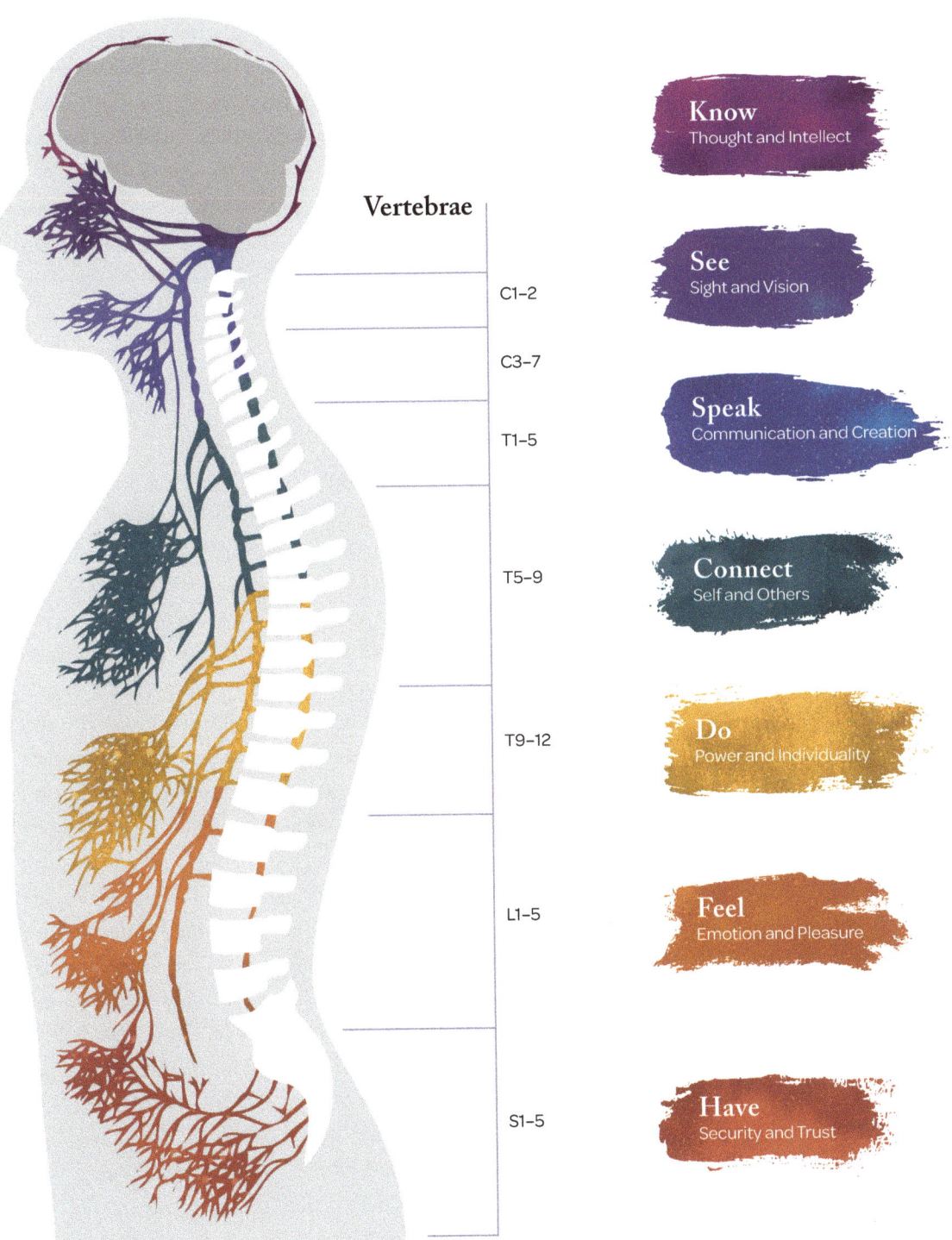

Vertebrae

C1–2

C3–7

T1–5

T5–9

T9–12

L1–5

S1–5

Know
Thought and Intellect

See
Sight and Vision

Speak
Communication and Creation

Connect
Self and Others

Do
Power and Individuality

Feel
Emotion and Pleasure

Have
Security and Trust

Mobility is compelled by the desire to touch, taste, and see its surroundings, and with the safe foundation of an attentive and trusted caregiver, the baby bravely begins to experiment with exploration. Feelings and emotion are the early form of communication: spontaneous crying, laughing, and fussing in response to arising internal needs and changes in the surrounding environment. This is when we expressed our early feelings and learned what our emotions meant through the mirrored responses of our caregivers.

The Third Hub: The Toddler—Initial age of development is 18 months to four years of age. When a toddler begins to assert its individuality and independence, the phase is often called "the terrible twos." The toddler is building confidence in its ability to operate in the world, but is still vulnerable and dependent on caregivers and is primarily oriented around self-gratification. Healthy development encourages freedom while respecting boundaries and limitations of oneself and others.

The Fourth Hub: Early Childhood—Initial age of development is from approximately four to seven years of age. At around four years old a shift begins to take place as a young child becomes interested in friendships with other children, and often there's a delightful move toward compassion and altruism. Now, expressions of kindness along with blossoming social awareness bring in a golden era. This stage is not without its challenges for children: it can be difficult to fit in and young children will often alter their behavior to be accepted (and will experience emotional turbulence as they navigate early socialization).

The Fifth Hub: Late Childhood—Initial age of development is from seven to approximately 13 years of age. Communication begins to blossom with a rapid expansion of vocabulary and an ability to express thoughts and feelings. As communication skills evolve quickly, a child may begin to journal and to talk to parents, friends, and siblings to process its experiences and to learn how to reconcile outer events with its inner life. Children may be taught to behave and to be polite to the extent that they hide what they think and feel. If the expressions of fear, emotion, anger, and sadness aren't allowed, they often burrow into the subconscious and hide. Allowing ourselves to process thoughts and emotions by using words and creative expression is essential to finding integrity in this hub.

We may say we "hate" a teacher or sibling in the heat of the moment, but if we're allowed to talk it through or write about it, we realize that feelings are not facts and that one's personal truth often requires some processing to figure out. The difference between truth and falsehood is experienced and explored as children become aware of discrepancies between what people say and what they do. As adults, feelings may arise that scare us because they are impolite and socially unacceptable (*Sometimes I hate being a mom.*). If we're not used to processing difficult feelings and allowing them to pass, we can find ourselves suppressing and even denying them, fearing that they are absolute truths rather than passing emotions.

The Sixth Hub: Early Adolescence—Initial age of development is adolescence, starting at approximately 13 to 14 years of age. Image and appearance—clothing, haircuts, and style trends—communicate identity to the outside world in attempts to attract specific people. There's interest in experimenting with personal style, and teenagers often bond by connecting over shared taste in music, hobbies, sports, and entertainment. Outward appearance becomes a focus while internal imagination and fantasy are also part of a teenager's life. Observing musicians, artists, and characters is a way to experiment with and to try out different aspects of identity. Taking in images and information builds a library of inner knowledge that's both conscious and subconscious; these are the raw materials for our ideas and imagination, and the more we see, the more material we have to work with when we build and create our lives.

The Seventh Hub: Late Adolescence/Young Adult—Initial age of development is late teens and early adulthood. Teenagers begin to ask big questions about the meaning of their lives and ideas like spirituality. How these questions are treated and how answers are provided shape this hub. Are the answers given as facts that support strict cultural or familial belief systems, or is there encouragement to develop critical thinking and form one's own beliefs? This hub connects us to wonder, awe, knowledge, wisdom, and divinity. Indoctrination and rigid belief systems restrict the potential of this hub; a head filled with beliefs has no room for new information. Interference with learning or access to information blocks the ability to connect to the full expression of this hub. Teenagers, having young adulthood on the horizon, are thinking about what comes after childhood: college, university, trade school, or starting a job—there's a sense of important decisions needing to be made that will shape the rest of their lives. Many teens will contemplate their relationship to the larger world outside of their family and childhood communities. If a teen graduates from a highly controlled learning curriculum at home and high school, perhaps it may start to experiment with what it finds naturally interesting. Because some folks continue to live under the programming of family and culture (and avoid exploration of the beliefs, conditions, capacity, and holding patterns of lower hubs), this hub doesn't develop in all adults. This can be an outcome of fearing change or ambiguity, of having a reluctance to consider differing beliefs—seeing them as disloyal and disrespectful to the family and community of origin.

BASICS

Each hub contains a component of our seven-layered self and specializes in a suite of specific qualities:

- *The First Hub* is self-preservation—Physical security, health, predictability, stability, physical boundary, trusting that basic needs will be met, and a sense of being wanted

- *The Second Hub* is self-gratification—Nurture, sensation, touch, movement, nuance, change, flexibility, coordination, feeling, emotion, and preferences, such as pleasure and disgust

- *The Third Hub* is self-definition—Individuality, confidence, independence, personal power, will, autonomy, freedom, action, and motivation

- *The Fourth Hub* is self-acceptance—Generosity, gratitude, belonging, connection, socialization, altruism, empathy, and devotion

- *The Fifth Hub* is self-expression—Speaking, listening, personal truth, sound, silence, and creativity

- *The Sixth Hub* is self-reflection—Pattern recognition, ideation, curiosity, imagination, appearance, dreams, metaphor, memory, perception, and decision-making

- *The Seventh Hub* is self-transcendence—Consciousness, meaning, belief systems, inquiry, knowledge, wonder, awe, grace, and divinity

THEMES

Even when a hub is well-established and high-functioning, there are dynamic, ongoing themes that elaborate on its basics with ever-increasing nuance and complexity that benefit from inquiry.

The First Hub: Can you relax, or do you remain vigilant? All the foundations of this hub are involved in feeling physically safe, wanted, cared for, and trusting that needs will be met. This trust is ongoing in our lives and profoundly affects our ability to navigate change and stresses on our bodies and physical environment.

The Second Hub: How much change and ambiguity can you handle? As a baby there isn't much subtlety or nuance: things are either good or bad, yes or no, black or white. But as we grow and mature, our intellectual capacity should be able to incorporate nuance and ambiguity. Maturation should support the reality that the truth always contains at least some nuance. Development in this hub eventually grows toward thinking on a spectrum—instead of black and white, there are infinite shades of gray. Because people don't fit into predictable boxes, and a black-and-white worldview leads to insular and isolated groups of so-called like-minded people who unintentionally minimize their lives in an attempt to make the world fit their limited capacity for nuance.

The Third Hub: Do you feel powerful and strong? The so-called dependency paradox is the balance between safety and freedom. We all need freedom and adventure, along with safety and boundaries. As young children develop their independence, their bravery is profoundly affected by their trust in safe, attentive, and loving arms to return to after venturing into the world.

The Fourth Hub: Do you feel worthy of love and acceptance? The balancing act of this hub is between giving and taking—generosity and gratitude. Fulfilling adult relationships involve reciprocity and consideration for both our own needs and the needs of others, similar to a balanced inhale and exhale. Mature relationships are also demonstrated by consistently showing up for them. Some folks exhaust themselves through giving but struggle to receive, and others tend to take and struggle to give.

The Fifth Hub: Can you speak up for yourself? The balance in this hub is between speaking and listening, between expressing yourself and being receptive to self-expression in others. How open are you to what people have to say and how much listening do you expect from them? An overall balance allows us to both speak and be heard, and to listen to and hear what we're told.

The Sixth Hub: Are you curious and receptive to seeing new things? In this hub, we see patterns in new information by using past experiences—we create our current experience and shape our future by what we see in our mind's eye. Along with previous experience, our perceptions and belief systems are largely shaped by important people early in our lives. The balancing act of this hub is the discernment of considering if something is insight and intuition or an unconscious bias, and being able to tell the difference between inner knowing and the social programming and holding patterns from previous hubs.

The Seventh Hub: Can you navigate the paradox of both knowing and remaining curious? The balancing act of this hub is to remain confident, curious, and open-minded instead of becoming rigid and cynical with certainty—rigid certainty cuts off our aliveness and connection to a changing, evolving world, and in this hub, excessive certainty will masquerade as confidence and intellect but is actually an excuse to be closed off, disinterested, and to resist change. To be intelligent, thoughtful, and aware in this hub, we ask questions and are receptive to hearing answers without feeling threatened or defensive.

INTERRUPTIONS AND STRESSORS

Stressors are events and phenomena that interfere and interrupt the naturally occurring and healthy development of a hub. They include the events and behaviors we directly experience happening to us and those we witness happening to others—a resulting interruption is how these events and behaviors affect the development of a hub. *Healthy* and *normal* are subjective assessments without clear definitions; they are more commonly identified by what they are not: *That's not normal*, rather than an explanation of what normal could be. The psychiatric profession defines all kinds of so-called abnormal psychology but has no agreed upon standard of normalcy; there's too much dynamism in psychological functioning—normal simply doesn't exist. Healthy, in *The Parinama Method*, simply means that the human rights and boundaries of the hub have not been significantly denied or invaded.

We won't remember the stressors from our early years—especially those from the development of the first three hubs, before episodic memory is neurologically possible—and we don't need to. But reflection and excavation can help connect rational cognition to make sense of deeper subconscious reflexes—that is, unless remembering causes distress (or even retraumatization). A relatively simple way to test for interruption in a hub is whether you resist (or believe) that a human right or boundary is a birthright or a privilege to be earned. Interruption separates us from our humanity, having us believe we need to *earn* dignity.

The point of exploring interruptions and stressors is not to find people to blame. Nobody wants to be incapable, and folks don't tend to consciously understand why they cause harm. Expecting people to take responsibility for hurting us is often above and beyond their capacity, and holding them accountable is often a challenging, ongoing process. There are many ways people cope with the pain of hurting you, such as through denial, diminishing, and dissociation. Psychologist Alice Miller wrote in *The Drama of the Gifted Child*, "Someone who was not allowed to be aware of what was done to them has no way of telling about it except to repeat it." The purpose of exploring interruptions is to better understand and evaluate the events that shaped your life so that you're better positioned to evaluate how you want to proceed with protecting yourself by creating boundaries, holding people accountable, and becoming aware of your own behavior. Our awareness of stressors and interruptions serves us by bringing our own behavior into the light of consciousness but be mindful to stay within your window of tolerance. This exploration of early experiences can be distressing and disturbing if it's rushed or forced. You may find yourself questioning (and recoiling at) the notion that human rights are to be given without having been earned, but the fact is that they can only be taken away, as they so often are, which can lead to belief systems, such as *Experiencing difficulty is a necessary evil*.

HUMAN RIGHTS AND THE CONDITIONS OF LIFE

Many of us live in so-called meritocratic cultures—the idea that we get and deserve what we earn. There's a lot of cultural mythology supporting the cruelty of meritocracy, and the simplicity of this belief crowds out the harsh reality of the inequality of opportunity distribution. The token animal of meritocracy is the lion, an apex predator. But what this mythology doesn't include is the reality that apex predators tend to be bad at hunting: a lion's kill rate is about 25 percent. It gains its apex status by stealing and scavenging the kills of so-called betas, such as African Painted Dogs (APDs), which have a successful kill rate closer to 90 percent. While believing in meritocracy often causes disdain for so-called losers, ultimately, it's a torturous pattern of outrunning feelings of unworthiness, resulting in burnout and punishing standards for the so-called winners.

The following human rights for each hub are every person's birthright, and the process of reclaiming them—even though they were always ours to begin with—can be difficult. It starts with knowing that simply being alive establishes worthiness: existence is the only merit required for a human life to be valuable and important.

First-Hub Human Rights: The right to be here, the right to take up space. Working on this right can feel deep and confronting. When we reclaim the first hub, we get better at caring for our physical body and build trust in ourselves and in our self-worth. The central tenet of this hub is trusting that you will have your essential survival needs met.

- The right to exist and take up space
- The right to physical security
- The right to have what you need to survive
- The right to sovereign ownership of your physical body

Second-Hub Human Rights: The right to feel and express emotions, the right to want things for yourself, and the right to experience joy and pleasure. Judith writes, "If we cannot feel, it is very difficult to know what we want." She points out how cultures that frown on emotional expression or consider sensitivity a weakness infringe on the basic right to feel.

- The right to feel
- The right to express emotions
- The right to want
- The right to need

Third-Hub Human Rights: The right to personal autonomy and the right to act freely from personal integrity. Judith writes, "Cultures with narrowly defined behavior patterns impair the right to act through punishment and the enforcement of blind obedience." Many people fear straying from a path of conformity and obedience because as children they were punished and taught to be well-behaved. For people who have been victims of oppression and injustice, it is their human right to express their natural and justifiable anger if it does not cause harm to others.

- The right to act
- The right to be free
- The right to be an individual

Fourth-Hub Human Rights: The right to love and be loved, and the right to be treated with dignity—all human beings, regardless of perceived merit, are worthy and deserving of love and compassion. This doesn't mean that you are personally responsible for supplying it. There are people who are shocking, and their actions may be unforgivable to you. You do not need to love or accept their actions, but it is their human right to receive the redemption and healing power of love, and to interfere with this is an act of interruption. A lack of compassion for other people is almost always the result of (or results in) a lack of compassion for ourselves.

- The right to love
- The right to be loved
- The right of human dignity for all people
- The right to feel worthiness without conditions

Fifth-Hub Human Rights: To speak and express your personal truth, and to be told the truth—mature adult functioning in this hub uses constructive outlets for expression. If your truth is being suppressed, the first step is to be aware of it, and the next step is finding the right outlet. There's also the matter of speaking up against injustice, which can be interrupted by cultural programming against breaking ranks with the status quo (speaking for the safety of others can put your own safety at risk).

- The right to speak your truth
- The right to be told the truth
- The right to be heard
- The right to self-expression and integrity

Sixth-Hub Human Rights: The right to be seen as who you are without punishment or cruelty. This is the right to express yourself with integrity and imagination so that your outside reflects what you feel inside in a way that is right for you, and to do it without experiencing retaliation or cruelty. This right is the visual expression of your embloom (see Chapter 3) to the world and can be experienced by recognizing yourself when you see your reflection.

- The right to see
- The right to be seen and validated
- The right to dream of possibility and potential
- The right to explore and develop inner vision

Seventh-Hub Human Rights: The right to inquire—the right to know and the right to receive answers—this is the right to information, education, and knowledge; to have your own thoughts and ideas and to explore your interests without being controlled or indoctrinated. This hub also contains the right to have a spiritual practice (if it doesn't interfere with the individual rights of others).

- The right to education and spiritual exploration
- The right to your own beliefs, both intellectual and spiritual
- The right to experience peace
- The right to change your mind

BOUNDARIES

The first spell aspiring magicians learn is one of protection. To safely operate in the world (as a magician or otherwise), we must uphold parameters with discernment.

Boundaries are part of the standards we keep for ourselves. Therapist Nedra Glover Tawwab writes in *Set Boundaries, Find Peace* that when we create healthy boundaries, "[I]t leads to feeling safe, loved, calm, and respected." According to Tawwab, healthy boundaries involve self-awareness, clear communication, and action. If they were not taught and respected during your childhood, they were likely disregarded or invaded. Similar to the human rights, if these feel overly sensitive, there's potential for interruption in the associated hub.

Each hub has a specific boundary, and healthy containment happens when it's neither too porous nor too rigid. On the one hand, if we always say yes—despite being chronically overwhelmed, resentful, overextended, disrespected, and needing approval—we have what Tawwab calls "porous" boundaries. A common fantasy for folks with porous boundaries is wanting to escape, hide, and run away from the demands of others. On the other hand, if we always say no—regardless of circumstance and without exception—we have rigid and excessive boundaries, acting overly guarded and walling people off without communication as a defensive reflex. When boundaries are like impenetrable walls, they often involve disdain for behaviors like delegation and asking for help and can involve perfectionism and protective isolation from other people masquerading as feelings of superiority over them.

By increasing awareness of our boundaries, we can grow the capability to calmly uphold and enforce them. Having the awareness that they exist is the first step toward developing them. The second step is having the ability to communicate and uphold limits that keep you feeling safe and protected, removing the feeling that the only options are to escape or hide behind walls.

A boundary is like a force field that allows you to decide who is let in and how close they're permitted to be. Since boundary invasions often occur because we're unaware that we can and should set and enforce them, we may feel odd or even second-guess ourselves when they're broken. And it goes both ways: if we don't understand our own, how can we understand them for other people? Sometimes they get interpreted as rejection, coldness, and/or folks feeling unworthy or unwanted. Folks who don't appreciate when boundaries are being upheld often will be those who've benefitted from the lack of them; expect them to be vocal about your enforcement, expressing their belief that you're being selfish and uncaring.

Objection to a stated boundary is a clear indication of a boundary invader. Telling someone you'd like physical and mental space should be the final word on the matter. It's a red flag if the response you receive is being told you're being too sensitive or that you're wrong for asking. If telling someone that something makes you uncomfortable doesn't immediately cause the person to back up or make space, that person is a boundary invader—and that's all the information you need to further enforce. Boundaries are yours to know and enforce, and the more you know your own, the more you can see and respect them for others. People who know their boundaries feel safer within themselves, and people who interact with boundary-aware folks may feel a greater trust and ease, which they usually can't identify specifically but do sense and appreciate.

THE SEVEN HUB BOUNDARIES

The First Hub: Physical boundary

Your body is yours—you alone decide who is allowed to touch you. You choose where this boundary starts; it can be at your skin, or it can be a parameter surrounding you. The more subtle aspect of this is related to social touching, physical closeness, and any other situation related to body autonomy, such as medical procedures, massage, and dentistry. The physical boundary also includes respect for what Tawwab calls "material boundaries"—your possessions, including respect for borrowing your things or your money.

The Second Hub: Emotional boundary

Your emotions and feelings are your own. *You're too sensitive* is an assessment from someone who doesn't have the emotional capacity to hold space for you. It's not an objective assessment of you; it's a reflection of that person. Part of a healthy boundary in this hub involves paying attention to how people make us feel and making decisions about who we want to spend time with—people who are emotionally safe for us. Boundary invasion in this hub can involve oversharing and mistaking inappropriate levels of personal disclosure as emotional closeness. Also, there are people—psychic vampires—who drain our energy and take advantage of the so-called politeness of an inability to uphold this boundary. It's best to create distance with them—lots of it. Sex is the potent combination of both the physical and the emotional boundary. Consent is required to cross it—without consent, an action becomes an invasion and possibly an assault. An indication of interruption in this hub is second-guessing your gut feeling and not acting on it. Interruption in this hub separates you from trusting your feelings, which can cause denial or distrust of one's emotions.

The Third Hub: Personal power boundary

This boundary awareness is respect for time and energy. When it's healthy, we keep out people who lack respect for our time and energy along with people who always need to be right (by proving us wrong); these folks will try to manipulate and dominate interactions using relentless attempts to overpower you and get you to do what they want. An invader of this boundary will show limited interest in your opinion, perspective, or the value of your time. When someone doesn't respect your time, it's an invasion of your power—everyday examples are conversations and meetings that run long without consent, leaving you feeling drained and frustrated.

The Fourth Hub: Relationship boundary

This is the protected space of chosen social, familial, and intimate connections—again, you decide who's allowed in. Like our home, it's a force field with levels of intimacy—who comes to visit and who lives here? There are people who come in uninvited and are oblivious to their invasion. There are folks we let in who cause distress in our lives. There are also those who are already in, such as family, who may look through the cabinets, judging and criticizing. In the boundary of your inner circle, you decide what type of access you're willing to offer so that you can know when it has been overstepped or disrespected. These invasions are painful, especially when people who cannot love us or do not respect themselves come into our inner circle and make us feel unsafe where we're most vulnerable.

The Fifth Hub: Sound and verbal boundary

This is the boundary of protection from noise, negativity, and hostility. When we hear negative comments, verbal threats, loud noises, or yelling, this boundary has been broken. We should feel safe within our boundaries—if there are words or sounds that make us feel threatened, it's the signal to create distance and enforce. Music that's too loud and people who yell are invaders. Sometimes this one is hard to trust and observe when we believe we're at fault for our preferred tolerance of noise and hostility (perhaps thinking we should be able to "handle it"), but these are your boundaries, and you decide what they are. Threats and the words you experience as hurtful are all outside this boundary that you get to determine and enforce.

The Sixth Hub: Visual boundary

This boundary includes invasive eye contact and curiosity. Studies show that a conversation should have about 60 percent eye contact to be effective; 90 percent is intimidating and invasive. Another invasion of this boundary are graphic images you can't unsee, particularly when it's age inappropriate. Similar to the fifth hub, awareness of this boundary can create major shifts in what you're personally willing to tolerate. For young children, seeing intense images can be very disturbing. As adults, sometimes we can feel the need to be tough and not enforce against invasions like leering (and other intrusive eye contact) and terrifying images. Most of what enters our visual field is either consciously or subconsciously absorbed into our inner-reference library, so awareness and discernment of what you want to put on your shelves are conscious acts of empowerment. Awareness of this can be particularly difficult because effective manipulation, mind control, and indoctrination can all fly under the radar. Social media algorithms are designed to keep us engaged and, as a result, break this boundary, often without our conscious consent.

The Seventh Hub: Intellectual and spiritual boundary

This more complex boundary involves all the previous six, affecting the questions we ask and what we believe. It can involve spiritual invasion with guilt and fear, using religion to control and restrict behavior with doctrines of perfection and purity. People have the right to their beliefs, and when those beliefs are disregarded, disrespected, or undermined, this boundary is being invaded; an inconvenient truth for some folks is that all individuals have their own perspective, and imposing one over another's is a seventh-hub boundary invasion. When the inquiry becomes protectively walled off, nothing new gets in and life is reduced to an insular, limited experience filled with assumptions and assertions.

Another aspect of the seventh-hub boundary is the containment of thoughts, which when agitated can act like a shaken snow globe and appear to take up as much space as they're given. Boundary enforcement requires noticing a repetitive thought or worry and doing the challenging work of evaluating and addressing the fixation. By introducing awareness and applying perspective when a thought is consuming all available space, contain it by writing it down (use the journaling practices for processing, see Chapter 11).

Some preboundary relationships only require attendance, which isn't a particularly high bar to clear. When boundaries are observed, communicated, and upheld, they deepen intimacy with the trusted people who respect what we tolerate and allow in our lives. Children who experience lack of development and respect for age-appropriate boundaries in a given hub endure stress that results in the creation of necessary survival protections (adaptations), some of which become holding patterns of behavior that remains for decades (or lifetimes) long after the initial stressors and interrupters have passed.

ADAPTATIONS AND HOLDING PATTERNS

When we experience stress from interruptions that is either intense and acute or low-grade but ongoing, we adapt so that we can maintain safety, dignity, and belonging for our survival. But often without our knowing it, the behaviors that helped us survive early in life can hold us back as adults; adaptations and holding patterns are often maladapted outside the environment that caused them, in both childhood and into adulthood. Initially our behavior changed, but sometimes, if the interruption was severe enough or went on for too long, the adaptation became a holding pattern that got coded into the physical and psychological reflexes in our body-mind. Children are completely reliant on the care of others and innocent as they adapt to do what's required to survive. People who grew up in stable environments may not understand and/or may lack compassion for adapted behaviors, mislabeling them as moral shortcomings. An adaptation is a behavior pattern of either inflating (overcompensating) or shrinking (avoiding) that protects a developmental dilemma within a hub. In each hub there's a survival reflex that supports us in small doses, but it can become a shadow when it takes an ongoing, fixated hold on our behavior. In the adaptations and holding patterns section in each chapter of Part 2, I discuss the hub's shrinking adaptation, inflating adaptation, and an additional theme or two related to holding patterns and shadows.

AN ALIVE BODY MOVES

An alive body is always moving. Watch a pet or a baby sleep and it will stretch, make little noises, and twitch. Your alive body wants to respond and to move. On the one hand, if we've been over- or understimulated in a hub we may shrink by becoming physically guarded and mentally defensive, and we may use separation and isolation to control and protect ourselves against stress and stimulation. On the other hand, we may inflate and respond by getting louder and puffing up physically and mentally in defense. When we stay in one response pattern for too long, we get stuck and lose natural dynamism and movement, and our capacity in the affected hub can either atrophy or never develop at all. An effective, short-term protection becomes a long-term pattern separating us from our full range of feeling and movement. Adaptations are strategies, not pathologies—the full range of a hub can be developed and enlivened again.

CHARGE

When you hear a good song, your body may begin to move spontaneously, or you may begin to sing along. Where does this surge of energy come from? It's an impulse we feel but it can only be observed in the movement it generates. I use Judith's term, "charge," to describe it: a life-force energy that moves within our bodies and connects us with all other life through reflexes, reactions, and conscious movement. When you take in energy in any form—eating, encouragement, rest—you charge. When you release—run, yell, work—you discharge.

Practicing the Parinama Method physically and psychologically restores and grows the fluid, dynamic movement in the hubs. If you value your ability to be intense and commanding at work, you won't lose these abilities—you'll simply increase your range so that you can be intense at work, and patient and acquiescing at home.

Alexander Lowen and Wilhelm Reich, the founders of bioenergetics, believed that our bodies are created to store and manage charge, depending on the adaptive strategies we develop for responding to stimulation. For example, if you grew up in a home in which being an easy child was appreciated, you may have downplayed your needs and reduced the appearance of them—perhaps becoming physically (and psychologically) compressed and small. On the one hand, a smaller body is energized (charges) quickly but doesn't store much charge and rapidly becomes overstimulated (and drained). But because it charges easily, it tends to reenergize without a lot of downtime. On the other hand, a larger body will take longer to charge but has more storage capability, along with greater requirements for space that are commanded merely through its existence. As we examine the hubs, we can look to our bodies to offer clues to which hubs have particular adaptations and holding patterns for storing charge.

Paying attention to what energizes and depletes you gives important insights about yourself, enhancing enjoyment as you consciously appreciate the sensation of being positively charged by something or by noticing when something is over-stimulating, overwhelming, or draining. You can pay specific attention to the stimulation that becomes distressing and use boundary awareness and enforcement to limit or eliminate exposure when possible.

Pert was able to isolate neurological proteins (neuropeptides) and to identify their cellular receptors (see Chapter 1). She found that there is a two-way communication and coherence between the brain and the body that neuropeptides make possible. Pert spoke of how we adapt to stressors through rigidity, that is, our brain cuts off the neuropeptides that encourage oxygenation of certain muscles, causing an amplification of pain to distract from unpalatable and over-whelming feelings and emotions. This is how emotions get trapped in muscles. In fact, in certain cases, revisiting our interruption origin stories may intensify rigidity in the muscles, so consider that the associated stories of stress events are not essential for releasing the physiology of the stress response. This is an important point when considering the individual hubs: again, it's not necessary to excavate all the stories of your history to release restrictive holding patterns. There's a minimum viable dose of intellectual awareness that helps uncover and determine the affecting patterns—pay attention to any sense of rising overstimulation and either proceed with caution or stop. This unifying approach satisfies all three parts of the triune brain (see Chapter 1):

primal-reflexive, emotional, and thinking-logical. When we try a singular approach, whatever we don't include will rebel—especially the primal reflexes that keep us safe—and will override with reflexes and reactions that may be interpreted by the thinking mind as self-sabotage.

VOLTAGE (Chronic and Acute)

Like electrical voltage, charge occurs on a range of intensity—both in the moment and over time. Think of the Goldilocks principle—an analogy of the fairy tale used in cognitive science and developmental psychology: Goldilocks tried three bowls of porridge, one too hot, one too cold, and one just right. Acute experiences that involve invasion and abuse of any or all boundaries can and do create long-standing damage. A single experience of intense shock and voltage, such as assault or abuse, can create a holding pattern in our body-mind. However, interruption and trauma can be experienced as too much, too soon (the porridge is too hot) *or* as too little, for too long (the porridge is too cold).

Another way to look at this concept is to think of a plant being over- or underwatered. If a plant is overwatered, its roots become waterlogged, so it will need time to dry out. Or, in the case of too little for too long, if a plant is underwatered the soil becomes so dry that water drains out before it can reach the roots. It needs to receive water slowly—it can't receive more than it can handle. Someone who has been overwhelmed (overwatered) by charge needs time to process. Someone who has been underwhelmed or ignored (underwatered) needs slow, steady, and patient care over time. Children get overwatered when experiencing acute or chronic trauma and shock and are underwatered through chronic loneliness, neglect, and boredom.

As Lowen and Reich asserted, when it comes to the intensity of charge, body size matters, but for a young child this can present a challenge—all children are small relative to adults. An average four-year-old is about three feet, three inches tall and weighs between 34 and 40 pounds. The average American adult is about five feet, eight inches tall and weighs about 170 pounds. If we convert this size differential to our adult lives, it would be like having a 10-foot tall, 720-pound person towering over us—we'd be helpless to defend ourselves if the person wasn't kind. We'd either hide (like trying to be an easy child who adjusts to the capability of the caregiver), or we'd fight (perhaps at the cost of being shamed then labeled as disruptive or bad).

If a hub receives too much voltage before it's developmentally capable of handling it, such as with abuse, it can get blown out like a circuit or it can become a live wire when activated by touch or stimulation. The energy that gets trapped in a hub with a traumatic amount of voltage must be released carefully. As we grow and mature, the development of each hub sequentially increases its capacity and integration with the other hubs.

Examples of age- and size-inappropriate voltage include being hit or physically restrained, being verbally abused, or being screamed at or shamed for a behavior that's developmentally impossible. For example, children are not developmentally capable of sharing until they're between three-and-a-half to four years old, but research has shown that 43 percent of adults believe children can and should be able to master sharing by age two; studies have shown that when forced sharing happens too early, it interrupts the development of generosity in young children. High voltage sent through a tiny body can also be experienced when children are expected to behave with adult-level maturity. If a hub gets overstimulated by what's seen, heard, or experienced before it has developed the capacity to have perspective, there's a shock to the system and adaptation is necessary (and inevitable). Exposure to pornography, flirtation, and sexual inuendo is common for many children, and the stimulation for a little body can lead to confusion when being interrupted feels exciting. What a child believes it can handle versus what's appropriate can often be two different things. A caring adult who helps with the processing of the voltage-inappropriate experiences can be lifesaving for a child.

Sometimes these experiences are walled off in the fog of our early cognition; other times they are memorable but muted and rationalized—memorable because of the shock to the system and rationalized to protect the perpetrator(s). In adulthood, a common protective response is, *I turned out fine.* Adults will talk nonchalantly about mistreatment—of childhoods witnessing violence or being exposed to age-inappropriate sexual material. Why do these memories persist when so many others do not? In some cases, the interruption was so severe that the memory of it is walled off, but then trouble with emotional regulation arises, which can feel like a mystery. Sometimes, if we're holding a lot of charge, we can surprise ourselves by the intensity of our reactions when we see or experience injustice, abuse of power, insincerity, or deception. We may find ourselves getting activated and not understand why.

Energy is the currency of our lives. We receive energy as food, touch, encouragement, and money. We're familiar with how to release and discharge energy through work, physical activity, talking, dancing with joy, and yelling at sports events and concerts. We release with spontaneous reactions until we're taught to control our behavior (perhaps to avoid punishment) and to gain acceptance (perhaps to avoid embarrassment). As children, we learn how to fit into our environment, sometimes in ways that shift us out of our natural responses and inclinations. If there are stressors in the home or the environment like a death, an illness, or unmet needs, we instinctively learn to adapt to survive. Life finds a way; anything that is alive adapts to its environment to the best of its ability. However, if survival adaptations are not consciously evaluated, they can become hardwired reflexes, which later in life interfere with the quality of our lives.

ADAPTIVE HOLDING PATTERNS: SHRINKING AND INFLATING

Each hub has its current level of strength (or weakness) coming from innate inclination along with the age-appropriate, healthy development it received early in life, but there are also survival responses that affect a hub: long-term adaptations in response to stressors and interrupting experiences, both shrinking and inflating. Under stress, the inflating response gets bigger and more demanding, while the shrinking response gets smaller and less demanding—and although these responses behave and appear to be very different, within a given hub both adaptations differ in strategy but orbit the same dilemma. For example, the third hub is personal power and individuality: on one end of the spectrum is the overcompensation (inflating) of dominance, authoritative behavior, and overconfidence that may appear powerful yet rely on having power over other people to feel strong. This means that without hierarchy there is no personal power—it can only be felt relative to others, but not from within. On the other end of the spectrum, the shrinking adaptation is more visibly lacking in confidence, feeling most comfortable in submission, and being protected by people it perceives to be powerful. Neither adaptation inhabits its own, sovereign individuality and personal power. They both require external validation, but in different ways. A strong and developed third hub feels and emits personal power from within, along with deep ownership of worth and capability.

Under stress, adaptations will tend to exaggerate—after all, they're outcomes of stress: if a shrinking adaptation is tired and hungry it will tend to become extremely quiet, and an inflating adaptation will tend to complain and get louder. A couple with opposing adaptation patterns under a mutual stress can experience exacerbated tension by how one or the other person responds.

If a hub is underdeveloped or affected by interruptions, there can be fixation and obsession—often subconsciously generated—that overcorrect on one or more of the basics or themes of the hub. For a given hub, both shrinking and inflating adaptations are two sides of the same coin reconciling the same dilemma using different strategies. However, once the dilemma is reconciled, the fixation recedes, and the preoccupation is either reduced or eliminated.

THE ADAPTATION DILEMMAS

Again, each hub has a central issue that its adaptations and holding patterns orbit. Like the above example of dominant and submissive behavior in the third hub, both inflating and shrinking adaptations fixate on power due mainly to the inability to directly experience it. The life-changing process of conscious reclamation and releasing the grip of holding patterns is a reconciliation and restoration of a hub's central capacity, a process that begins with awareness that a dilemma exists. Following are the dilemmas of each hub and prompts for consideration and contemplation.

The First Hub: Physical insecurity—If we're constantly anxious about money, basic needs, or physical safety, all other hubs are affected. Maslow's hierarchy of needs (see Chapter 1) is a reminder that our full capability can only be possible with the safety and trust that come with essential physical needs being met. This dilemma is both subconscious and unconscious, so it can be difficult to spot. But anxiety, chronic hypervigilance, feeling disconnected from your body, or general distrust about whether your needs will be met (resulting in fixating and obsessing on potential scarcity) are some indicators of disruption in this hub. A central issue of this dilemma is taking up space and having the ability to obtain, keep, and maintain physical things (with extremes in either excessive minimalism or hoarding/collecting). Prompt: *Do I have trust in my physical safety?*

The Second Hub: Emotional unavailability—This hub contains the self-gratification impulse that is essential for experiencing pleasure—unapologetically wanting more. Part of this dilemma is the permission we may believe is required to feel and express emotions. It's common in this hub to be disconnected from feelings, emotions, and wants—to either suppress and hide them (shrinking) or to be intense and lack containment (inflating). This dilemma can be expressed through who we believe is responsible for how we feel, either completely blaming oneself (shrinking) or completely blaming others (inflating). Without significant adaptations within this hub, there's a dynamic balance between personal responsibility and holding others accountable. Prompt: *Can I have emotions and allow myself to want what I want?*

The Third Hub: Feeling powerless—The dilemma here is self-esteem and confidence and is ultimately about the bravery and courage required to stand alone and to express individuality and personal power. As children our will, confidence, and self-esteem can be interrupted by seemingly well-meaning folks trying to teach us how to behave and fit in (see Chapter 6). This particular dilemma orbits the locus of control. Is power given by others (shrinking) or must it involve having power over others (inflating)? Prompt: *How powerful can I be without making myself or others uncomfortable?*

The Fourth Hub: Feeling unlovable and unworthy—This is the hub of loving, belonging, and balance. Unfortunately, part of belonging often involves hiding parts of ourselves for the purpose of outer harmony and the reduction of social friction that allows us to remain part of a group. We learn to keep secrets about our behaviors or characteristics that may cause embarrassment or estrangement, and we develop personas for different parts of our life. This dilemma is focused on the conditions of belonging: How much of ourselves must be hidden as a condition for being accepted and loved? Central to this dilemma and the overall development of this hub is the balance between giving and taking (between generosity

and gratitude), which ties into our behavior in relationships. Prompt: *How much of myself do I need to hide to belong?*

The Fifth Hub: Believing that the expression of truth is dangerous—Confidence and social acceptance from the previous hubs affect the willingness and the ability to speak out. In some cases, we risk our safety and belonging when we speak our truth, especially when challenging what people in power and family members want to hear. When we suppress our emotions and thoughts, we may keep the peace but make war inside ourselves—outlets that can include journaling, therapy, and trusted friends support the management and resolution of this dilemma. Central to this dilemma and to the overall development of this hub is the balance between speaking and listening. Prompt: *How much of my truth can I speak without punishment, retaliation, or putting myself at risk?*

The Sixth Hub: Distrust and second-guessing inner vision, insight, and ideas—Things we're not ready to see are hidden in our subconscious. If we don't feel safe, powerful, and securely connected, there are truths we may not be ready to face. We may hide secrets we're ashamed to reveal, pretend to believe things, or be in denial. Curiosity is the domain of the sixth hub, and there are many questions that arise when evaluating this complex, multifaceted dilemma. For example: Are my belief systems mine or do they contain unconscious biases? Can I express my ideas and dreams without fearing criticism or being ostracized? Does my appearance express how I feel inside, or does it serve the cause of fitting in and pleasing others? Central to this dilemma is our level of curiosity: what we allow ourselves to see (and reveal). Prompt: *What will I allow myself to see?*

The Seventh Hub: Intellectual insecurity—The physical location of this hub is our PFC (see Chapter 1), which offers the uniquely human function of advanced consciousness and the ability to understand and consider alternatives. Developed and balanced behavior in this hub is the ability to consider opinions that are different from yours without fearing it will weaken or contaminate your own point of view. Complete dismissal of a person by making sweeping, unexplored assumptions happen in both shrinking and inflating adaptations, but the strategies differ, from expecting others to convert to your worldview (without any willingness to consider theirs) all the way to rationalizing the dehumanization of people holding conflicting opinions. A central issue of this dilemma is certainty, with know-it-all (shrinking) and don't-care-to-know (inflating) attitudes. Prompt: *Can I change my mind?*

RESTORING FLOW

In animals and young children, we see the body in natural states of buoyancy and flexibility. Our bodies are shaped by posture, coordination, rigidity, and flexibility in response to our surrounding environment, and like a cramped muscle, patterns from the past can remain frozen or blocked until they're released. Ideally, we stay dynamically responsive to what's going on around us, but especially when we're young, repetitively adapting can turn into holding patterns that keeps us stuck in reflexes and behaviors from the past. A mature and fairly conscious adult should be expected to manage responses and find outlets for healthy release. Short-term restraint, such as blocking our natural response to an unreasonable boss or remaining patient with a child when we're exhausted, is essential behavior for a mature adult. If we get angry at our boss, we know expressing rage and anger risks our employment and professional standing; if someone we love makes us angry, blocking an immediate impulse gives us the time to form a response that won't cause harm. But if a block is sustained and not dealt with, it will begin to build intensity and lead to either an explosion (usually at someone who is blameless) or get stored as stress in the body. Blocking the immediate expression of emotions can maintain harmony in the world around us, but often at the cost of the harmony within us. When we express ourselves, we don't want to have a backlog of emotion that results in outbursts and out-sized feelings relative to the situation. We need to discharge and release blocked responses in a way that's safe for ourselves and others. Blocks can take physical form as muscular tension, a tight jaw, tooth grinding, obsessive/compulsive patterns, body fat, water retention, addiction, and other repetitive behaviors. There are also behaviors related to our adaptations that are part of our unique suite of talents, identity, and personality. When we restore flow, we don't lose the benefits of our holding patterns when we unblock them: we can access these qualities when appropriate and release them when they're unnecessary, such as being able to remain consciously objective and emotionally distant while negotiating a business deal and then coming home to connect deeply with our children.

Our adaptations are evidence of our extraordinary capacity to survive and evolve. It is our unique ability as human beings to adapt and evolve *consciously* to greater heights and levels of joy, freedom, happiness, connection, purpose, and contribution. The ideas of achieving balance and of staying so-called centered are conceptually elegant, but the practical reality is more like the dynamic equilibrium of homeostasis. Homeostasis is maintaining a relatively central position that's achieved through shifting up and down and in and out of a central axis. When we restore flow, we're incorporating a wider range of responses and behaviors within the spectrum of a hub. We look to remain responsive to what's arising in the moment instead of getting stuck in automatic reflexive reactions, regardless of the nuances within what's occurring.

THE SHADOWS

The shadow of each hub when acute is a natural, healthy reflex, but it becomes dark and disabling if it becomes a chronic, overwhelming, maladaptive behavior pattern. In the first hub, fear as an acute reflex protects our physical safety by using rapid, reflexive action—you jump out of harm's way—to support your survival. But as a chronic condition, fear can become immobilizing anxiety and hyper-vigilance that affects sleep, health, and relationships and can even lead to terminal health conditions. Each hub has a shadow that will be explored further in Part 2. Here, an overview.

The First-Hub Shadow: Fear (*as an active, reflexive response)* is lifesaving. As a chronic and immobilizing condition, fear is life-taking. Because of our advanced brains, we have the ability to imagine and to anticipate stressors, and our imaginings cause stress and anxiety. Fear is effective when it leads to immediate action, but as an ongoing state of mind, it can hijack and overwhelm the day-to-day functioning of our lives. Fear is a shot of adrenaline, and anything that doesn't require immediate or near-term action builds up and causes stress in the body, transmuting into the shadow of this hub.

The Second-Hub Shadow: Guilt and Shame are naturally arising impulses to fix a mistake, especially if the mistake involves hurting someone. When guilt is healthy and natural, it supports corrective action. When guilt becomes a shadow, we're chronically fixated because guilt becomes an enforcer, often of unrealistic standards for ourselves. When guilt naturally arises and encourages a reparative action, we tend to not feel good until we make things right. As a shadow, unhealthy guilt blocks us from feeling good or attaining satisfaction. Guilt stops the cascade of enjoyment before it can achieve the fulfillment of pleasure: *I shouldn't be doing this* interferes with the pleasure of objectively benign activities. Eating and resting are common behaviors in which shadow guilt is found—they often metastasize into shame. With guilt, we feel bad about a specific action; with shame, we believe the action is evidence that we're fundamentally flawed.

The Third-Hub Shadow: Anger (*a natural defensive response to being shamed*) is an expression of our innate requirement for human dignity. In its acute form, anger is the action of holding people accountable and responsible for mistreating you. But it becomes the shadow of this hub when it's not allowed healthy expression (which is common) and gets buried in our psyche then transforms into rage, becoming destructive and internalized as self-doubt, depression, and self-destruction or externalized by harming others. Anger is a response to having your humanity and will disrespected, subdued, and undermined. It's a form of grief over mistreatment (and even trauma). Shame—from the second hub—is also present because shaming is an underlying cause of anger and rage. When shamed, especially in our early years, we feel faulty, unworthy, isolated, and uncomfortable within ourselves. Because this goes against the integrity of our humanity, an impulse to fight back will arise in defense of our dignity. To compound matters, anger is often considered forbidden and can get expressed as chronic impatience and irritation. Anger in response to being shamed and undermined can lead to further shaming for making people uncomfortable about how we feel—and if suppressed and undermined for too long it often becomes rage, which is met with even greater social disdain.

The Fourth-Hub Shadow: Sadness and Grief are unavoidable parts of the human experience; when we love, we eventually experience loss—the greatest pain we'll ever know. Even if we try to protect ourselves by putting up emotional walls and distancing ourselves from others, grief is experienced as loneliness in the pain of isolation. Allowing yourself the time you need for processing and feeling loss is the healthy expression of grief, even when it takes longer than others think it should—you alone determine the time you require. When grief becomes the shadow, it immobilizes and closes us off from love and connection, because of the aversion to and fear of more hurt and pain. We can work with the shadow in this hub by allowing ourselves to feel the pain of grief and by accepting that it can (and will) change us—and letting it happen. As a friend once said, "I could control when I die by killing myself, just as I could control love by closing my heart."

The Fifth-Hub Shadow: Lies and Deception carry tremendous stigma. Lies can be used to protect us in acute situations. A child may lie to its parents about being LGBTQ+ because the child fears retaliation. In acute situations, lies can buffer us from danger, but when they are used chronically to suppress our personal truths, they create both inner conflict with ourselves and outer conflict with others.

The need to tell lies can indicate that the truth is (or was) not safe for any number of reasons—also, there are socially sanctioned lies. Being polite to people when they're not respecting you; living outside of your integrity by pretending to be happy; working at a job or living a life that pleases others but actually feels terrible to you—these are lies and deceptions. When people talk about having zero fucks left to give, they're often referring to the diminished or eliminated need to be polite when it's out of alignment with their personal integrity: this expression is code for no longer being able to tolerate the deception of politeness that makes life easier for everyone except ourselves.

We may lie when we don't feel good about ourselves, when we're attempting to elevate our stature when we don't feel good enough as we are, and when we're avoiding an exhausting, difficult discussion. Lies become a shadow when we hide our true self from others (and from ourselves); lies and deception are shadow behavior when we give misinformation and misdirection that lead others to make poor or dangerous decisions based on bad information. When we give misinformation that leads to harm, we should be held responsible.

The Sixth-Hub Shadow: Denial is protective on occasion and can get us through difficult situations. But when denial becomes chronic, we get stuck believing illusions that will be challenged eventually when we interact with the outside world. As children, we need to survive within our families. This can mean that we choose to look the other way or to believe a creative interpretation of our environment or circumstances. Denial is a survival tool that becomes a shadow when the delusion doesn't allow us to see the truth about ourselves (eventually) or to respect other people's lived experience—for example, if we refuse to believe people when they tell us who they are and tell us their personal truth because these things conflict with our worldview. Your own denials act as a retaining wall for truths that you may not be ready to see about yourself, your family, and your culture. We all maintain a certain amount of denial that's mostly subconscious and can become distressed when faced with the discomfort of cognitive dissonance (see Chapter 9). In this hub, the dysfunction and shadow surge when we actively deny our own truths and the truths of others based on reflexive biases.

The Seventh-Hub Shadow: Certainty is inflexibility in our beliefs or ideas to the point that new information is reflexively rejected without consideration. A healthy level of certainty is having confidence and conviction in important beliefs while remaining open to hearing dissenting opinions. We can know some things for certain, such as the importance of human dignity, but if we deny the dignity of someone who disagrees with us about, say, human rights, we accidentally counter our own strongly held belief. Healthy certainty can be necessary to fight for what we believe in, but the ability to have our minds changed is essential for our growth and development. Our personal truths are relative based on our own circumstance, experience, culture, education, and unique disposition. The inability to be willing to consider another person's perspective when it conflicts with yours or to discount them without consideration is a shadow activity. We liberate ourselves by knowing that all human beings contribute to the collective experience. You do not need to agree with everyone, but if you are brave enough to be curious, you learn about yourself and grow through being open minded. (A notable exception to this is exposure to people who don't see you as fully human—exposure to these attitudes is harmful and dangerous.)

We can know things that are central to our integrity and truth, but because life is dynamic and constantly changing, new perspectives are introduced as we age and as our life circumstances change. The seventh hub is where we fully comprehend the profound and ingenious paradoxes, perspectives, and ambiguities in all the hubs.

TECHNIQUES AND EXERCISES

At the end of each chapter in Part 2 there's a series of techniques and exercises for both expanding the capacity of the hub and restoring its dynamism. This combination of movements with theory and contemplation is surprisingly potent and powerful. Any implication that a person needs to be healed, fixed, or corrected is an adaptation. We are natural and beautifully, perplexingly, and astonishingly able to survive and adapt in wild ways. Everything in *The Parinama Method* offers the chance to consciously govern your life and to be more dynamic and responsive.

In the techniques and exercises section for each hub chapter, you'll find prompts that consider the physical location of the hub on the body (and in this chapter, seven short exploration-awareness prompts); practices for growing the capacity and integrity of the hub; and exercises for charging and discharging.

PRIMARY LOCATIONS OF THE HUBS ON THE BODY

The First Hub—HAVE: bottoms and tops of feet, knees, legs, bum, perineum, and base of spine (physical boundary: parameter of the entire body)

- **Awareness prompt:** Bring attention to the soles of your feet. Are they on the ground? Bring attention to the surface of your body. Can you feel your physical presence and sense the surface of your body?

The Second Hub—FEEL: hips, pelvis, genitals, lower abdomen, lower back, sensations on entire body (includes pleasure or pain)

- **Awareness prompt:** How much mobility do you have when you make Hula-Hoop or figure-eight motions with your hips? Do you have pain or discomfort in your lower back? Do you have chronic pain in any area of your body that despite diagnosis and treatment does not go away?

The Third Hub—DO: abdomen, mid-back, digestion, posture

- **Awareness prompt:** Abdomen and posture are mobile, taut, and upright; digestion and metabolism are effective and effortless.

The Fourth Hub—CONNECT: chest, upper back, heart, lungs, arms, hands

- **Awareness prompt:** Bring awareness to any tightness in your chest when taking a deep breath. Pay attention to the balance between an inhale and an exhale: Is one more comfortable than the other? On an exhale, extend your arms out as if asking for a hug; on the inhale draw them inward, placing hands on heart. Pay attention to any feelings that arise in either direction—asking, giving, taking.

The Fifth Hub—SPEAK: neck, tops of shoulders, jaw, ears, voice

- **Awareness prompt:** Are your jaw, neck, and shoulders loose or tight? Is the tone of your voice pinched and high, loud and domineering, or resonant and comfortable? Bring attention to any constriction on your vocal cords when you speak: Do you have a vocal effect that you're aware of? If so, what do you believe it helps to amplify or project about you?

The Sixth Hub—SEE: eyes, forehead, brow, third-eye space (related to the pineal gland), memory (can be an indication of the condition of this hub)

- **Awareness prompt:** Is your brow relaxed or furrowed? Do you often squint or are your eyes generally relaxed? Do you close your eyes during any activities that involve your body? Toward middle age we begin to see lines between our brows and on our forehead if we have chronic tension here—when we furrow our brow or squint our eyes, we constrict this hub.

The Seventh Hub—KNOW: crown of head, PFC, and subtle, felt sense of the body

- **Awareness prompt:** Sustained concentration and focus are the domain of the seventh hub experienced through reading comprehension, attention span, ability to tolerate silence and stillness.

CHARGE AND DISCHARGE

For each hub, I provide techniques for both energizing (charging) and releasing (discharge). Charging involves light stimulation and gentle activation; discharging includes muscular release through mild tremoring. Lowen believed that humans function best when their charging and discharging are balanced. We blow off steam when exercising or when we need to vent frustrations verbally to a friend or partner; these are everyday ways that folks release and discharge. Again, when charge is held in the body without release it leads to chronic tension and stress. The longer we hold the stress and tension, the heavier it gets, and we can get so used to the heavy load we almost forget we're carrying it. Releasing can cause initial discomfort and pain, but with that release, sometimes an astonishing amount of energy becomes available. Charging is how you energize your body with any kind of activity that restores you, such as music, time with friends, enjoying food, and rest.

SAFETY FIRST

We need to feel safe before we can be brave. Indeed, yoga can feel good at first, but I've heard folks say, "It feels so good, I'm not sure why I stopped doing it." When we start to open up and release long-held tensions in the body, the feel-good period of yoga can shift into experiencing emotional discomfort. Both as a yoga student and a teacher, my experience with guidance and support around release was woefully inadequate. Directions like, "Explore that," and "Be gentle with yourself today," are like driving without a map; we don't know where we're going, so there's an inability to offer directions back to safety.

The Parinama Method is a map but going too fast can overwhelm, so similar to thawing frozen fingers and toes, it's best to go slow. This work must be handled with care. It's common that the actual exercises can feel relatively easy—some clients who are used to constantly pushing past limits ask to heighten the intensity. Yet afterward, the intensity causes them overwhelm and emotional flooding—so we work to find their zone of tolerance through a gentle and patient process of trial and error. So many of us are used to pushing ourselves. Sometimes I see growing alarm or distress in clients' eyes as they ask to be pushed harder, and I've learned to slow down or stop to check in at the earliest signs of this.

Psychologist Dan Siegel coined the term "window of tolerance" in *The Developing Mind: How Relationships and the Brain Interact to Shape Who We Are*, referring to how much of something we can comfortably tolerate. A window of tolerance is not something to take lightly or to disregard when doing transformative work—part of this process is developing and building trust in ourselves, and blowing past limits to be so-called strong or superior interrupts our progress. Within this zone we can function effectively and are typically able to receive, process, integrate information, and otherwise readily respond to the demands of everyday life. If we extend beyond it, we can become overwhelmed with either hyperarousal (frustration and agitation) or hypoarousal (numbness and feeling spaced-out).

A SANCTUARY: CREATING A SAFE PLACE

Before you need them, identify the friends, music, and other constructive comforts to turn to if you feel overwhelmed (see Chapter 11). Pets, partners, books, walks, relaxing playlists, a bath, a massage, therapy, naps, friends, and podcasts have been and continue to be safe harbors for me—a place to regain my footing when experiencing overwhelm.

AFTERGLOW, RECOIL, THEN INTEGRATION

After anything that expands our capacity, such as a challenging and revealing conversation, a performance that's a new personal best, or insights from a retreat or vacation, we initially can expect to feel good (the afterglow), which is followed by some discomfort that comes later (the recoil), and eventually by a leveling out (the integration).

THE AFTERGLOW

The afterglow can occur after therapy, yoga, a positive experience feeling vulnerable with someone, exercise, and any kind of peak-performance achievement when we actualize greater levels of our capabilities and talents. We walk away from these experiences feeling lighter and more free.

THE RECOIL AND THE INTEGRATION

Soreness after a challenging workout is the physical version of this: it may hurt to walk the next day but ultimately, greater fitness is achieved. Integration happens after the recoil discomfort settles down. Rome wasn't built in a day and for a little while, the afterglow will have us feeling like it could've been.

The recoil is the darkness before the dawn, and it can be hard to remember this when it's happening but by allowing it to pass, staying with yourself instead of resisting it, integration occurs.

Be gentle and keep showing up for yourself—a practice that slowly opens and expands capacity offers protection. This work is powerful, and a rapid, immediate, dramatic change can be disruptive and distressing. You've spent your entire life living within your current capacity, adaptations, and holding patterns. These are big shifts, and as tempting as it can be to want rapid change, nothing is more important than cultivating acceptance of yourself exactly as you are within any given moment.

SURGEON GENERAL'S WARNING

The Parinama practice is not a substitute for medical care: it's intended to help support attending to and cherishing your body-mind, and in fact, building a support team is part of growing capacity. The denial or delay of medical maintenance and physical needs is part of maladaptive holding patterns that diminish the importance of your connection to your body and yourself. Your care-and-support team comprises doctors, dentists, therapists, and medications that are essential for self-care that respects your body-mind. I've witnessed many cases of a dangerous, dissociative denial in the yoga and new-age spiritual community. People forgo medical help for treatable matters because of magical thinking about the power of yoga, meditation, fasting, and eating so-called clean diets. I saw someone die of starvation from so-called spiritual fasting, and because Western medicine is so stigmatized in some communities, I've seen treatable medical conditions lead to permanent or near-fatal conditions. Another dark side I've witnessed is blaming people with diseases like cancer and mental illness for these conditions and implying that a lack of green juice and yoga is at least partially responsible. My own experience with this practice has led to my now-proactive medical and dental care—my previous fear of doctors and dentists was intense, yet when love and respect for my body(-mind) became central in my life, those fears became secondary to love and care.

GOOD PRACTICES

When we feel the positive disintegration of falling apart (see Chapter 1), we're feeling behavior patterns and beliefs that have outlived their usefulness trying to fall away.

As you read and do your practice, keep your journal and pen handy; thoughts will inevitably arise, so write them down for later exploration—again, journaling can help with processing thoughts and feelings (see Chapter 11). Writing something down is particularly useful because you will likely find that some of the insights are potent in the moment when they arise, but quickly fade from memory. If there's a particular hub or topic that you feel compelled to prioritize, consider following this impulse to explore.

Set a specific time of day to practice at least four days a week; remember, consistently showing up for yourself is an act of self-love. I discuss the essential importance of devotional discipline and of showing up for the people you love, including yourself, in Chapters 6 and 7. As you familiarize yourself with your hubs, you may find yourself identifying with specific needs and adaptation patterns—and as you go through your day, you'll likely begin to see things differently. Add the movements and intentions from specific hubs as you check in with yourself (see Chapter 11) while standing in line, riding an elevator, or commuting. This practice supports an ongoing love and commitment to yourself and your life.

In Chapter 3: The Method—Entering the Void: Paradox, Ambiguity, and Nuance, I discuss some of the larger concepts of the Parinama Method ethos.

Chapter 3

THE METHOD—ENTERING THE VOID: PARADOX, AMBIGUITY, AND NUANCE

Do I contradict myself? Very well then I contradict myself,
(I am large, I contain multitudes.)
—Walt Whitman

OUR PHYSICAL BODY IS as magical and mysterious as the enlivening force—sometimes called the soul—within it. For millennia, world cultures have contemplated many of the same questions: What's the meaning of life? Why are we here? What creates life and enlivens a body? Astronomer Carl Sagan said, "We are made of star stuff," because the atoms in our body were once scattered across the cosmos. So perhaps the greatest question of all is this: Within a body made of cosmic matter, what's the invisible essence that enlivens it? The answer may be that it's the essence comprising the spark of life, destiny, uniqueness, with interconnectedness to the larger force of the universe.

Aristotle considered the intersection of what we are and what we can be a hylomorphism (*hylo* means *matter* and *morph* means *form*), that is, our body-mind is matter and morphism is the potential and destiny that form it. Aristotle also connected *entelechy* (the realization of potential) to his concept of matter and the ability to *become*—the vital principle that guides the development and actualization of the potential within in every human life.

This most remarkable thing that we have (and that we are) is the unknown force within our body that requires no effort: the miracle of life within you, the embloom.

Perhaps the embloom is like an eye that can only see itself in a mirror because it's the core of what we are, the witnessing presence within us. And perhaps the evolution of consciousness is this witness seeking to see itself, attempting to understand what it is.

The embloom can often be bothersome, making life difficult because it wants to follow its destiny. It doesn't preoccupy itself with physical needs and safety, yet because it's in the flow of something larger than we understand, it can deliver us to abundance beyond comprehension. But for all its magic and mystery, the embloom exists within the practical needs of the body-mind and our physical needs must be established before we can truly surrender to the embloom's mission. Imagine (or believe) that your soul is born into your body and must stay alive to achieve its mission, that is, to learn its lessons, to make its contribution, and to have the experiences of being alive. You have this body-mind experiencing the world, you are an embloom with an important purpose. Again, the embloom has a mission, and the practicality of life keeps getting in the way—or is it an essential part of the experience?

Our destiny doesn't leave us alone: craving authenticity, mastery, and purpose haunt us, even when we don't know exactly why or what we're supposed to do. Plato believed that our soul selects our parents before we're born, recognizing that once we're born it won't remember its destiny and, for better or worse, the selected parents will help it to know. Because your embloom is invisible and can only be perceived in subtlety, it expresses and recognizes itself in metaphor and mythology. It's difficult to put into words the strong feelings we get from movies, books, and other forms of storytelling—universal themes, such as the hero's journey, can be deeply evocative and transcend explanation (see Chapter 4). We only come close when we express a sense of recognition, often using metaphors—in words, visual art, movement, or music.

You are an effortless original. Acting teacher Keith Johnstone, who pioneered improvisational theater, writes in *Impro: Improvisation and the Theatre* that when we try to be original, we block our innate originality. According to Johnstone, "Striving after originality takes you far away from your true self and makes your work mediocre." The performative aspects of behavior, often intended to charm or to intrigue, do the opposite as they often create behavior that's contrived and fake. The effortless and unaffected expression of who we are gets contaminated when we believe we should act in ways that are more interesting. We're only boring to ourselves because we're so familiar. We fear we're unremarkable (or unworthy) but attempting to appear interesting robs us of the innate appeal of our authenticity. Actors' charisma partially arises from their ability to be organic, authentic, and spontaneous, and there is a noticeable magnetism in people freely expressing themselves. The expression of your embloom is always spontaneous and organic, and restoration of the natural rhythm and flow in each of your hubs allows more of your authentic self to be revealed.

Many of us don't know how to access the nature of our embloom because we hide important parts of ourselves so we can belong. The need to belong is a practicality of our physical existence that often interferes with authentic self-expression. And after all, most schools—where we learn socialization—don't value or develop all aspects of intelligence, instead focusing narrowly on math, science, reading, writing, and a curated version of history. Developmental psychologist

Howard Gardner challenges this narrow scope in his theory of multiple intelligences, which identifies eight specific forms of intellect:

- **Naturalist:** understanding living things and nature
- **Bodily/kinesthetic:** coordinating mind and body
- **Intrapersonal:** understanding yourself, what you feel, and what you want
- **Interpersonal:** sensing people's feelings and motives (emotional intelligence)
- **Linguistic:** the ability to find the words to express yourself—closely tied to reading and writing
- **Musical:** discerning sounds, their tone, pitch, rhythm, and timbre
- **Spatial:** visualizing the world in 3-D
- **Logical and mathematical:** quantifying things, making hypotheses, and proving them

Logic, math, and linguistics are important skills and talents in our professional lives, but the skills and talents supporting career advancement include many of the other intelligences, specifically inter- and intrapersonal ones. There's more than a passing alignment with Gardner's multiple intelligences and the hubs of the Parinama Method; for example, the second hub with bodily/kinesthetic, the fifth hub with linguistic, and the sixth hub with spatial. The narrative that most people work under protest and are mediocre is not scientifically validated: we work under protest when we're not afforded the human dignity of autonomy and independence, the opportunity to get better at something, and the opportunity to connect with purpose. Mediocrity is a condition of hopelessness placed on a human: it is not human nature.

Unaffected people are not afraid to be themselves—the adult advice to early adolescents that they should just be themselves is well-meaning and wise but falls short because it doesn't acknowledge a practical caveat: being fully yourself is hard to do when your identity is tied to social belonging. But the charisma that we surrendered for social belonging at early school age is still present; restoring and strengthening our hubs around personal integrity and thawing frozen behavior patterns not only transforms how we feel, but also how people respond to us.

The realization of the consequences of conformity (as an outcrop of the need to belong) can come when it's too late. Former hospice nurse Bronnie Ware's book *The Top Five Regrets of the Dying* explores in detail what she learned as she cared for people in their final days. Ware cites the most common deathbed regret: *I wish I'd had the courage to live a life true to myself, not the life others expected of me* (see Chapter 13).

OUR NATURE IS NATURE

When we don't connect with the natural world, we tend to feel disconnected from our lives; when we bring attention to our connection to everything around us, we better understand ourselves. The radical acceptance that's possible produces a charisma and a dynamism that exists in the full experience of life and rejects the punishing notions of purity and perfectionism. When we're in rhythm and feeling connected, we experience ourselves as part of life rather than apart from it. And as the natural world shows us, the path isn't a straight line—it's cyclical and rhythmic. We continually come back to things we thought we understood to find deeper truths.

The transformation process has practical limits for what we can tolerate and what to leave alone. As we see in nature there's no sanitized perfection or complete resolution of anything. There will always be memories, pain, and issues—we have the attics, basements, and junk drawers of our lives. There's no fixed state of physical perfection, and purity is a conceptual standard—instead we seek personal integrity. Ideals like perfectionism, full resolutions, and purity can control us through disgust (*impure! gross! fat!*) and/or shame (*sloppy! unworthy! fat!*) and cause the false belief that you are fundamentally flawed—a problem needing to be solved, optimized, and/or fixed—and that you must be productive to deserve dignity.

None of these things is true: it's the belief in these controlling ideas that's the problem. We are all alive, changing, moving, and messy. We have partners, children, and pets (and plants) that show us (if we allow ourselves to see) that life is moving, reorienting, and shifting. If we're rigid and frozen against natural rhythms of the very nature of life, we miss the experience of it.

We're better able to understand ourselves and to navigate life's fluctuations by being aware of the rhythms, cycles, and patterns of our natural world. This theme is repeated in different ways throughout the hubs, but here I provide a primer on perspective through parallax, paradox, and ambiguity.

PARALLAX: AN EVER-CHANGING PERSPECTIVE

Your perspective on life is the result of your unique inclinations combined with specific experiences, circumstances, level of maturity, and other variables that add up to being a life that is completely yours. Parallax goes deeper into our concept of what it means to have perspective: it not only considers your relative position to something, but also how the direction and speed of travel influence perception. Instead of *perspective* or *context*, I use *parallax* because how we're oriented and how we approach something affects how we perceive it. Also, orientation and approach shift and change throughout our lives, and parallax introduces the reality that perspective and context are always moving and changing.

We may agree with people on important things, but if we're honest, we rarely if ever agree on everything. Even choosing how and what we focus on influences our perspective: try taking a picture of the moon—the camera's viewfinder introduces a broader perspective until we actively shift its focus. Until we zoom in, the massive moon seen with the naked eye is a pinprick of light in the vast sky. Grasping the reality that our perspective (and the factors that affect it) is unique to us not only grants us our singular version of reality, but also opens the aperture for awareness and respect for the views of others. We all hold certainties based on the experiences that shaped our lives, but if we feel like someone wants to understand us, we're more likely to hear them out (and vice versa). Your perspective and internal truth are woven into the cloth of the shared humanity, which in turn is woven from eight billion threads—we are all entwined, sharing the same experience from different positions.

PARADOX: COMPLEMENTARY OPPOSITES

We encounter paradox when seemingly opposite things enhance the existence of each other. For example, activity makes rest satisfying, black makes white stand out (as white does black), and we can feel most alive after having come close to death. When we look closely, we can notice that opposites tend to be complementary and together contribute to an emerging property—and even breakthroughs—of possibility.

Each hub has one or more of these dichotomies in which one polarity cannot exist alone, such as pushing into our feet (or seat) to rise upward. A central, repeating paradox is the need to belong that exists with the need to be free, the need to both follow your own arrow and find safety in the quiver. Below I list some of the paradoxes in our hubs:

- Roots to grow (pushing down to rise)
- Attraction and repulsion (magnetism)
- Intimacy and distance (absence makes the heart grow fonder)
- Individuality (personal freedom) and belonging (connection)
- Gratitude (receiving) and generosity (giving)
- Speaking (finding the words) and listening (seeking to understand)

- Creating (self-expression) and validation (being seen)
- Knowing (certainty) and remaining curious (openness to new ideas)

Complementary opposites (see Chapters 6 and 7) are strengthened by the existence of each other, as if on a spectrum of hot and cold with infinite possible temperatures in between. Awareness of complementary opposites helps us better understand ourselves: sometimes we want to be with people, sometimes we want to be alone. These dichotomies in our lives are dynamic, constantly evolving and changing, and exist on a continuum in the ambiguity and nuance of infinite possibilities. The difference between paradox and hypocrisy is that in a paradox, two polarities can be simultaneously true, which is the opposite of hypocrisy. Hypocrisy confronts us with two irreconcilable demands, such as a mother who tells her child, "You're not affectionate enough," but when the child shows affection says, "You're acting like a big baby." Hypocrisy says one thing and does another, a double bind of *damned if you do, damned if you don't*—and there's no way to win. But paradox strengthens its opposing force, and like a cool drink on a scorching hot day, greater capacity is realized through opposition—hot and cold accentuate each other, unlike mixed messages that negate one another.

AMBIGUITY AND CONTINUUM VERSUS POLARITY

Ambiguity is the infinity between two seemingly polarized opposites. There are countless shades of gray found between black and white, and when we attempt to pick a paint color, the different hues and tones appear endless. An apple in the grocery store and an apple core in a trash can are seemingly two different things, but they exist on a continuum from seed to compost. An apple is a moment in time, and gray comes in numerous tints that can all be called by the same word—*gray*. Between apple and core and black and white is a field of infinite possibility. We expand our ability to see and appreciate nuance through awareness of the extensive possibilities between so-called absolutes.

Absolutism (*This is good, that is bad*) is suitable for the level of brain development in younger children, but as adults, part of maturation is expanding our belief systems to consider options outside our current thought patterns. Folks who are prone to absolutism tend to see the world as a place where nothing but the so-called best is acceptable. We can know a lot about people when they speak in absolutes—specifically, that they could benefit from compassion. And when we are prone to speaking in absolutes, we can know a lot about ourselves—specifically, that softening absolute positions opens us to greater possibilities.

We often resist ambiguity because it points to a less certain and less controllable universe. First hub stability supports the inner sense of containment and solid ground needed to feel more secure in and tolerant of the intellectual ambiguity necessary to understand yourself—after all, we contain multitudes (see Chapter 5). A polarized worldview makes understanding ourselves difficult. In an absolutist worldview, when we do something considered bad, we may believe ourselves to be a bad person. Making a mistake doesn't make you a mistake. Without the range of ambiguity, there is no room for redemption; without the continuum between absolutes, there is no way to fully accept ourselves—and only when we accept ourselves can we be free to accept others.

NATURAL RHYTHMS
CYCLES

The patterns we follow with calendars and clocks track the cycles of nature, specifically, the cycles that are connected to Earth and its relationship with the cosmos—after all, we are made of star stuff. We're deeply affected by the natural world because we're part of it. We experience predictable patterns: seasons, day and night, and days containing a ratio of light and dark that predictably shifts with the time of year—longer days in summer and longer nights in winter. But again, when night falls in our lives we tend to forget that it's always darkest before the dawn (regardless of how many times we've experienced dark times)—the dawn always comes.

EBBS AND FLOWS, HIGHS AND LOWS:
PREDICTABLY UNPREDICTABLE

In Chapter 1, I briefly discuss Ayurveda and states of tamas (rest), rajas (action), and sattva (reflection). As long as we're alive we cycle through all three states and, as much as we may try to distance ourselves from this, our bodies are natural. The earthy, low-energy tamasic state can be profoundly uncomfortable when we're from cultures in which work and accomplishment are heavily emphasized and so-called laziness is stigmatized. But no matter how unhappy or low energy we may be now, we will be energetic and happy again—and the cycle continues as long as we're alive.

This is an assurance in life—that ebb-and-flow rhythms are reliable. If we can ride the waves with a sense of curiosity while we experience the ups and downs, we can become relatively peaceful about the fluctuations. Our up-and-down cycles are complementary opposites that support each other in the homeostasis of life. The truth is that nothing lasts forever, except perhaps this invisible life force within us, and although this realization initially can be depressing, it can also be liberating.

When we look back, we can see how hard times taught us lessons and brought us blessings in cycles—just as the rich, full, good times brought us peace and joy. Your life centers around the expansion and contraction of your heart and the inhale and exhale of your breath. Through good times and bad you are alive, and whatever may be in front of you, you're where you're meant to be, doing what you're meant to do, and experiencing what you're meant to experience. Most of the pain we experience comes from the tension of believing that things are supposed to be different from what they are, but if you can watch your life with even a slight amount of distance from it (perspective), everything changes.

DIRECTIONALITY

Progress is rarely linear. An arrow needs to be pulled back to be launched forward. Still, the perception of regression can lead some archers to drop the slack in their bow and lose sight of the target. If you were to be promoted from a junior position in your company to president, you'd probably be happy and perhaps a little overwhelmed (in a good way). But if you were demoted from CEO to president, you may feel slighted and overwhelmed (in a bad way). Directionality matters, so much so that people will throw away relationships rather than roll them back or quit jobs rather than endure the indignity of being placed in a role that technically represents a reduction in status but may be a better fit. The same position can represent gaining ground or losing it—it all depends on where you're coming from.

We perceive time with a directionality of a familiar past and an unknown future. Because our brain equates familiarity with safety, the devil we know (the past) can have a rip current's pull. Whenever we do something new (the future), we have deep reflexes that set off alarms signaling danger. Nostalgia is a past sanitized of its previous uncertainty. Your future is infinite and unknowable. Although this may sound wonderful in principle, the deep survival reflexes that have been doing such a nice job of keeping you alive are not particularly excited about uncertainty. The reflexive lizard brain speaks softly and carries a big stick while the executive-functioning logical part of our brain seeks forward motion but gets steered off course by the wonky wheel of subconscious programming and will look for a culprit, often placing blame on itself for not understanding underlying influences. This push-pull force is the internal conflict of survival and progress, and although progress continues to win the long game, it loses many battles along the way.

TWO DIRECTIONS: MOVING THROUGH THE HUBS

There are two primary directions that we navigate within our hubs. In Part 2 of *The Parinama Method*, I focus on the bottom-up approach toward greater self-awareness, starting from the first hub (Chapter 4—HAVE) and progressing to the seventh (Chapter 10—KNOW) in chronological correspondence with the first 21 years of life (see Chapter 11). The opposite and complementary direction is the top-down approach of conscious creation: finding ideas and bringing them into reality starting with the expansiveness of the seventh hub to capture inspiration and descending all the way down to the practical and grounded first hub. Chapter 12 explores this approach, which can be used as a method of transformation through manifestation in the later phases of life (and is easier to follow and enact after reading Part 2).

THE FOUR PHASES OF LIFE

Some yogic traditions believe that a life is 1,008 cycles of the moon around the Earth (84 years) and that our life is divided into four phases. These phases of life are childhood (0–21), early adulthood (22–42), middle age (43–64), and old age (65 and over). The first 21-year phase is profoundly affected by parents, caregivers, and early social experiences. The phases that follow are opportunities to edit, elaborate, and shift holding patterns from the first 21 years. As I discuss, the truth of our embloom can be inconvenient (with its sense of purpose and mission), but it will tend to allow some leeway in childhood and early adulthood. However, the third-phase midlife crisis usually reveals truths that have been avoided. Much of these revelations and their release are stigmatized as selfish, self-indulgent, irresponsible, and even childish because they release and express unresolved, trapped joy that can be decades old. This so-called crisis usually dies down after an initial period of release and expression and clears the way for greater self-actualization.

The first phase (0–21 years old)

The first phase of development happens during the first 21 years of life. Although there is some functional use of all hubs at birth, their capacity increases sequentially, corresponding with the development of the nervous system and maturation of the body. For example, a toddler will be able to use words in the service of getting what it wants, but more highly developed communication and creativity starts around age seven or eight within the fifth hub. The hub chapters in Part 2 provide an in-depth examination of this first phase.

The second phase (22–42 years old)

Many of our patterns and beliefs are like contracts or subscriptions that automatically renew. If we don't periodically review the terms, we can spend our lives in personal, social, and cultural contracts that we're used to but that don't serve our best interests. Ideally, at the beginning of this second phase young adults should transition to early adulthood and take the wheel to drive their own lives. Young adults get their own apartments, begin to have intimate adult relationships, a career, and to find their society—communities that they choose and create. The onset of this phase can be a difficult transition because it's the beginning of surviving alone and doing the work of living one's own life. When entering the second phase, young adults have to start from the bottom after being on the mountaintop of high school and college as seniors. It's humbling to be in the unfamiliar world of adulthood, with its drudgery and practicality. After 21 years of receiving, young adults are dropped into the deep end of the pool, and when they struggle, they're often admonished and made to feel small by the same system that previously told them how special they are. This, like all transitions, can be difficult and lonely while young adults grieve the end of their childhoods. But this phase is also exciting: it focuses on establishing security, autonomy, purpose, and building a family of one's own.

The third phase (43–64 years old)

The third phase, starting at about age 43, is marked by an assessment of life—how to spend the rest of it. Up until the beginning of this phase, we tend to live our lives with the illusion of unlimited options and time, as if we have money-stuffed pockets and are deciding what to buy. At middle age we reach into our pockets and find that half the (fantasy) money's gone and that we need to act, or we may face regret. During this phase, parenting young children is usually winding down, and for some folks who felt undecided about having biological children, there can be a sense that this decision is now final. This is a phase for contemplating one's impact on the world, that is, giving back and making life-defining contributions. The previous four decades give perspective and there's more to come—still young but also having some wisdom and understanding the consequences of not taking action.

The fourth phase (65 and over)

In this phase, we harvest the fruits of our lives through activities we enjoy, family, and the release of regrets and grievances. This is the phase of wisdom, experience, and context, and yet there's so much more to learn and experience. The previous phases were busy and had plenty of distractions. Now, a greater emphasis is placed on the upper hubs of connection, truth, inspiration; the contemplation of one's life contribution often becomes a focus. If we have invested in good health, this phase can be relatively calm and enjoyable. If security, physical health, emotional health, connection, community, and personal power are underdeveloped or stuck in holding patterns, this phase can be difficult, lonely, and painful—but it's never too late for transformation.

TRUST YOURSELF: YOU KNOW MORE THAN YOU THINK YOU DO

In 1946, Benjamin Spock's groundbreaking *Baby and Child Care* revolutionized parenting and child-rearing. The first chapter is titled "Trust Yourself *and* Your Children," and the first sentence is, "You know more than you think you do." No one knows more about you than you do—there are no gurus. But there are teachers and lessons that have survived for decades and centuries, helping to guide us by using education to draw out our inner truths. True education develops our ability to find and draw out truths. Indoctrination tells us what to think, often selecting information to enforce a preferred worldview. Is your experience with education one of drawing out your truth, or is it one of indoctrination? There's no person better qualified to steer your life than you.

CURIOSITY AND THE MYTH OF PERMANENT HAPPINESS

What is happiness? An elevated mood, absence of pain, forgetting problems, and feeling good? On the continuum of feeling states, it's one of the best but as dynamic, living beings we should always expect to be moving through the spectrum of different feeling states. Paradoxically, our negative feelings only increase when we believe we should feel differently from how we do, perhaps feeling pressure or shame about not being happier. Happiness is an easy product to market: we part with our hard-earned money to get it and surrender more than we care to admit chasing illusions of it. The myth of a state of permanent happiness haunts many of us, so much so that when we're unhappy, we may even feel that we've done or are doing something wrong.

Instead of wishing for permanent happiness, try cultivating attention and curiosity for all feelings—enrich your experience of being alive through the good and the bad. Notice how mentally present and accepting you can remain in any situation, how curious you can be about exploring experiences in your life by watching and allowing—with awe or acceptance (a reduced ability to remain present is often a response to interruptions, which I discuss in Part 2). Before naming or categorizing something, try standing in awe and looking—really looking—to see that even within pain, sadness, and drudgery, there is an astonishing, wonder-inducing experience happening. If something is happening to us, we can get lost and/or overwhelmed, but when we see the same scenario in the lives of others, we view them with semi-detachment—even amusement. Now imagine being able to have this perspective within the power of the direct experience in your own life. Even feelings of happiness can be enhanced by paying attention to the direct experience of them. If we're unafraid of what we may see, curiosity can heighten and become a very powerful tool. If we attempt to create stability in a changing world by remaining rigid in our perceptions and beliefs, we become a fossil, a living relic of our past. Being walled off and protected with reactions like *That's how we've always done it* and *You're overthinking it* if presented with new ways of doing things blocks the experience of the world as it is. And what time has ever been one without change? Author Steven Pressfield writes in *The War of Art: Break Through the Blocks and Win Your Inner Creative Battles* that "[T]he levels of revelation that can unfold . . . in any art are inexhaustible." There is so much to see and experience, and as we pass through the transitions of life, awareness and presence give us a much richer experience.

CHANGES IN RELATIONSHIP WITH OTHERS

Relationships can struggle to right themselves when we change, and this can be difficult and sometimes painful. Some adaptive behaviors, such as tolerating poor behavior from others or showing very little emotion, can act as load-bearing beams in existing and long-standing relationships. Even the change of becoming more loving—and expecting that love to be returned—may disrupt a relationship that had previously functioned around relatively low expectations for connection, empathy, and reciprocity. When you combine the enactment of boundaries with the self-awareness for needing them, such as telling a demanding loved one that you've reached your capacity for talking about an issue, they may have a negative reaction. Sometimes they will stop coming to you, which initially may feel like rejection. There can be a period of loneliness—and even some grief—as you allow yourself to see the true nature of some of the relationships in your life that may be holding you back. But the space you make with boundaries creates room for new, enriching, and fulfilling relationships—it just requires a little patience, which also can be challenging. Finding support with a therapist, uplifting communities (sometimes online), or spending more time with existing, positive friends can be a lifesaver. This is a common theme that people ask to discuss during ongoing Parinama sessions: they experience positive transformation and joy while partners, family, and friends struggle with how the changes are impacting their own lives. For example, a man was showing more emotion and his wife told him she wanted her strong, silent husband back. He felt free, and she wanted him back in his box—they had to find a new way to relate to each other.

AN INSIDE JOB

The work of the Parinama Method can only be self-administered; attempting to fix people around you is procrastination and avoidance of the task at hand. Finding new ways to categorize people is a new way to judge them, although seeking to better understand folks can help with developing connections with them. You can attempt to change people by conversationally exploring the topics I discuss in the coming chapters and by encouraging the method's techniques without expressly explaining what you're doing. Depending on how receptive and trusting of you they are, there can be brief, brilliant shifts, but without their willing participation, they always steer back to their original patterns. No matter how well-intentioned you may be, trying to change people without their consent is manipulation that doesn't respect their autonomy. We should all be at the wheel, responsible for driving our own lives, and should incorporate and integrate changes when *we* choose them.

This work is an inside job and when we change within ourselves, the people around us change. It's also natural to initially read *The Parinama Method* with someone in mind other than yourself: your parents, a significant other, or anyone who causes you pain would be a natural choice. This is a standard way to make sense of these ideas (see Chapter 7). When we change, the people around us can also be positively affected, but ultimately, any change has to come from inside ourselves.

YOUR OWN EXPERIENCE

When we compare ourselves to other people, we compare ourselves to what is either visible or what we imagine about them. Most of us make efforts to appear happy even when we're not, and we hide things we don't want people to see. Almost everyone does this because it's part of conventional adulthood, so what we see and imagine in other people is always only part of the story—and often, an astonishingly small part. Our direct experience is not in imagining what other people will think, nor is it in seeking their validation of our worthiness. It's experienced by looking through your own eyes and feeling the sensations within your body. What we see in others is what we choose to see, colored by the filters of our own perception. How we interpret the actions of others is a projection of our own worldview, our own personal truth, not an absolute or universal one; the better we can see in ourselves, the more we can draw it out of others.

Let's face it, there are mysteries about ourselves we're still trying to figure out, which is an important consideration for relating to other people and for keeping relationships fresh. And this is essential for understanding how change works: people change when they're ready to. Isn't that how it works for you?

Next, in Part 2 of *The Parinama Method*, I discuss each hub at length in its own chapter, using the Map of the Hubs provided in Chapter 2.

Part 2

THE SEVEN HUBS

HAVE: INFANT, SELF-PRESERVATION

Basics	Themes	Interruptions and Stressors	Adaptations and Holding Patterns	Techniques and Exercises
Home	Physical Boundary	Absence and Loss	Characteristics of a Balanced and Out-of-Balance First Hub	Sanctuary and Grounding
Secure, Grounded, and Tidy	Solid Ground	Nurture and Nourishment	Inflating and Shrinking	Physical Boundary
Body	Routine, Consistency, and Reliability	Boundary Invasions: Medical Procedures, Accidents, and Illnesses	Intellectualization Replaces Embodiment	Consistency and Completion
Food and Rest	Ancestry, Origin Stories, and Owning Them	Instability and Insecurity at Work	The Shadow: Fear	Charge and Discharge
Work	Birth: Welcomed and Wanted			
Money and Prosperity	Death			

Chapter 4

THE FIRST HUB—HAVE

SAFETY AND SECURITY

To fully embody the right to be here is essential for the ability to experience security.
The right to take up space, have your essential human needs met, and be a unique
individual. Without establishing the foundation of these rights, the ability to succeed
and thrive may be possible to achieve but difficult to impossible to sustain.
—*Anodea Judith*

THE FIRST OF THE seven hubs, the HAVE hub, is physical. Our overall sense of trust and safety began to form at the dawn of our life with every subsequent experience being built on the previous one, all the way up to this moment. Albert Einstein, responding to a reporter's query, said, "I think the most important question facing humanity is the following: Is the universe a friendly place?" Our relative position to Einstein's question begins at birth—remember that even then, we're carrying information from our experience in the womb—establishing the sense of whether the physical world is safe and can be trusted, thus marking the foundation of our faith in it. Without connection to and relationship with our bodies, we're disconnected from our life, pushing ourselves to exhaustion, injuring ourselves with physically punishing exercise (or not exercising at all), and skipping or avoiding bodily care and regular medical checkups.

As infants, we experience life through sensation because the nervous system and brain don't have the capacity for words and intellectualizing. As a result, we cannot rely on intellectual memory to recall this stage of life. Early experiences and the environment we're born into train and shape our bodily reflexes. The lives we have now were built on the relative solidity of these early moments; these sensations were where our taproot into the world first developed, beginning with the feelings and sensations experienced in our mother's womb.

Physical awareness is the first layer of our experience. It begins to form in utero and at birth. In a 2010 interview, therapist and somatic pioneer Peter Levine describes the body as a container that everything experienced in your life is felt from, either as a response to your surroundings or from what's rising within your body. How physically safe and secure you feel affects everything about your trust in the world: it's the foundation from which everything grows.

If at any time life feels mundane, consider what mathematicians and scientists have determined: your chance of being born was one in 400 trillion (see Table 4.1). We would probably be better at appreciating the extraordinary odds of our birth if everyone we know had not won the same lottery—and it's significantly more likely that you would win a lottery than be born. Part of appreciating the improbability of your birth involves shifting the belief that being extraordinary involves exclusion; but if you insist on exclusion, consider it from a universal perspective of all human existence being cosmically miraculous compared to anything else in the known universe.

Odds of being hit by lightning	1:500,000
Odds of winning a lottery	1:300,000,000
Odds of being born	1:400,000,000,000

Table 4.1: Odds of Being Born

Your mother was born with about one million eggs; of those, between 300 to 400 are released over her lifetime, but only one became the foundation of your body. The egg that determined half of your biological source code encountered millions of spermatozoa in the marathon of fertilization. Now consider the lines of your forebearers reaching back eons before recorded time. You are the outcome of the lives of a vast network of ancestors—so many babies were born, grew up, and had babies themselves for you to be here. They are part of your story, and you are their legacy. Perhaps this moment—the one you're in right now—feels mundane. Nonetheless, the circumstances that have made it possible—every force that conspired for your body to be here now—are cosmically and mathematically improbable. Yet here you are.

You may think that if you don't remember something, you can't trust that it matters—it's a good point and one I discuss in this chapter. The present-day state of your first hub and how it feels to live in your body right now is evidence we can examine. On one hand, it can seem ridiculous to consider birth trauma and early life so profoundly formative and influential on our adult selves. On the other, we have reflexes and behaviors that operate from programming outside of our conscious control. If we consciously decide we want to do something, that decision should be the final word on the matter—but it isn't—many self-sabotaging behaviors have their origins (and are addressable) in this hub. If we have anxiety about security or we fear change even as we crave it, the HAVE hub is where we explore a conscious relationship with trust, stability, safety, and boundaries.

ORIENTATION

Physical location: Feet, legs, knees, bum, and perineum, the physical boundary of our bodies

First cycle: Third trimester through one year old

Task: To claim the sense of boundary and physical security within the body

Rights: The right to have, the right to be here

Identity: I am what I have, I am my body, I am my physical possessions.

Reconciliation: I am physically safe and secure; I feel my physical boundary.

According to developmental biologists, the timing of a human birth is when an infant's head can fit through the birth canal. This timing is the result of brain size, not readiness for survival in the world. As a result, we rely on our caretakers for the first year of life in a way that is mostly unprecedented in the natural world. Our infant requirements for survival and the demands placed on our parents are significant. Further complicating matters, the capacity to attend to a child gets disrupted by the stress, illness, and trauma in parents' own lives, and even those with the best familial blueprints of nurture and childrearing cannot control unpredictable external stressors like accidents and illness, which can knock a life out of its orbit.

The primary needs of a newborn are food, shelter, and nurture. Consistently meeting these early needs is essential for physical survival and for forming a solid physical and psychological foundation. Right now, bring your attention to your feet and notice if they are both planted on the ground. Then notice if you tend to shift in your seat and observe the physical boundary of your body where your skin contacts your clothing and the air. Everything within the skin is you and it is *yours*. If the body feels everywhere and nowhere (without a clear boundary), focusing on this hub will be helpful. Lightly tapping or gently patting on your body helps you arrive at this moment as you place both feet on the ground. As the foundation and container for our feelings, power, connection, communication, and creative expression, finding physical security within our bodies supports all the hubs.

The work of the HAVE hub is to instill the senses of trust, safety, and protection within our bodies. Not everyone has the same access to resources to meet fundamental needs. Understanding our own basic human requirements should enhance the empathy and consciousness that are essential for the actualization—and transcendence—in the upper hubs while we learn how to cultivate boundary, ground, and consistency from within ourselves.

INITIAL DEVELOPMENT

Life begins in a warm, comfy place where needs are effortlessly met. It's the definitive experience of excellent, anticipatory service. In the womb, before we can even want something, it's provided. As adults, there are times we seek unconsciously to return to this comfort when we feel vulnerable, sick, or sad. In the womb, we're merged as one with our environment, touched and held from all directions. We're unified with our mother's diet, health, and emotional state. When we're born, we are pushed into a world and experience cold, light, and hunger for the first time. Sound is louder, and when placed in our mother's arms, we return to the familiar sound of her heartbeat and the comfort of her warmth. We have just survived the most extraordinary transition of life: being born. When we look at our baby pictures, there's usually a combination of awe and estrangement—*How could that be me?*—combined with a charmed sense of recognition.

How our HAVE hub developed began with what that newborn experienced and carries patterns and programming into adulthood. For example, self-sabotaging behaviors partially arise from early disturbance in the development of our sense of safety and trust in this first hub. In our first months of life, getting our needs met was beyond our control, and the only way to communicate hunger or discomfort was through crying. Out in the world, there are periods of hunger, cold, and discomfort—sometimes even pain. Our experience during this transition taught us whether the world was a safe, kind place or a hostile, withholding one or somewhere in between.

Psychologist Erik Erikson called this early developmental stage "trust versus mistrust," referring to whether the infant establishes a clear sense that it can trust its caregivers and environment. The infant experiences mother and the surrounding environment as merged with itself and has only a dawning sense of its physical boundary, so trust or mistrust is internalized in its sense of trust within itself. According to Erikson, that successful resolution in this stage leads to a sense of hope carried forward into the following stages of development and adulthood. Judith writes, "Without trust, your survival feels constantly threatened, and because there is nothing you can do to meet the threat, the anxiety is unbearable [see Chapter 2]." Table 4.2 lists other psychological-development theories that correspond to this early period of life.

Developmental Theory	Age and Stage	Purpose of Stage
Erikson	Trust versus mistrust (birth to 18 months)	Care the infant receives is consistent, predictable, and reliable—in this case, it will develop a sense of trust that it will carry with it to other relationships, and it will be able to feel secure even when threatened.
Maslow	Physiological needs	Food, water, warmth, rest
Freud	Oral (birth to 18 months)	Chewing and sucking produce comfort (some overlap with second-hub development).
Piaget	Sensorimotor (birth to 2 years)	The infant is discovering the relationship between its body and the environment using senses (some overlap with second-hub development).

Table 4.2: Infant Psychological-Development Theories

Parents, family, and caregivers are responsible for meeting all our needs in the early development of the first hub. We're born with a suite of survival reflexes that include turning toward touch, grasping, and sucking when the roof of the mouth is stimulated, all originating from the brain stem. We're born ready to receive. There's no beam-me-up-Scotty option—we cannot return to the mother ship and try again. This is our life, and we need to make it work or otherwise perish—and surviving may require adapting in ways that affect the development and expression of a hub. We're born to survive, and we find ways to make the most of our circumstances. It is often a safer adaptation to believe our own shortcomings affect our security than it is to comprehend the terrifying notion that our caregivers are incapable. Perhaps it's less overwhelming to think that our survival is within our control rather than tethered to an out-of-control environment. Judith writes, "A smooth first year of life creates a solid foundation that can better withstand or recover from difficulties later on."

If our caregivers didn't meet our early needs, we found ourselves in the impossible position of relying on ourselves, which we were developmentally incapable of doing effectively. Although our time in the womb, birth, and the first year of life are not part of conscious memory, those early experiences will implant the sense of security or insecurity in our bodies that we carry into childhood and adulthood. The interruptions, traumas, and even abuses from this stage are not simply a matter of intellectual processing (although cognitively understanding this hub supports the restoration of trust and of feeling safe in our bodies). Restoration and reclaiming involve the physicality of our bodies.

Maslow's hierarchy (see Chapter 1) emphasizes that at the foundation of our psyches is the need for consistency and predictability of basic needs. As adults, we may find ourselves either rigid and fixated on routines or we may be unable to create and/or uphold them. A routine helps create embodied security, but if it's too rigid, disruptions result in destabilization. The opposite adaptation is the tendency toward constant chaos and disorder, which becomes so familiar that it's soothing (even though it drains our energy and often leads to adverse outcomes). In the techniques and exercises section, I emphasize the body-based approach and address first-hub behavior tendencies as holding patterns in the body. Through this combination of awareness and gentle shifting, we can support and minimize the impact of early interruptions (see Chapter 2).

BASICS

Here, I discuss the functions within this hub, which is where we possess—our home, material belongings, and physical body. As we ascend the hubs, without the balancing and conscious reclaiming in the HAVE hub, we may look to possess through emotional manipulation, overpowering people, plagiarism, or perhaps by (possessively) believing our friends and partners belong to us. But through self-possession in this hub, we can access greater expression of higher hubs by creating inner security and releasing possessive inclinations. The practical effects of this hub on our lives occur in five areas:

- **Home and shelter:** Do we have a place where we feel safe and nurtured?

- **Body:** How do we relate to and care for our body?

- **Nourishment and nurture:** What is our relationship with the need for food, touch, and rest?

- **Work and livelihood:** Do we feel fearful, overwhelmed, or anxious about our job?

- **Money and physical possessions:** Do we hoard or have a hard time keeping money and prosperity?

HOME

Home is both where we live now and the place(s) where we grew up. We have a homeland of familiar sights, sounds, and faces that soothes us with nostalgia and connects us to our early formative life. This specific feeling of returning home to familiarity—the place where we felt and loved for the first time—is universal. While I was writing *The Parinama Method* in October 2020, Nigeria was in political upheaval. My Nigerian friends living in America were struggling to explain the depth of the loss they were feeling, to put into words the meaning of *home* and how it feels when you cannot return to it. Whether it's a diner your dad took you to for pie or spending time with a beloved grandmother or driving around your town, home is a feeling we can return to, and the pang of nostalgia grows as places tied to our history slip away. This sense of home is a shared human experience, fundamental to being human. Perhaps we don't return often, if at all, but knowing this place is waiting forms a type of emotional bedrock in us, one that my Nigerian friends were grieving as I wrote these words.

SECURE, GROUNDED, AND TIDY

As adults, the home we create for ourselves is the fortress and foundation we return to after venturing into the world. Home is a place to restore ourselves, to rest, and to feel nurtured and protected, a place of our own—perhaps shared with people we love and trust. Our inner harmony is expressed by and through our dwelling. In this context, it should be a safe and comforting place. Making room in your home by removing clutter affects psychological peace and harmony. If we're going to have possessions that we house and care for, they should be life-affirming. There are many methods and resources available that support organizing and decluttering your home, which helps to strengthen stability in this hub.

An important aspect of a home is the boundary of who is allowed into it. Do the people who enter respect your sensitivities and your belongings, or are they oblivious to them? A house guest who comes empty-handed, makes a mess, takes things before they're offered, and invites strangers along without your permission disrupts calm in the HAVE hub.

If you have ever experienced housing insecurity—even for a moment, such as moving—you know how disruptive it can feel. The physical structure of home is the protective boundary for the body, sheltering it from the elements. It's unrealistic to expect anyone who's experiencing housing insecurity on any level to focus on the pursuits of other hubs. Even relatively benign experiences, such as fighting with people we live with or being locked out, show us that the stability and safety of our physical environment is a primary, fundamental human right and that without it, fully focusing on anything else is just not possible. When folks who are struggling with meeting basic needs appear unstable, it is because they are operating without a foundation.

BODY

It's been said that without our spirit we're a corpse, and without a body we're a ghost. We need a body to experience our life, and the care we give it extends into all other areas of our lives. Many of my yoga students would talk about experiencing their bodies as a patchwork quilt of pain, stiffness, and sensation, with areas described as either numb or blank. When we feel sick or get injured, do we walk it off, wait it out, or go to the doctor? If we work when instead we need to rest and if we avoid calling the doctor until we're in terrible condition and need the emergency room, this is where behavior changes that are relatively minor can result in major positive shifts. In this hub, I discuss the activities of essential care like brushing our teeth, showering, changing our sheets, eating healthy food, drinking enough water, and resting when we're tired as high-impact acts of reclamation.

Physical care and rest can be surprisingly difficult for many (seemingly) high-functioning people. And like home, as I discuss above, all humans need the foundation of the basic needs of nourishment, rest, medical care, and shelter—again, it's universal. To be born is to deserve to live, and anything (a system or a person) that obstructs this dignity interferes with a person's humanity and first-hub capacity. When individuals can take better care of themselves, they begin to feel more connected to these essential, fundamental rights for all people. During the 100-plus interviews and consultations I conducted for *The Parinama Method*, one executive told me, "I'm tired, but I'll sleep when I'm dead," yet she was eager to address her anxiety about her job performance, so we worked together using the method. She also said, "I used to fall asleep working on my laptop in bed and forget to brush my teeth. I hadn't seen a dentist in years because I was ashamed to be an executive with a mouthful of cavities. Now, as I've started tuning into my physical awareness when I feel scattered, I turn to my body, ground myself, and feel my physical boundary. My consciousness has also expanded, and I understand why physical needs are so important for all people." The foundation of the first hub involves body care that includes annual doctor visits and your medical team's engagement in supporting the care of your body-mind.

FOOD AND REST

Recall the discussion of cycles and the Ayurvedic quality of tamas (see Chapter 1): by trusting the down cycle and allowing ourselves the time to rest, ground, and restore, we can rise when the time is right. We can return fully from tamas, rested and ready to tackle whatever we want to accomplish. Without rest we are diminished and function at a fraction of our capacity.

Food, nourishment, and nurture blend into deep and soothing comfort in both the first hub, HAVE, and second hub, FEEL. In utero through infancy, a baby is in a merged, unconscious oblivion with its mother (the first hub); in the second hub, a deepening sense of pleasure, sensation, and preference come online as an infant begins to experience the world beyond mother through its dawning senses. But in the HAVE hub during these early weeks and months of infancy, nurture and responsiveness with food are deeper and more primal, laying the foundation of physical trust.

Consider the warm, enveloping comfort of sleep after a good meal or zoning out with entertainment—it's a deeply comforting, safe (even infantile) state as we lie down and allow for this deep, simple satisfaction. Allowing ourselves this experience without judgment and with acknowledging our need for this kind of comfort is restorative. We already rest and sleep (perhaps not very well), but by bringing the restoration and comfort of these activities into consciousness without shame and guilt, they can become deeply nourishing and satisfying.

If you need babying, offer yourself comfort. First-hub disembodiment and its relationship with food and rest can carry a lot of shame and guilt, making self-compassion, self-awareness, and self-worth challenging. But if we allow ourselves to see that needing time for resting and eating is likely related to first-hub needs, perhaps we can be gentle with ourselves.

If we eat for comfort or use food like a sedative, we are asking for something that is fulfilling a deep need. When we war with our bodies over urges and cravings we can't seem to control, we may believe our body is betraying us when it is actually crying out for nurture and comfort. If the precious baby in you wants to eat a lot of food—feed this sweet, innocent baby. When you need a nap, swaddle yourself and try putting a big, sweet, satisfied smile on your face. Accepting and allowing are necessary to integrate this fractured sense of ourselves.

Another part of care in this hub is seeking help for our mental health. If we feel depressed and need care, it is through this self-care that we nurture ourselves by seeking support and service. Remember, there's nothing you can do that's outside the spectrum of human behavior, and there is no agreed upon professional definition of being psychologically normal. In my interviews with people who were self-soothing for comfort, I would often hear about how lonely they were feeling, and they would discuss how they felt astonished by the paradox that loneliness is one of the most widely shared human experiences.

WORK

Our livelihood meets many needs for us. It provides an income that feeds and shelters us, can connect us to others, and can provide us with a sense of purpose. Regarding money, meeting essential needs is the domain of this first hub, and creating wealth above and beyond this is in the expression of the action-oriented third hub—DO. Still, the ability to have and maintain money for essential needs is in the HAVE hub, where we contain, support, and secure our physical existence.

A 2018 Purdue University study looked at the association of money with happiness. In an article about the study, lead author Andrew T. Jebb states, "We found that the ideal income point is $95,000 for life evaluation and $60,000 to $75,000 for emotional well-being." Furthermore, the study found that once the maximum threshold for life evaluation was met, further increases in income tended to be associated with reduction in life satisfaction.

According to the study, the amount of money required to achieve physical and emotional well-being for a single person is $4,000–4,500/month in take-home (after-tax) pay—of course, there are variations depending on the cost of living where you live, the impact of inflation, and whether you have a family. If housing, food, health insurance, basic needs, and some pleasures are met and saving is possible, we can live in relative first-hub peace. If you receive noncash assistance from family, friends, or support programs for any of these needs, the cash value contributes to the $4,500 a month for physical and emotional well-being.

In the first hub, our relationship with work focuses on whether we feel secure in our means of earning income. Do we trust that we will receive a consistent paycheck and is our work physically and mentally sustainable? A volatile boss, a stressful work environment with high turnover, high performance pressure, and unclear goals and objectives all lead to instability in our sense of livelihood. Further affecting physical instability is work that does not pay a living wage. If work cannot meet our basic, essential human needs, we will be distracted, destabilized, and produce lower-quality work that is beneath our true potential. As Maslow's hierarchy clearly illustrates, before we can ascend to greater levels of purpose and actualization, our mortgage, bills, and food need to be taken care of. We can't reach upward toward our aspirations when we stand on the shifting ground of physical instability.

MONEY AND PROSPERITY

Experiencing insecurity with basic needs—especially early in life—can have a lasting effect that complicates our relationship with money. Early insecurity can lead to holding patterns, such as hoarding or dissociative spending, which create debt and so, put financial security at risk. Since the pulse of this hub beats below the surface of our conscious mind, no amount of wealth consciousness will override disrupted and interrupted security programming. A relationship with money gets stored in our bones and tissues—sometimes, it reaches back into our ancestry. Long after the Great Depression, many who survived were still fearful and retained hoarding habits. Children of survivors born decades later were affected by the intensity and severity of the lasting trauma they witnessed in their parents and grandparents.

Money empowers our efforts and expresses our values—whatever they may be. Money is an amplifier: consider it neutral potential energy that's neither good nor bad until it gets turned into action through spending. When we have it, some of our true nature is revealed. If we're miserly, petty, or cruel, our money will amplify our ability to express these qualities. If we're generous, creative, and kind, these qualities also become magnified through the power of money. How we spend money is individual and an expression of what we value. It is beyond *The Parinama Method*'s scope to discuss healing a money relationship—and unnecessary because there are many excellent books on the topic.

Physical possessions are in the domain of the HAVE hub, but they cross over into the second hub when we become emotionally attached to them. Young children often form an attachment to a toy or blanket—what psychologists call a "transitional object"—that they rely on while they navigate transitions into independence and autonomy. The consistency of a physical object supports confidence as they make their way during the separation from the merged state with the mother or primary caregiver. This is common, as reports show two out of three children who attend nursery school have a transition object. If a transition to secure emotional attachments with people isn't made, as adults, we may find ourselves with strong material attachments. If we tend to personify and feel a connection to our possessions, this can interfere with our ability to let go of things when we need to release them. An inability to part with items affects first-hub holding patterns—specifically, the inflated adaptation of hoarding.

Prosperity and manifestation require repetitive, mundane work. Although we can experience a flow state and periods of ease in creation, a paradox exists because we need to show up for the work every day; this is a paradoxical complementary opposite—both things seemingly conflict while simultaneously being true. It's an appealing idea that, if we're excited enough about something and that it seems meant to be, it will be effortless to attain. But to make something happen we need to spend time with it; although the initial attraction can be effortless, there will be work to do.

I discuss discipline and action further in the third hub (see Chapter 6) and go even deeper into activating the top-down current of creation in Part 3 of *The Parinama Method*. For now, I underscore the reality that succeeding in any venture requires mundane repetition that persists through challenges, disillusionment, and failure. Showing up every day is how we transform an idea into a physical reality as an expression of love and intention. Every hub plays a role, and the first hub is the practical reality of the importance of consistency. Boundary and containment are essential themes in this hub because having something requires holding and keeping it. What we create in the higher hubs will slip through our fingers if we cannot maintain and contain with a solid first-hub boundary.

Professor and mythologist of the human experience Joseph Campbell told us to follow our bliss and described the hero's journey: it starts with the call to adventure and is followed by a departure from the life that the hero has previously known. Next come trials, tribulations, and an abyss. Last, the hero, if persistent, returns to society with the treasures gained from the journey (see Chapter 9). Understandably, we prefer the call-to-adventure and the return-with-glory parts. The trials, tribulations, and abyss are less popular, which is a shame because they are where the profound transformation happens. And we may like to imagine mythical, action-packed battles with dragons, but the trials, tribulations, and abyss are the lonely, isolating, inner struggles with ourselves as we work past insecurities, limits, and fears through long hours, days, and years of devoted discipline. It's hard; manifesting takes work. In a twist of new-age irony, manifestation requires limitation and consistency, as we must choose one course of action over all the others. This process of bringing a dream into reality means focusing on something to the exclusion of other activities. Manifestation is about being grounded through this limitation. Judith speaks of the "[U]nrealistic attachment to freedom in the yoga and new age spiritual community." We paradoxically break through limits and experience greater freedom through growth by practicing restraint and discipline. Developing any kind of fitness or education requires showing up consistently for what really matters (see Chapters 6 and 7). It's an expression of love.

THEMES

PHYSICAL BOUNDARY

In our early years, our caretakers do their best to help us grow and may believe that because they are responsible for us, we belong to them; but the body you are born into is sovereign: you are the sole owner of all it contains. Throughout your life you will live with—and love—family, friends, community, and intimate relationships—and still, your body is yours.

A newborn baby is a soft and delicate miracle—everyone who surrounds a birth gets a contact high from the magic of new life. The inclination to delicately wrap it in loose blankets is counterintuitive to the fact that snugly swaddling the tiny body helps a baby feel the safety of containment within its physical boundary.

The self-advocacy of caring for our body through awareness and enforcement of physical boundaries is part of adult functioning. The only reasonable time to expect to be cared for without verbally communicating our needs was when we were preverbal. Expecting others to intuit and/or anticipate our needs and punish any shortfalls with anger or withdrawal can be related to the needs of the first hub. Again, infants experience their body as bonded and merged with mother or a primary caregiver. If this early experience of deep safety is not fulfilling and internalized, we may be fixated on achieving warm, dark, zoned-out states as adults.

Teens and adults with short- or long-term disabilities who need physical assistance require the dignity of their physical boundary to be respected. When caretakers don't ask permission or have not established trust, their caretaking can be an invasion. Any unwanted touch, especially by force, is profoundly damaging to this essential foundation of physical security. A boundary is crossed by unwanted hugging, close-talking, or a handshake that lingers a little too long. Many of us were raised without this understanding and received unwanted hugs and/or touch from adults and medical examinations without consent or were pinched, prodded, and grabbed by other children.

The first step to establishing our physical boundary is to bring awareness to it. Awareness, observation, and enforcement of the physical boundary leads to greater inner security and confidence with boundaries of the other hubs (see Chapter 2). When our boundary is broken, we feel uncomfortable, but sometimes question ourselves about the validity of that feeling. The rule is simple: if you feel uncomfortable, it's not right for you. Keep in mind that overt abuse isn't the only breaker of the physical boundary: hugging and/or touching people who are not 100 percent okay with it is inappropriate, so don't do it; and if you don't want to be touched or hugged, you can simply say so.

Folks who don't understand boundaries will protest and resist us when we try to enforce them. Boundary invaders are often unconscious abusers, and if they don't respect your requests, it's best to create distance or cut ties altogether.

One of the hallmarks of a healthy physical boundary is the ability to say when we've had enough of an unfulfilling relationship or situation. But if we still crave the merging and connection of this first hub, we may (subconsciously) fear potential loss and separation if we draw the line. *Enough* is hard to understand if there's a deep need to be held and attended to, coupled with a fear that we don't deserve more or that we'll experience alienation if we don't gratefully take whatever is offered, regardless of its quality.

Another sign of a healthy physical boundary is not apologizing when your body needs to get through tight quarters. There should be no *I'm sorry* for existing and taking up space. We should say *Excuse me* or *Pardon me* to people who are oblivious to seeing that they need to move. Then, saying *Thank you* will feel more appropriate as we step by someone in our way. So, a new rule: only apologize for making a mistake (your body and existence are not mistakes). Your body is a container, and without containment we feel perpetually exhausted, often without understanding why. For many people, experiencing the physical boundary is a simple yet astonishing practice. The techniques and exercises below help bring the sensation of boundary into your body.

SOLID GROUND

Judith writes, "Many people who cannot find their true path in life have simply not yet found their ground. Sometimes they are busy looking up instead of down, where the feet meet the path." Solid ground is a calming and energizing feeling that's reliable and consistent. Even though falling will hurt, the ground always catches us. When we sit and lie down, it welcomes us with the subtle, profound, nurturing support of consistently and predictably holding us. How connected are you to this solidity? If you're seated, pay attention to the bottoms of your feet: Are they planted on the ground or are they on tiptoe or perhaps with sides down, but insoles and toes elevated? Adjust your body and place both feet on the floor, bringing attention to the bottoms of them, and notice how it feels. My own first impactful revelation for *The Parinama Method* came from gaining awareness when I brought attention to my feet.

We savor the sensations of our bare feet in the grass and our toes in the sand. These experiences feel good and relax us because we are part of the natural world. In addition to the physical grounding, the surrounding nature soothes us as we connect to the land, plants, animals, and sky. In the techniques and exercises below, I discuss the practices of charging and discharging using the physical ground and the Japanese practice of Shinrin-yoku: forest bathing.

The physical connection to solid earth and consciousness of the effect it has on us (and of the relationship we have with it) gives us a place to find deep comfort within ourselves—it's simple and profound. When we're in contact with the ground and we push down into it, the counterreaction is the sensation of wanting to rise upward. A paradox in this hub is that pushing down prompts upward extension of the spine and body, a movement that embodies power, which I discuss in the third hub. To rise, we need our feet on solid ground.

ROUTINE, CONSISTENCY, AND RELIABILITY

The ground, the existence of our body, and gravity are constants that anchor us to the physical world. I discuss discipline and action in the third hub; here, I focus on the solidity of repetition and how it creates trust. For better or worse, anything we repeat (anything we consistently do), becomes real. Our routines orient us, and without them we may feel untethered and even anxious.

During the testing phase for Food and Drug Administration approval of antidepressants, scientists needed depressed rats, and so they developed a protocol they named CUS for the chronic, unpredictable stress they used to manufacture depression. Instead of a dramatic or life-threatening event, they introduced constant change and interruption to the rats, including tilted cages, damp bedding, new cells, altered cycles of light and dark, and the smells and sounds of predators. As a result, the animals developed depression-like symptoms: they became lethargic, apathetic, stopped grooming themselves, stopped building nests, and stopped using running wheels.

In an uncertain world, anchoring to consistency and routine can create calm. Once we've embodied and grounded ourselves, we can feel our body as the container for feeling and emotion in the second hub—benefitting from first-hub solidity, we can minimize anxiety, insecurity, and tolerate change.

ANCESTRY, ORIGIN STORIES, AND OWNING THEM

Our lives are like a play in which the stage was set before we were born, with characters, circumstances, and an environment in place when we joined the plot. We may envision the drama coming to life when we're born, but we joined a cast of lives that were already in progress—with their lives also shaped by those who came before them. Knowing our origin story helps us understand the multifaceted circumstances of our arrival. Learning our origin story doesn't relegate us to the past; it helps us understand the circumstances and precedent that built who we are right now, so we can better know ourselves. We inherit the patterns of our parents and ancestors through genes, traditions, and epigenetics that can incorporate unprocessed traumas of previous generations.

The storyline that we join at birth affects who we become, and it can be illuminating to learn it. Our origin story is the root that unites our lives to the natural world and to our ancestors. Although we are physically separate, we are both part of the natural world and part of a lineage. When we lose our connection to either one, we tend to feel anxious. This grounding unification, through our ancestors, birth, and early life, weave us into the fabric of humanity and the entire natural world. Judith writes, "Our roots represent where we come from: the earth, womb, our ancestors and family, and

our personal history. We cannot simultaneously deny our past and maintain our roots." Our origin story provides context for understanding the conditions and circumstances of our birth: the political and cultural climate when we were born, the surrounding family events, the economic and cultural stressors, the critical early incidents, and any difficult occurrences never talked about, such as accidents, deaths, and illnesses. At birth our parents were godlike heroes to us; maturation involves the reconciliation of this view, a rightsizing of parents into fellow humans who have a special connection with us that is the blueprint and foundation for all our relationships.

If you want to leave your past in the past or if you consider your family history and birth story unnecessary, it may indicate that there's something in your subconscious you don't care to resurface. There are no rules for what needs to be done here and leaving these matters unexplored is a reasonable choice. Still, the memories (and even the physical movements) of our ancestors are passed down through the behaviors of our primary caregivers. If we did not feel welcomed and wanted at birth—before there is a boundary between us and the world—these feelings are internalized. Without compassionate, conscious awareness, it can feel like living a haunted life with unseen forces shifting our sense of stability and well-being. When we can surface and explore this facet of our identity, we uncover part of the mystery of who we are and have the opportunity to consciously embrace or release the parts we choose.

During gestation and birth, feeling unwanted or unsafe creates patterns (reversible) that require nurture and responsiveness in adulthood. Your origin story, specifically as it relates to the first hub, includes your mother's experience carrying you during pregnancy and the events and circumstances of your birth. Who was present? If possible, ask your parents and family members what they remember about your birth and early months of life—and keep in mind that what you hear will be a mix of fact and revisionist history.

BIRTH: WELCOMED AND WANTED

Dante Alighieri wrote in *La Vita Nuova*, "In that part of the book of my memory before which little that can be read, there is a rubric, saying, "Here beginneth the New Life." For better and sometimes for worse, we learn about our formative events because they have been installed like programming in our bodies. When we were born, did we feel wanted? Were we conceived in love? Were we embraced, attended to, and cooed over? Were we watched with wonder and adoration or were we treated as an obligation and duty? What was the transition like, and how did we first experience the world outside the womb? Was the room quiet and warm with soft light or was there the beeping machinery and cold air of a delivery room? Imagine waking up from deep, satisfying sleep to the described conditions of your birth. How would you expect the rest of your day to go?

For some people this exploration is pleasant and fun, but for others it's upsetting. Feeling unwanted, for example, creates interruption that can require adopted children to reconcile their birth mother having surrendered them (regardless of their loving adoptive home). This is a feeling that is deeper than rational thought and deserves gentle patience when it's explored; examining it can help us to understand some important experiences that shaped us before our memory could record them.

The maternal physical role runs deep. The connection to our biological origin and the fused sense of identity during gestation is a connection that reaches into our bodies and minds. The new fathers I interviewed spoke of knowing the relationship was biological, but it was still hard for them to have their child prefer their wives or partners for the first year or so. Even in the same-sex couple interviews there was a distinction that was less about gender and more about a primal sense of maternal and paternal roles. A gay father told me of his children's matter-of-fact explanation that he was the dad, and his partner was the mom, which he had struggled with because housework and nurture was shared equally and the couple had made conscious efforts to avoid gender labeling. "David does the cooking," he said. "I don't know if that has anything to do with it." Neither do I.

Knowing your birth story, however, is not essential for restoring ground and stability in this hub. It's nice to know, but if it exposes you to a hurt you don't want to endure, don't pursue this information. Adopted children or those of us who cannot be in touch with family, say through estrangement or death, can simply explore the birthing practices common at the time and even meditate on it if that feels right. The modern delivery and labor room in a hospital is a recent development in human history; the past 50 years have seen a great deal of progress in making birth a gentler transition.

But many of us were born under bright lights in clinical surroundings and then got slapped on the bum and poked and prodded in our first moments of life—all of these things were shocks to our soft and vulnerable body. And keep in mind that the remnants of old methods remain stored in our cultural consciousness and ancestry.

DEATH

As soon as we arrive in our body, we want it to survive, but even our most valiant and perfect efforts will end in death. We fear death instinctively—remember, our reflexes are tuned for survival—yet we tend to believe it's our conscious efforts that keep us safe. But everything that keeps us alive, from our heartbeat to our fight, freeze, or flight reflexes, operates from behind the locked door of the unconscious like a guardian angel yanking you out of harm's way before the conscious mind has a chance to form a plan. This profound suite of protections is deep within the roots of the first hub. The ancient Bardo Thödol (The Tibetan Book of the Dead) states, "Soon we all will die. Our hopes and fears will be irrelevant." Consider facing the root of all fear: everything we're intellectually scared of relates to the fear of death. You're alive now, so why not make the most of it?

Death presents a paradox: to live fully and courageously, we must accept death as inevitable. In Himalayan ashrams, there's a Bhutanese saying spoken repeatedly by practitioners to constantly remind them of death: "To be a truly happy person, you must contemplate death five times a day." The notion of death has a psychological hold on us, but once we can accept some manner of its inevitability, we become more free. Acceptance of the eventual death of ourselves and others can spark despair and anxiety, or it can invigorate and heighten the awareness of being alive right now. The courage, activation, and urgency to live with bravery and depth is happening *now* as we realize that life is a limited-time engagement. By accepting death, we can fully live. When we expand the aperture and see the paradox of our lives as both miraculously improbable and relatively insignificant, we can set ourselves free to do and be with complete integrity.

INTERRUPTIONS AND STRESSORS

Interruption in this hub is caused by instability, inconsistency, and inattention to the human right of having fundamental needs met and by invasion of the physical boundary. For infants and children, inconsistency creates anxiety: we were helpless and vulnerable, and if we couldn't trust that we'd be fed and attended to with regularity it was a threat to our survival. A parent's consistent lack of attention (or outright neglect) creates distrust within a child's body. The reality is that the world is uncertain, and safety is not assured for anyone. In this hub, we establish a safe harbor within ourselves: a trust that our reflexes protect us and that our bodies can be a safe place.

If we were attended to, protected, and fed with consistency, we will be more likely to have a healthy tolerance for uncertainty and can trust that hard times pass when we weather a storm. If this seems hyperbolic or far-reaching, remember that the infant body is small, soft, and vulnerable. It has no defense against its environment except to adapt to it and interpret it in a way that makes it feel safer and reduces anxiety. This tiny body begins adapting, and an imprint of our early experiences is found within our present-day being until it's consciously addressed and worked on.

Interruptions and stressors that directly refer to oppression, trauma, and abuse are not specifically addressed here, although they are without question interruptions that have massive effects on the first hub's stability and functioning (and deserve special attention and professional support). Many of the examples provided here can trigger intense feelings and, in some cases, may retraumatize. Fully immersing oneself in the memory of an event is unnecessary for releasing resulting adaptations and holding patterns. The somatic techniques and exercises deal directly with the bodily imbalance and only require peripheral knowledge of interruptions to help recruit all levels of the triune brain. Techniques that can help reduce stimulation include imagining an experience from a physical distance (as if it's at the end of a long tunnel) or from the psychological distance of imagining how someone else would experience an emotionally loaded event. This psychological-distancing technique is to guess what the experience would be like for someone else. If this or any interruption ever starts to feel uncomfortable or too intense, permit yourself to skip it. A therapist is excellent support and can help guide you through these explorations and help you determine what is safe and what should be left alone.

ABSENCE AND LOSS

Cinderella and Snow White were children of abandonment. Bambi lost his mother to violence at a young age; so did *The Lion King*'s Simba, who lost his father. Fairy tales and Disney films are full of themes of childhood neglect, abandonment, and loss—these stories and many others are standard entertainment for children. In the 1970s and 1980s, a free-for-all style of parenting resulted in a generation of so-called latchkey kids, whose unsupervised after-school hours were spent in a lawless land of siblings and neighborhood children. For the first hub, neglect and abandonment are experienced through the lack of a consistent physical presence of a caregiver, leading to deep, internalized feelings of loneliness, isolation, and unworthiness.

Any form of abandonment during the formative years often results in first-hub overcompensation through clinging to security, routines, and loved ones. Abandonment also creates a tendency to self-abandon through leaving things unfinished, being inattentive to bodily care, behaving in ways that we imagine will be pleasing to others, and believing others won't like our true selves if they really knew us. Self-abandonment, fear of separation, and even fear of endings and departures all link into first-hub interruption of absence and loss.

When a separation is prolonged or permanent, such as a divorce or the death of a parent, children experience how essential people can change and/or leave for reasons they cannot fully grasp. Their emerging-but-incomplete cognitive capability, coupled with lack of context, will create a narrative that puts a child at the center of the story, often blaming themselves for events outside of their control. Adoption can also lead to insecurity in this hub, because an infant or child is separated from its birth mother long before it can know what happened. This birth-mother connection transcends intellectual explanation—even as adults it's hard to fully comprehend. For folks with a secure, uninterrupted upbringing, all of this can be hard to fathom but understanding how lived experiences can be different from our own is part of the development of the upper hubs.

Sociology professor Karl Pillemer conducted a Cornell University study on family rifts and found that 27 percent of adult Americans are estranged from a close family member. An article in *The Economist* about the research quotes Pillemer saying that because people often "[F]eel shame, the real figure is likely to be higher. The most commonly severed relationship is between parent and adult child, and in most cases, it's the child who wields the knife."

NURTURE AND NOURISHMENT

Physical touch and nurture used to be considered secondary to primary survival needs for food and shelter. But as anthropologist Ashley Montagu learned in his research for *Touching: The Human Significance of the Skin*, extreme lack of touch and nurture can be deadly for infants, even when their other primary needs are being met. Montagu uncovered alarming mortality rates of 90 to 100 percent for turn-of-the-20th-century eastern European institutionalized babies who had not been held or touched. This condition—touch starvation or touch deprivation—refers to infants who are fed and housed but waste away and perish without touch and physical contact.

Touch and nourishment are fused in the early development of the first hub. As adults, it may be hard to understand why eating evades our conscious control when our relationship with food is affected at this hub. Food and how we relate to it primarily tells us a lot about which hub has been affected: if we use food as a sedative, we can be reasonably confident that

we're in the first hub. Sugar creates a spike in energy and then a crash, which can be great for napping. Eating to support emotional regulation (so-called emotional eating) is the domain of the second hub and food comforts us; also, gaining weight can be a subconscious, protective, emotional boundary that can guard a body from emotional overstimulation. It's worth noting that first-hub food sedation usually involves eating while lying down—a return to the comfort of infant life.

Criticizing this behavior creates a painful carousel of guilt, shame, and blame for lack of self-control, which leads to the repetition of these comforting, protecting behaviors. If we're not conscious about it, this can lead to self-hatred, depression, and despair. But from a developmental perspective, these protections and comforts are profound acts of love and reclamation. Punishing and cruel self-hatred has never led to meaningful or lasting change, but we can transform these food experiences if we self-nurture with the same loving acceptance we'd offer a child in need of comfort. Everybody on earth is a miracle, regardless of age, appearance, or physical condition, and everybody deserves love. There are no exceptions.

BOUNDARY INVASIONS: MEDICAL PRACTICES, ACCIDENTS, AND ILLNESSES

Unwelcome and unwanted touch invades the physical boundary—even infants will demonstrate a preference for how they want to be touched by fussing and squirming. If a boundary is either ignored or invaded in the initial development of this hub, early responsiveness and affection will profoundly affect a baby's relationship with touch—one that carries into adulthood.

Our nervous system has deep, ancient roots, and although medical practices can be lifelines, medical care can be experienced as invasion and even trauma. Giving injections to infants can be lifesaving, but the procedure is an invasion of the physical boundary. And according to Judith, time spent in incubators can leave prematurely born children with the sense that relationships are surreal, because their first impressions of caring faces are seen through glass and plastic. Any events for which we must surrender control of our body, such as being anesthetized, breaks the feeling of complete governance over ourselves, even though these practices can save our lives and keep us healthy.

In *Waking the Tiger: Healing Trauma*, Levine discusses how these events disrupt our sense of safety and physical security—we have a feeling of helplessness. He writes that unless these reactions are expressed and released, they can become trapped in the body as frozen shock and stored as stress. "Traumatic symptoms are not caused by the event itself. They arise when residual energy from the experience is not discharged from the body. The energy remains trapped in the nervous system where it can wreak havoc on our bodies and minds."

Some events, such as car accidents, natural disasters, illnesses, and injuries, are beyond our control. Regardless of circumstance, being trapped, shocked, or restrained can lead to long-term stress in the body if the tension is not discharged.

INSTABILITY AND INSECURITY AT WORK

Income insecurity and the destabilizing fear of not meeting your basic needs can be devastating to the sense of solidity in this hub. Feeling unsafe at work can also be extraordinarily destabilizing to our general sense of safety. If your boss is critical and threatening, his predictably terrible behavior affects your health, quality of life, stress levels, and relationships. When we feel secure, we perform better—without physical security, we behave out of fear and become more likely to steal, to protect our interests at the expense of others, and in some cases to act more emotional and get labeled as disruptive. This insecurity and its resulting behavior are seen at all levels of an organization, including in the executive suite.

Paul Santagata, Google's head of industry, telecom, and consumer electronics, studied workplace performance and his findings reveal that the most significant predictor of a team's performance is the sense of psychological safety within the group. Teams in which members feel safe to take risks and trust in fairness outperform those with cutthroat environments.

When individuals feel unsafe, they will shift into protection mode and do what they need to save themselves. Self-protection, risk avoidance, and defensiveness will include behaviors that are bad for the long-term health of a company, such as taking credit for others' work, plagiarism, blaming colleagues, creating confusion, and withholding information that could help others.

Further creating anxiety for teams is the lack of a plan and/or the occurrence of constant change. One way to make employees feel unsafe is by constantly changing direction and goals. We tend to intuit continuous shifts in strategy and direction within an organization as a lack of strong leadership. For some leaders, there can be a false attribution to chaotic conditions producing their best work—they overlook the level of power and visibility they have in times of turbulence, not considering that it isn't a driver who gets carsick. After all, who can function well in a state of constant, unstructured change—especially if they are not at the wheel?

ADAPTATIONS AND HOLDING PATTERNS

Adaptations and holding patterns shape our physiology, worldview, and personal beliefs; the effects from our earliest childhood experiences inform how we perceive teenage and adult experiences. We are born with an innate inclination, then our adaptations vary depending on several factors, including the amount of strength and development we had at the time when the initial interrupting or stressing events occurred. Although the resulting behavior patterns of adaptations tend to get moralized, Zen-meditation teacher Cheri Huber writes in *There Is Nothing Wrong with You: Going Beyond Self-Hate* that "What happened to you, not who you are, makes you angry, fearful, greedy, mean, anxious, etc." Our adaptations and holding patterns are survival strategies.

Sensory-motor development in children has been a long-standing area of focus for developmental psychologists and biologists. The simultaneous development of the psyche and the body of a child form lasting behavior patterns (see Chapter 2). The Bodynamic Institute, a school of somatic-developmental psychology, studies this link and theorizes that our patterns form relative to when interruptions happen during our development. Using grasping as an example, if a baby has a toy consistently snatched away in the early development of its grasping musculature (when it is most weak), the baby may learn that grasping is pointless and that there's no point in trying. Therefore, the baby gets less development in the associated musculature (a shrinking adaptation). Or perhaps, later in its development, a parent may decide the child has become too old for a toy. But now, when the parent attempts to take the toy away, the child has the strength to tighten its grip. If this happens consistently, it may result in overdevelopment of the grasping musculature and increased intensity in the physiology and psychology of grasping (inflating adaptation). A pattern is created, and instead of the dynamic ability to hold on or to let go (depending on the situation), there's a reflexive response pattern of either giving up without a fight or holding on whenever there's a real or imagined challenge or threat. These are holding patterns that carry into adulthood. By this theory, we can consider that early interruption in a hub's development leads to shrinking adaptations while interruptions occurring later in development lead to inflating adaptations.

In the first hub, when we experience insecurity at work, a physical illness or injury, a money problem, or any issue related to the security in our home, we may find ourselves leaning into our dominant pattern of first-hub adaptation by either diminishing our needs (shrinking), overemphasizing (inflating)—or both in some cases. When we're under even relatively mild stress in a hub, our adaptations tend to amplify. Supporting ourselves when stresses happen involves knowing that all feelings and thoughts eventually recede. Regardless of how overwhelming they feel in the moment, a mixture of acceptance that this too shall pass balanced with the techniques and exercises below (and see Chapter 5), helps us weather life's turbulences and manage the amplification of adaptation behavior patterns.

Fixating on a stressing event amplifies the intensity of the adaptation response while we feel overwhelmed and emotionally flooded. For example, if you just received an unexpected bill and a first-hub behavior adaptation is surging, allow yourself to set aside additional thoughts about insecurity until the immediate feelings about the unexpected financial stress recede. During a first-hub stress event, it's not a good time to start thinking about how you hate your job or about a needed repair on the house or to wonder if a recent pain in your body could be cancer. Additional stress will only heighten the activation of the initial first-hub stress event.

CHARACTERISTICS OF A BALANCED AND OUT-OF-BALANCE FIRST HUB

Our adaptations can lead to estranged relationships with ourselves, so restoring a dynamic balance between the polarities of adaptation can increase the capacity to be more responsive in life. Many of us have developed some level of disconnection and distrust with our body, and in a mind-over-matter culture the body becomes the subordinate, either carrying out orders or disobeying them. In *Dubliners*, James Joyce's short story "A Painful Case" effectively describes this disconnection: "Mr. Duffy lived a short distance from his body." When we're dissociated from our bodies, it's difficult to feel fully alive and to appreciate and respect the aliveness in others. The first hub represents the physical container for every experience we have during our lives: everything happens within it. Balanced integration in the HAVE hub means you

- are comfortable and well-grounded in your body;

- are able to sit and to stand still;

- are able to relax;

- have an overall sense of safety and security;

- are stable and prosperous; and

- have general good health.

Imbalance in the HAVE hub can include

- aches and pains, especially in the knees, feet, legs, and bones;

- disconnection, dislike, or distrust of your body;

- low job satisfaction;

- anxious feelings about work;

- a cluttered, unclean, or ridiculously minimalist home;

- unmanaged finances, excess debt; and

- hypervigilance and/or low energy.

Keep in mind that holding patterns were created when we were small and helpless, so we benefit from rightsizing into our adult reality. According to Judith, there's an epidemic of disconnection with the biological reality of our existence. Reconnection (healing) begins with understanding our first hub and the ongoing practices to bring awareness to it. As the numbness in this hub wears off and we become more fully alive, there can also be some pain and sadness that arise and need to be released. As adults, we may suspect that intense and deep emotions will overwhelm us and threaten our survival. The response of disconnection can act like a circuit breaker that cuts off sensation, sometimes even creating a sense of exhaustion—excessive sleeping can be an adaptive behavior for this hub.

INFLATING AND SHRINKING

We reflexively adapt ourselves to our families. The two primary adaptation strategies for creating physical safety are needing less and becoming smaller (shrinking) by restricting and constricting or taking up more space and stockpiling (inflating). In extremes, both strategies will be driven by the same sense of insecurity, fear, and anxiety that arises from first-hub stressors. Although one may seem preferable to the other, both drain our energy. We need to occupy space to have comfort within our bodies, and there is also room for getting cozy and curling up: the aim is to restore natural dynamism and to have access to broader overall responsiveness.

We can all identify, at least a little bit, with both ends of the shrinking and inflating spectrum. It requires energy to hold our behavior in these patterns. The effort required to uphold an adaptation recedes when we strengthen the hub by expanding our capacity within it, allowing access to greater joy, aliveness, and creativity in our lives.

Inflating qualities can include

- heaviness;

- exhaustion;

- hoarding;

- materialism and shopping; and

- catastrophe planning.

Paradoxically, hypervigilance on amassing financial and physical security often increase feelings of fear and anxiety: *It's all going to come crashing down.* Constant preparation for disaster and catastrophe leads to feelings that overwhelm day-to-day functioning. The inflating response for some folks can involve obsessively watching market fluctuations of their retirement portfolio, even though retirement is 40 years off. Inflating behaviors can be the daily tracking of net worth and saving for a rainy day to the point of miserliness, or even hoarding and collecting (with a reluctance to throw anything away in case it could be useful or potentially valuable in the future). In a marriage, if one spouse wants to save and be frugal while the other desires to live more freely, the first-hub tensions can run very deep. If one partner has early experience with loss, such as a bankruptcy or other reversals of fortune, they may want to be prepared for the worst and so, exhibit an inflating adaptation. And if the other person desires to spend and enjoy money, it requires conscious management and sensitivity because the resulting behaviors can get intense and emotional, regardless of the marriage's present-day financial reality.

Shrinking qualities can include

- being underweight;
- anxiousness;
- restlessness;
- vagueness; and
- excessive minimalism.

I interviewed Lucy, who fixates on money (her adaptation is to need less of it—a lot less). She describes herself as anxious to the extreme and takes comfort in believing that the financial system will collapse anyway, so why bother to have any savings? She has a freemium blog that gives tips for penny-pinching, finding deals in her city, and how to get free food. She spends an enormous amount of her time and energy chasing deals and jokes that all the time she spends searching clearance racks and saving money leaves little time for full-time employment. Lucy is a freelance writer and struggles every month to scrape rent money together. Other behaviors for a shrinking adaptation involve trying to take up less physical space. During my interviews I noticed this tends to be verbalized as disdain for others who do not observe the fixation—unapologetic space-taking was scrutinized and disdained.

In both shrinking and inflating holding patterns, the energy to pursue greater aliveness, fulfillment, and purpose remains stuck by fixation on safety. Feeling justified in these fixations—believing adaptations are absolute truths about life, not malleable survival strategies that can be shifted—affects relationships with others and ourselves. The techniques and exercises to restore dynamism and build strength in this hub primarily focus on our relationship with our physical bodies and the surrounding physical environment, and can be enhanced regardless of our health, finances, and possessions. Having money does not necessarily release a bind in this hub—money cannot keep us safe, though it can get some important needs met—if we continue struggling to survive or attempt to reduce the size of our needs, we'll understandably fixate on this hub until we can feel safe.

INTELLECTUALIZATION REPLACES EMBODIMENT

Lowen and Reich demonstrated that the developing mind influences and characterizes the shape of the body (see Chapter 2). They believed that what you think and do changes your physical form. According to Lowen, when the physical foundation of security is not developed and supported, children tend to intellectualize rather than physically feel. Living in their heads cuts off feeling and is what Lowen called "the schizoid"—Judith more charitably uses "the creative." There is disassociation between thought and feeling, and a tendency to think through life rather than feel. The schizoid/creative fears becoming overwhelmed by feelings and is easily flooded emotionally by relatively minor issues. Deep love or deep joy are usually avoided, and intimacy is rare. These folks are afraid of letting go and of trusting others, preferring cerebral relationships over physical and emotional ones. They also have a deep fear of needing or wanting anything they can't control. Lowen asserted that as children, no one came to comfort them in their fear, so now, as adults, they believe others will not be there for them. Often, when bodily sensation is deadened, it's replaced with a tendency to intellectualize. This so-called character structure often presents as slender with cold hands and feet.

THE SHADOW: FEAR

A little bit of fear is activating, and a lot is debilitating. When our immediate survival is threatened, fight, flight, or freeze get activated, as this suite of reflexes moves faster than thought to get us to safety. Fear serves our survival as an acute response, but when it becomes maladaptive, it leads to stress-related physical and mental illness. When we become overwhelmed by worry, the life-affirming (and lifesaving) quality of fear becomes life-taking. When we become overwhelmed or worried over a boss, a phobia, or an imagined catastrophe, the life-affirming and lifesaving quality of fear gets hijacked and becomes maladaptive. Keep in mind that our brains evolved to keep us alive—not to be good at relaxing—and to constantly scan the horizon for threats. When we consciously reclaim fear, we can change our relationship with it. To work with fear, we can contain it by identifying the specific event that caused it and compartmentalize it with techniques and exercises; instead of being flooded, overwhelmed, and reflexive, we work with the arising response and allow it to pass.

Part of managing our first hub is incorporating physical release and discharging muscular holding, which I discuss below. If we must suppress a natural reaction to fear, which adults must often do, a cascade of neuropeptides floods our body, and with no way to exit they're trapped as a stress response that gets held in our body. Because the foundation of this first hub is precognitive and preverbal, it can lead to an often-perplexing inability to feel completely safe or to trust the physical world. But when we speak to this facet of ourselves in its nonverbal language of physicality, we have the chance to communicate, to build trust, and potentially shift long-standing patterns.

Next, and in all the following Part 2 chapters, are techniques and exercises for how to create the sense of stability, boundary, and ground within the body.

TECHNIQUES AND EXERCISES

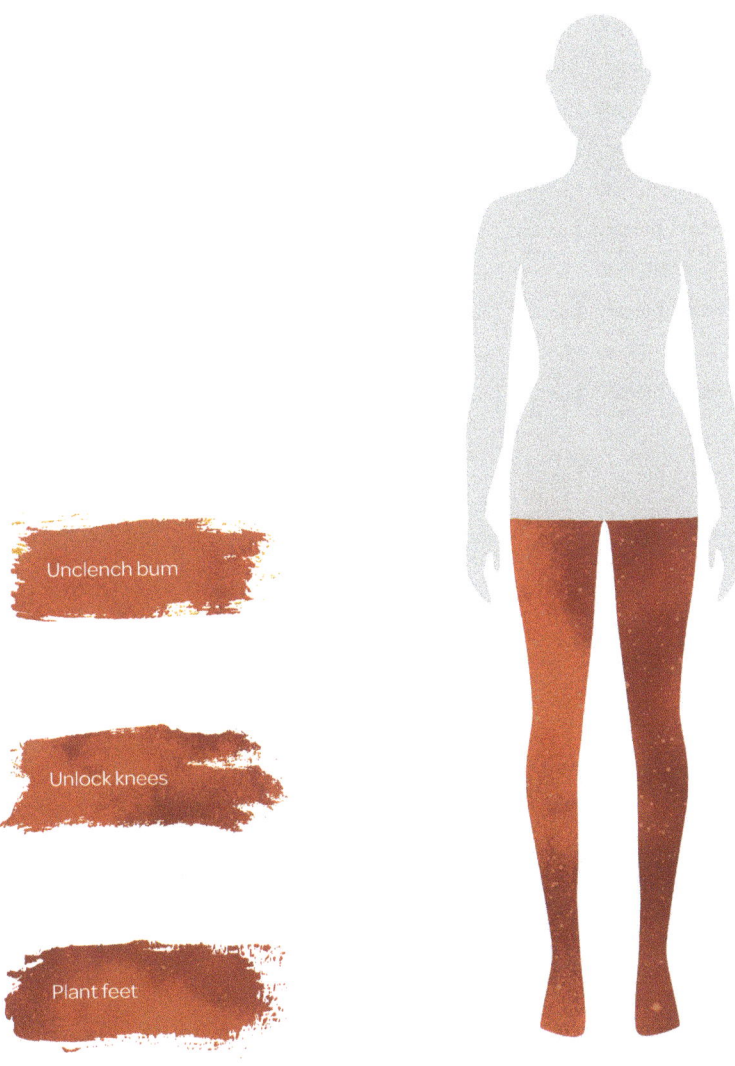

Figure 4.1: First-Hub Body Prompts

THE PARINAMA METHOD FIRST-HUB FUNDAMENTALS

Reclaiming the first hub involves conscious reclamation of rest, nurture, and trust—all nonverbal and restorative. In the first hub we practice grounding, physical boundary, consistency, and completion (not abandoning things before they're done). You are already caring for and living in your body by eating, bathing, sleeping, and clothing yourself. The distinction in reclaiming this hub is surrendering to nourishment with conscious intention and performing these acts with intent that builds and restores trust and physical connection within yourself. If you find yourself lying down a lot, curling up on the couch or in bed—first-hub activities—notice what keeps this from being restorative: a subtle resistance of guilt or shame *(I shouldn't be doing this)*. First-hub restoration requires surrender by deeply relaxing into nurture and nourishment by reducing self-consciousness along with distractions from external stimulation. Thoughts like *I shouldn't be doing this* block the fullness of what's possible. Instead think, *What would a newborn do?* and just wiggle around a little bit, snuggle up, take up as much space as you want, and snooze in a cozy blanket cocoon. A cute newborn sleeps with its tummy relaxed and its adorable, squishy body in whatever form is most comfortable; try doing this and give yourself permission to release the need to be or do anything: just be.

Receiving in this hub is simple but not easy. We tend not to pay close attention during everyday acts like resting, cleaning, eating, and spending time outside. They can get mistaken as interfering, distracting, and delaying us from so-called higher accomplishments and functions. Sleeping and eating can be considered a waste of time and can be rushed through or minimized. The cognitive reclamation of grounding, boundary, nurture, and consistency is a process of intentionally babying yourself. The embodiment of bathing, cleaning, and cooking with intention restores this foundational connection within yourself.

In *The Parinama Method* there are pointers for preparing for a practice (see Chapter 2), and you will find practices that integrate all seven hubs (see Chapter 11). Throughout Part 2, the techniques and exercises are intended to offer an introduction to the practice. For each of the hubs I discuss

- body prompts;
- conscious reclamation in seemingly simple behaviors;
- techniques and exercises for building capacity in the hub;
- the accordion technique for releasing tension; and
- charging and discharging to restore dynamism in the hub.

SANCTUARY AND GROUNDING

This is a potent practice, and when you feel intensity rising, unless you feel safe and supported it's always better either to slow down or stop, returning to a sense of safety. The first step in your practice is to establish a safe place you can return to for rest and sanctuary. Remember that the first spell a magician learns is one for protection (see Chapter 2).

A safe place to land and conscious reclamation

The physical boundary of a home is a good place for acts of comfort and restoration: being surrounded by people you trust, listening to music, having a comfortable place to watch TV or read, eating a meal that provides comfort, taking a bath, caring for a pet, having a comfy blanket and pillow. Reduce stimulation by playing some calming instrumental music at low volume, dim the lights, and lie down. Establishing this infant vibe is a first-hub essential and how we allow ourselves to surrender to comfort and nurture has everything to do with how restorative it can be (and can often be reflected in the quality of our sleep).

Some folks experience shame with these innocent activities—a high-performing executive I interviewed told me she'd be more comfortable telling me details of her sex life than disclosing the amount of time she spent on the couch and in bed watching TV. And the urge to rest resists attempts to be subdued and can even slide into denial; people who spend hours a day streaming TV and consuming social media have this urge just to slip outside of their self-awareness when zoning out replaces restorative rest. Screen-time tracking apps can leave us a bit shocked when we see our behavior displayed objectively. The trick to getting the most out of this time is to give it to yourself as a conscious act of recreation and restoration without guilt, shame, or denial.

In times of anxiety and overwhelm when the home is not available, find the sense of safety within your physical body by grounding yourself in the current moment without over intellectualization: feet on the earth (stand in the grass) or the Vu exercise of gently humming the vowel sound "vuuu" (see Chapter 8). Overwhelm is often felt as expansion beyond the direct experience of the body and can involve massive, unnamable feelings. Try to bring yourself back into the sensation of your body through becoming aware and alert, which is different from hypervigilance which is an activated nervous system prepared for an incoming threat. This exercise can help by bringing awareness to the senses that are all happening within your body. Look around and find

- five things you can see;
- four things you can touch;
- three things you can hear;
- two things you can smell; and
- one thing you can taste.

Clutter from outstanding tasks can turn a sanctuary into a visual reminder of feeling overwhelmed and not having enough time. Reconnect with your physical space by decluttering and cleaning to reduce this subtle tension while clearing space for new things. Sometimes the same physical objects that feel like they are creating safety and security actually weigh us down. There is a distinct difference between something that you're using that sparks joy and something that takes up space that you've held on to for a future need or emergency. The inflating adaptation will tend to hold on to things and to have more clutter, and the shrinking adaptation will often be excessively minimalist. It doesn't matter which tendency you have; the focus of the Parinama Method is to find dynamism that supports feeling good in your body and your home as often as possible, with the ability to appreciate belongings while also being able to let them go.

Grounding

Sometimes you may find yourself feeling mentally and emotionally frayed at the edges: concentration is difficult, resentments arise easily, and assuming negative intent in others becomes reflexive and combined with a general low-key impatience with people. This fussiness can happen when we've been working too much, not eating well, not caring for our health, and/or exposed to people and societal factors that diminish our dignity. It can make it hard to connect with ourselves and can cause tension in our relationships, especially when they're also struggling. Fussiness comes from disconnection to ourselves, and although it can be supported by connecting with other people, the natural world has a unique capacity to absorb and restore equilibrium in the body.

What I am about to describe will require a leap of faith for some folks because it's simultaneously simple and a little weird: it's the practice of grounding and spending time in nature. Simply bringing attention to keeping the soles of your feet on the ground can be a game changer. But for the premium experience, take off your shoes and socks and stand barefoot on the ground—direct contact, with nothing between you and the earthen surface. Unlocking your knees with a slight bend is essential (locking can act like a circuit breaker cutting off the connection to the rest of your body). Unclenching your bum also increases the benefit. When you're feeling disconnected, you can use grounding to rehumanize yourself or you can use it to get a second wind if you need to get more work done. Grounding restores connection with the natural environment as it absorbs excess charge and synchronizes with your body. The process is passive: just stand on the ground, unlock your knees, and let it happen; notice the solidity and consistency of the earth and extend the feeling to the sense of being held and supported by something that's always there for you.

When there's a disconnection with the body, the first step is to notice how you feel without minimizing or downplaying it. Rather than seeing spikes in agitation and combative thoughts as moral shortcomings, view the fussiness as needs to be met and take responsibility and support yourself. When you have needs, attend to them with care instead of turning them into negative narratives. Consider this layer of your psyche an infant requiring adoration, loving attention, and responsiveness—assume positive intent with yourself as you return to the nature of your first hub: innocent, reflexive, and new. This is the nature within yourself that you're returning to with patience and understanding. It's unreasonable to expect a fretting baby to be anything other than what it is, and what it needs is soothing and comfort—not fixing.

An important note for those of you who are inclined to nurture others: nurture and rest are not restorative for you when you're providing them for others. Caring for your own needs to ground and be nurtured is essential, especially when you're attending to the needs of others. Again, I discuss altruism in the fourth hub, but for our purposes now, remember that self-nurturing and conscious reclamation are forms of altruism for a part of ourself that needs to be embraced and held.

Grounded Squat Using K1

Located on the soles of our feet are the K1 acupuncture points. Between the ball of your foot associated with the big toe and the ball of your second toe, you'll find a connection point that is like the prong of an electrical plug. Notice the difference when you press into the ground with the K1 area versus pushing down indiscriminately into the entire foot. To maximize the connection, remember to unlock your knees so they're just slightly bent, relax your lower back, and unclench your bum.

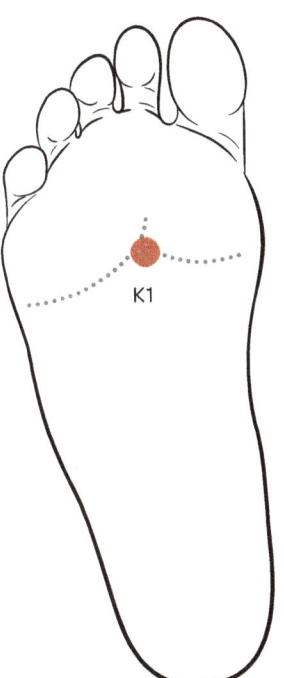

- Place your feet a little wider than hip distance apart.

- Squat by lowering your bum into a seated position, with your toes visible in front of your knees.

- Keep your back upright like you're sitting in a chair.

- Dip down until shaking occurs, allow the shaking for two full breaths (inhale and exhale).

- Stand for one full breath, and squat back down for two more full breaths.

- Come back to standing. Take note of which muscles engage and if and where there was tightness or discomfort.

- Next, bring attention to the K1s and push them into the ground.

- Drop back into your squat and notice the difference for three full breaths. Does this require more or less effort?

- Come back to standing and take a moment to notice any difference when grounding with K1.

Figure 4.2: Techniques and Exercises, K1

Nature

Spending time outside with your senses immersed in the sights, sounds, smells, and sensations of the natural world will shift how you feel, even if it's for only five minutes. Evidence-based clinical studies have repeatedly demonstrated the measurable, positive effects on our immune and nervous systems from time spent near trees; diffusion of natural essential oils (especially from trees) has been found to promote measurable, positive effects on our sense of well-being, and even boosts the immune system. Diffusing essential oils provides an accessible, achievable daily grounding practice. Adding plants, wood, stone, and other natural materials into your home supports the first hub.

Balance

Standing involves the strength to hold your ground and the agility to maintain balance in a constantly moving world. Practicing balance brings strength and agility into the body. Activities like barre, Pilates, and yoga involve strengthening stability, but you can practice it simply by standing on a single foot, then alternating to the other: lift one foot off the ground and notice what happens to the grounded foot. Explore the need to activate more of the standing foot, and how pushing down through the K1 while extending upward through your perineum and torso support and stabilize balance. This can be practiced while waiting in line or even when talking on the phone. Simply lift one foot slightly off the ground. Balance on each foot for five full breaths each.

PHYSICAL BOUNDARY

You are the only person who should decide who enters your physical space. To reclaim this, we first work on ownership. Your body is your domain, although many of us have been socialized to be polite with folks who casually invade the physical boundary and so, we struggle to uphold it. Once you become uncertain of your boundary, maintaining and enforcing it becomes a challenge of second-guessing and making uncomfortable exceptions.

Feel the container

The first step toward owning your body is to establish its perimeter. You do this when you wash your body in the shower, dry off, and apply lotion. Adding the conscious element makes this a first-hub practice. Say to yourself, *I am here*, and *This is mine*, as your hands are on your legs, arms, and torso; lightly pat your body. Next, move your hands on the same path and again say, *I'm in here, this is mine*. This can also be done during the day, fully clothed, by tapping the perimeter while quietly or silently repeating *I am here, this is mine*. This phrase is particularly useful if you're feeling overwhelmed, because big emotions tend to feel bigger than our bodies. The human right of this hub is a reminder that your birth alone is what establishes your right to exist and to take up space. There is no merit to be earned; the proof of your worth is your existence.

Take up space

Many of us—especially women—are socialized to believe that taking up space is impolite. It's rude to have the flesh of your leg take up more than your seat while men—often without knowing they do it—are more likely to feel comfortable taking up extra space by manspreading. For a woman to be excessively self-conscious and apologetic about the amount of space she needs is often considered charming and socially desirable. This respects others' boundaries over consideration for one's own need to occupy space and is also related to power (see Chapter 6). There are subtle, profound implications when apologizing for needing space for your body. The hypervigilance about invading someone else's boundary can lead to apologizing when someone invades your space by bumping into you or squeezing by you in tight quarters. It's challenging to feel personal freedom and power when you're trying to be physically smaller and (apologizing for) existing. Before you practice comfortably occupying the area your body requires in the larger world, grow your inner practice in places where you feel safe. Taking the space you need starts in your own private life by allowing your thighs to flop out on the couch and giving yourself a little smile when you see yourself standing tall and unapologetic when inhabiting the space you require.

Hug yourself

Somatic therapists use the self-hug or the hands-on-heart to reduce a stress response and to begin releasing oxytocin (the comfort hormone). This is something you can do for yourself: simply place both your hands, one over the other, on your heart and direct your focus to this act of connection.

As Levine explains, the body is the container of all your sensations and feelings. Two of his practices help settle the nervous system.

1. Place your right hand under the armpit of your left arm. Place your left hand on your right shoulder. Get a feeling of what is going on in your body—many people report a settling feeling. Hold for a few moments or a few minutes, whatever feels right for you.

2. Place your left hand on your heart and your right hand on your forehead. Feel what goes on between the hands. Hold for a few moments or longer. Once there is a sense of connection, move your right hand from your forehead to your stomach and allow yourself to feel that connection between the hands.

Both practices can be used before sleep to relax the nervous system. Tapping is also helpful to soothe and manage feelings and emotions (see Chapter 5).

CONSISTENCY AND COMPLETION

We tend to feel trust when a person or a thing is reliable. In the first hub, you build this trust within yourself and bring it into the experience of your body. A body has practical realities of care and maintenance that are repetitive, and they can become joyless because their subtlety gets crowded out by the busyness of modern life. The practicality and necessity of these activities, when tied to a more sublime aspect of existence, offer an opportunity to ground yourself; again, when you take care of your body, cook, and clean, you're attending to your physical needs.

By making reflexive behaviors conscious, that is, cognitively reclaiming them with consistency and completion, we strengthen internal trust. Sometimes we may do something at a standard lower than what we'd like for ourselves: producing poor quality work, skipping a workout, or eating so-called unhealthy food. Afterward, perhaps we wonder what other people would think if they knew. But the impression you make on yourself and knowing your own tendencies is far more important than any external perception of you. When you finish what you start and show up for yourself, you build trust and faith that you carry within yourself wherever you go. This starts with giving yourself a break for making mistakes when working toward consistently showing up for yourself as an act of love and devotion. Leaving things incomplete—books unread, projects around the house partially finished (or unstarted)—can be related to a fear of loss or abandonment. Saying good-bye and letting things go can evoke a subconscious sense of loss, so we often avoid doing it. Be gentle but work with yourself to begin to let go of things that are taking up the space that new and positive things entering your life will need when they arrive.

An exercise for completion: make a list of three unfinished projects or tasks—books, emails, and any other matter that has been left unresolved. Next, assume positive intent and practice being patient with yourself as you complete them. Pay special attention to sensations that arise, such as anxiety when donating your belongings or uncertainty about a next step. And own up to the very human reality that when something is left incomplete long enough, it becomes more complicated (and sometimes more embarrassing) to address it—try not to let this stop you. Complete your list, notice how it feels, and give yourself credit for taking steps to create a new, better pattern.

CHARGE AND DISCHARGE

Shake it off

You've probably noticed how animals reflexively shake their bodies after being overstimulated from a threat (either real or perceived) or, if you have a pet, from receiving extra affection—even tail-wagging corresponds with releasing stimulation. Animals don't tend to store stress in their bodies; they release it in real time, as it happens. Although humans can control reactions, we still need outlets to discharge and release or the suppressed reaction becomes spring-loaded in our nervous system. If we hold back responses long enough (and over an extended period), it's not surprising that they eventually shape our muscles and nervous system. These trapped patterns shape our bodies and psyches, and sometimes become rigidity, inflexibility, and even pain. Suppose you hold back a response when a demanding boss upsets you. In this case, it's not only the boss's words, but the need to hide physical reactions that disturb your inner peace: an elevated heart rate, heightened nervous-system arousal, and perhaps a clenched jaw (even holding back the urge for fight or flight). Our never-let-'em-see-you-sweat socialization rewards us for not showing strain when we're under pressure. If you talk to your spouse about what happened, it's a verbal release (venting) or if you go for a run, it's a physical release (blowing off steam). However, if you don't discharge the adrenaline of that moment, it can set in the jaw and body as muscular tension.

The action potential of a neuron or muscle cell is a cycle that's activated when the threshold of stimulation is achieved. The cell is stimulated, tension begins to build, and when the rising tension hits a critical point, it's released into action. Then it's followed by a brief period of absolute refraction, when restimulation is temporarily impossible—as the cell catches its breath, so to speak—and restores itself by repolarizing to be prepared for the next stimulation event. This cascade is the natural response to stimulation and its reflexive reactivity was a premier feature of a nervous system until the PFC came along and introduced choice and conscious management of reflexive responses to stimulation. Humans, with our PFC, can't stop the spring-loading of the nerve or muscle cell in response to stimulation, but we *can* block the resulting behavior. This conscious control keeps us from doing things we'll regret later, but also leaves the response within the body, which over time builds into stress and pain.

Squeeze and release for resting

In the techniques and exercises in the second hub, I introduce the accordion technique for managing pain and tension (see Chapter 5). The accordion technique exaggerates a tension or stiffness further by first squeezing into it before slowly releasing and expanding it. Keep in mind that conscious intervention to stop a reaction happens before we reach the peak of the action potential—so to release the trapped response, we need to complete it and squeeze out what needs to be released from our tissues before we release and relax. However, for the first hub, release using the accordion allows for a deep relaxation in rest. Simply squeeze your bum to the point of shaking and slowly, slowly, slowly release and allow it to melt. Squeeze your thighs, tummy, arms, and face, and exhale your body into the melting sensation of release—and rest.

Discharge

On one end of the spectrum, folks with shrinking adaptations often struggle with fully taking up space and indulging needs and so, they benefit from activities that build charge, for example, eating and resting. On the other end, inflating holding patterns and adaptations tend to overdo rest and nurture to the point that they're no longer restorative and instead create lethargy, and thus need discharge.

There are many forms of everyday discharging, such as sweating, talking, and physical exertion. Other, more intense discharging activities, such as laughing, sobbing while crying, and orgasming, rely on shaking that releases muscle tension. Charging, which is generally energizing, can lead to feelings of exhaustion and low energy when done to a body that has not been discharged. Here I focus on a specific muscular release for discharging stored muscular tension by using shaking and tremoring. It's an unusual sensation—a certain loss of control that takes some getting used to, especially if the chest cavity and diaphragm are so rigid that they can no longer do subtle movements like the quivering in crying or the rollicking abdominal movement of a deep belly laugh.

Some familiar places where tremor is experienced are in a good laugh, in holding a contraction during exercise, and in orgasming. In a world that favors civilized behavior, we're socialized to police our responses from a very early age. Natural reflexes are suppressed in favor of social belonging, and it's hard to draw a definitive line of where and when restraint shifts from being responsible to restricting our humanity. Excessive restraint, which is common, is how we can become adults who think we don't cry, don't dream, and aren't emotional. It's a matter of how good you become at hiding and/or suppressing your responses—a concealment that's eventually hidden even from ourselves, locking reactions into our bodies as rigidity, stiffness, exhaustion, and soreness.

A discharge involves a slight electrical shaking, which can feel like a live wire and is perplexing in that it's a little out of control. But these brief, often awkward moments offer a significant reward, ultimately restoring natural responsiveness into your body by increasing blood flow to stressed, rigid muscles, which leads to laughing more easily, restoring movement and coordination, physical satisfaction, and even ease in speaking with greater confidence.

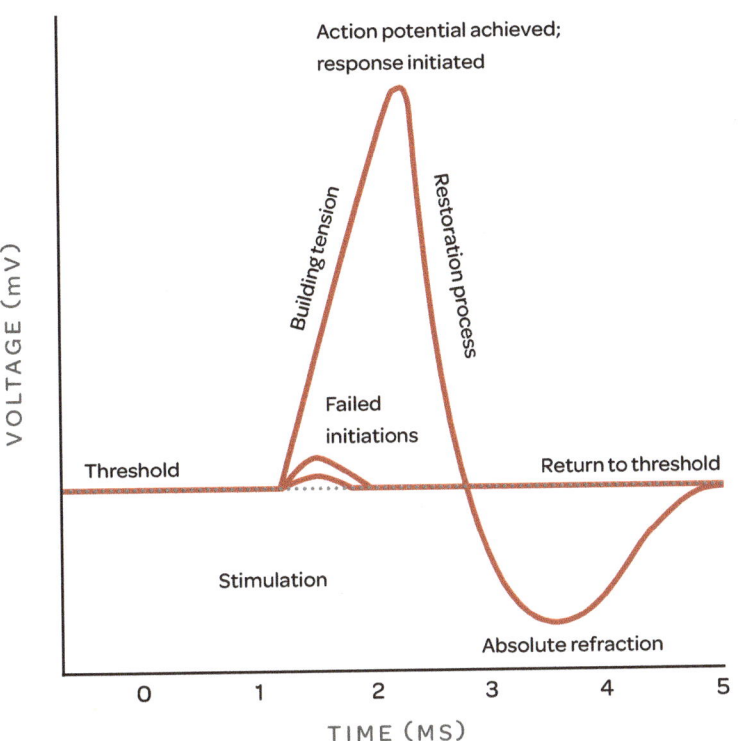

VOLTAGE (mV)

Action potential achieved; response initiated

Building tension

Restoration process

Failed initiations

Threshold

Return to threshold

Stimulation

Absolute refraction

0　　1　　2　　3　　4　　5

TIME (MS)

Figure 4.3: Techniques and Exercises, Action Potential

Squat and strap around the foot for lying down

Starting with your bare feet on the ground, step into a sumo stance with your feet pointed slightly outward and do the grounded squat with K1. Relax your lower back, engage your lower abdomen, keep your knees back so you can see your toes, and squat down with your legs from anywhere between 180 and 90 degrees. Find a position in which you can withstand the quivering for up to five full breaths. Stand, then repeat up to three times.

This can also be done lying on your back with a strap held with one end in each hand, looped around the bottom of your foot—for this exercise we do one foot at a time alternating from left to right. The foot with the strap is elevated with the knee at about a 90-degree angle (the other leg remains on the ground). Use the pressure of your foot against the strap to access the tremor. This can take some exploring—you're looking for a tremor that's practically effortless. Hold for up to five breaths, and switch legs—repeat up to three times.

Next, release the strap and while still lying down, with the bottoms of your feet flush to the ground and knees bent so they point upward, lightly slap or even stomp the bottoms of your feet on the floor to feel an additional release. Then, relax your legs out like a gingerbread figure, maybe adding the gentle action of your hands slapping the ground (even adding a playful *no, no, no* with each stomp-slap can offer an outlet as a little, contained, adult tantrum).

Holding in charge is exhausting for a body, so discharging is essential for readying your body for restoration. In addition, chronic muscular holding of rigidity, stiffness, and inflexibility takes a low-grade, ongoing, energetic demand to maintain—stored charge in your muscles blocks full relaxation. As a result, you may initially become tired when you discharge, but ultimately—over time—you free up more energy and feel more energized.

Charge

The charging in the upcoming hubs more closely resembles the type of active stimulation one would expect during the initiation of the action potential. But in the first hub we look to the restoration period after stimulation—the absolute refraction—within the cycle of activation and discharge. Thus, in the first hub, charging is both gently stimulating and restorative, and although I discuss charging by introducing consciousness to deep rest, in this hub we also charge through subtle and soothing stimulation.

Energizing the bottoms of feet

This can be done standing, seated, or lying down using a tennis ball, physio ball, or a yoga strap.

Standing: Unlock your knees and notice any sensations in the bottoms of your feet. If you're using a ball, it works best on a soft surface like a carpet or a yoga mat, so the ball doesn't roll away. Start with your left foot planted on the ground with the ball under your right foot. Roll the ball around the perimeter of your foot, keeping a slight bend in your standing knee. Next, allow the sensation to guide where you roll the ball. Do each foot for five breaths each and repeat up to three times.

Seated: Make sure your chair is sturdy and firmly plant your left foot on the ground, placing your right ankle over your left knee or thigh. Give yourself a foot massage—it's remarkable how sensitive the bottoms of our feet can be. Switch feet when your foot is no longer feeling stimulated by the touch. (If this places strain on your joints, place a ball on the ground and do the standing exercise with a ball from a seated position.)

Lying down: Start on your back on a yoga mat, couch, or bed. Slide your feet up and plant the soles on the ground by bending your knees and pointing them toward the ceiling. Form a loop using a strap, scarf, or even a piece of soft rope, hold each end in a hand, and slip it under the bottom of your right foot; next extend the foot into the air, supported by the strap. Rub the bottom of your foot with back-and-forth polishing motions. Do this for five breaths, and switch to your left foot.

These containment practices will become a refuge in all the following hubs, along with the grounding practices that bring conscious reclamation into the body. The sense of trust and solidity in the first hub establishes the foundation and container for the fluidity, movement, and change that come in Chapter 5, the second hub—FEEL.

FEEL: BABY, SELF-GRATIFICATION

Basics	Themes	Interruptions and Stressors	Adaptations and Holding Patterns	Techniques and Exercises
Feeling and Emotion	Pleasure and Aversion	Chronically Distracted, Distressed, or Emotionally Immature Parents	Characteristics of a Balanced and Out-of-Balance Second Hub	The Right to Feel: Expanding the Container
Sensation and Touch	Change and Ambiguity		Inflating	Working with Feelings: Tapping
Attunement and Attachment	Laughter	Enmeshment: Lacking Emotional Boundary and Differentiation	Shrinking	Emotional Literacy
	Movement and Coordination		Combination	Charge and Discharge
	Boundary and Differentiation	The Museum: The Emotionally Intolerant Home	Balance	
	Hidden Self and Projection	The Circus: The Emotionally Chaotic Home	A Shrinking Strategy: Intuition and Intellectualization	
		Intermittent Reinforcement	Tolerance for Touch	
		Trauma	Pacifiers	
			The Shadow: Guilt	
			Chronic Pain and Suppressed Emotions	

Chapter 5

THE SECOND HUB—FEEL

MOVEMENT AND EMOTION

Baseball is the president tossing out the first ball of the season. And a scrubby schoolboy playing catch with his dad on a Mississippi farm.
—*Ernie Harwell*

IT'S AGAINST THE LAW of nature for anything alive to remain unchanged and still be living. Rigid standards for our bodies are only temporarily achievable from day-to-day, and depending on stress, sleep, food, physical movement, and water intake, our appearance can shift from glowing and rested to puffy and exhausted. Again, an alive body is constantly changing. Every day, our physical ability, body shape, size, appearance, and health change. The signatures of the second hub are movement, sensation, emotion, and change, but if we tend to block out what we feel and desire, we become out of sync with ourselves and the world and grow increasingly rigid and resistant to change.

The safety and solidity of the first hub is essential for having a positive relationship with change. Without the sense of protection—in the case of a baby, a trusted caregiver to return to—being brave and adventurous isn't realistic. Autonomy requires a safety net. During the initial development of the second hub, children begin to explore, wishing to taste and touch their surroundings to figure out what they like and what they don't like. A facet of your identity is your unique profile of likes and dislikes, preferences, and desires. As adults, joyless grinding at work and in life creates friction, and friction overloads a motor, eventually burning it out. Jung said, "It is not the meaning of life we seek, but a greater feeling of aliveness." The resilience, vitality, sensation, and integrity experienced in movement and joy within our changing body is how we experience our aliveness.

Our body-mind holds buried feelings and thoughts—and as they surface, like warming frozen toes and fingers from the cold, we experience discomfort as flow is restored. This flow brings aliveness in the form of the second-hub sensation, pleasure, and vitality. Once we have this feeling of aliveness, the meaning of life becomes self-evident.

ORIENTATION

Physical location: Pelvis, hips, lower back, genitals, sensations of the skin, and all movement

First cycle: Six months to approximately two years old

Task: Mobility

Rights: The right to feel, the right to express emotion, the right to change

Identity: I am what I feel, I am my desires.

Reconciliation: I am allowed to express my emotions and desires.

The first months of life outside the womb are a continuation of gestation as mother and child feel merged through feeding and familiarity. In the early months, a baby stays where it's laid down. Its primary language is crying and fussing; parents and caregivers communicate back with responsiveness and touch. Responsiveness signals safety and soothing, providing a profound and lasting sense of inner comfort and security.

At about six months of age, most babies can sit up on their own and as their eyes begin to focus, they become aware of their surroundings. As babies begin to explore, having caregivers who are emotionally connected and responsive provides a haven that builds trust and confidence. As the outside world comes into focus, there's a growing temptation to examine it through the sensory stimulation of touch, taste, hearing, and sight. There's a dawning awareness of separateness. This desire to explore inspires the mobility of crawling and walking. In this stage, caregivers introduce solid foods and reveal the sensory world of different tastes and textures. During this period of neurological development, most of our brain's progress isn't through the creation of new brain cells but in the connections between them. Columbia University neuroscience professor and pediatrician Kimberly Noble explains in her April 2019 TED Talk, "How Does Income Affect Childhood Brain Development?" how when newborn brain tissue is viewed under a microscope, there aren't many visible connections between the brain cells. But by age three, there are 1,000 trillion visible connections—a lot happens in the early years to shape the brain.

Again, an infant is born into a preexisting ecosystem of household responsibilities and activities swirling around its arrival. Caregivers must deal with the ongoing stressors of adult life as they incorporate the care of a new baby. The quality and responsiveness of attention may fluctuate; sometimes a parent may be warm and attentive, but other times distracted and distressed. A baby reflexively adjusts to its environment as it shifts into a role that best supports getting its needs met: it learns how to navigate life in a home with a variety of people all with their own individual wants and needs.

As the desire to explore increases, caregivers provide safe, attentive, and predictable arms to return to—a safe harbor in the choppy and potentially dangerous waters of early mobility. No parent can always be there, and many developmental biologists believe that manageable and well-supported challenges are suitable for a developing child. Pediatrician and psychoanalyst Donald Winnicott coined the term "good enough mother" in *Playing and Reality*, and observed that children benefit when parents fail them in manageable ways; however, he also wrote that if a primary caregiver doesn't adequately respond to the baby (if the challenges are too great), the baby "[L]earns to become the mother's idea of what a baby is." If the safe harbor of predictable and attentive caregiving is consistently missing, much of the energy a baby would use for exploration goes into fixating on security, which can result in a combined fixation on safety that carries into adulthood, in addition to discomfort in managing difficult feelings and emotions.

INITIAL DEVELOPMENT

Developmental psychologist Jean Piaget called the first stage of development "sensorimotor," because the infant begins to know the world through movement and sensation—an acknowledgement that our senses and emotional reflexes develop in lockstep with our physical bodies. In Freudian terms, this is the oral stage, referring to the pleasure and curiosity of an infant placing things in its mouth. As feelings arise in the baby, emotions reflexively communicate through the universal human language of cries that express anger, sadness, surprise, and fear. The baby and its parents start to establish patterns of response and validation. The unique identity of each child reveals itself in a suite of preferences and aversions. Many parents of multiple children marvel at the significant differences between siblings raised in the same home—the age for the first word or step, the tolerance for discomfort, food preferences, and general temperament vary from child to child. The physical needs of the first hub change with the introduction of solid foods: the baby no longer needs to be held while being fed while the demand for nurture and emotional connection is becoming more pronounced and increasingly sophisticated.

A baby knows instinctively that belonging within its family is tied to its survival. Emotional connection signals safety to the developing brain. Humans experience physical security in groups by sharing the load of vigilance, a behavior we share with many animals. A solitary animal must keep its head on a swivel and spend energy on its preparedness for threat; a group can share in the task and, as a result, feel greater safety while using less energy.

Bonding with our parents starts with learning the language of emotion, the precursor to verbal communication. As feelings are experienced from both the external world (sounds, temperature) and from inside the body (thirst, hunger)—the emotions arise, and reflexes react. Trusting your feelings as valid comes from how parents responded to us, which either strengthens or weakens confidence. If parents do not respond to their baby's emotional expression, it may struggle to trust itself and may sense that its emotions are unwelcome and out of sync with its environment.

BASICS
FEELING AND EMOTION

According to Charles Darwin in his 1872 study, *The Expression of the Emotions in Man and Animals*, emotions initiate movement, and these movements restore us to safety and physical equilibrium. He noticed this effective communication in bodily and facial signaling in both animals and humans. In many psychology disciplines, emotion is viewed as a response to a physical or mental feeling, and feeling is a response to (internal and external) sensation and stimulation. Simply put, a feeling/sensation comes in and the emotion moves out, expressed through thought and behavior. Emotion is the expressed response to feeling, and it's how we're in relationship with ourselves, others, and the world. As babies and children, we learn—usually from parents—emotional expression through our primary relationships and what we learn is carried into our teenage and adult lives.

During the initial development of the second hub, a baby's emotions are natural, wild, inconvenient, self-serving, spontaneous, and unaware of time. As an adult, watching a baby—chasing it around as it explores and as its emotions arise—can be exhausting. When expression of emotion causes harm, they need to be contained, but otherwise, a baby should be free to explore and experiment.

For a baby, the maturation of emotional control is still on the developmental road map—and becomes a progressively appropriate expectation in the subsequent hubs. As children, physical expression in body language and facial expressions of things we tried to hide could result in punishment or disapproval from the people we needed most. Learning to control emotional responses becomes both practical and responsible for maturation but taken too far it becomes a holding pattern (and if introduced too early, it cuts us off from our relationship with ourselves).

When children are allowed to be free, spontaneous, and self-serving, conflicts with others can arise. Mature emotional expression involves short-term compartmentalization, control, and evaluation of how we affect others. As adults, sometimes we must put our immediate emotional responses on ice for responsible, respectful, and mature behavior—but this can go too far. As adults, excessive and chronic suppression and rejection of feelings and emotions extinguishes aliveness and creates blind spots in our self-awareness, getting stuck in our bodies when not effectively processed. Yet some emotional containment *is* necessary—by harnessing their primal strength with awareness and effective management, we can feel fully alive and find healthy outlets for their expression. When fresh emotions go into the emotion-control refrigerator, they can get pushed to the back and forgotten—and when we forget about them, they tend to spoil. Later, when we pull them out, they're in a different form from what they went in as and can be messy, but by clearing and moving them out, we make room for what we want to hold within ourselves.

SENSATION AND TOUCH

The language of the physical world is sensation communicated through temperature, texture, tension, auditory vibration, visual stimulation, taste, and touch. Human touch is the sensation that's also an essential need; for a baby, through responsiveness and tenderness, touch expresses the relationship with its parents. Sights, smells, sounds, and tastes contribute to the exciting, sensate experience of early life, but experiencing touch is our earliest understanding of feeling loved and safe.

The early touch and responsiveness of our primary caregivers forms our emotional bedrock. Our first anger comes from inattention or separation. Hunger or physical discomfort is distressing, but our first strong emotions come from separation and distance. According to psychologist John Bowlby, considered to be the first attachment theorist, anger, rage, and sadness in infants and toddlers are common responses to disconnection and neglect. The central tenet of attachment theory is that young children need a relationship with at least one primary caregiver for their healthy emotional and social development.

Psychologist and researcher Harry Harlow's baby rhesus-monkey experiments in the 1950s and 1960s clearly underscore the importance of comfort and touch (that said, the experiments' design was unethical and disturbing). Harlow separated baby monkeys from their real mothers for varying amounts of time (from months up to one year of their lives) and built them surrogate-mother structures of wire and cloth. He provided the babies two wire mothers: one that produced food and one covered in fabric but without food. It was observed that the babies would only feed from the wire mother, and then return and cling to the cloth mother. When Harlow eventually resocialized these monkeys, the effect on their ability to integrate was devastating: he made note of "[S]evere deficits in virtually every aspect of social behavior" for the monkeys that had never been nurtured by an attentive mother. These monkeys were disinterested in sex, but if they did have babies themselves, they were abusive and had to be removed from their cages.

Old parenting-practice styles include the children-should-be-seen-and-not heard concept, the I'll-give-you-something-to-cry-about threat, and perhaps more saddening, the spare-the-rod-and-spoil-the-child rhetoric. Some folks express pride in having survived what they refer to as "real" childhoods and shake their heads at how "soft" kids have become (and fear for their lack of preparation for the "real world"). Others speak of emotional needs using words like *indulgent* as they recall their parents managing tremendous stress and overcoming hardships—having learned to compartmentalize their hurt, loneliness, and pain. These crossed wires of familiarity and safety can lead to repeating patterns of harm—and because this part of our development happens before we have the capability for memory, it's coded into our reflexes and risks being passed down to the next generation unless it's consciously evaluated and reclaimed.

Emotional literacy and physical sensation can feel like both a mystery and a vulnerability. Healthy development in this hub leads to awareness of feelings and emotions, including when we should postpone our own needs so we can be responsible for children or maintain adult relationships. But eventually our own needs, feelings, and emotions must get time and attention, or we face chronic pain, numbness, stiffness, and blankness in our bodies, which can go unexamined and be misattributed as completely due to aging.

When emotional needs are not respected, feelings get dysregulated and our connection to sensation is experienced from a distance; due to this detachment, any sensation and craving in our bodies can become adversarial when we fear and vilify natural impulses and meet them with harsh judgment, such as disgust at the sight of body fat, emotional neediness, or exhaustion. We may respond by pursuing punishing food restrictions and intense exercise, by escaping into workaholism, or by tuning out, then tuning in to a screen. And for many folks, there's a false correlation of restriction with moral superiority.

Living fully and expanding capacity in this hub involves increasing how much pleasure and enjoyment can be felt before discomfort arises—how big your container for joy is. Your ability to do this is often an inheritance from generations of your family before you. If these people's lives were interrupted by war, poverty, or violence, we often carry the effects of the traumas of our ancestors, passed down through parenting and even genetics. The source of our trauma and the hold of addiction come from sensation and stimulation that are above and beyond our existing capacity to process and handle them. Psychologist and associate clinical professor Daniel P. Brown at Harvard Medical School identifies five essentials of early experience with caregivers—these are the real thing:

- safety and protection;
- attunement;
- soothing and comfort;
- expressed delight (your parents express delight in your existence); and
- support and encouragement (for your self-development).

Compulsive or addictive behaviors are ultimately unsatisfying replacements for the real thing, and counterfeit soothing through adult pacifiers may be the only tool we know.

No childhood is all good or all bad: there are always happy things and always upsetting things. Struggle makes us strong, but sometimes this strength comes at the expense of softer qualities that support the joys of feeling fully alive. Building emotional capacity increases the power to maintain the fullness of life and acts as an accelerant to fulfilling achievement. Brown's power-exercise video, "Imagine Ideal Parents," can be soothing and healing for this hub.

ATTUNEMENT AND ATTACHMENT

A growing understanding of the importance of parental attunement, originating from Bowlby's development of attachment theory, has made *attunement* a familiar term. Attunement is like a game of catch: there are cycles of receiving, holding, and throwing; with attunement, there's receiving sensation, feeling it, and expressing it with emotion. How a recipient responds to our throws informs the quality of the exchange. A good game of catch should involve awareness, attention, turn-taking, responsiveness, synchronization, support, and staying within range, along with a gradual expansion of limits. We learn how to trust ourselves through our ability to throw (and the responsiveness of a catcher) as we build confidence by managing to catch what's thrown to us.

When a parent is even relatively developed in the second hub, playing catch is a source of joy. The child's experience is the parent's focus, so they will gently throw to where the child can catch the ball (keeping aware of the range) and so, slowly encourage the building of the child's skill. Attuned parents learned this from their parents—an ability to experience the delight of their child's existence is often tied to their own childhood experiences (though not always).

This balanced turn-taking shows up in adult conversation skills and shows mature attunement through the responsiveness of talking and listening (see Chapter 8). Are we aware of and do we respond to a facial expression or body language communicating what the words do not say? In friendships, do we stay in touch with people even when we don't need anything, or do we only think of people when our own needs are inflamed? Do we sit waiting for incoming texts and calls when we feel lonely, or do we send a communication and initiate a friendly game of catch? Adult loneliness can be an outcrop of underdeveloped attunement if our early childhood outreach did not provide results—outreach may not be a developed reflex.

Parental emotional attunement is one of the more significant factors that lead to our development of an attachment style in our adult relationships: secure, anxious, or avoidant. In the fourth hub I discuss how these attachment styles affect adult relationships (see Chapter 7).

THEMES

PLEASURE AND AVERSION

Feelings register on a spectrum from pleasure to disgust; each of us has a unique pleasure profile of what we like and what we do not like—arising as a spontaneous response uniquely tuned by our innate biology and psychology and inevitably incorporating social conditioning and the associated belief systems about appropriate behavior.

Self-gratification in the second hub takes what it wants, not as an act of malice but out of exquisite joy without fixation on consequence. Unless it's fun for them, babies and toddlers don't like to share *(mine, more, give me, I want),* which is healthy. However, they may have been shamed for being selfish, which is an interruption before the consideration of others was a developmentally appropriate expectation and even possible. As adults, surrender and absorption into pleasure—to unhook from perceived control's safe harbor, to only want more, and to freely and openly express rapture and delight—can be considered taboo. Pleasure is unapologetic, can't tell time, and takes without considering reciprocity. If we experience chronic guilt and shame, which I discuss below, the disdain for this type of surrender can be particularly strong. Some folks attempt to control pleasure by reducing it to a concept (rather than a sensate experience), and by verbally expressing enjoyment without feeling it. There is growing evidence that brain structure and chemistry play significant roles in an individual's ability to suppress desire, which can be considered an asset for high levels of professional performance but a liability for overall quality of life.

A repressed culture that fears what it regards as sexual contamination pushes pleasure into the shadows, where desire can become cold, hungry, and even predatory. When we see joy and self-satisfaction as either a provocation or disturbed behavior, we protect ourselves from sending the wrong signals with overcompensating rigidity. Predatory behavior and adultification—when adults think adult-level maturity in children is possible—are violent to a developing psyche and being victimized interrupts the relationship with pleasure and joy—the relationship with life itself.

As uncomfortable as the investigation of this hub can be for some folks, it's important to reclaim the narrative around the innocence of pleasure. Emotionally mature parents understand that responsibility requires that their helpless baby's needs come first, even when they are sleep deprived and feel miserable, and that this is a temporary containment and there is room for their own joy in another place and time.

Mature adults experience pain and discomfort and must manage their feelings, knowing they tend to come and go. The ability of a parent to maintain perspective and to allow the time needed to process the discomfort of unpleasant emotions contributes to positive second-hub development in their children. This is the same adult restraint used if our boss unfairly criticizes our work. We can't yell, hit, or storm out of the office without risking negative consequences. If we are professionals, we maintain an even tone, acknowledge the feedback, and discuss any necessary changes. Afterward we may seethe, but where does that rage go? That surge of adrenaline (an impulse to hit and/or storm out) will need a healthy outlet. When we suppress our pain and aversion for extended periods, we are no longer fully attuned to ourselves, which degrades the trust we have in our feelings; yet when we listen to our discomfort and allow ourselves to hear it, that trust begins to reemerge and grow.

Pleasure does not play by these rules: it's pointless and timeless. Reclaiming pleasure requires surrender. We can lose a connection to delight when ambition becomes so intensified that everything we do is in the service of future gains. But in the service of joy, the impulse for passion is in the second hub and happens in the moment—desire and passion also fuel our power in the third hub; before focused action is taken (see Chapter 6), we should first know what we want.

CHANGE AND AMBIGUITY

In Walt Whitman's *Leaves of Grass*, the poem "Song of Myself" cites the uncomfortable edges of ourselves and the paradoxical tensions of who we are: "I contain multitudes." We are dynamic, nuanced, and fascinating in our vicissitudes, yet there are many societal forces that encourage reductionism and simplicity that does not reflect our true nature.

Traditional children's stories teach morality through stock characters like heroes, villains, and damsels in distress. As we mature, we learn that no single person is completely bad or completely good; we're all a mix of positive and negative behaviors. If we mature in this hub, we accept that we're the hero in some stories and the antagonist in others. In breakups, negotiations, and conflict, sometimes we learn we're the villain in someone else's story. A mature mind can claim this ambiguity within itself and release unrealistic standards of perfection—reducing reflexive defensiveness—and increase self-acceptance and awareness.

Along with the ability to embrace ambiguity comes the capacity to accept change. In the initial development of this hub, as babies and toddlers, we're capable of understanding simple polarities—along with a strong need for routine and consistency—as we establish our sense of safety. The world of the baby and toddler is black or white, right or wrong, yes or no. Aversion and attraction are binary at the dawn of our psychological development. It's hard to imagine a young toddler saying *maybe*. Toddlers are rude, judgmental, and lack diplomacy: *Yes*, that's interesting and *no*, that's not interesting.

They haven't developed the ability to incorporate nuance and the preferences and opinions of other people. Ambiguity is not part of this hub's initial development, although it's essential for its maturation.

We often face a moment of truth as adults. Perhaps we become a boss or parents, and as we consider the magnitude of our new responsibility and calculate the limitations in our qualifications, we often have the astonishing realization that there are no adults—everyone is just making their best guess. Rulings passed down to us as children were essentially judgment calls, and now as adults we try our best to be fair. But fairness itself is a matter of opinion and perspective. Life is ambiguous. We're all making it up as we go along. Sometimes it's overwhelming, especially if we expect our final answers to be absolute truths.

In *Liminal Thinking: Create the Change You Want by Changing the Way You Think*, change and innovation leader Dave Gray writes about thinking in the "space between" and ambiguous opinions; he calls this "neither and both." In the maturing of this hub, we become aware of the relativity of our perspective that influences our beliefs and grows a willingness and ability to consider someone else's opinion in earnest without feeling threatened.

Two-handed thinking is a practice for developing the capacity for ambiguity. We practice holding our opinion in one hand and then consider the alternative in the other; we don't agree with or adopt the other perspective, but by considering and respecting a conflicting viewpoint, we increase our emotional and intellectual capacity for nuance, which has the added benefit of improving our relationships with others. Following is a sample of the practice:

- **Your opinion:** On the one hand, I feel very strongly that dogs are perfect judges of character.

- **Any opinion different from your own:** On the other hand, I understand that sometimes dogs can be mistreated, leading them to display unpredictable behavior.

Another practice that expands advanced capacity for ambiguity is laughter and the ability to be lighthearted—to not take ourselves too seriously.

LAUGHTER

Laughing feels good—an authentic, spontaneously arising laugh shakes our body and delights the senses—it even feels good to see or hear someone else really laugh. Laughter is contagious and can create positive attunement between people. The things we find funny have some universal themes, but what delights you is part of your unique identity—and laughing with someone builds intimacy and connection in personal and professional relationships. Real laughter can't be predicted or controlled, making it an ideal demonstration of the FEEL hub expression: it incorporates an element of surprise that sparks genuine joy. Of course, there's also laughter that's used to signal social agreement or to reduce an awkward moment—that is not what we're talking about here. In the second hub, laughter and giggling can be an outlet for percolating emotions that are not yet fully understood—a signal that can be misread as not taking something seriously, a lack of sensitivity, or even falsely attributed to agreement or acceptance of an awkward situation. In the seventh hub, laughter is part of our ability to not take ourselves too seriously, which also helps to release mental rigidity.

MOVEMENT AND COORDINATION

In *The Body Keeps the Score*, Van Der Kolk (see Chapter 1) describes the lack of coordination in children affected by traumatic upbringings that he witnessed during a canoe trip. His insight was that physical coordination and grace are the products of attunement with early caregivers; physical clumsiness and lack of coordination can be the result of poor early attunement. As I discuss earlier, attunement is synchronization between the child and mother (or primary caregiver) with responsiveness and awareness that teaches a child to coordinate with both itself and its environment—the nice game of catch. We can be in conversations that are out of rhythm as we interrupt and struggle to read the other person. Early attunement teaches us to trust our signals through synchronizing and coordinating with our caregivers. A consistently distracted and/or inattentive parent does not support motor development and emotional attunement, and thus, children may become hesitant and distrustful of their reflexes and reactions. Parents who probably didn't experience an attuned parent themselves may be distracted, impatient, performative, belittling, and focused on themselves rather than their child.

With attentive and attuned parents, grace and the effortless flow of coordinated movement gets baked into the body early in life.

BOUNDARY AND DIFFERENTIATION

The FEEL boundary includes the ability to be around other people without becoming absorbed in their emotions. There's also an inner containment, which helps us to avoid becoming flooded by our emotional states and to avoid becoming disconnected from reality. A young child throws a tantrum when it cannot have what it wants: its emotions completely overwhelm and hijack the child. As we mature and develop, we can understand the transient nature of feelings and know it's unnecessary to immediately act on them—and that often, waiting for the strength of an emotional reaction to pass leads to better outcomes.

Children in a home environment that's quiet but tense can become overly attuned to the emotional states of others. They become vigilant and able to see around corners with respect to others before they develop an understanding of their own internal state. This high sensitivity can lead to becoming overwhelmed in social situations and so, these children prefer to limit their exposure to people because they reflexively absorb their emotions. A person who is highly attuned to the emotional states of others can be drawn towards distressed or underappreciated people, often leading to advocacy, and drawing out people who need support; this can be draining if the person's own emotional boundary is unformed or porous. In the fourth hub, I discuss the continued importance of emotional differentiation (see Chapter 7).

Containing emotional boundaries allows us to remain secure within ourselves rather than being anxious or avoidant in intimate relationships. A lack of boundary leaves folks vulnerable to their identity being dependent on other people (in codependency and enmeshment patterns). Emotional differentiation helps us to understand that our friends and partners can have different experiences from ours, which helps to avoid getting overwhelmed or jealous or sucked into others' turmoil. When overwhelmed by people, it's an excellent practice to take personal responsibility for our own capacity and boundary rather than to incorrectly assert that someone is being objectively "too much."

Intimacy is the softening of our emotional boundary with

someone special. In adults, physical intimacy is the apex for the expression of this hub. Sex is connection, pleasure, sensation, and attunement, and it relaxes the distinction between two people as separate. The voltage intensity of sexual activity is appropriate for a consenting adult. Invasion before a boundary forms causes profound damage. Suppose a predator invades the emotional boundary before it formed. When this happens, a child is affected for the rest of its life, and as an adult may either leap into intimacy very quickly or avoid it entirely. Before we can allow someone into our boundary, we need to have one. This requires a somewhat stable sense of personal identity (see Chapter 6); otherwise, we need others to supply validation. Relying on others to tell us who we are leaves us vulnerable to manipulation and to extreme devastation in breakups when intimacy ends.

Children benefit from the guidance and support of a responsible, mature adult. When these aren't provided in the home, kids depend on peer relationships for emotional fulfillment and insight. Physician and addiction expert Gabor Maté writes in *In the Realm of Hungry Ghosts*, "Kids are not cruel by nature, but they are immature." If peers (or adults) who are at the same developmental stage as us play a role in raising us, there's no context or perspective to support maturation. Furthermore, when we're young, the only perspective we have is of our earlier childhood; it's all we knew, and as children we often mistake it for wisdom.

A sign of a developed boundary is the ability to say *no* when something is enough, based solely on your own assessment of the situation. A developed boundary is semipermeable, can intercept invasion, and allows entrance to the right people. However, a boundary becomes a protective wall when we reflexively reject change, saying *no* to almost everything new. A protective boundary can be a survival adaptation and can become physical vigilance and heightened defensiveness, with an emotional wall keeping people at a distance. An inability to understand or respect boundaries with other people can result in unintentional and oblivious, intrusive behavior. Someone who's unsettling (creepy) is often someone who does not respect our boundaries. By the simplest explanation, a creep is a boundary invader.

HIDDEN SELF AND PROJECTION

Similar to how plants grow toward any light when placed in dark corners, the conditions of our lives shape us—all living things adapt to survive. Babies instinctively learn to repeat the behaviors that gain them the most favorable response, pruning natural predispositions to gain nurture and to get their needs met. In one home, we may learn that we get picked up if we scream and cry, and in another we may learn that screaming and crying get punished (and we adapt to be more agreeable). This initial adaptation to the family (and later to social relationships) will continue to evolve but stems from our earliest patterns as an outcome of two variables: who we were naturally and how our environment responded to us (nature and nurture).

There's no shame in surviving and adapting; adaptations are not sinister or dark when they're occurring. But when they hide too much of who we naturally are, they begin to change who we think we are. And because whatever threat we experienced was true when the hiding occurred, we subconsciously fear and consider a piece of our true nature dangerous to our survival. There may be a surge of disgust or resentment when we see others authentically thriving in their ideal conditions. If we had to hide things we see others showing, the adult responses can range from *That's just wrong; that's irresponsible;* and *that's disgusting* to *They deserve bad things to happen to them.* But dig just a little deeper and you hear the voice of an inner child say, *That's not fair.* What we want for ourselves is buried under layers of social approval, hurt, protection, and resentment. The voice that says *That's not fair* is young. The adult voice that is an overbuild of this says things like, *I had to make sacrifices; I must work and be responsible; I was not accepted as myself;* and *I had to suck it up.*

The hidden self begins to get buried long before episodic memory is operational, cataloged in a subconscious language of reflex, aversion, and where we choose to direct our attention. Keep in mind that the early reflex that does the hiding does it to protect us: it wants us to survive and doesn't understand time, so it doesn't recognize when the immediate threat has either passed or been reduced.

We bury the hidden self under strong responses like disgust and aversion—Judith writes, "Through judgment, we attempt to remove stimuli that might awaken our shadow." If we seek to surface and integrate our hidden self, strong reactions to matters not concerning us combined with complex rationalizations are an excellent place to excavate. The initial excavation can be anxiety provoking and destabilizing. The reward for seeking out and accepting our hidden self is the ease and the effortless charisma of self-acceptance. It takes a lot of energy to keep a secret, and even if we don't know we keep it, our bodies hold the information.

We see our hidden self everywhere we look; it wants us to reconnect with it—our true nature—by showing it to us in everything we see, revealing itself in what we project on others. But it gets intercepted by the same protective reflexes that initially kept us safe, and this requires the recruitment of consciousness. The repressed hidden self can become dangerous when it leads to behavior that invades, abuses, or otherwise interferes with others who are openly expressing themselves. You're not necessarily gay if you have a substantial, adverse reaction to LGBTQ+; you may be resenting the freedom of living bravely in personal truth. Still, there may be something about your own sexuality or gender identity that you're hiding from yourself.

We didn't hide parts of ourselves because they're objectively wrong, we hid them because they didn't support our safety during our early years. I discuss more about the hidden self, projection, and social personas in the CONNECT hub (see Chapter 7).

INTERRUPTIONS AND STRESSORS

The courage to change, to try new things, and to take risks—along with emotional confidence—comes from being attended to with responsive care. For this facet of ourselves, our early caregivers play a profound role in shaping us. Consider how, after a long day of sightseeing in a foreign country, getting a good meal can be challenging—perhaps we're hungry but don't know the language beyond a few conversational phrases and we're unable to read the menu. Maybe we point and use hand gestures, but ultimately the service we receive determines the quality of the meal. If the waiter is patient with us, we will likely get something we like; if the waiter is distracted and annoyed by our inability to speak the language, we'll eat whatever's brought to us or otherwise risk conflict. In the case of the distracted and annoyed waiter, that bad meal will likely make us feel *less* adventurous, and the next time we're hungry, we're more likely to go to terrible tourist restaurants with English language menus. However, if we had a patient and attentive waiter, we either return to the restaurant or feel good about our ability to dine in a foreign country and venture farther off the beaten path, buoyed by the confidence gained from the positive experience. In either case, we will likely internalize the experience and view it as an expression of ourselves and our capability. The patience and responsiveness of our early caregivers gave us the confidence to explore and to experiment, and how emotionally responsive they were with us became our own self-concept of what we deserve and what we are capable of doing.

In *Mating in Captivity: Unlocking Erotic Intelligence*, therapist Esther Perel writes, "It's important to point out that our parents' behavior, what they do, is only part of the situation. Another part is our interpretation of their actions. Each child brings an individual resilience to the lottery of life." The very delicate matter of reconciling parental shortcomings is sensitive work, but like all teachers, the education parents provide is likely very similar to the one they received.

We can consider that many parents are working with an incomplete tool kit passed down through generations (before the revolutions of Dr. Spock's work (see Chapter 3) and Bowlby's attachment theory). Spock introduced the importance of children's emotions to a culture unfamiliar with the notion, and Bowlby introduced the essential importance of nurture, which has continued to be strengthened by a growing body of research.

The children of parents who effectively attuned to them and encouraged individuality often become adults who can be more objective about their parents. The ability to withstand the paradoxical tensions of ambiguity make it possible to deeply love our parents while seeing them as fallible human beings. Emotionally mature and secure parents are comfortable being viewed as human, and by nature imperfect.

Parents who tell their adult children how to feel when asked about difficult memories—*You didn't have it so bad*—tend to enforce a loyalty code with an underlying threat of estrangement. When parents of adult children still require obedience, these children feel protective of their parents' fragility and are fearful of the consequences of speaking up. A continuation of polarized, binary thinking is often a requirement for loyalty—you are either entirely in or entirely out. This can lead to exile and ostracism when the teenager or adult child will not adhere to the parents' restrictive standards.

It's been said that the two early heartbreaks in life are realizing that your parents are people with flaws and that love alone cannot make a relationship work. Our hurt and pain are not dissolved by understanding the circumstances that led to them, but understanding our interruptions can support the process—be gentle and mindful of becoming overstimulated. This section helps the process but is not always necessary, especially if the events of this hub have been traumatic. Fairy tales are filled with caregivers who are absent, careless, clueless, and in some cases, "evil" (see Chapter 4). It's usually with animals and the counterculture of the forest where fairy tale protagonists go to heal—and in many ways, what we do in the Parinama Method is similar to this.

CHRONICALLY DISTRACTED, DISTRESSED, OR EMOTIONALLY IMMATURE PARENTS

When attuned parents teach their child to play catch, they're aware of their child's ability and determine appropriate distance, trying to keep the ball within a reasonable range. These parents can tell when a child has had enough, and they end the game. For attuned parents, this activity focuses on their children—the joy of spending time with them and teaching them new things. When emotionally immature parents play catch, the game has a performative quality for a real or imagined audience. The emotionally immature parent may throw the ball out of the child's range, throw it when the child isn't ready or looking, hit them with the ball or throw it too hard, and claim to be teaching something. These parents may be out of sync, may blame the child when it doesn't catch the ball, may give authoritative advice, and may laugh and taunt when the child struggles. When parents feel the need to assert superiority over their children, they demonstrate their own underdeveloped emotional capacity. A child raised under this parenting style often hears the rationalization of being prepared for the harsh world—a world that distracted, distressed, or emotionally immature parents (upon examination) don't seem to be able to effectively navigate themselves.

There are many reasons parents can be distracted, distressed, or emotionally immature. They may have become sick, lost a child, experienced trauma, have currently or previously lived in poverty, or had parents of their own who were emotionally immature and unable to support their emotional development. The level of emotional immaturity of parents is often inherited. I interviewed a man who told me how his mother, "Sat and listened to me until one o'clock in the morning, and she had to be at work at six a.m. I remember what that felt like, so now I do it for my kids. I don't try to solve their problems, and I only give advice when they specifically ask for it. Mostly, I just take the time to listen. I'm always surprised by what I learn." During interviews, I listened to folks struggling with difficulties in their own parenting as they tried to give their children more love and attention than what they had themselves received as children, and these parents often found the reflexes from their own childhoods to have perplexingly deep roots.

ENMESHMENT: LACKING EMOTIONAL BOUNDARY AND DIFFERENTIATION

Enmeshment occurs in a relationship lacking boundaries and differentiation between two emotionally immature people. It's often intense but never emotionally deep. For babies or young children, immaturity is developmentally appropriate; they are naturally self-centered, focused on their gratification, and for the most part oblivious to how their actions affect others. Mature parents teach children how to develop emotional awareness. Parents who enmesh with their children cannot teach what they don't know, acting like the bigger kid and taking advantage of their adult position of power, often using conditional attention to reward a child in the service of their own interests. In these cases, children will attune to trying to maintain a parent's emotional stability and happiness at the expense of attending to and developing their own. A young child with distracted, distressed parents may do a developmentally inappropriate amount of housework or may spend their allowance on gifts to try to make their parents happy. But the appreciation is inconsistent: sometimes the child receives affection and attention, and other times the parent barely notices what the child is presenting them.

One common form of enmeshment uses a child as an extension of the parents' ego (*Look what my child accomplished*), often with hobbies and activities suited to their own interests or failed dreams getting forced on the child. These parents may wish to live vicariously through their children, instead of allowing the child to explore their own interests. The hallmark of enmeshment is when a parent either overidentifies with the child or uses the child for emotional gratification. In a relatively

consistent home environment, children will not need to fixate on the physical and emotional stability of their parents and can direct their energy toward the things they want to do.

THE MUSEUM: THE EMOTIONALLY INTOLERANT HOME

Parents who have limited emotional capacity with a shrinking adaptation may create a home environment in which children feel like they are walking on eggshells, attempting to avoid disdain or punishment. In this home, children are told they're too sensitive when they express emotion. Being *too sensitive* is not an objective assessment: it's subjective and relative to the parents' capacity for handling the emotions of others. These parents are simply referring to their incapacity to handle their children's emotions. Young children cannot understand this and will likely internalize this assessment as a personal flaw, which can feel like a bind when parents don't provide tools for understanding and processing feelings and emotions—leading to guilt, frustration, and shame.

The emotionally intolerant home will usually be very polarized, with parents speaking in black and white absolutes and showing very little curiosity about the inner lives of their children. Small talk will be familiar, and many circuit breakers will be used to stop the flow of emotions, perhaps using some of the following responses:

- **Dismissing:** "You have no right to feel that way."

- **Manners and politeness:** "You're being rude; that's not very nice."

- **Prematurely pushing for positivity:** "Look on the bright side."

- **Correcting:** "I think what you're trying to say is . . ."; "Hate is a strong word."

- **Fixing and advising (rushing to a solution):** "You're talking about this when you could be doing something to fix it."

- **Polite cutoff:** "Well, that's nice, honey. It sounds like you have a strong opinion about that."

- **Silent treatment:** Used as punishment when a child becomes upset, and the parent becomes impatient or angry about it—calling out any emotional expression as insubordination.

This home is like a museum; it feels cold and quiet. Meals can be repetitive or bland, and the only nurture children receive happens when they're sick (because illness falls within the responsibility of physical care). Some children raised in these homes will fake being sick or become hypochondriacal to experience nurture and rest—a pattern that can extend into adulthood.

In cases of moral or religious severity, children can seek the approval of their parents by becoming rigid. Rachel, a woman I interviewed, strained to please her strict parents by being a perfect teenager: no sex, no drinking, earning excellent grades, and following all the rules. The only approval she can remember receiving was when she would parrot the restrictive values of her parents' faith. She wanted their support and resented the means required to receive it. The only television that was allowed was religious or G-rated. Her mother would say (in a small, pinched voice that concealed her intense, punitive disposition) that there was no point in so-called dark entertainment.

As an adult, Rachel avoided all movies that were dark, dramatic, suspenseful, and horror-based. When she and her boyfriend, Jamal, started dating, she repeated her mother's words about dark entertainment as her own, and Jamel said, "I think you're afraid of emotions," which gave her pause—but elicited her curiosity. Rachel had seen a scary movie the previous year and had been disturbed for days afterward. After considering Jamal's words and doing some conscious reclaiming of her emotional awareness (see the exercises below), she watched the film again. To her surprise, this time was different. "It was dark and scary, but I was able to pay more attention to the message and social commentary and not get overwhelmed."

THE CIRCUS: THE EMOTIONALLY CHAOTIC HOME

Parents' generally control the emotional climate in a home, and emotionally immature parents can be emotionally unregulated yet chastise their children for being emotional, further adding to a child's confusion about its emotions. In both the museum and the circus, nothing emotional is dealt with directly. In the museum, a child's emotions are usually dismissed or invalidated while the parents emote, criticize, and complain—using lack of expressiveness or labeling their feelings as facts to disguise their underlying heightened and emotional nature. But in the circus, the home is full of excessive emotional expression that's often loud while there will be one (or more) elephant-in-the-room issue that never gets mentioned. In both the museum and the circus, talking about complex emotional topics happens behind people's backs, never directly with them unless it's in an explosion of frustration or anger. One example is a mother who complains to her child about its father's inconsiderate behavior, but when the father comes home, says nothing to him about her frustrations. Also, a pattern in divorce can be parents who don't communicate with each other but complain about or insult the other parent in the child's presence. Children who are starved for attention may bathe in parental engagement that's in short supply, not realizing that their parents are using them to process their own emotions, often without awareness of or concern for the effect on their children's emotional development and the inner conflicts this creates.

Infants and children amplify and act out emotions and learn to understand what they are and how they work by how parents and caregivers react to their behavior. Attuned parents respond by mirroring back, which teaches children how effective their emotions are at communicating inner wants and needs with others. A child learns to understand its feelings through this mirror. But suppose parents are highly inconsistent or absent when responding. In these cases, children grow to distrust the effectiveness of their emotional communication, questioning their ability to communicate rather than questioning the parents' ability to respond. Invalidated or failed attempts to mirror with young children can shift into the behavior pattern of emotional contagion (the attempt to understand the overwhelm of arising emotions by wanting others to feel the same way). A child or adult may use emotional contagion if it becomes emotionally overwhelmed, often amplifying irritation and frustration in an effort to use mirrored pain or fear in the eyes of its loved ones to see the emotions that are arising within itself. This can be a contributing factor to the escalation of an argument if the people involved need to see their feelings of pain in others to fully understand what they're feeling themselves. Emotional contagion is an outcome of emotional illiteracy and is not within conscious control. The inability to attune, to handle emotional voltage, and to contain and manage intense feelings comes from a lack of development that becomes a profound blind spot for self-awareness—remember that this development happens before memories can form. A perpetrator of emotional contagion creates an environment in which the rest of the family tiptoes around this potentially explosive person, which hijacks the expression and development of the emotional capacity of others within the household and so, the pattern often gets passed to the next generation.

INTERMITTENT REINFORCEMENT

Intermittent reinforcement is any conditioning schedule in which rewards and punishments are not consistently tied to behavior. Consider the analogy of a consistent paycheck providing stability and a framework for budgeting and paying bills: on the one hand, the energy spent worrying about money is reduced or eliminated; on the other hand, if we get paid the exact same salary with the only difference being an unpredictable payment schedule, there will be worry, anxiety, and the fixation caused by intermittent reinforcement. In the case of the inconsistent paycheck, we would likely spend excessive time checking for the money, planning contingencies, and worrying that it may never come. This takes extra time and energy, while folks in a consistent model don't have to think about it and can direct their focus and energy on things that lead to greater productivity.

Children cannot control the vicissitudes of moods and circumstances within their family, but they don't know this yet. When there's no consistent pattern of emotional connection (love, affection, and validation), children can become fixated on figuring out how to bond, wondering if or when connection will ever come. If parents are chronically distracted, distressed, or emotionally immature, how they treat their children will be an inconsistent expression of how they feel on any given day. As a result, children can strain to find correlation and meaning and are often left feeling helpless and frustrated. The outside world is unpredictable, and children seek safe haven within the home; when it's not consistently available, they may work futilely to try to create it by changing themselves. Surprisingly, good times ultimately can cause the most hurt for children raised in either the museum or the circus: having good times shows that good times are possible, raising the question of why they're infrequent. A chaotic and unpredictable house requires children to develop adaptations for emotional survival, which I discuss next.

TRAUMA

We do not consciously decide to become rigid, block our memories, or even adopt the spacey responses of dissociation, but again, our body's deep, ancient technology is programmed to survive and to consistently seek to find a way, even if it reduces function and feeling. Most of us like to see ourselves as resilient and robust because *we are*: resilience and strength are coded into our being. Wounds heal, we survive and carry on living despite tremendous loss and difficulty. We share the same responses to shock and surprise that many animals have: fight, flight, or freeze. We are wild, strong, and resilient, but also fragile and vulnerable. The human body has narrow and specific requirements for temperature, nutrients, oxygen, and hydration. Our bodies are relatively delicate, while also resilient and committed to our survival, sometimes in the face of conditions, events, and circumstances that can be shocking and incredibly brutal.

Trauma is most commonly known as being the result of surviving acute and severe violence, but trauma is a complex phenomenon, one that can result from events and causes not commonly considered traumatic. Trauma is any disruption to the harmonious functioning of the body. If we get yelled at, honked at, or even jostled or shoved in a crowd, it's socially responsible and mature to turn the other cheek, shrug it off, or proceed as if nothing happened. But if the jet fuel of adrenaline and stress hormones are released into the body and don't get used in response to a threat, again, where do they go?

If we feel but can't express surprise or shock (or can't fight back), it doesn't make these feelings disappear; instead, they become rigidity, stress, and even underlying, unpredictable frustration and aggression. Our feelings and emotions, when suppressed, will rebel and show up in mysterious ways, such as misplaced anger and rudeness (*Hurt people, hurt people*). The fight, freeze, or flight responses are deeply coded reflexes for escaping and/or surviving danger and distress.

Levine describes the freeze response seen in nature as serving "a last-ditch survival strategy" to buy time (see Chapter 4). In the example he uses, an impala attacked by a cheetah may freeze (play dead). If the cheetah believes its prey is no longer mobile, it may lower its guard, giving the impala a potential chance to escape. This freeze response to shock is more common in so-called civilized society than are fight or flight. Some folks express shame and feelings of regret for not responding in the moment when shocked by the actions of others. Anyone who has mentally replayed a past event and imagined a perfect response to an insult is familiar with this. However, the shock response—even in social situations—can take hold and not release for minutes, hours, weeks, months, or even years. Victims of violent trauma get shamed for not speaking up sooner, but the body-mind will hide overwhelming memories until it's physically (and emotionally) safe for them to come out and be processed.

Levine's revolutionary discovery of somatic therapy for healing trauma emphasizes a reduced role in the story of the initial event of a trauma (see Chapter 4). Although talk therapy can and does play a role for discharging a traumatic experience, Levine asserts that revisiting the stories alone can lead to retraumatization, and how we remember the stories contain clues: "The condensation of an entire event into a single image is characteristic of trauma . . . what most people don't know is that seemingly benign situations can be traumatic." Examples of this include simple early-childhood experiences of discomfort in the cold, fear of the dark, or even lifesaving medical procedures that involved being restrained. These situations represent disruptions to harmonious and spontaneous responses and movements and cause stress in the body, and their voltage can overwhelm a small body that's still learning an unfamiliar world. Oppositely, neglect—not getting enough stimulation over longer periods of time—can also produce trauma.

Children can be brilliantly inventive at self-soothing with transition objects (see Chapter 4): carrying a blanket or stuffed animal, sucking their thumbs, playing with their pets, seeking a screen, eating food, reading, or any other behaviors that simultaneously numb and gently stimulate. However, if a child cannot discharge or express its response to shock or neglect, the stress is stored in its body until it has an outlet for release. For many teens and adults, alcohol is used for self-soothing because it temporarily relaxes and lowers boundaries and increases capacity for emotional expression. Alcohol can lead to blowing off steam, but it doesn't expand this hub's capacity because it only opens us up temporarily—any received gains of emotional capacity contract the next day, perhaps with a hangover.

Abuse on young bodies, especially sexual, invades boundaries before they are formed and overwhelm a body with high-powered voltage that blows out circuits and fries wiring. Trauma from this abuse is astonishingly more common than people like to believe, and it's the survivors' decision when and how to tell their stories and process the experience. All survivors deserve the care and support of a professional and loved ones.

ADAPTATIONS AND HOLDING PATTERNS

Our adaptations and holding patterns in this hub can be challenging to see because the interruptions that shaped them happen so early in life—so early we literally can't remember life without them because they happen before we can form memories. Second-hub holding patterns are easy to see in others but are uniquely challenging to see in ourselves. Psychologist Pierre Janet, as quoted by Van der Kolk, said, "Every life is a piece of art, put together with all means available [see Chapter 1]." The patterns and composition of the art that we observe in others is visible to us, yet we often remain blind to our own if we do not choose to consciously look.

CHARACTERISTICS OF A BALANCED AND OUT-OF-BALANCE SECOND HUB

There is no reliable prediction that determines how one child raised in the same emotional environment will adapt compared to another. However, brain scans show that some children are born with more activity in the so-called executive functioning of the PFC, and others are born with more activity in the emotional limbic system. Furthermore, children with higher PFC activity tend to be better at delaying gratification than those with high limbic-system activity. The compounding effect of judgment and moral assignment on a child's natural tendency toward feeling (limbic) or over thinking (PFC) can escalate into guilt and shame and can further drive destructive behaviors within an adaptation.

Evidence of a dynamic, strong, and balanced second hub:

- feeling deeply without becoming overwhelmed;

- having strong emotions and expressing them when appropriate, and holding back when it's necessary;

- having grace and coordination;

- being content with self and accepting of own feelings (even when they are negative);

- being able to enjoy pleasure without guilt or shame;

- being able to understand subtlety and nuance, and able to hear different points of view without trying to change them; and

- having effective emotional boundary observation and enforcement with other people.

Holding patterns in this hub affect our ability to grasp ambiguity, tolerate reasonable amounts of discomfort, and have coordination and emotional literacy along with the ability to change. Evidence of second-hub imbalance:

- deep discomfort or awkwardness with feelings and emotions from self and others—both positive and negative;

- clumsiness and lack of coordination;

- moodiness;

- either discomfort with or fixation on pleasure;

- tendency to feel guilt and shame;

- believing that your perspective is completely right, and others are completely wrong;

- difficulty being in the presence of strong emotions without becoming overwhelmed or absorbed by them;

- addiction (excessive adult pacifier use): avoiding feelings above the threshold of emotional capacity by using distractions and the oblivion of overindulgence;

- rescue fantasies: believing that parents will change and become more caring or that problems will be miraculously solved by other people (often, a romantic interest or relationship);

- chronic pain, especially low-back or pelvic; and

- stiffness or hypermobility in the hips.

INFLATING, SHRINKING, AND COMBINATION

The two primary adaptation patterns are shrinking, avoidance and minimization of emotions, and inflating, expansive and unpredictable emotions. One adaptation hides feelings (shrinking), and the other fills a room with emotional expression (inflating). Neither have full awareness, governance, or control of feelings and emotions, and both tend toward being emotionally unavailable. A rule of thumb for determining a second-hub adaptation is to ask yourself if, when overwhelmed with emotion, are you are more likely to want to be alone (shrinking) or do you want to be around people (inflating)? Also keep in mind that it's perfectly natural to relate to some of both, but there is likely a primary behavior pattern.

INFLATING

The inflating response is expansive and finds comfort in getting attention: in school, it can be the child who tries to get the class to feel the way it does (for example, the class clown or the rebel disrupting class). On one end of the spectrum, the second-hub inflating child can feel betrayed when others don't take on the intensity of its feelings. This child is often waiting impatiently for parents and others to take responsibility for the disappointments in their experiences—and waiting for an apology can become a fixation carried into adulthood. On the other end of the spectrum, the shrinking adaptation tends to overemphasize their personal responsibility while the inflating adaptation blames others and can resist (and feel overwhelmed by) accountability—the shrinking adaptation is more likely to criticize and blame itself. The inflating response is the so-called difficult child, who often expresses what the shrinking child can only dream of saying. As children, usually they are outwardly rebellious and at times shocking, with near-constant button pushing of one or both parents. They wonder why the parents will not solve everything and they may have difficulty knowing how to control their temper and emotions. Fierce, unpredictable, and social, this overcompensating adaptation may feel protective and possessive of their shrinking sibling but resentful and envious of the approval received for their perceived perfection and easiness. Because they are bold and brave, often speaking truth to power, the inflating child is often vilified and made to feel that it is too much. Although there is often the appearance of excitement and aliveness, this adaptation tends to have trouble emotionally regulating and can be unpredictable, which can lead to feeling defensive or ashamed. The fear of vulnerability leads to dominant social positioning, seeking people who will look up to (and not question) them. They tend to live in the past and spend time with younger people who lack confidence—and so, they can become controlling and sometimes can abuse their power. Despite the appearance of being unapologetic, the inflating second hub wants to be attended to and cherished and is often mystified and ashamed of the outcomes of their unregulated and expansive emotional behavior. But without emotional literacy they are likely to feel helpless and even identify themselves by their lack of emotional control (*That's just who I am*) as a way to manage the shame and discomfort about it.

Because folks with the inflating adaptation are so misunderstood and can be a bit scary when their emotions are intense and out of control, they're often met with a lack of sympathy and compassion when they suffer. Combined with relatively weak connections and volatility, they can despair at their lack of real friends, but forget the craving for authentic bonds as soon as an adoring crowd surrounds them again. They get angry about boundaries and need them but will only be open to working on themselves when they feel low—a state that can change quickly. The truth is that someone who has a robust second-hub inflating adaptation is less likely to read any self-improvement book, including this one, unless they're facing a crisis.

Inflating Behaviors

- Is frustrated by others: *They should've known; Why didn't you _____?; I'm surrounded by idiots.*

- Craves change; is easily bored

- Is impulsive, impatient, and seeks immediate gratification

- Is highly social, has social dependency with a fixation on others who look up to (worship) them

- Feels lost and anxious with quiet or when alone

- Has a sense of conquest versus intimacy with sex; openly talks about sex or discloses private information about partners

- Gets absorbed in strong feelings, tries to pull others into them, and often views the lack of emotional participation by others as disloyalty or even betrayal

- Gets absorbed in the intense emotions of others

- Is unaware of their own boundaries, with a tendency to invade those of others

- Is pleasure-seeking

- Is soothed by immediate gratification to alleviate mounting frustrations and difficult emotions

- Social persona: the so-called bad one

- Body: numb unless highly stimulated

SHRINKING

Folks with a shrinking adaptation tend to take complete responsibility for interruptions and developmental shortcomings. They blame themselves and use control to comfort and soothe themselves. The shrinking, easy child (so-called mature beyond its years) is contained, restricted—and these qualities are carried into adulthood, often leading to success in professional environments. In a classroom, these children are excellent candidates for teacher's pet: well-behaved, responsible, and with a strong desire for self-control through perfectionism. They often seek parental validation through being so-called good (a validation that never comes from emotionally immature parents—but these children blame themselves and just try harder). Complicating matters, emotionally immature parents may even feel competitive with them, just as they may get wrapped up in the drama associated with an inflating child. Also common with a shrinking child is the assumption by adults that their good behavior indicates that they're doing fine and don't need help.

The second-hub shrinking adaptation needs permission for self-gratification, believing that everything needs to be earned. This correlates with taking blame and responsibility for negative things that have happened that were outside of their control. There is discomfort with being in debt to anyone because of the vulnerability. Folks with a shrinking tendency make their emotional needs smaller and become exhausted trying to earn and deserve enjoyment. This pursuit can become so exhausting it's often avoided altogether. Any so-called debt of gratitude becomes guilt and asking for what they want feels especially scary because it risks the devastation of rejection.

Disordered eating of all kinds, such as fixating on healthy eating, calorie guilt or fixation, restrictions of any kind, cleansing, and obsessive exercising can be a sign of imbalance in this hub. Fixation on dieting and perfection of the body indicate that working to strengthen and balance this hub can be rewarding and bring greater peace to the emotional relationship with food.

The shrinking adaptation manages emotions by diminishing them: when flooded with feelings, the escape is deciding that it's *just not that big of a deal*. Conversely, the inflating will make a big deal out of the problem but be unlikely to address it directly with a person who has upset them and instead, complains to everyone except the offending person. When (or if) they do address the issue directly, it's likely to be explosive and combative. A shrinking sibling will simultaneously admire and resent its inflating sibling, and seethe at the attention and special treatment it receives for poor behavior. Higher expectations placed on the behavior of the so-called easy, shrinking child means that when they do misbehave, they're told, "I expect that from your [inflating] sibling, but not from you." Again, the inflating sibling can carry resentment toward the so-called perfect, well-behaved shrinking brother or sister. These are naturally occurring dynamics between siblings that get brokered by attentive parents, but when parents lack maturity, complexity and intensity are added to an already fraught connection.

Shrinking Behaviors

- Use a defensive strategy: are low-maintenance

- Are uncomfortable with change

- Soothes by controlling

- Have unrealistic levels of responsibility and accountability, take the blame, blame themselves: *I'm the only person I can trust to do this right; I must solve everything.*

- Get upset when others don't have the same intense level of responsibility: *Great, now I have to take care of this.*

- Use food for control, such as with disordered, restrictive eating and obsession with health

- Control and delay gratification (good for careers, but can be bad for happiness)

- Prefer to be in small groups or one-on-one situations; alone time energizes and feels safe

- Can have difficulty staying in the moment during sex; often uses alcohol or watches the clock; doesn't mind celibacy

- Have numb or diminished sense of importance of emotions

- Have low tolerance for others' neediness and emotional behavior and move to find a solution before emotions are expressed. Have guilt for their emotions, see them as a burden, and apologizes when expressing them

- Have boundaries with big walls around inner self but lacks full awareness of these boundaries. Feel overwhelmed by people invading their boundary while not fully understanding what's happening.

- Have social personas as the so-called good one

- Have numb bodies with lowered ability to sense needs

COMBINATION

It's not unusual to identify with behavior from both adaptations or to believe one is morally superior to the other. The common denominator in both adaptations is twofold: they don't have strong emotional literacy or emotional availability in relationships, and they struggle with attunement to others. The purpose of this section is to bring awareness to our patterns so that we can manage them and accept ourselves (and others) as we are, along with having optimism for the possibility for greater capacity and development in the hub.

BALANCE

When we're balanced and dynamic in this hub, we can have a differentiated identity from family and social relationships enough to build a life for ourselves separate from the expectations of others. When this hub is developed, we have both impulse control and expression of emotion, along with the emotional intelligence that supports empathy and compassion. Empathy is knowing how something feels while remaining present in your own experience, unlike weak emotional boundaries that mistake empathy as becoming immersed in the same emotional state as another person. When there's strength in this hub and we have a problem with another person, we can deal with it directly to smooth out differences; we can be objective and know ourselves well enough to admit weaknesses. Balance in this hub also means we don't second-guess ourselves when we've had enough.

A SHRINKING STRATEGY: INTUITION AND INTELLECTUALIZATION

A reliance on intuition (in the sixth hub—SEE) can be used to avoid the direct experience of sensation and emotion in the second hub. This is an adaptation in which a shrinker is insightful about others but is a mystery to itself. Intuition is pattern recognition, and in the absence of attuned parents, someone with the shrinking response can develop a heightened sensitivity to patterns. The child who knows its mother is about to get angry may quiet itself after hearing a barely audible intake of breath signaling her exasperation. This highly developed sensitivity around emotional patterns grows increasingly strong. Folks with this adaptation often become so insightful that they seem to be able to see around corners and to predict outcomes. But there's a subtle insecurity because these observations are perceptions that are secondary to the sensation of direct experience—feelings are substituted with a very informed guess that over time can become disconnected from reality. Following our gut feeling can drive us

in surprising and counterintuitive directions toward a more correct path of action. Intuition guides us by patterns of what we have already seen and may unintentionally keep us stuck in what's familiar.

When we rely on the sixth hub before it's developmentally optimal, we become spectators rather than directly feeling our aliveness—our sixth hub carries a heavy load before it's ready, replacing feeling and sensation with observation, which can lead to the sense that life is happening at a distance. Instead of building our capacity to feel, we watch and become fascinated by so-called normal and abnormal behavior. We develop an orientation of looking outward to avoid the mystery of what is inside us. Folks with this holding pattern may be great with people in business and casual friendships, but struggle with personal intimacy. When what is seen overrides what is felt, this holding pattern can lead to manipulative behavior or relationships that rely heavily on appearances.

TOLERANCE FOR TOUCH

Physical intimacy and sex are apexes of the adult expression in this hub. This is high-voltage attunement with the softening and dissolving of boundaries. Intimacy can strengthen and balance this hub with a secure partner who attunes and supports safe exploration while respecting limits. Our relationship with sex can shed light on the state of this hub. As with body weight, extreme fluctuations in sexual activity can also point to adaptations and holding patterns.

A person with an inflated adaptation is going to be more likely to have trouble with boundaries. When we don't have them for ourselves, it may be harder to be aware of them in others and makes it difficult to imagine that a person wouldn't enjoy the same things we do. Just as an appropriate amount of emotional expression is subjective, pleasure and sexuality are uniquely individual matters: it's your right to determine what makes sense for your life—and your life alone. If a person is a so-called hugger and pulls people in for a handshake and a light embrace, some people may find this warm and charismatic. The same gesture can be alarming and unwelcomed by folks who bristle at the lack of appreciation for their range of comfort with touch. The same behavior that is experienced as warm and welcoming by one person can be experienced as a boundary invasion by another—and there should be no judgment on a person's preference. Although the intention of a hugger may feel defensible, we should always respect the physical boundary of another person. Each of us should decide who is allowed in our physical space, and even with the best intentions unsolicited physical contact is always at risk of being unwelcome.

PACIFIERS

A pacifier is a device used to provide comfort in times of overwhelm. In the case of parents, they offer a pacifier if they cannot immediately attend to the discomfort or distress of a baby. As adults, we continue to use this device, but with greater specificity for the comfort we crave in times of overwhelm and overstimulation—smoking, eating, sex, sleeping, shopping, drinking, scrolling, or any other thing that can help us escape the discomfort of a given moment. I have yet to meet a person who does not use some manner of a pacifier. They're all substitutes for the five primary human comforts and encouragement that we learn above from Brown: receiving someone's complete and concentrated attention, experiencing affection, being cherished and adored, feeling safe and supported, and being seen and listened to by someone who wants to understand you. These experiences are profoundly soothing and satisfying. They differ from pacifiers in that primary comforts lead to a deep sense of satisfaction, completeness, and resolution—while pacifiers leave us craving more. There's a tendency to judge pacifier use, but judgment just leads to shame and guilt—and these feelings are usually at the core of the hurt, so feeling them just leads to more pacifier use. Guilting and shaming people doesn't lead to meaningful or long-term behavior change.

Before judging the use of pacifiers, consider that our compulsions and addictions are related to our capacity for processing feelings and expressing emotion that we didn't choose or get the chance to shape. The brain and nervous system we're born with determine our ability to delay gratification and tolerate discomfort, depending on their unique biological predispositions in concert with the early environment that shape their development. I discuss this further regarding the Stanford Marshmallow Experiment, along with its long-term findings (see Chapter 6). Further complicating matters, the human nervous system cannot evolve at the same rate of change as the increase of stimulation in modern society over the past hundred years.

THE SHADOW: GUILT

If we say something that hurts someone, the pressure of the bad feeling can drive us to make an apology to relieve the internal tension. When guilt is tied to specific wrongdoings toward others, it's acute and moves us to corrective action. It's that nagging feeling that won't go away until we do the right thing to make good on what we've done wrong. If we do something that negatively affects someone, we tend to feel bad, and the discomfort eventually leads to a corrective action or if unaddressed perhaps becomes regret. When functioning in its acute capacity, guilt is a meaningful contributor to a homeostatic, self-correcting, inner ecosystem. If it leads to kind and corrective action, the system is functioning. As a dynamic equalizer, guilt naturally restores peace, but when it becomes a holding pattern of chronic guilt and shame, it becomes a punishing inner enforcer.

Chronic guilt is the circuit breaker for satisfaction that interferes with attaining the achievement of satisfaction in pleasure, which often can lead to repetitive and compulsive behavior. When guilt is chronic, we may fixate on enjoyment and pleasure but characterize them as indulgent or sinful—gluttony, lust, and sloth. When guilt is reflexive, as it often can be with a shrinking adaptation, achieving a satisfying response to enjoyment gets interrupted with feelings of unworthiness and disdain. In this cruel moral universe, only a so-called perfect body can eat what it wants and be allowed to enjoy sex. We may even seek out people who reinforce these distorted, disturbed values because we tend to find comfort with the familiarity of belief systems formed during early programming.

CHRONIC PAIN AND SUPPRESSED EMOTIONS

Pain protects us—it directs our attention and prioritizes our actions. Like the shadows of each hub, when it's acute it helps us, but when it's chronic it will hijack us. Chronic pain can leave us adrift in despair, having cut away our mental anchor. It creates feelings of hopelessness and immobilization and can feel like a betrayal (being trapped in your own body), with the sense that living a full life is no longer possible. When chronic pain receives a therapeutic diagnosis without resolving the pain itself, the sense of limitation can be devastating.

If doctors, therapists, chiropractors, massage therapists, and alternative medicine have been unable to provide relief, things can indeed feel hopeless.

When our demanding careers and tight schedules don't allow the time for inconvenient emotions, pain can slow us down and provide so-called acceptable reasons for rest. This is reminiscent of parents who are distant with emotional comfort but can nurture physical injury and illness in their child because it falls under the duty of physical care. Perhaps we notice that back-pain flare-ups seem to happen when the stakes are the highest. If we allow ourselves to listen, the pain has a voice: *I'm nervous about whether this project will succeed; I don't know if I can handle this stress any longer;* and/or *I'm afraid of looking stupid.* As the voice of the repressed emotional self, it will be vulnerable; as an adaptation it became a part of us early in life, when we didn't have tools or support for processing feelings and emotions. Pain makes staying present and calm difficult, because its function is to create urgency and narrow our focus on resolving the discomfort—and it's very good at its job. For folks suffering from chronic pain, an understandable strategy and response is disconnection and disassociation from the body. There's a common tendency to distract ourselves from our bodies when pain and discomfort are overwhelming.

Some folks will say that they don't get angry or lonely or they altogether deny other difficult emotions yet will be familiar with a suite of chronic ailments like migraines or back pain. In *Healing Back Pain: The Mind-Body Connection*, rehabilitation-medicine practitioner and Professor John Sarno called the syndrome of denied emotions shifting into chronic pain and health problems "tension myositis syndrome" (TMS). Sarno noticed the following traits in patients who tended to have physical pain in lieu of expressing emotions (I've added the adaptations in parenthesis):

- perfectionism, people-pleasing, stoicism (shrinking);
- rage and hostility, anxiety and fear, dependency (inflating); and
- tendency to be highly polarized with a severe judgment, low self-esteem (combination).

Understandably, accepting this can take some getting used to, but as those suffering from chronic pain know, the pain will be waiting until we choose to face it. Sarno's method involved an initial step of identifying the syndrome and accepting it—and this one step alone has tremendous effect on chronic pain. The next step is to consciously surface and process feelings and emotions.

If you can, listen to what your body is trying to say: the chronic pain is real. When addressing it as solely a physical injury or infection doesn't provide relief, it can be confusing. This phenomenon is considered biopsychosocial, meaning that biological factors play a role, but social and psychological factors are also involved. When we are detached from our emotions, physical pain can signal the path back to finding peace through acknowledging truths that can be difficult, but by facing it we can ultimately gain access to having more energy and in many cases, can bring an end to chronic, mysterious, physical pain. Communicate with your body and ask pain, stiffness, and discomfort directly (but gently) if there's something they want to tell you. Bring some movement like gentle rocking into the affected area when possible. (I provide more practices to find and express emotions in the techniques and exercises below. In addition, there are also multiple journal practices for what I call "emotional hygiene," the daily practice of clearing out residual emotions (see Chapter 11). Instead of actively agonizing against pain, it can be surprisingly powerful to simply accept that we're in it—beware of how self-talk can express impatience and frustration when your body needs patience and encouragement the most. This is not always doable, but I introduce it as a possibility.

When we bring more dynamism and responsiveness into adaptations and holding patterns, it can be like removing load-bearing beams from how our relationships function. When a daughter stops filling the air with polite chatter, the silence can be deafening. When a wife finally asks her spouse for the affection she craves, an outright rejection may be shocking. Perhaps a husband wants to be more emotionally expressive, and when he is, his spouse's disdain may cause deep pain. Remember that adaptations were early compensations for our environments; when we shift holding patterns, we can disrupt the balance of adult ecosystems that have been created in the image of the early dynamics of home.

TECHNIQUES AND EXERCISES

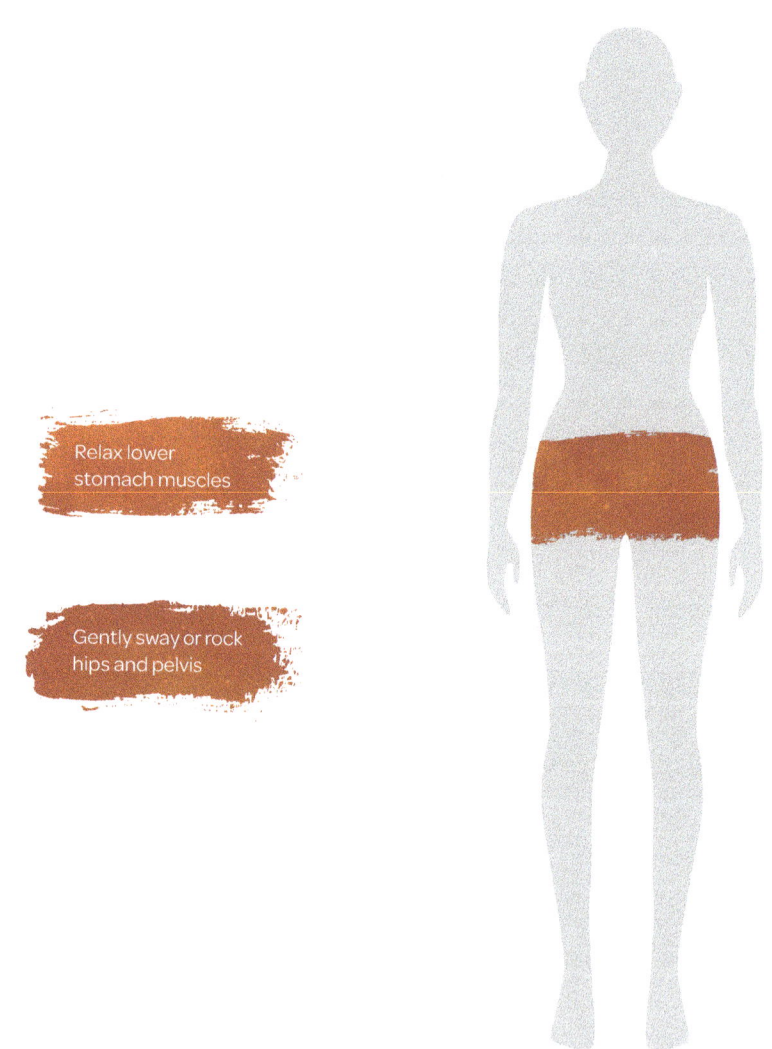

Relax lower stomach muscles

Gently sway or rock hips and pelvis

Figure 5.1: Second-Hub Body Prompts

The measurement of health in the second hub can be observed in our capacity to embrace change without losing our sense of self and in movement without pain or discomfort. Change is movement: for anything to change, it needs to move. Movement in the second hub is driven by curiosity and sensation—we move because it feels good and reclaim a relationship with feeling that centers around an uncomplicated, simple sense of curiosity. We reclaim our emotions as naturally arising, knowing they communicate with the world around us when we express them. Next, in the third hub, preferences and aversions inform directed and focused action, but before we get there, in the second hub we establish movement that doesn't require a specific outcome and is simply satisfied by exploring sensation.

Once you feel physically safe, change and movement become a welcome counterbalance—movement and change thrive with the solidity of a first-hub foundation. The second hub can hold a surprising amount of emotional intensity. In second-hub restoration, we don't look away from discomfort and pain: we want to hear it out and let it pass through. If we don't have time and bandwidth to process it, we can at least tell our pain, "I may not be able to do anything right now, but I can listen. Tell me what you need me to know." Emotions and pain tend to pass when expressed in ways that are safe and contained. Stay with yourself, go slowly, and pause when needed. If at any point you begin to feel distressed while practicing these exercises, bring yourself back to the safe place established in the first hub: put your feet in the grass, use the Vu sound (see Chapter 8), or reach out to a friend or professional for support. Restoration of all hubs consists of the knowledge that you're important and deserve physical and emotional support—regardless of previous experience.

The primary physical locations of the second hub are in the hips, pelvis, lower back, and abdomen, and the hub is expressed in both physical and emotional movement. The epicenter of the second hub is the psoas muscle that tethers the legs to the back. As the deepest muscles in the human body, they affect balance, flexibility, range of motion, joint mobility, and even organ function. In yoga, the psoas is sometimes called the "muscle of the soul." The nerves associated with pelvic pain, back pain, and sciatica run through the psoas, and the extension and stretching are associated with the surprising emotional releases experienced when people stretch in their hips. (There's a light psoas release (stretch) below.)

THE RIGHT TO FEEL: EXPANDING THE CONTAINER

This hub has a sweet and special quality taking its cue from the baby version of ourselves, with unselfconscious self-gratification coupled with unapologetic aversion to things we don't like. Reclaiming this part of ourselves means finding the capacity to say, "I want more," without feeling the need to earn it or feel guilt, and saying "no" or "that's enough," and allowing ourselves to dislike something without second-guessing it. Of course, the adult version of saying "yuck" to something benefits from a little more diplomacy than we'd expect from a baby or toddler—but still carries the strength and clarity of preference.

Guilt

This is the hub of gratification—and guilt, the shadow of this hub, interrupts the achievement of satisfaction. However, self-gratification is often considered taboo; not many so-called responsible people are great at fitting it into a balanced identity. Thoughts like *I shouldn't be doing this*, or *This* is *irresponsible* when resting, eating, having sex, or otherwise indulging cut off satisfaction before it can be fully achieved—and when satisfaction isn't achieved, the craving doesn't get subdued. If we truly savor a dessert, rest, or a glass of wine, without the circuit breaker of guilt, the compulsion to have more naturally recedes as we enjoy.

Believing that guilt or shame is the only thing keeping us from becoming reckless or dangerous is part of the foundation of self-loathing—our nature is not inherently bad and not in constant need of policing. But unexpressed guilt and shame inflicts suppressions that *can* make people unpredictable and even potentially dangerous. When anger and rage as natural responses to insults on our dignity are pushed into the subconscious realm, they *can* become triggered at unpredictable and inconvenient times.

Growing the capacity to feel

Pleasure is not time-bound, has no goal, and is numinous, and as a result, surrendering to pleasure provides an important release from the intensity of working and living a busy life. As a counterbalance to intensity, enjoyment supports greater success and performance in all areas of life. Some folks often imagine the solution to unhappiness is more money, things, fun, and so-called better people surrounding us—and although this may be true to a certain extent, if you can't enjoy the good things you already have, your capacity for pleasure does not grow just because you get better stuff. Opportunities for enjoyment and satisfaction exist in everyday moments. It can be as simple as savoring a hard candy, smelling a flower, spending time with a pet, or reading a few pages of a book. But if you have not expanded your capacity for pleasure, the enjoyment of getting more things is like trying to fit two gallons of water into a one-gallon pail. It pours in for an instant but doesn't get fully experienced as it spills over. We grow our container by finding and experiencing pleasure in the simple things in life.

Our belief about pleasure fits within the vessel we provide for it. Psychologist Gay Hendricks writes in *The Big Leap* about what he calls your "zone of genius" and how to expand it to contain greater feeling and capacity for living. The limits on your zone of genius, according to Hendricks, can be explored by asking the following questions:

- Do you keep yourself comfortable by deflecting compliments, criticizing yourself or others, and sabotaging relationships with conflict or worrying?

- When you imagine yourself feeling good all the time, what objection pops into your head?

- Is it that your worrying is foresight and keeps problems from occurring?

- Is it that criticism drives improvement?

- Is it that deflection is a sign of humility?

- Is it that you have high standards in relationships, family, and you are unwilling to compromise on them?

Take a moment with each of these questions and notice how your reflexively respond. These beliefs cannot be used discriminately: they either affect all of your life or none of it. Bringing conscious evaluation to these helps release their grip.

Emotional containment

If your early development involved enmeshment and contagion, you may have learned that entering the same emotional state as someone else is how to support that person. A byproduct of interruption in the second hub is believing you must match someone's outraged or strong emotions to demonstrate your solidarity. Holding space and maintaining your boundary is a mature way to be in the presence of someone who is experiencing strong emotions. Some folks feel betrayed when their anger is not being mirrored—likely a throwback to very early experiences lacking attunement—but healthier relationships are possible when this response is better understood and addressed with consciousness and emotional literacy practices. However, keep in mind that many folks without emotional boundaries may interpret maintaining one as aloofness, detachment, or even disloyalty. One technique that can feel a bit goofy—it can be done in a private place—until you try it is to use your hands to form an invisible pod around your body to represent your emotional boundary. Sense how your emotions are happening within the pod and view others' intense emotions with the appropriate amount of presence but stay aware that you're safe within your pod. If the pod feels invaded, find a way to distance yourself, perhaps by stating that the intensity extends past your capacity or by physically leaving the situation. For example, I was shopping with a friend recently and she became tired, hungry, and aggravated. I started to feel overwhelmed by her, so I stepped into the store's bathroom and formed my invisible emotional boundary using my hands. When I returned to shopping with her, I felt immediate relief and began to enjoy myself as she complained; I heard her from inside my pod but didn't feel my own emotions being invaded.

WORKING WITH FEELINGS: TAPPING

Part of being alive and dynamic involves experiencing other people's behavior, getting disappointed and upset, and a host of other challenging emotions that can arise on a typical day. No matter how hard we may try to be, we are not isolated, and feelings are inevitable as we interface with the world. Having tools to manage negative and/or intense emotions and physical sensations can help you stay present during a difficult day. Studies show that tapping reduces PTSD in veterans, reduces food cravings and anxiety, and decreases cortisol levels in the stress response by as much as 43 percent. The following technique of applying delicate taps to nine points on the body while repeating a validating statement can shift physical discomfort and challenging emotions in a matter of minutes.

In *The Promise of Energy Psychology: Revolutionary Tools for Dramatic Personal Change*, clinical psychologist David Feinstein and energy-medicine practitioner Donna Eden present the following technique for tapping:

Scan your body and mind and locate a concern, feeling, emotion, physical pain, or discomfort. In this exercise, we find and identify the feeling because we will work with it to soothe and release it.

Once you have located the sensation—examples: tight shoulders, butterflies in the stomach, tightness and burning in the throat, back pain, sore knees—whatever you find, give it a number on a scale of one to 10, one being almost unnoticeable and 10 being excruciating. If it's a 10, you may want to consider getting additional help or do this exercise with someone present who can support you; just having someone capable of holding space with you can increase the power of these exercises. Write down the location, description, and number.

Sit in an upright position or lie down. Close your eyes and take a breath in through the nose and out through the mouth. Now open your eyes and say your phrase out loud two times:

For physical discomfort and pain: *Even though I have discomfort and pain in my _____, I deeply and completely accept myself.*

For emotional discomfort and pain: *Even though I am feeling _____, I deeply and completely accept myself.*

Repeat the phrase two times as you tap the outside of both your hands (sometimes called the karate-chop location), with the pads of your first two fingers. Start with one hand, and switch to the other.

Tapping with the pads of your fingers with a light and steady rhythm in the following pattern, say your statement at least once at each location. Then, repeat your statement and tap as you speak.

TAPPING LOCATIONS

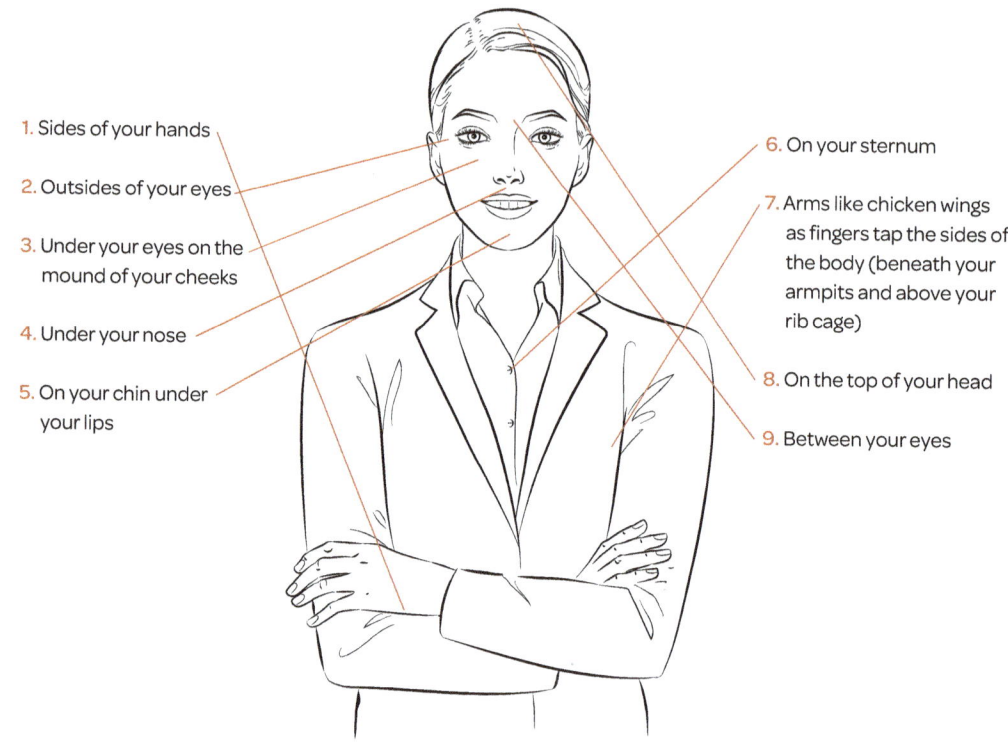

1. Sides of your hands

2. Outsides of your eyes

3. Under your eyes on the mound of your cheeks

4. Under your nose

5. On your chin under your lips

6. On your sternum

7. Arms like chicken wings as fingers tap the sides of the body (beneath your armpits and above your rib cage)

8. On the top of your head

9. Between your eyes

Figure 5.2: Tapping Locations

Once you have gone through the sequence, check in with your physical sensations and feelings and notice if anything has shifted. Has the number changed? Repeat as many times as feels good.

EMOTIONAL LITERACY

Feelings and emotions happen regardless of control and denial. Folks with the inflating adaptation tend to be focused on the behavior of others: *You made me feel this way* or *You make me want to give up.* These sentiments place the control outside of oneself, making others hold ultimate responsibility for how we feel. The shrinking adaptation will tend to sweep an experience under the rug immediately as a lesson learned: *I should know better—I shouldn't have trusted them* or *It isn't that big a deal, a lot of people have it far worse than I do*, along with sentiments like *It could've been worse, I consider myself lucky*, instead of holding people accountable. A more balanced and literate emotional response will consider that other people need to be held responsible for their actions, but also that we play a large part in choosing how we respond.

Emotional literacy requires acceptance and awareness. Knowing the words to own and contain your emotions may not come easily at first, so be patient and kind with yourself as you work to increase and develop this capability.

I noticed the pattern of a friend who would send me texts with intense and emotionally fraught detail about their health, career, and personal life. The text exchanges were rapid as this friend kept piling on more and more information about what happened and about the specific disappointments. Eventually, I'd ask, "How are you feeling about all this?" which is when the exchange would stop abruptly. I felt a bit used initially, thinking that this person had dumped all these problems on me and then had stopped texting mid-discussion. Then I tried something different: instead of asking, "How do you feel?" I asked about a specific emotion, for example, "Do you feel relieved?" After providing a specific emotion that my friend could confirm or deny, the conversation continued. For some folks, the prospect of naming emotions without some help is overwhelming.

There is no way to avoid feelings and emotions—work, children, bills, relationships, low energy, and the stresses of living are ongoing. All emotions and thoughts pass eventually but resisting and denying them keep us in holding patterns; until they're resolved or given the chance to be processed, the same feelings and emotions will keep attaching themselves to different narratives. If we're not practiced in emotional literacy, we may need some help identifying feelings and exploring their causes and triggers before we can release them. The emotional-hygiene practices in the Parinama Method help us wash them out of our system; otherwise, how we feel gets gunked up, weighed down, and even fatigued. In our hard-charging, competitive world that reveres stoicism and can view emotion as weak, simply acknowledging and respecting them can create meaningful shifts.

A sudden downshift in your mood that seems to be out of nowhere can lead to confusion. Sometimes it happens when I'm scrolling through social media: suddenly, I feel bad and when I scroll back up, eventually I find the post that sparked a feeling of inadequacy, loss, envy, or regret. Part of emotional literacy is connecting the stimuli to the feeling(s) and naming the specific feeling(s). The ability to effectively name something takes away its expansiveness. Following are four steps for increasing and developing emotional literacy: pause, name, contain, and process.

1. Pause

The first step in emotional literacy is to pause when feeling(s) arises. Expressing emotion is not about unbridled catharsis or knee-jerk reflexes. Brain scientist Jill Bolte Taylor explains that in 90 seconds an emotion can be noticed, identified, and (in many cases) will fade if we allow it to. Feeling and emotion are interpretations and when we let some time pass, we can see what remains when the dust settles and can have a better chance of having a constructive response and processing without causing distress or harm.

2. Name

Once we have paused, the second step is to acknowledge that emotion is happening and to identify it. Find the feeling that most closely matches yours on the wheel; next locate it in your body without trying to change it—examples include upset stomach (butterflies), jaw tension, eye strain, or headache. With a sense of curiosity, seek to understand and tune into it before asking the emotion how it would like to express itself. You can also approach this by finding the sensation in the body and based on its location, connect it to the associated hub—then think through what has happened in the past day or so that relates to the hub—examples include tension in the throat (from not feeling understood), tightness in the chest (from grief or loneliness), and having an upset stomach (from feeling undermined). See Figure 5.3 for the Parinama Method Wheel of Emotions, which is color coded for a variety of emotions as a suggestion for association with certain hubs.

3. Contain

The third step is containment: differentiate what's happening inside you and what's happening around you (I use the invisible pod). Levine draws the boundary with skin sensation, bringing attention to what's inside versus what's outside, and bringing awareness to the knowledge that there's a difference.

4. Process

The fourth step is to explore and release. Once you have found sensation in your body, see what it wants to do: does it want to shake, squeeze, hit, yell, or be listened to? If you're comfortable doing this, ask it sweetly, "Baby, what do you need" and just listen—allow it to communicate. You can do this with nondominant-hand journaling: with your dominant hand, write the question, "Baby, what do you need?" and let the nondominant hand write the answer. (In Part 3, I provide journaling practices for emotional hygiene, see Chapter 11.)

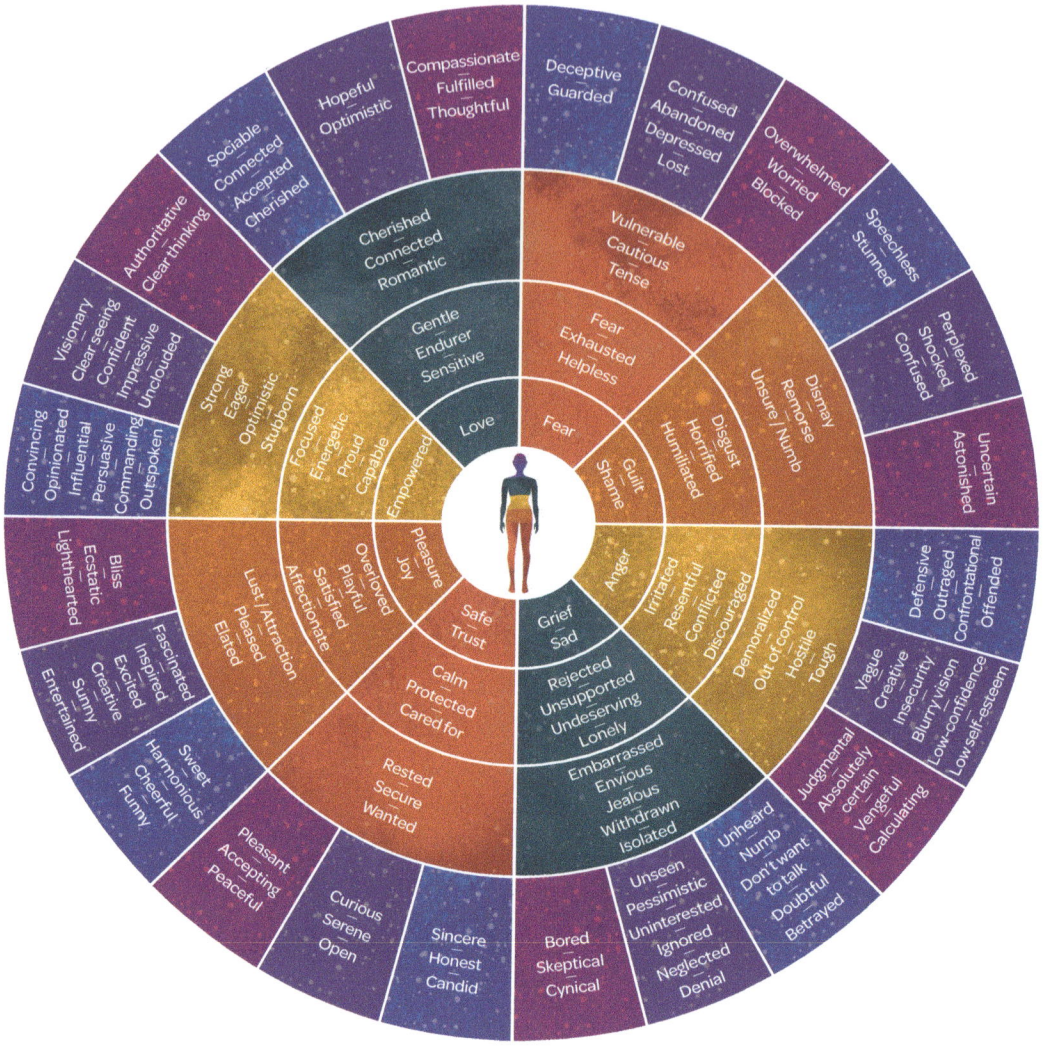

Figure 5.4: The Parinama Method Wheel of Emotions

CHARGE AND DISCHARGE

In the second hub, our aim is the restoration of natural flow and movement. Thawing and increasing capacity for a shrinking adaptation restores the natural charge/discharge of movement and emotion. For an inflating adaptation, we're looking to contain the expansiveness of the charge/discharge. Containment is the goal for folks who tend to emote easily and expansively. Excessive and reflexive catharsis can lack self-awareness and synchronization with others, so without conscious awareness, charging and discharging can wear a deeper groove in already excessive behavior patterns. Excessive emoting affects the people around us, so becoming aware of the physical and emotional boundary (all your feelings are happening within you) can help contain and manage overwhelm. When experiencing a surge of emotions, press pause when possible and do a safe physical discharge or journal through it. Uncontained, frequent, and intense discharging in this hub can cause unintentional harm to people around you, specifically those who don't have the power to speak up and those who do not have strong boundaries.

The Accordion: Focus and Exaggerate

When a muscle feels tight, a natural inclination is to try stretching it out. But here we consider contraction to be a frozen and incomplete response to a stimulation or stress event (see Chapter 4). Again, the accordion is an exercise that aims to complete the contraction and then slowly release. It's called the accordion because a full contraction needs to occur before we can get full expansion.

The accordion is an essential technique in the Parinama Method that can be used throughout the body, in every hub. Therapist Stanley Keleman, an early innovator of somatic practice, told his students and patients that "less is more," and offered this five-part accordion exercise:

1. Identify the pain or discomfort.
2. Lean into and intensify the muscular tone by exaggerating it, holding it to the point of tension.
3. Move at a glacial pace and slowly, slowly release the contraction (consider the action of a spring-loaded coil—don't snap it back too fast or it will recoil).
4. Pause and allow the release to settle in, noticing any shifts without making any movements.
5. Make a note of what you have experienced and repeat if it feels right to do so.

Charging (Stimulating)

As you read this, try making a gentle rocking-chair motion with your body. Many people report that this feels soothing. This is a gentle stimulation, sometimes called "stimming"—repetitive movements that self-soothe, such as nail-biting, knuckle-cracking, foot-tapping, hair-twirling, fidgeting, or whistling (or gently rocking your body, as I suggest here). These common examples of stimming may seem like discharging but notice the subtle stimulation they provide. In the first and second hubs, we charge with subtle and soothing motions; remember that we're going for soothing, infant-and-baby energy. To charge this hub, we bring our attention to the effect of these subtle movements, focusing on the pelvis, hips, and lower abdomen.

Rocking, windshield, and bridge pose

Start by lying on your back with your feet planted and knees pointed toward the ceiling. Lightly massage the sides of your bum, upper thighs, and lower abdomen to increase circulation. (Sometimes just the contact of the lower back to the floor can feel soothing.)

With a gentle and subtle motion, rock your body up and down toward your head and then your feet, similar to what happens when you hear a good song, and your body can't help but move to the rhythm. Pay attention to your lower back and enjoy the sensation of being rocked. Inhale through your nose and exhale out through your mouth for eight rocks.

Next, move both knees to the left and then to the right like windshield wipers, maintaining a comfortable range of motion (four times back and forth). Pause and find a word to describe how your body feels and note that you're paying attention to yourself.

Then bring your attention to your lower back and lower stomach. Push into the bottoms of your feet, and on an inhale raise your bum off the floor, pelvis toward the ceiling, and on the exhale lower your bum back down to the floor. Repeat five times pulsing with the breath. On the last exhale, lower to the floor and notice any arising sensation.

Next, keeping your feet and shoulders on the floor, lift your bum and extend your pelvis toward the ceiling (sometimes called a "bridge pose") and hold for three full breaths. On the third exhale, bring your bum down and extend your legs out into a gingerbread-figure position. Tune in to how your body has responded. Does it feel stimulated, numb, distant? Without judgment, take a moment to observe your relationship with physical sensation and contain it with ownership—*This is mine*—and own your feelings and remind yourself there's no correct way to feel other than exactly how you feel right now.

Discharging (Shaking)

The second hub has the most famous discharge of them all: the orgasm. For some people with rigid musculature and even trauma, this can be difficult to access. The exercises here help release trapped muscular stress but do not focus specifically on sexual release. Following are three specific modes of second-hub discharge: shaking the body to music, discharging tension in the hips, and a gentle psoas release.

Free dance/shake your body

Play some music and move your body. Pick a song that makes you want to move and follow where the movement wants to go—bounce, shake, and wiggle. This is dancing focused on how it feels, not how it looks (that's a concern that comes later in the sixth hub). Some cues can help: start by shaking out the hands, stand up and wiggle your body, stomp your feet a bit, and wiggle your head. After a tough day at work, try finding this release in your body before engaging with your family. If you are becoming frustrated with a spouse or partner, try discharging a bit by shaking out your body, releasing some tension so you can have a more constructive interaction.

The discharge bridge: abducting and adducting

Start from the supine position with feet planted and knees pointing toward the ceiling. Place a rolled-up towel or a yoga block at its narrowest position between your thighs.

Adduction moves inward: lift your bum into a bridge pose and squeeze the block or towel between your thighs for two breaths; bring your bum to the floor for one resting breath and lift your bum again. Repeat two more times. When squeezing the block or towel, try to find the light tremor without straining muscles.

Abduction moves outward: before removing the block, loop a yoga strap or a belt around your thighs—you want a few inches of distance between your thighs—once the loop is in place, remove the block. Next, lift your bum and squeeze outward into the strap, seeking the same tremor for two breaths, release the bum down for one breath, and then up again. If raising your bum for either exercise is too uncomfortable or causes pain, both adduction and abduction can be done with your bum on the floor. When you are finished, loosen the strap and march, or stomp your feet on the ground to release any excess tension—sometimes slapping the palms of the hands on the floor can also help with release.

Psoas stretches

Fold a towel in half the long way and roll it up so it's shaped like a log. Lie down in the prone position, placing your towel roll horizontally under your upper thighs, an inch or two beneath your pelvis. If a fully rolled-up towel increases your lumbar curve to an uncomfortable degree, only partially roll it. Push into the ground with the towel for a count of three, then relax for three breaths. Repeat up to five times, and then relax for at least two minutes with the towel still under your thighs.

The second hub builds from the solid ground and boundary of the first hub that created the stable container for the flow of emotion, increased tolerance for change, and the enjoyment of unstructured pleasure and desire. Now, the baby's second hub ambivalence shifts to the more focused and determined actions of a toddler as we move into the third hub.

In Chapter 6, I discuss power and individuality. Our feelings and emotions show us what sparks desire and what we want. Knowing what we want, how we feel, and containing and managing the associated emotions from the second hub support the growth and development of authentic power in the third hub. We're easily overpowered in life's negotiations if we don't know what we want, or if we simply accept what's offered; in the former example we're easy to control and manipulate because we lack self-awareness, and in the latter because we lack conviction. The emotional literacy and attunement of the second hub is essential for understanding and managing personal power and individuality in the third—DO.

DO: TODDLER, SELF-DEFINITION

Basics	Themes	Interruptions and Stressors	Adaptations and Holding Patterns	Techniques and Exercises
Combustion, Metabolism, and Transformation	Resistance	Authority: Discipline and Punishment	Characteristics of Balanced and Out-of-Balance Third-Hub	Power and Posture
Courage	Failure	Dominance and Submission	Shrinking	The Power Trio
Individuality, Independence, and Freedom	Productive versus Busy	Shaming, Criticism, and Failure	Inflating	Push Down, Rise Up
	Time		Inflating: The Classic	Boundary and the Physical *No*
Confidence versus Self-Esteem	Mastery	The Permissive Helicopter Parent	Inflating: The Endurer	Metabolism and Digestion
Focus and Discipline	Leaders, Followers, and Cults	Corporal Punishment	Risk-Taking	Charge and Discharge
Purpose and Passion	Responsibility	Imposed Maturation	Inner and Outer Critics	
Motivation	Status and Hierarchy	Abuse of Positions of Power	Judgment, Criticism, and Feedback	
	Negotiation and Conflict	Imbalance of Power	The Shadows: Anger and Shame	
	Power: Masculine and Feminine	Unfair Compensation of Labor and Bad Deals		

Chapter 6

THE THIRD HUB—DO

POWER AND INDIVIDUALITY

The most common way people give up their power is by thinking they don't have any.
—Alice Walker

THERE'S NO SUBJECT MORE taboo than power. As an unseen force influencing all human dynamics, even sexual tension pales in comparison to the ubiquitous signaling and status grappling that occur in every human interaction—from two toddlers fighting over a toy, to a patron placing an order with a server, to a more obvious example: bosses and employees. Freud's psychosexual stages of development missed the mark; sexual tension is limited to a relatively narrow, specific range of interactions while the overarching dynamics of power include them yet also shift and shape every encounter we have with another human being. In our culture, the understanding of our individuality, self-discipline, and personal power have become conflicted and disembodied—are the qualities of individualism and independence selfish and egotistical or inspiring and empowered? Traditionally, we tend to look for power through a mix of external validation, approval, and the influence we have over other people, but to be truly powerful we must be capable of standing alone, and to do this we must feel the force emanating from deep within us that both elevates us and radiates into the world. In this chapter, I discuss the ultimate taboo (and the forbidden practice) of reclaiming and cultivating greater personal power.

A well-known quote from Marianne Williamson's *A Return to Love* begins, "Our deepest fear is not that we are inadequate. Our deepest fear is that we are powerful beyond measure." And this fear, one of breaking ranks—and of breaking free—has deep roots that reach into first- and second-hub needs for safety, security, and attunement with others.

The work we do every day, in whatever form it takes, is how we express our power and effect on the world. We may work in environments with micromanagers, repetitive tasks, and carrot-and-stick compensation models, often without a clear link to our sense of personal purpose. If we operate within a system that rewards obedience (at all ages), we can feel disconnected from the dignity of autonomy, the challenge of mastery, and the activation of a sense of purpose for our lives. This hub is about reclaiming your power and understanding how you may have lost the connection to it in the first place—often before you could know it was happening.

ORIENTATION

Physical location: Abdomen, postural muscles, torso (specifically, the area above the belly button and below pectorals), and digestion

First cycle: 18 months–three years (the so-called terrible twos)

Task: Autonomy

Rights: To act, to be an individual, to be free

Identity: I am what I do.

Reconciliation: How powerful can I be without punishment?

We learned about power when we asserted ourselves as toddlers during the development of our autonomy, through the expression of our uniquely distinguishing characteristics and qualities. Our personal power operates within a paradox between freedom and control (along with individuality and loyalty)—this dynamic between independence and belonging builds momentum when toddlers begin to self-assert. They learn about their power through the brute force of their will and in the responses that it receives. Our parents were physically larger than us, and they decided (or enforced) what would be permitted and what would be punished—these decisions are at the core of our esteem and confidence. This was the dynamic of how we first practiced and learned about our personal power. As children, well-behaved and obedient (so-called good) boys and girls are generally praised and favored, but this often comes at a cost when children strain to please others by hiding their thoughts, feelings, and emotions and, as a result, dull their distinctive shine. When the requirement of obedience overrides our integrity, we create external peace with others, but a war within ourselves. The symbols of this hub are fire and combustion—repression in this hub becomes explosive with anger, which I discuss below, and an eventual outcome of this can be rage. If our power, identity, and individuality have been suppressed and lost their voice, they will eventually find an outlet to express the grief in the form of frustration, anger, and then eventually rage. The radiant magnificence of a self-possessed, emotionally secure person is undeniable, yet it can provoke people who have repressed their power as they adapted to survive, so the quest for authentic personal power is not necessarily the easy road, but it's ultimately one of the most fulfilling in the Parinama Method.

INITIAL DEVELOPMENT

Toilet training is the first significant battleground in the early months and years of third-hub development; a child navigates holding and letting go. The timing of a child's readiness for toilet training is individual to the child who's learning to restrain and release in a rhythm uniquely its own—Freud famously called this the "anal stage." Personal power has a dynamic that exists between what we express and what we contain.

Caring for a toddler is a maddening balance between allowing freedom and avoiding a trip to the emergency room. There's a short period of life when the child is mobile but has limited capacity for language and reasoning. This emerging will and curiosity can be dangerous, and for some exhausted, overwhelmed parents, preemptive discipline to keep a child safe can be an outlet for their own arising frustrations.

The first- and second-hub development days while a child is physically and emotionally merged with caregivers are for unconditional love and connection: and any discipline or punishment only causes distress and confusion for a baby who cannot intellectually reason—they can only develop reflexes. In third-hub development, a toddler has awakened to the awareness that it's an individual, and the shift can be jarring for everyone involved. During the terrible twos, with autonomy shifting into high gear, a toddler learns the words *mine* and *no* as it becomes increasingly mobile. When anchored by caregivers' safe, familiar comfort, a toddler grows the confidence to explore while its parents help it navigate its abilities and limitations. It's a challenging line for parents to walk, and perfection is impossible. Erikson (see Chapter 4) called this stage of balancing self-control and self-esteem "autonomy versus shame and doubt." If children are encouraged and supported in their increased independence, they become confident in their ability to thrive in the larger world. But if they're criticized, overly controlled, punished, and/or not allowed to assert themselves, children feel inadequate in their capabilities. If they don't learn to inhabit their own sense of self, they may become overly dependent, may lack self-esteem, and feel a sense of shame or doubt about their abilities. Some parents insist on preparing their children for a harsh world by creating one in the home, but research repeatedly shows that trust and security (see Chapter 4) in the home are the foundations for resilience and confidence in the larger, and at times harsh, world. Having a safe place to return to after venturing courageously into the world is essential for development of bravery, confidence, and independence. This hub benefits from encouragement, containment, and focus. This is the hub in which the sense of urgency that compels us forward emerges, where the time is always *now*.

Children need to be able to practice their personal power while (paradoxically) living within limits and learning control. Age and developmentally appropriate self-control are essential for functioning in the world, and the ability to delay gratification magnifies confidence and personal power, although self-control comes more easily for some children than others. In the early 1970s, Stanford University researchers studied self-control in children between the ages of three-and-a-half to five-and-a-half years old in what has come to be known as The Marshmallow Experiment. In the study, each child was offered a choice between one immediate reward or, if they were able to wait (hence, delaying gratification), they would receive two rewards. As the participants aged over the following decades, they were tracked and studied. The children who delayed gratification had better SAT scores and were assessed to be more socially competent than the children who took the singular, immediate reward. There was conjecture and moralizing that this so-called ability to delay gratification was evidence of superiority and strength of character. But in 2011, the participants from the original experiment, now middle-aged, took part in a brain-imaging study and the images showed more activity in the PFC of the study participants who had delayed gratification. The non-delayers had more substantial activity in the ventral striatum of their emotional (limbic) brain system—put simply, the adults who had been children unable to delay gratification had more activity in the areas of the brain that heighten feelings. This begs two questions: Are self-control and emotional regulation naturally easier for some people than others; and should we replace the moralizing about impulse control with support and appreciation for folks who feel more deeply—those who must work harder than others to achieve self-control and focus?

For all children, learning to control their emotional reflexes, taking responsibility for causing harm, managing disappointment and failure, and learning to understand strengths and weaknesses should be cultivated during the initial development of the third hub. The delicate balance between too much and too little power can be compared to a single match that can either burn something down or be extinguished with a puff of air.

BASICS

Our lives are shaped by the decisions we make and the actions we take. Our world is like a democracy in which the deeds we perform are like votes cast for the reality we want: our choices and the resulting actions we take reflect back on us, forming our self-perception and, to a certain extent, creating our view of how the world operates. Perhaps we worry about how others will judge our behavior, overlooking the important point of how the things we do shape our relationship with ourselves—our actions become what we know ourselves to be capable of doing. Although an observer may have an opinion, you carry the awareness of your tendencies and capabilities with you everywhere you go. This profoundly affects who you believe yourself to be. The answer to the question, *Did anyone see that?* is always: Yes, *you* did.

What we do is just as much about choosing inaction as it is about choosing action: both carry implications. Action and inaction—and the profound intensity of these opposites existing simultaneously (paradoxically) is demonstrated in the image of Buddhist monk Thích Quảng Đức immolating himself in 1963 in protest of religious persecution as he sits in meditation.

Some spiritual practices encourage surrender as radical acceptance to whatever arises in our lives, but there's a significant difference between surrender and passivity: surrender allows for the acceptance of what is, as the foundation of constructive action; passivity allows for docile and avoidant inaction. Passivity waits to be rescued and turns a blind eye, allowing others to suffer. Personal power is the surrender to the sometimes-painful acceptance of what is real, which demands action in the courage to either walk away, continue (with full acceptance), or stay and create change. Taking responsibility is at the pinnacle of authentic power and leadership.

COMBUSTION, METABOLISM, AND TRANSFORMATION

When power is compressed, it becomes volatile: if it's not contained and focused, it can dissipate or become explosive. In this hub there is a balancing act between action and inaction on a spectrum between destruction and impotence. Fire without limitation or direction inflates, dominates, and consumes everything around it, but with restriction and direction it shrinks, submits, and is extinguished.

The third hub is central to any transformation, and change requires the horsepower of strength and courage. Digestion of food and our metabolism are practical examples of our physical ability to access and transform power from our environment to use in our bodies. The literal transformation of food into energy happens in our digestive system. Knowing which foods our body responds to and effectively digests and knowing if we have allergies or autoimmune issues helps us consciously manage the process of optimizing and fueling our lives.

COURAGE

At least some degree of bravery and courage are necessary for change. If we want to change anything about our lives but struggle to make it happen, there tend to be things that we're attached to—usually related to feelings of familiarity, safety, and comfort—that need to be released. To be brave enough to make change, we need security in the first hub and to have the fuel of emotion and desire in the second hub. Ware notes in *The Top Five Regrets of The Dying* (see Chapter 3) that at the end of life, "Almost every regret came down to a lack of courage." She lists the top-five deathbed regrets as

1. I wish I'd had the courage to live a life true to myself, not the life others expected of me.
2. I wish I hadn't worked so hard.
3. I wish I'd had the courage to express my feelings.
4. I wish I'd stayed in touch with my friends.
5. I wish I had let myself be happier.

You'll notice that these regrets are simple: people don't regret not becoming billionaires or not impressing people. In fact, it seems like those types of accomplishments are more likely to be tied to significant regrets.

When we are brave, we fight the potent illusion that obedience keeps us safe. Many folks who've supposedly done everything right by following a prescribed path in their lives—say, of college and career—one day may find themselves lost and feeling powerless, aware that the most important decisions that shaped their lives were not made by them. Think of the great and powerful Oz: a little man behind a curtain who "gave" powers to questing heroes who already possessed them. If we're not careful, life will have passed us by when we realize that the people who prescribed these paths for us—those who professed to give us our powers—were lost and frequently fearful themselves.

Again, individuality requires having the courage to stand alone. It's not an easy road, which is probably why people fantasize about it so much, yet never take action.

INDIVIDUALITY, INDEPENDENCE, AND FREEDOM

When we stand up for our freedom and make decisions that reflect our unique values, we must be prepared—at least initially—to stand on our own. (In Chapter 7 I discuss activism as the ability to stand for what we care about and believe in.) But before we can stand for others, we should be able to stand for ourselves. If we don't find independence in the third hub, we won't have the necessary underpinnings to ascend to increasing levels of self-expression in the upper hubs. Instead, we risk experiencing the regret that comes from stifling the expression of our unique truth and giving away too much of ourselves so we can continue to belong in places that accept us under the condition of hiding who we are.

To stand in our uniquely personal truth, we must first break with invisible forces and wrestle with the impulse to remain hidden and safe. Our individuation can awaken a sleeping giant in some people: they may react by being afraid, may feel threatened, and may project their insecurities onto us. We don't live in a world in which individualism is widely practiced in real life (only fictional heroes do). During our most vulnerable moments of bravery, the sleeping giants of others' projections and adaptations are often the most unkind—that is, until they see you conquer and succeed. But after the initial dark nights of the soul (and they get dark!), our individuality eventually leads to more fulfilled belonging with people who accept us and enrich us for who we are, not for a role we play.

Many of us have unseen and unspoken yet ever-present conditions of belonging that bind our behavior, profession, clothing, and other forms of self-expression. Some family and social bonds require that we either be completely with or against a person or a group, and there can be no in-between position—it's understandable that most of us try to hold on to the safety of our in-group for as long as possible. It's hard to be an outsider.

In the legend of the search for the holy grail, King Arthur and his knights each enter a forest, alone, at a dark place without a path. Campbell suggested that if they saw a path, they could know it belonged to someone else—it wasn't theirs. A common narrative frames people who are free as selfish, egotistical, self-involved, or even worse, so-called crazy. The balancing act between freedom and belonging is a paradox that becomes increasingly nuanced as we move up through the hubs. In the fourth hub, during our early social belonging, spontaneous self-expression is put in a bind because our social identity is shaped by a randomly selected happenstance of peers at school, the children of our parent's friends, and the kids in our neighborhood. When we were young, we had to work with what we were given. As adults, we continue to navigate this dichotomy between individuality and belonging in our professional and personal relationships. The balance of authentic self-expression and the compromises we make to belong and be considerate of others are dynamic and ongoing.

CONFIDENCE VERSUS SELF-ESTEEM

Self-confidence is belief in your ability. Self-esteem is acceptance of yourself regardless of abilities. Self-esteem or self-worth has a relatively consistent quality that doesn't rely on abilities or conditions. Esteem is the baseline of how people feel about themselves, regardless of circumstance, external approval, and capability. The Parinama Method is an exploration for the repairing and right-sizing of self-esteem and self-worth. Positive self-esteem is unconditional, optimistic self-regard and does not require external validation (even though it is appreciated).

Confidence is tied to ability and, as a result, is highly conditional. It's trust in your capability to be effective in a specific area, and because this is relative to the folks who surround us, it's fragile. Unlike esteem, confidence tends to be uneven and dependent on situations and environments. For example, someone may be the best athlete in their school, but is bested when competing in a larger venue. Some folks enjoy being a big fish in a little pond when they rely on confidence to bolster low self-esteem. One of my interviewees said, "I already feel bad enough about myself, so I choose to spend time around people who respect me even if that means I'm not reaching my potential."

Increasing confidence—contrary to common opinion—is not how to create sustainable self-esteem. When we build confidence in our abilities, we place conditions on our worth. If your confidence comes from being a great singer, what happens if you lose your voice? We build self-esteem when our sense of value comes without conditions. Many people I interviewed feared that unconditional self-esteem would affect the quality and urgency of their work; some even took offense, bristling at the suggestion that self-acceptance without accomplishment is positive or even possible—and to be clear, it is absolutely

possible. But these interviewees were correct about the effect on their professional lives: if we have better self-esteem, our tolerance for unreasonable demands and unfair treatment declines and we direct more energy toward the overall quality of our lives. Also, if we stop performing to outrun criticism, we can connect to our own desires and achieve satisfaction in the name of actualizing our potential—an internal drive that despite what our conditioning may have led us to believe about ourselves is inherent for all humans.

FOCUS AND DISCIPLINE

Devotion is the ardent dedication and loyalty of consistently showing up for what we love and giving it our best, even on days when our best isn't that great. A parent or anyone in a committed, loving relationship knows that love involves consistently showing up—and this includes the days we don't feel up to it. Every day will have different capacities; some are close to perfect and others far from it.

Through discipline and devotion, we experience our integrity and learn that we can trust and rely on ourselves. If we were taught discipline as punishment, we may resist it or recoil from it. Some folks who have been abused by discipline may either avoid it entirely or overuse it with an excessive, punishing force of willpower, seeking to attain perfection while hoping deep down for the much craved but illusive sense of love and acceptance. Devotional discipline—showing up for the things that matter even when it doesn't feel good—deepens our love and respect for ourselves; punishing discipline further separates us from it. Even a lousy workout supports momentum more than not working out does. We tend to show up for family, friends, and work, but how do you show up for yourself every day and receive the demonstration of your commitment, love, and acceptance in devotional discipline to yourself?

Perfectionism blocks progress: if we wait to be motivated with high energy and a good mood, it may never happen. Perfection is an unattainable ideal and changing our relationship with perfectionism transforms our relationship with ourselves. Devotional discipline involves a lot of imperfect work; perfection is never achieved, but the work to get close to it can be gritty and satisfying.

When we have a daily practice of anything, we see how our body and mind fluctuate every day, and we learn to appreciate and know these fluctuations, understanding that we'll be there for ourselves through them all. Show up, even when your best for the day is unshowered, in stained sweatpants, and hungover; after making choices that negatively affect the body-mind, the natural consequences of how we feel help us make better decisions, so we make changes from love and care instead of judgment.

Just show up for what you care about—relationships, exercise, meditation, writing, or anything that matters to you—in the best form available today. On good days and bad, just show up. If you need to look great every time you show up and to be well-rested and well-dressed, you reduce your attendance to a fraction of what's possible. Being good at being bad at things is a brilliant ability.

If you've been heartbroken by a parent who could not show up for you consistently (or at all), or if you had a parent who showed up but struggled, I get it. My daily yoga practice taught me how to find the unconditional love of showing up within myself, not because it was yoga but because I consistently did something for myself every day by spending time on and paying attention to my body-mind. Previously, I'd been unable to fully accept love because I was afraid of my bad days. I would think, *If you only knew.* In any consistent practice there are days when it's so hard that it's unbearable—and days when it's so easy it feels like cheating. A body feels different every day, depending on factors that can be identified and others that cannot. I've learned that the hard days are the ones that make the easy ones extraordinary; I know I can trust myself. Love is found in devotional discipline and it's the domain of both the third and fourth hubs. We examine it here in the third hub because the over- and misuse of punishment and shaming actions interrupt our relationship with discipline, but in the fourth hub, we continue to build on this practice as part of what it means to love: showing up.

PURPOSE AND PASSION

In the poem "On Houses," in *The Prophet*, Kahlil Gibran warns us that comfort enters a house as a guest, then becomes the host, and eventually the master with a hook and scourge that "makes puppets of your larger desires." Comfort offers itself in trade for the desires, dreams, and passions that help us know who we are. When our desires are denied, they go underground. To find them, we excavate our memories, envies, and judgments of other people. Perhaps you believe everyone desires the same things; your excavation will prove this untrue—what you *truly* want is unique to you.

If you feel cut off from desire and its aliveness, tune back in: make a note every time you feel a spark of joy, such as sunshine, reading about a specific topic, a certain person, or seeing something beautiful. Pay attention to the things that make you feel. We wake up every morning to days packed with responsibilities, busyness, and duties. You know you're highly capable of doing hard things, but by tracing back to where you find joy, you source the power to energize your life. Finding passions that energize and magnetize you is like having a compass that directs you homeward.

Before our activities and interests were labeled as either practical or a waste of time, there were things you genuinely liked to do *just because*. What was your favorite subject in school? How would your earliest friends describe you as a kid and what would they remember you loving to do? What books and music affected you in your early years and what hobbies did you have? Why did you love them? Is there something you've always wanted to try? What type of problems do you find satisfying to solve—in other words, what's the work that doesn't feel like work to you? Everyone has different answers. Believing a hobby or interest isn't practical can stop us from spending time with it, yet spending the time enriches and helps us to uncover our relationship with enjoyment.

MOTIVATION

The carrot-and-stick model of work assumes that people only work to make money. Research consistently tells a different story and doesn't support the narrative that employees are like pawns that require ongoing oversight and constant direction. Instead, it reveals that people need autonomy and support to do their best work. A spirit-crushing, authoritarian management style is demoralizing, dehumanizing, and often mislabeled as the remedy—not the cause—of mediocrity and dissatisfaction. Through an investigation of the existing research, author Daniel H. Pink's *Drive: The Surprising Truth About What Motivates Us* explores the fact that humans are driven by three primary things in their work: autonomy (the ability to make decisions and be trusted), mastery (the opportunity to get better at something), and purpose (the sense that their work matters). As Pink writes, "Control leads to compliance; autonomy leads to engagement."

Confidence, action, individuality, and the pursuit of personal purpose are components of a strong, developed third hub. In an early-1970s interview with Bill Moyers, Maya Angelou said, "You are only free when you realize you belong no place—you belong every place—no place at all. The price is high. The reward is great." The third hub's about taking action that's ultimately in the service of the freedom to be our most authentic self, an ongoing process of revelation experienced through the work of our life.

RESISTANCE

As we know from the first hub (and the brain stem), change signals possible danger; so, we tend to reflexively stop doing things that will change us. As a result, discipline is hard. There are endless examples of projects and activities we enjoy, find satisfying, and feel are important, yet we abandon them. They start with a burst of adrenaline and suddenly, seemingly out of nowhere, meet with resistance. Pressfield (see Chapter 3) writes in *The War of Art* that "[T]he stronger the resistance, the more important the work." He considers resistance a mythical—even spiritual—force that tests our resolve and commitment when it comes to the important work of our lives (the expression of our embloom). When we start the work that will transform us and reveal our truest nature, resistance will be relentless. Any distractions—writer's block, an illness, a cute cat to pet—and any justifiable obligations will suddenly surge when the work begins to really take on momentum. When you know to watch for it, it's astonishing how the force of resistance will send its horsemen as soon as it detects devotional discipline in the service of an embloom. Resistance is so clever and insidious that it created a belief that meaningful work should, and will, be easy—and a belief that if work gets difficult, it must be a sign that it's not the right thing for you. This can make you feel crazy, lazy, irresponsible, ungrateful, afraid, or even stupid. The idea that it just flows when it's the right thing is astonishingly incomplete. The paradoxical fact is that the important work of your life is both easy *and* difficult. Overcoming resistance is difficult because it's a genuine force to be reckoned with; moreover, there's a distinct difference between the difficulty of showing up against resistance for the important work of our life and the difficulty of showing up for meaningless, repetitive work. If you believe that everything that is meant for you comes in a flow of easy positive energy, your life will slip away. The paradox is that there's an ease and flow within the most meaningful work *and* there is resistance and struggle. You will be transformed through the effort and become the person capable of achieving the best work of your life by doing it—not by having the prerequisites of previous success to undertake it. And you can expect that resistance will consistently show up to test your conviction; for those who stay with it, the rewards are extraordinary.

FAILURE

We're often socialized to believe in a polarized system of pass/fail or win/lose that casts failure in absolute terms. Yet within an infinite spectrum of possible outcomes, failure is subjective and simply provides a lesson, a speed bump, or an embarrassment. What's typically considered failure is simply the disappointment of missing the mark you intended to hit. The fortitude to try again is largely tied to how much energy we have after a disappointment, so the trick's to not let disappointment be what Buddhist's call "the second arrow." In the parable of the two arrows, the first arrow is the disappointment itself, which we can't always control; the second arrow is our reaction to the first—the second arrow is optional.

There's a powerful paradox in complementary opposites when we can simultaneously hold on *and* let go, that is, having the courage to pursue something you want with passion and focus but also understanding that in the larger context of things, everything is impermanent and so-called failure is okay. The Bhagavad Gita references this power of detachment: "[D]o thy work, O winner of wealth, abandoning attachment, with an even mind in success and failure." This is an esoteric concept, but it has practical applications: intense execution of a business plan in concert with the counterforce of ease—simultaneous intensity and ease together exert a powerful force. And there's nothing that can diminish your power in a high-pressure situation more than appearing desperate or nervous about failure. George Orwell alluded to this in *Down and Out in Paris and London*: "It is fatal to look hungry. It makes people want to kick you."

To internally cultivate a counterforce to pressure, make a list of what matters to you that doesn't change if you miss your mark. It can contain people (and pets) who love you, things you enjoy doing, and personal truths that are the bedrock of your values. Hold on to them also knowing that there's not a single person or transaction that can be completely responsible for shaping your destiny. Then go fight for what you want—the likelihood of a favorable outcome will be fueled by the energy of your conviction, your focused determination, and your ability to learn and iterate when things don't go as planned.

PRODUCTIVE VERSUS BUSY

Success and fulfillment require decisive action about the things that matter. Distracted, chronically rushed people who place significant value on how busy they are often miss the boat when they're spread too thin. In the third hub, we ask ourselves if we have the ability and willingness to focus on substantive achievement or prefer to spend our time being chronically and chaotically busy. The prompt here is to do fewer incidental things and more of what matters. A few good places to make cuts are time with people who don't appreciate you; responding with urgency to non-urgent issues; talking to customers who are either not going to buy or will drain your energy when they do; giving more to people than they would

ever wish to provide for you; and spending time on details that don't really make a difference. Are you willing and able to see the difference between busyness and actions that contribute to the things that matter?

TIME

In the third hub, unlike the second, we're aware that time is finite—and even though they can't read a clock, toddlers expect certain things at certain times. In *The Marriage of Heaven and Hell*, William Blake wrote, "Eternity is in love with the productions of time." Time is limited, precious, and not to be squandered. Pleasure in the second hub is unaware of time and its limitations. In pleasure, attention to time detracts from enjoying sensation. Transcendence and the feeling of timelessness are essential for indulging in pleasure, yet time marches forward regardless of our awareness of it. While there can be academic discussions about the nature of time, we abandon them if we must catch a plane. Most people trade their time for money, and because it's limited, it's an asset regardless of how much value you place on it. There are 24 hours in a day, and how we spend those hours (and money) tells us about our values.

By valuing our time, we express power—time is a primary measurement of power (and a common way to invade third-hub boundary). When people take up your time, they steal your autonomy. When you give your time where it's not appropriately valued or when you are so busy that you don't have time for yourself, it's a direct corollary to how you own your power. Wealth is a secondary measurement of power to time because wealth ultimately can offer the freedom to spend your time exactly as you wish and trading a lifetime of doing things you don't want to do in exchange for wealth and authority is diminishing to your personal freedom (and power). It doesn't matter if you have power over other people if you don't have power over yourself. If you already love what you do, great. If you don't, make a plan and start taking action.

MASTERY

Mastery comes from working through and triumphing over limitations. Meaningful accomplishment is achieved through doing the work that forms us into the person capable of doing it—we don't begin the process being everything we'll need to be. To build skill (to pursue mastery) you need to be challenged, and by facing the challenge you will be changed. If we repeat something we already know we're good at, we're just keeping ourselves busy, which from a growth perspective is like running in place. The difference between busyness and flow—both states in which time disappears—is that flow is uplifting and satisfying, and busyness is draining. Busy people are perpetually exhausted and disenfranchised (especially when they don't connect what they're doing with what matters to them); those who expand their abilities are exhausted but satisfied. Our work ethic and behavior either build or diminish our confidence in ourselves.

Sometimes the only option for making the money we need to survive is to work at a soul-sucking job. When this is the case, become clear about who you are and about your long-term plan—don't let the situation define you (reminding yourself of this should be done daily). When we know a job isn't developing skills in us that we care about, isn't allowing for the dignity of autonomy, or isn't connecting us to a sense of purpose, we can choose to show up for ourselves by connecting with how the job helps our short-term situation while we build a plan for a better future. This can be really difficult—but worth the effort.

When we're pursuing mastery, the good, hard, intense, focused, and aligned work of our lives is deeply fulfilling—we want rest but once we're rested, we want to get back to it. Rest after completing challenging work feels fantastic. Struggle and rest together build strength. When we exercise, we push our muscles, and when we rest, they repair—that's when increased strength gets created.

Some parents and leaders try to eliminate struggle, and others can cause harm by pushing too hard. Some get it just right: they support and develop self-empowerment in their children. Good parents, coaches, and leaders allow struggle while holding a safe space for rest and support when it's needed. It's hard to watch someone struggle without stepping in. Observe your own inclination to interfere with and manage a child as it struggles, then watch its frustration if you take over before they've finished trying. Sometimes a task is too challenging, and a child needs help, but if it's empowered, when it's ready the child will ask to receive it. Alternatively, if a child keeps having the challenge snatched away, it becomes dependent and less likely to try. Watching talented, experienced people do difficult things can be inspiring, but to make a skill

our own, we need to try and struggle with it to learn. If we allow struggle within safe parameters for our children and the people we lead, they have the opportunity to grow. If we do the work for them, we rob them of their growth.

LEADERS, FOLLOWERS, AND CULTS

A basic definition of leadership is the ability to take responsibility and to make the best possible decisions for the greater good of the group. Leaders should be able to communicate their plan to the group so that everyone is aware of the bigger picture, helping folks to understand why their contribution matters. Of course, when you make decisions there will always be disgruntled people who don't get what they want, and leaders need to know how to manage the discomfort of being questioned and/or disliked when this happens. A leader does their best to make a decision based on incomplete information—you will never know everything—which can turn risk-aversion into paralysis and can result in avoidance of making important decisions. Responsibility is the primary indicator of leadership (power is a cross to bear): the difficulty of shouldering the load contributes to the appeal of following gurus, teachers, and bosses who volunteer to do the heavy lifting on tough topics in exchange for unquestioning loyalty. Cult leaders broker an exchange of obedience and sacrifice from their followers. The result is an infantilized utopia in which followers are unburdened and relieved of the difficulties of responsibility. However, the challenging (and rewarding) work of managing the paradoxes and ambiguities in life cannot be outsourced: eventually, all leaders placed on pedestals experience corrective falls that bring them back to their appropriate position as fallible human beings.

When our will has been broken or diminished; if we fear responsibility because of the potential for failure and embarrassment; and if we don't know how powerful we are, we won't know we're capable of facing challenges and being leaders in our own lives. You're more powerful than you've ever imagined possible, and when we reflect on the people who had lasting positive effects on our lives, they tend to have taught us about our unique inner capabilities and how to access them.

As leaders we learn there's a spectrum between love and fear. Too much love and there will be a lack of respect—the team will feel that there are no consequences. Too much fear and the team will resent you, doing the bare minimum while investing most of its energy into serving individual interests. Leadership, like so many things, rides a line of balancing complementary opposites. A teacher, coach, or parent knows that sometimes your people will love you and sometimes they will hate you—and you need to comfortably occupy either state to gain leadership's powerful middle ground.

On a good team there should be room for healthy descent and for everyone to have the opportunity to feel heard. Chris Voss, former FBI hostage negotiator and coauthor with Tahl Raz of *Never Split the Difference*, discusses the meaning of *You're right* versus *That's right*. During hostage negotiations Voss uncovered that when people say, "You're right," they consent to end the conversation by using a superficial resolution that leaves the negotiator feeling good but leaves the negotiation unresolved. When people say, "That's right," it's evidence that they feel understood—and then the process can move forward. Superficial agreement never advances a process. In the case of leaders and followers, without the dynamic of active, authentic engagement, it's only a matter of time before the scales are corrected and folks find a way to be seen and heard through disruption, withdrawal, or departure.

RESPONSIBILITY

Regardless of our age and position, there are three developmentally appropriate levels of responsibility: a child's, an adult's, and a parent's. These levels or roles can fluctuate depending on circumstances and situations. A child makes a mess that others clean up; an adult cleans up its own mess; and a parent cleans up the mess of others. It's good to be able to play all three roles, that is, to be taken care of, to take care of yourself, and to take care of others; it's also good to cultivate awareness of which role we're playing in each situation. Owning and taking responsibility for your mistakes, shielding your team by taking the blame, and proactive communication are behaviors of leaders and individuals who have both confidence and self-esteem.

STATUS AND HIERARCHY

When people are unaware of their power, it's easy to extract it from them. The way to get people to participate in predatory, hierarchical power structures is to pretend they don't exist or to convince folks that they're receiving protection—or better

yet, that any negativity they perceive is a figment of their imagination.

Power structures are always in play with any interaction, with extremes in excessive domination and subordination. Johnstone's introduction of physical expressions of status revolutionized theatrical dynamics (see Chapter 3). "Every inflection and movement implies a status," he notes, and asserts that theatrical scenes aren't believable unless actors incorporate the body language and mannerisms of status. According to Johnstone, every interaction in life between people involves high- and low-status behaviors, and depending on whom we're interacting with, we assume a status position relative to the other person. If we're unaware of how power is expressed and communicated, we can be vulnerable to people who take advantage, manipulate, or overpower us. Following are examples of indicating high or low status using Johnstone's method:

Person A: I just came back from Spain.
Person B: It must be nice! I've always wanted to go (low status).
Subtext from person B: You're doing better than I am.

Person A: I just came back from Spain.
Person B: It's beautiful this time of year. Have you tried El Primo in Madrid? It's excellent (high status).
Subtext from person B: I'm doing better than you—the things you're doing, I've already done.

Person A: I just came back from Spain.
Person B: [disinterested] How fun. (high status)
Subtext from person B: You're not important.

Person A: I just came back from Spain.
Person B: [overly enthusiastic] How fun! (low status)
Subtext from person B: I want or need you to like me.

In some cases, status grappling competes in a race to the bottom to have it worse than everyone else in the conversation. An example is sharing bad news but losing status to worse news: "Our trip got canceled," is met with "We can't even afford to think about a vacation. I'd be happy with a canceled trip; at least I'd be able to dream."

Johnstone says, "Normally, we are forbidden to see status transactions except when there's conflict." Conscious awareness supports our ability to operate more effectively in a maneuvering-for-status world. He believes his students should be able to act convincingly as either low or high status (see Table 6.1)—depending on what a role calls for. To become more conscious of status positioning, Johnstone offers specific behaviors and physical cues. Using voice and sound, posture, eye contact, and relationship to surroundings, he provided techniques that allow for consciously influencing how others subconsciously perceive your status. Awareness allows us to play with hierarchy by operating in subtext rather than overt statements and actions.

Low Status	High Status
Unnecessary movements (fidgeting)	Still and composed
Moving head while talking	Holding head still while talking
Eye contact: looking away and quickly glancing back	Eye contact: looking away, not looking back (but if you do, it's a long look)
Adding short and hesitant *er* or *um* to the beginning of a sentence (shows uncertainty)	Adding an extended *errr* or *ummm* to the beginning of a sentence (controlling the conversation by not allowing anyone else to speak)
Trying to be small and inconspicuous or acting uncomfortable	Taking up space and owning it, showing comfort and ease with surroundings
Crossing arms, toes pointed inward (shrinking)	Open arms and hands, sitting back, and toes pointed out with legs spread (inflating)
Uncoordinated, rapid, panicked, and frantic movements	Smooth, slow, and flowing movements

Table 6.1: Signaling High and Low Status

We can incorporate Johnstone's methods using posture and ease to signal power, calmly taking up the space we occupy while using slow, commanding movements *and* be aware that we signal lack of power when we fidget, make rapid movements, and contort our bodies to take up less space.

Zoologist and author of *The Human Zoo* Desmond Morris asserts that to be the top baboon in a colony requires an imposing physical or mental presence—our physical presence and mannerisms signal our relative position in a hierarchy. Morris's 10 commandments of dominance "[A]pply to all leaders, from baboons to modern presidents and prime ministers." The commandments include the display of postures and gestures of dominance, the occasional acknowledgment of extreme subordinates, and the use of brutal force when challenged. Taking up space and physical presence matter when it comes to power: a survey of Fortune 500 CEOs revealed that on average, they are six feet tall—approximately two-and-a-half inches taller than the average American man. Having relatively small bodies and being pretty may put some women at the top of a social-power pyramid, yet these qualities signal low status when holding positions of ultimate power. This leads to a complex conflict that can be difficult to resolve. A woman will have to reconcile the two conflicting power structures she participates in: desirability and professional power. Along with cultural biases that favor small women, who are perceived as charming and alluring, the notion that men are somehow more authoritative and influential is a Darwinian bias—meaning that it prevails because it's selected for out of perceived advantage and is not an absolute truth.

Hierarchies exist in all human organizations and families. Even in so-called flat organizations there will be jockeying for status—again, the best way to use hierarchy to exert control of others is to pretend it doesn't exist. Office politics uses psychological tactics instead of brute physical force, so having a few tools in your kit to demonstrate and express power with your body and manner can only help you. These signals are so deeply buried in the subconscious that people are often unaware they're being transmitted and received. But also keep in mind that similar to a baboon colony, threatening the top baboon can be bad. Johnstone teaches his students to be dynamic. Despite any wishes for it to be otherwise, there are times when it serves our best interests to play low status.

Hierarchies are always organized around power, with rituals and obligations for the members to observe in different tiers. Common phrases like *top of the food chain* and *apex predator* are used to describe power and domination; lions have long been considered the archetypal apex predator, although their top-of-the-food-chain status isn't necessarily due to their ability to eat what they kill (see Chapter 2). This is how power works: in hierarchies, it's not about capability but dominance; the most proficient predator in the natural world is the dragonfly—not typically considered apex—with a successful kill rate of 95 percent. It uses selective attention and the ability to calculate, predict, and intercept the trajectory of its prey (using less energy on chasing), leaving the kill

rates of the so-called apex predators in the dust. The lion does not achieve apex status as a result of talents and abilities—it uses brute force; the dragonfly uses focus, concentration, and perception to accurately predict the route of its prey, arriving in its path ready for the kill. It may be the most talented predator of them all. Usurping traditional systems of power requires the ability to outsmart them, which first requires becoming aware of the game we're playing.

NEGOTIATION AND CONFLICT

No discussion of power is complete without the acknowledgment that our individual interests eventually collide with others' and that we must negotiate or remain in conflict. The sunny, early days of personal and professional relationships eventually cloud over when conflicting interests threaten disruption. Any otherwise harmonious relationship reaches a point at which some priorities and expectations will need to be reconciled.

When I interview job candidates, they usually present two versions of their work history: one that reflects the past performance as it relates to previous employers' evaluation of them, and the other reflects the candidate's proudest accomplishments, which include the different projects they took on outside the scope of the role and the unique ways they excelled above and beyond expectations. Understanding the candidate's innate talents and passion helps me to see how they can provide unique and fulfilling value to the organization and team. This process with a candidate who's a fit for the role is usually upbeat and enjoyable. But when it comes to negotiating salary, this dynamic tends to shift, and a candidate will frequently become tense and defensive. People tend to regard salary as an assessment of their worth, so negotiating a job offer is loaded, complex, and enters an intersection of personal value and beliefs around money. I interpret this as a first- and second-hub imbalance and try to work through it. The task at hand is to broker an arrangement in which all parties are satisfied, minimizing, or eliminating any loss of goodwill. The hallmark of a good negotiation is a resolution that involves clear expectations for how to move forward. Legal contracts are often maligned for their rigidity and robotic language, but they are a paragon of clear expectation setting. Contract language is the balancing of an equation: *If you give me that, I'll give you this.* It's straightforward and deals in trading things that can be measured—it's a high-level transaction that balances measurable variables and leaves out almost everything else.

There are mindset considerations to address related to the first two hubs, in addition to the classic negotiation advice of knowing what you want and knowing your bottom line: not taking things personally (avoiding emotional contamination); considering what matters to the other party in order to gain leverage; knowing your worth; and reducing or eliminating shame around wanting what you want (usually money and respect, which are often closely tied to emotional contamination). Consider the following four practices for effective negotiation:

Avoid emotional contamination. Some years ago, an employee came into my office and, after the initial pleasantries, matter-of-factly said, "I've been on your team for almost a year. I've hit or exceeded all my goals, and I hope it's fair to ask for a salary increase. When is a good time for us to talk further about this?" I was used to nervous chatter and unnecessarily charged emotional exchanges, so when I was approached in a levelheaded manner it was refreshing and effective—I've used this approach ever since, to great effect. We naturally become defensive when people come at us loaded with emotion; coming into a negotiation either tense or creating an emotionally loaded atmosphere stacks the deck against you and interferes with clear thinking on both sides of the table.

Understand what matters to the other parties involved. My own compensation negotiations used to start with lists of what I was most proud of—unconventional things I was doing to drive the performance of my team, which weren't part of my boss's perception of my value to the company. When negotiating for promotions and compensation, it's not the time and place to make the case for methodology. When I learned to focus on the specifics of what my boss valued and spoke using their preferred terms and language, I got better outcomes (more money, more promotions, more freedom). In salary negotiation, know how your performance measures up to targets and expectations and come to the table knowing your metrics. Don't make it more complicated than it needs to be.

Know your worth. You need to be clear about your value without over- or understating it—without fully owning your worth, you become vulnerable to hosting a parasitic relationship. On the one hand, when we downplay ourselves, we risk being taken advantage of and losing opportunities. On the other hand, when we overstate our contribution, we lose credibility and possibly make it difficult to gain an effective negotiating foothold in the future because our self-assessments get discredited. Self-assessments are sometimes given to staff members to determine their self-awareness (seeing that someone is out of touch with reality can be a red flag). It's important to remember that your performance toward meeting your goals is your professional leverage, so if you don't have clear performance goals and expectations, advocate for them as early as possible. Leaders should prioritize building and providing clear frameworks for evaluation (and the rationale behind them) and should communicate that anything outside the stated priorities is appreciated but not necessarily part of the job. And we can apply this practice to all relationships: communicate what matters and point out what is appreciated but not essential.

Reduce or eliminate shame about wanting what you want. A strong position in a negotiation requires clarity about what you need, along with an understanding of the wants and needs of the other(s) involved. The measurable, quantifiable language of business is through transaction: know what you want, translate it into the language of the party that holds the most power in the negotiation, and know what it wants, or else you may find yourself overpowered and undermined.

POWER: MASCULINE AND FEMININE

Contemporary corporate warriors' bookshelves usually have a copy of Sun Tzu's ancient pillar of strategic wisdom, *The Art of War* (written 500 years before the birth of Christ). Before becoming a general and a preeminent military strategist, Sun was a Taoist farmer. His insights, which remain potent and profound to this day, came from observing the rhythms, patterns, and power of nature. Business consultant Chin-Ning Chu explained in *The Art of War for Women* that Sun wrote his 13-chapter treatise to get a military job, making it quite possibly the most effective job application in history.

A familiar Taoist symbol is the black-and-white swirls of yin and yang, in which each swirl contains a small circle of the opposite color (an enduring representation of paradox and ambiguity). Nothing is entirely black or entirely white, and there is no absolute in anything natural, including the notion of gender. Jung described the animus as the unconscious masculine side of a woman, and the anima as the unconscious feminine side of a man (like the opposing dots within the larger yin-yang swirls). Consider a football team, often viewed as a pinnacle of masculinity, yet it balances both anima and animus. The cohesiveness of the team— how players work together, the preparation of attending to details, and the big-picture strategy—incorporates the yin of feminine-energy principles, along with the yang of masculine-energy principles in the focused execution in each play as the ball advances down the field.

Feminine force is distributed energy, a unified field within all matter that's like energetic glue: it holds the universe together. Masculine force is the focused, directed energy of specific intention, causation, and transaction, a laser-like action that drives things forward without excessive consideration for far-reaching consequences. Masculine energy tends to win the battle but lose the war and feminine energy tends to lack focus in individual battles but win the larger war—consideration of long-term consequences tends to fare well in retrospect. Alone, each of these energies has considerable strengths and definite limits; together, they're formidable. This balancing is nuanced with dynamic complexities that are like the rhythms in nature—complexity that gets reduced to binary gender roles and heterosexual relationships, when instead of two singular expressions, the possibilities are actually infinite.

In Parinama Method practice, the foundation of gender identity first emerges in the individuation and personal power of the third hub. Social identity in the fourth hub will influence the expression of gender identity as it continues to blossom and evolve as we ascend the hubs, but under the strain of certain social influences—being shamed or disdained—it can also become part of the hidden self. Most of us learn gender as a set of socially prescribed roles and behaviors. Gender identity can be confused and conflated with these roles and social behaviors, but gender has ephemeral connections to our inner being and aspects of ourselves that transcend social roles and functions. Flowers have genders and express them in all manner of pollination and self-expression. Many iconic flowers—roses, tulips, daffodils, lilies—are intersex, containing both male and female organs. Pumpkins, mangos, and almost half the animal kingdom are intersex, including clownfish,

red kangaroos, and hyenas. There is awe in a flower expressing itself wherever and whenever it grows and blossoms. If a sunflower grows in a rose garden, why would we call it a rose?

Transgender activist Janet Mock's first memoir, *Redefining Realness*, states, "Gender and gender identity, sex and sexuality, are spheres of self-discovery that overlap and relate, but are not the same. Every one of us has a sexual orientation and a gender identity. Simply put, our sexual orientation has to do with whom we get into bed with, while our gender identity has to do with whom we get into bed as." Some parents fear teasing and harsh judgment of their children outside the home and rationalize their own harshness in the home as preparation for the so-called real world, but we'll never find bullies that hurt us worse than the ones in our own families. The delicate and small body, the psyche, and the soul of a child at any stage of early development just wants to be loved and accepted. In some families, the same parents who claim that the death of their child would destroy them impose a death by exile or denial of existence on a child born a sunflower in a rose garden over their beliefs or fear of embarrassment. Gender identity is part of early third-hub development— it's part of authentic self-expression—and although gender identity is often conflated with sexual orientation, they're two separate-but-related elements of the human experience; with sexuality as the domain of the second and fourth hub that come later in life along with maturation. As in nature, the evidence of masculine and feminine are always in complementary and dynamic flow everywhere we look—if we can see it. Some examples of yang (male) energy and yin (female) energy:

Male/Yang: Transactional (quantitative and measurable)

- Tactical
- Focuses intensity by completing tasks
- Loses the big picture
- Focuses on rules and specifics of contract language (the letter of the law)
- Organized
- Consolidates and simplifies
- Starts from the historical or current situation and looks forward

Feminine/Yin: Relational (quantitative and abstract)

- Strategic

- Focuses on the big picture

- Focuses on intent in contract language (the spirit of the law)

- Able to multi-task

- Expands and distributes

- Reverse engineers (starting with how things should be then envisions the creation of an ideal future state)

If you feel like you can relate to both, that's normal—we all contain dynamics from both ying and yang energetic qualities.

INTERRUPTIONS AND STRESSORS

Third-hub interruptions run the gamut from excessive and punishing authority to permissive lack of consequences and boundaries. As parents work through the hurts and wounding from their own childhoods, the pendular overcompensation of permissive parenting can occur. This can involve shielding children from struggle or allowing inconsiderate self-expression without any consequences. If a child is praised for absolutely everything it does while its parents fight with teachers and coaches who attempt to impose limits and restrictions, the child doesn't develop resilience and personal power. This child has no sense of agency, and advocacy is experienced as being done *for* them, not *by* them. Overbearing parents (the so-called helicopter, snowplow, or bulldozer parents) imagine themselves as the heroes they never had as they fight off demons, perhaps living out the fantasy of standing up against their own restrictive childhoods. But this happens at the expense of their children developing self-advocacy and personal empowerment.

By contrast, when shaming, punishment, and authority are overused, children are taught that the joy of freedom and independence can be stripped away without a moment's notice. Children learn to determine their next move by waiting for a nod of permission (external approval). If a child is shamed for behavior that's developmentally appropriate, it doesn't know how to avoid punishment. A race to become perfect enough to be beyond punishment begins before the child knows that winning is impossible. Understandably, hypervigilance around being perfect, virtuous, and obedient becomes a defensive adaptation strategy when parents, teachers, and other authority figures require obedience and overuse punishment and shame to force behaviors that can only be learned as a (fear) reflex. This can all happen before the PFC is developmentally capable of the reason, memory, and learning required to understand advanced behavior modification. A child's dislocation and interruption of personal power is almost always related to early life within the home, but school, sports, and religious groups can also contribute. For some parents, working through their own hardships may drive the requirement that their children be easier to manage, more respectful, and more rewarding for them. The age at which a toddler becomes willful is often a dramatic shift for parents from the challenges of caring for a helpless little being to containing a small tornado.

An adult outcome of power dislocation is the feeling of being perplexed at having done everything right—going to college, getting a good job, a house, and a relationship—but still feeling unsatisfied. A quote often attributed to theologian and writer Thomas Merton says that people "may spend their whole lives climbing the ladder of success only to find, once they reach the top, that the ladder is leaning against the wrong wall." Some folks will recall early achievement behaviors of sacrificing satisfaction and enjoyment for activities that look good on college applications. Conversely, people without conventional academic track records may feel ashamed and less intelligent because they didn't achieve academic success early in life. The fear and aversion created between these two behavior patterns strengthen shame in the nonacademic but enhances risk-aversion in so-called professionals. Professionals may fear losing privilege, even when having it requires a way of life that does not fulfill them. Nonacademics may fixate on the shame of feeling like a failure when they don't have degrees and high-paying jobs in so-called white-collar professions.

Adaptations resulting from early interruptions are often mistaken as identity and personality because they're so deeply familiar to us: they're all we can remember. Interruption in the first three hubs can lead to rescue fantasies, the hope that through love or leadership someone could come and change everything. The combination of physical disembodiment, emotional detachment, and the feeling that power happens outside of us creates the sense of feeling lost and confused by life. But the love of another person (or, say, a religious belief) will not resolve or transcend physical, emotional, self-esteem, and/or confidence struggles. This work is our own. The willingness to connect early childhood with adult behavior patterns is often met with resistance until the suffering becomes untenable and we are ready to explore transformational practices like therapy and other inward-looking actions.

AUTHORITY: DISCIPLINE AND PUNISHMENT

Consequences and limits teach us self-control and help us to avoid potentially damaging outcomes. Children raised without structure can struggle with self-awareness, self-control, and boundary, but a child's will can also be broken by authoritarianism and/or excess discipline that uses outsized punishment and consequences.

Authoritarian parents are often risk-averse themselves, and when they don't receive respect and admiration in the world outside the home, they demand it in excess within it. Children in strict homes are often taught discipline exclusively as a practice of virtue in doing things they don't want to do and are taught to respect their parents regardless of the parents' behavior—*Do as I say, not as I do.* The obedient child can become a rigidly disciplined adult with a has-to-do life: *I have to go to work; I have to go to the gym; I have to make dinner.* When bound together, unquestioning obedience and discipline are joyless (and again, discipline as devotion to the people and things that matter to you is the path to fulfillment and satisfaction). It's a powerful reframing to connect work and responsibility to things you truly desire and to the people who matter; it's enlivening, fulfilling, and it usually feels great to take responsibility and accomplish things that have meaning for you.

Overuse of authority is often applied at an age before episodic memory is possible. When the development of the nervous system is in its nascent period, the emerging will of a small child is frequently reckless, unpredictable, and beyond reason. This places strain on overworked, overwhelmed, and under supported parents. The cultural history of our relationship with authority contains conflicting messages. We tend to imagine ourselves as free, but conform to restrictive and unspoken social, cultural, and professional expectations. Western culture and values are a convergence of Christianity, Judaism, Islam, and European mythology. Aeschylus wrote *Prometheus Bound* around the same time that the Book of Job was composed. These conflicting stories—Prometheus' bravery and defiance and Job's complete submission and surrender—exemplify the conflict in Western consciousness (and subconscious). Job wins a bet for God by tolerating the destruction of his life without complaint (and he never receives an apology or explanation). Prometheus defiantly brings fire to humans and suffers the consequence of the endless, horrific wrath of Zeus. This dichotomy is, on the one hand, between the loyalty and submission of Job, and on the other hand between the bravery and defiance of Prometheus: both lock horns within our shared American psyche. We tend to identify with Prometheus' bravery, forming the inwardly defiant and outwardly compliant mentality that splits us into outward-facing, agreeable personas while on the inside we seethe. I discuss below how we are kept separated from and unaware of our power and how we tend to use (intentionally and unintentionally) our power against ourselves.

DOMINANCE AND SUBMISSION

When we cannot sense our own power, we tend to experience it through either overpowering others or by surrendering our power and submitting to others. There will always be power differentials between people, but with our embodied power we can decide what's best for ourselves (even though it may not be possible to in each moment). Children are often taught that all adults must be respected and obeyed, regardless of the adult's behavior—and children are often taught that their thoughts and feelings about elders are irrelevant. However, when we grow to be adults ourselves, it becomes clear how all adults do not merit automatic respect.

Again, some strict and domineering parents rationalize cruelty as preparation for the harsh reality of the so-called real world. But no real world could be more brutal than being treated poorly by your own family in your own home. And a child bullied in the home must adapt to survive and so, learns to either submit (shrink) or dominate others (inflate).

Look what you made me do is something bullies will say while dominating and abusing someone, displacing accountability for their cruelty onto their victim. It's confusing and distressing for a child to hear this coming from an adult. The phrase implies that the bully's free will has been hijacked. There's a distinction between holding people accountable for their behavior and hurting someone, then gaslighting them about who's responsible for the harm.

When Hitler rose to power, the surrounding global community watched in astonishment as this unremarkable, gesticulating, angry little man commandeered the human decency of an entire population. Miller (see Chapter 2), in her book, *For Your Own Good,* detailed the strict and unrelenting family lives of top Nazi officers. According to Miller, these men had been raised in punishing, authoritarian homes, and as adults were unable to resist the familiar commands of domineering authority. Hitler has been described as always carrying a sense of impending violence, and his officers obediently followed his sadistic, shocking orders without question.

Adolf Eichmann, a principal organizer of the Final Solution, sat scowling throughout his 1961 trial for crimes against humanity, but he reportedly blushed in embarrassment after being told he should be standing rather than seated for his sentencing. Eichmann, who had organized the logistics for the death of millions of human beings, was unmoved by the recitation of his crimes, but a slight embarrassment over a minor behavioral error caused a physical reaction.

SHAMING, CRITICISM, AND FAILURE

It's devastating to be shamed for behavior outside of one's developmental capacity (or outside the reasonable scope of awareness). When we're ashamed, our senses deaden to protect us from the hurt of losing our sense of dignity and, ultimately, self-worth. The voltage of yelling, slapping, and isolation-as-punishment causes distress by invading a child's physical and/or emotional boundary. Toddlers are messy and self-centered; altruism and selfless acts come later, when the brain and the nervous system further develop in the fourth hub. Rambunctious toddlers can be overwhelming and can become outlets for frustration, even for well-meaning parents.

A toddler is not yet capable of considering that criticism and judgment are subjective and related to the emotional state of the accuser. If shaming happens early and often, it creates a chronic shadow of what some psychologists call "toxic shame," a constant fear that the other shoe is about to drop. The implications of making mistakes become impossibly high when we rely on external approval for identity and power. With toxic shame, low-quality work, mistakes, and imperfection come to represent that *you* are of poor quality, a mistake, and imperfect. The pressure for perfection can be excruciating when so much is on the line. This understandably interferes with trust in happiness—the painful experience of having joy repeatedly ripped away without warning is hard to reconcile. As a protection, we may either drive ourselves to burnout trying for so-called perfection or decide that it's pointless and not even try to trust in achieving satisfaction.

Burnout and fatigue are natural outcomes of interruptions in this hub. A person with a stance of a collapsed midsection—think of Charlie Brown—is the physical act of shame. Like crimping a running hose, the flow of energy in the body is blocked; the collapsing of the torso (shrinking) physically expresses a sense of defeat and fatigue. We become easily tired, tense, and stressed if the torso is crimped or compressed, and struggle to access our energy. Combine low energy with a perceived drive for perfection to outrun shame, and burnout is only a matter of time. The symptoms of burnout are exhaustion, anxiety, insomnia, decreased motivation, becoming excessively emotional, and having hair-trigger anger and frustration. (The somatic practices and exercises below work on strengthening a centered, upright midsection.)

THE PERMISSIVE HELICOPTER PARENT

The helicopter-parent interruption comes when parents, teachers, and leaders diminish or remove children's challenges all together. We learn our capability by working through and overcoming manageable challenges and by bouncing back from mistakes and failures. When challenges are removed or diluted to the point that they exert no force, the empowering experiences of surviving disappointment and growing the ability to get up, dust yourself off, and try again don't happen. If we're not given chances to fail, our capacity to weather loss and disappointment either never develops or atrophies. A child has the chance to develop resilience if manageable challenges are presented so that both success and failure are experienced.

Helicopter parenting eliminates exposure to difficulty and consequence, usually due to parents themselves being unable to manage the emotional load of struggle and disappointment. Permissive parenting revolves around the parents' own relationship with difficulty, failure, and their level of discomfort with the challenging emotions that arise when their child feels letdown, frustrated, or sad. Although a child raised with overly positive parents may not develop the ability to handle any form of criticism, on the flip side, children raised with excessively negative parenting can become overly resilient as they struggle with confidence and self-worth, often feeling unable to ask for help when they need it.

Our struggles build strength, but they should be manageable or they overwhelm us and, as a result, can change our relationship with failure from one of reluctance to one of complete avoidance. If we're going to learn to do something we've never done before, we first must try and struggle—even people with natural talent need to practice. The first act of a good success story is a mistake: a failed company helps teach us how to avoid future errors, and an embarrassing experience can motivate us to work toward better outcomes. Again, purebred failure is hard to find; the closest thing to it is giving up or not trying at all.

CORPORAL PUNISHMENT

When a child is hit for misbehaving it's called punishment; when an adult is hit it's called assault. It's not uncommon for adults to tell stories of being hit as children and in the retelling, say they hated it when it happened, but now they look back at it with respect. You only need to look at the soft, sweet, small body of a child to see that either hitting or screaming at them is heartbreakingly inappropriate, especially considering that the expectations for self-control and behavioral awareness and modification are often placed on young children before they match what's developmentally possible.

Children who grow up in turbulent, violent homes can experience an increase in their threshold for stimulation, sometimes resulting in either seeking intensity (to feel alive) or in avoiding conflict (to the point of complete isolation). It's a cruel assertion (and misappropriation) that positive outcomes and professional success result from early punishment and violent discipline. The excruciating, unrelenting fear of making mistakes can fuel performance, but does not foster the resilience and cultivate the healthy tolerance for risk needed for innovation and leadership. Again, a toddler's developing brain has limited capacity for reason and logic, so physical punishment gets transferred to a child's body as reflexes, not rationales—and these reflexes are carried into adulthood.

Corporal punishment erases physical boundaries by stepping over them, causing anxiety and fear that's mistaken by parents for good behavior and obedience. A growing body of research, including a recent Harvard study in which brain imaging measures the effects of spanking on a developing child's brain, emphasizes the negative impact of physical punishment. The study, "Corporal Punishment and Elevated Neural Response to Threat in Children," shows that spanking, compared to more severe forms of violence, has surprisingly similar outcomes for a child's reflexive fear. Researcher Katie M. McLaughlin and study coauthor Jorge Cuartas report that "[T]here were no regions of the brain where activation to fearful relative to neutral faces differed between children who were abused and children who were spanked . . . we know that children whose families use corporal punishment are more likely to develop anxiety, depression, behavior problems, and other mental health problems, but many people don't think about spanking as a form of violence." They also state, "It's important to consider that corporal punishment does not impact every child the same way, and children can be resilient if exposed to potential adversities . . . but the important message is that corporal punishment is a risk that can increase potential problems for children's development, and following a precautionary principle, parents and policymakers should work toward trying to reduce its prevalence."

IMPOSED MATURATION

When children are made to perform the adult duties of their distressed, distracted, or nonfunctioning parent(s), they're burdened with developmentally inappropriate work that takes away from the activities and behaviors needed for their own growth and development. A child who takes on adult duties, such as caring for brothers and sisters, will always fall short trying to adequately support and provide for the same needs they have themselves. In addition, siblings of a child working to fulfill parental responsibilities may resent them because a parentified child doesn't have the capacity (nor should it) to take on adult duties, and so, grows to feel inadequate under the strain of adult-level responsibility.

Some children find themselves in developmentally inappropriate power struggles with authority figures who rationalize their own behavior by referring to certain children as "more mature." In *Minor Feelings: An Asian American Reckoning*, essayist Cathy Park Hong writes, "One characteristic of racism is that children are treated like adults, and adults are treated like children." When a child is mature beyond its age, it's not an indication that its emotional development is ahead of schedule; it typically means that the child has adapted to survive and still has the need for nurture and tenderness appropriate for its chronological age. There are wise children with so-called old souls, but their perceptiveness and thoughtfulness aren't indicative of their entire physical and psychological development. Exposing any infants, children, and teenagers to adult voltage harms and even traumatizes them. With forced maturation, adults hold negative and distressing opinions of children, interrupting the child's development and causing the reflexive formation of protective survival adaptations. Often, a child pushed into this pattern loses its childlike openness and receptivity while the adults that they must protect themselves against rationalize their own behavior based on the resulting, so-called mature defensive behavior they have caused.

Oppositely, children may put in extra effort to gain the respect of the adults who hurt them. Psychologist and professor Louis Cozolino writes in *Social Neuroscience of Education* that often, "[C]hildren are more deeply connected to parents who mistreat them, so don't assume that abused and abandoned children don't blame themselves for what has been done to them. A kind and attentive teacher may be attacked by a neglected student because being cared for activates her

sadness about the parents she never had." He also writes, "In general, the more disrespect a group has had to endure within a broader culture, the more being respected is important to each individual."

ABUSE OF POSITIONS OF POWER

When a boss, teacher, parent, religious leader, or anyone else uses trust and the power of its role to harvest adoration or to initiate a physical relationship, it's an abuse of its position. Students, employees, and children innocently admire and adore the charismatic, attentive leaders in their lives, which can make them vulnerable to abuse when the power of authority is in the wrong hands. There's love and trust that a leader will have our best interest at heart. If a leader mistakes this for the love that occurs when two individuals have relatively equal power, the leader may justify invasion and abuse. When predators groom children, the dynamic of adoration and trust is intentionally enhanced, and vulnerability and growing attachment will be used against the victim. As a boss in professional environments, I've seen the look of adoration on the faces of the people who work for me as I help them grow professionally and support them from my relative position of power. It's abundantly clear to me how in the wrong hands this could be opportunistically rationalized as an invitation. There are power imbalances in every relationship, but misuse and abuse occur when the relative power of one person is given in good faith and is used to take advantage and to abuse.

IMBALANCE OF POWER

Not all hierarchies are toxic, but cultures and organizations in which prosperity is hoarded while the majority suffers are dehumanizing to everyone involved. In hierarchies, power is often traded for a relative level of safety within the group, but the trade-off is often imbalanced and parasite-host dynamics so common that they become invisible—even though the effect can be felt every day as exhaustion, disillusionment, and hopelessness. Only when we bring awareness to the dynamic does it become possible to take action for positive change.

From birth, we absorb the dynamics of elaborate cultural hierarchies, some with values that have justified the dehumanization of others through formal and informal caste systems and beliefs that have been held so long that they're seen as absolute truths. For example, the belief that the difficult lives of poor and oppressed people are due to their flawed character and weak morals fuels ongoing dehumanization. If we believe everyone receives the same privileges and access to opportunity, the moralizing and marginalizing of oppressed communities becomes easier to rationalize. This rationalization sweeps under the rug the notion of being a beneficiary of a system that can be profoundly cruel; it's an unpleasant reconciliation to consider that one's accomplishments are not just the product of merit, but also a byproduct of a position of privilege relative to others.

UNFAIR COMPENSATION OF LABOR AND BAD DEALS

The enrichment of a few at the expense of many interferes with human evolution. The disempowering effect of having the value of your work undermined is a third-hub interruption. If the wages of someone working full time for a profitable company cannot meet the person's basic needs, it's a parasitic relationship. If a parasite kills its host, it actively engages in its own destruction—a shrewd parasite leaves just enough to keep its host limping along.

In the late 1970s and early 1980s, so-called shareholder value (the company stockholders and owners) overtook stakeholder value (the owners and the workers) through economist Milton Friedman's theories, which have metastasized in the past decades into increasingly jaw-dropping gaps in wealth distribution. A good business deal is relatively balanced and produces beneficial outcomes for all parties involved; a bad deal is significantly more beneficial for one party than the other, and imbalanced deals lack long-term stability. Some folks think that being good at business means creating uneven deals, believing it's simply good business to generate big profits while controlling wages (as full-time employees live without health care and don't make a living wage). I discuss the dehumanizing effect of the Industrial Revolution on human connection and belonging in Chapter 7.

ADAPTATIONS AND HOLDING PATTERNS

The conditions that shaped our third hub occurred when we were small, and even when these early conditions are no longer in effect, the resulting cognitive biases and beliefs can keep us seeking (and validating) a worldview that interferes with our freedom and fulfillment (see Chapter 9). Maybe we learned that if we speak up we'll be punished or that if we aren't domineering we'll be overpowered. The early adaptations in the first three hubs run so deep that the idea of losing them can feel like a threat to our identity. There's the story of a baby elephant pulling against a small stake-and-rope, which it learns it can't move. Later, as an adult elephant, the same small stake-and-rope can be used to keep it in place—the early learning persists because the animal has not periodically evaluated and tested it since it was a calf.

Our early experiences in this hub are reflected by whom we feel comfortable respecting and how comfortable we are with receiving respect. We may find that we're most comfortable respecting people who are critical of us, not realizing this is a holding pattern related to early authority. Mistaking kindness for weakness is also related to third-hub interruptions and holding patterns. Without awareness of interruptions and holding patterns, it can be uncomfortable to have someone treat us with more or less respect than we believe we deserve. It can be perplexing to be mistreated by people when we are kind to them, and we may find ourselves uncomfortable with leaders who are either too hard on us or who are so lax that we don't grow and develop.

CHARACTERISTICS OF A BALANCED AND OUT-OF-BALANCE SEVENTH HUB

Balanced Third-Hub Characteristics

- Energetic and at ease

- Good posture

- Responsible and reliable (not fixated or obsessed)

- Self-disciplined

- Has inner authority (listens to itself)

- Learns from losing and celebrates wins

- Reflects on past performance to fuel future improvements with minimal excuses or defensiveness

- Is open to feedback without being defensive

- Is spontaneous, warm, playful, and humorous

- Has a positive sense of self (usually tries its best, takes healthy risks)

- Can be firm and direct (but doesn't attempt to break another person's will to get its way)

- Hierarchy: *People with higher titles have more power than I have—but they're not more important than people with less power than I have.*

A sign of embodied power is the ability to take direction from someone considered lower status without feeling agitated or ruffled. When power is externalized, there's a near-constant inner turbulence because every interaction either supports or undermines our sense of confidence and self-worth. When we can sense our personal power emanating from within us, we know who we are regardless of how people treat us—and when we are treated poorly, we hold others accountable for their actions and do not second-guess ourselves.

Out-of-Balance Third-Hub Characteristics

- Believes status determines a person's value

- Exhaustion, burnout, low energy

- Midsection weak, bent, or abdomen distended

- Is overly anxious about disappointing people

- Uses caffeine, stimulants, and/or sugar for energy

- Has difficulty with back after failure (can be a sore loser or risk-averse)

- Is either grinding or exhausted (rarely in between)

- Is hardworking but risk-averse (fears mistakes and works with intensity to avoid them)

- How well its doing is almost entirely determined by how other people react to it

- Hierarchy: *People are more important than I am when they have higher titles.*

- Externally compliant and inwardly defiant

- Impatient and irritated: feels that others are either too fast or too slow

An adaptation in the DO hub, as in all the others, is a survival strategy—a shrinking adaptation wants to remain a passenger (with other people making the decisions) and the inflating adaptation won't give up the driver's seat. There's a time for both: dynamism and balance in this hub involves knowing when to drive and when to sit back and enjoy the ride as others take the wheel.

When our inner authority has not been established, we fear rejection, embarrassment, or even retaliation if we make mistakes. Balance in this hub is also a healthy relationship with our own errors—and the ones other people make. If we cannot forgive the mistakes we make, when we see other people make them we may consider them deal-breakers that cause excessive loss of respect, and may push them off imagined pedestals.

SHRINKING

The shrinking adaptation is fixated on power but fears the responsibility of the spotlight. There can be a false modesty and the use of *us* and *we* to avoid direct responsibility. A leader or parent with a shrinking adaptation will require loyalty from subordinates and children, but is unable to effectively advocate for the people who depend on it. The shrinking-adaptation pattern doesn't have much vitality and tends to struggle with follow-through and motivation. In conflicts, instead of directly dealing with people this adaptation often complains about people to others—but seldom to their faces. This adaptation will avoid accountability, and often resents power in others while secretly craving it for itself.

Shrinking Third-Hub Characteristics

- Compliant
- Victim mentality (often blaming others, attempting to appear sympathetic, and avoids accountability)
- Passive-aggressive
- Requires external approval before taking action
- Inwardly impatient and irritated
- Risk-averse
- Struggles with spontaneity
- Procrastinates, sandbags, is slow to act, hesitates (even when knowing what to do)
- Hides lack of confidence (asks for more information before deciding things)
- Hides from the spotlight
- Wants more but avoids asking for it
- Struggles with energy and motivation

INFLATING

Directly addressing an inflated third-hub adaptation is like poking a hornets' nest. Keep in mind that this adaptation needs respect and appreciation, which it doesn't tend to receive when it presents as defensive, harsh, competitive, and uncaring—all qualities that often cause folks to bristle. It's common to see inflation in the third hub combined with shrinking second- and fourth-hub adaptations, that is, minimized feeling and emotion in the second hub and diminished need for truly intimate human connection in the fourth hub (and overcompensating with a quest for power over others).

Working directly with our inflated third hub can be like trying to remove hornets from your home by attacking them with bare hands—you're likely to get stung—so we work around this by developing feeling, emotion, and connection to reduce inflammation and find ways to genuinely respect and appreciate ourselves.

When inflated and inflamed, this adaptation will absorb a lot of an individual's self-identification—*Do you know who I am?*—crowding out the expression of other hubs. Usually, this adaptation is only open to being helped when it's temporarily dazed and confused from burnout as it attempts to recharge or as it becomes aware that its tactics are not working or are not sustainable. But beware the hornet nest that appears to be dormant: without conscious evaluation and change, as soon as its energy returns it will start buzzing again and repeat the patterns that lead to burnout again.

Inflating Third-Hub Characteristics

- Controls others
- Is defiant
- Is authoritative
- Is aggressive
- Asserts: *I don't care what anyone thinks.*
- Is active
- Is stubborn
- Takes reckless, careless risks that affect other people
- Is strong-willed
- Sometimes displays shocking spontaneity (laughs at danger)
- Wants compensation for everything (*everything* is a transaction)
- Impatient (may undervalue orderly problem-solving)
- Reckless about how change affects others (but likes change when in control of it)
- Grandstands and condescends
- Believes it deserves more than others

HOLDING PATTERNS

Inflating: The Classic

The inflating adaptation has many characteristics of the highest-ranking baboon in Morris's colony and rules that apply to all power structures, from baboons to CEOs to presidents. The first commandment is that the top baboon displays the trappings, postures, and gestures of dominance, and in moments of active rivalry it aggressively threatens its subordinates when physically or mentally challenged: it must overpower them. In the extremely inflated adaptation, the primary concern is advancement of personal power, often at the expense of others. But according to Morris, the other nine commandments relate to responsibility for the group—breaking up squabbles between subordinates, protecting weaker members from persecution, making decisions about social activities, and repelling threats and attacks from outside the colony. In some human hierarchies, when we see an excessively individualistic and inflated third hub, these behaviors of responsibility are less common; it may have an overblown concept of the absolute value of competitive behavior—not understanding that true leadership is not individualistic, even in the jungle law of a baboon colony.

The classic inflated adaptation manages up while stepping on those below it, focusing on people who have more power than it does, such as authority figures or people in a position to support their personal aspirations. A particularly maddening example is a toxic colleague who targets coworkers it finds threatening, while hiding in plain sight from bosses—the so-called kissing up while kicking down. An extreme but surprisingly common example of overcompensating inflation is the narcissistic executive who can never get enough and who destroys lives of others in its relentless pursuit of power.

Extreme risk-taking appears brave, but when it's done without fully understanding or appreciating the consequences for others, it's reckless and irresponsible. Inflating tyrants will bellow commands, be greedy for power over others, and take shockingly rapid action that disrupts everyone around them. Perplexingly, they can also be brought to their knees by rejection from a singular source of approval, usually someone who rejected or disrespected them early in life. There can be a fixation on trying to win the respect and approval of a distant parent, typically assumed to be the father, but it's just as possible that it's a withholding, oppressive, authoritarian mother. When others see the tears of a tyrant, they may believe they're witnessing the person soften, when in fact they're witnessing an exit wound of pain. Beware: witnessing this vulnerability can be a liability because the recoil of inflators can be alarming, sudden, and self-protective. As a counter defense from the perceived loss of power, the inflator may seek to regain its footing and those who witnessed the softening may pay the price.

Inflating: The Endurer

A more common inflated holding pattern is "the endurer," a term coined by Judith for someone who takes great satisfaction and validation from outlasting and outworking others. This adaptation tends to have both physical and intellectual horsepower—a naturally strong third hub—but overspends its energy anyway, leaving itself exhausted and craving power from external validation. This adaptation is excessively active and often overwhelmed and on the verge of burnout and tends to get fixated on the importance of their busyness. It has very little realized personal power and exerts control through extremes in eating, exercising, and working—expecting others to be impressed by their intensity. The endurer is productive but always operating below full potential because it's taking on too much and is almost constantly overwhelmed, overworked, and tired. The endurer tends to believe that it holds everything together, so much of its identity rides on the importance of its contribution and it will feel devastated by the implication that things could succeed without it. The endurer gets tremendous satisfaction from outlasting others in terrible situations, believing that people who leave don't have what it takes.

Endurers are high achievers whose struggles with self-worth and confidence interfere with their ability to respect their accomplishments; they tend to see their ability to accomplish something as an invalidation of its difficulty. When the third hub is strong, balanced, and dynamic, we can celebrate wins and take responsibility for losses. The endurer struggles to celebrate wins and, fearing failure, is usually in a purgatory of grinding out work, always outrunning the sense of lacking success (despite its objectively measurable accomplishments), and rarely allowing the wins to feel like they matter.

Both the classic and endurer holding patterns are the result of overcompensating for underdeveloped self-esteem and both seek to have power over others to inflate the confidence they have in their abilities. But again, confidence involves feeling good based on performance, so it's tethered to conditions. These two holding patterns are difficult to address directly because they're highly defensive about their behavior—and may view moderation as a threat to their work ethic, which they will often perceived to be their greatest asset. These holding patterns fear losing their edge, unaware that intensity is what keeps them from being leaders people genuinely respect. By introducing more dynamism (and equanimity), the capabilities and talents remain, but life becomes infinitely more enjoyable.

The Overachievement Cycle

When we depend on work to avoid the other areas of our life as an outlet to pursue perfectionism or when we overwork to avoid potential embarrassment, we become the so-called perfect worker who relentlessly drives itself to outrun failure. But mistakes are inevitable, and instead of acting as reality checks on the futility of perfectionism, they tend to accelerate the overachievement cycle. This is a cycle of simultaneously avoiding risk and hungering for validation, like a wheel that builds momentum as it spins but ultimately steers us toward overwhelm and burnout.

Characteristics of the overachievement cycle:

- Works to outrun failure, criticism, and negative outcomes (although they are ultimately inevitable—we're all human and fallible)

- Making mistakes accelerates risk aversion due to heightened shame and embarrassment

- Pride in the ability to endure excruciatingly difficult situations and circumstances

- High pain tolerance and disdain for so-called weakness

- Perfectionism and high standards (resentment of so-called freeloaders and/or fears being one)

- Serves a master (and revels in having subordinates)

THE OVERACHIEVEMENT CYCLE

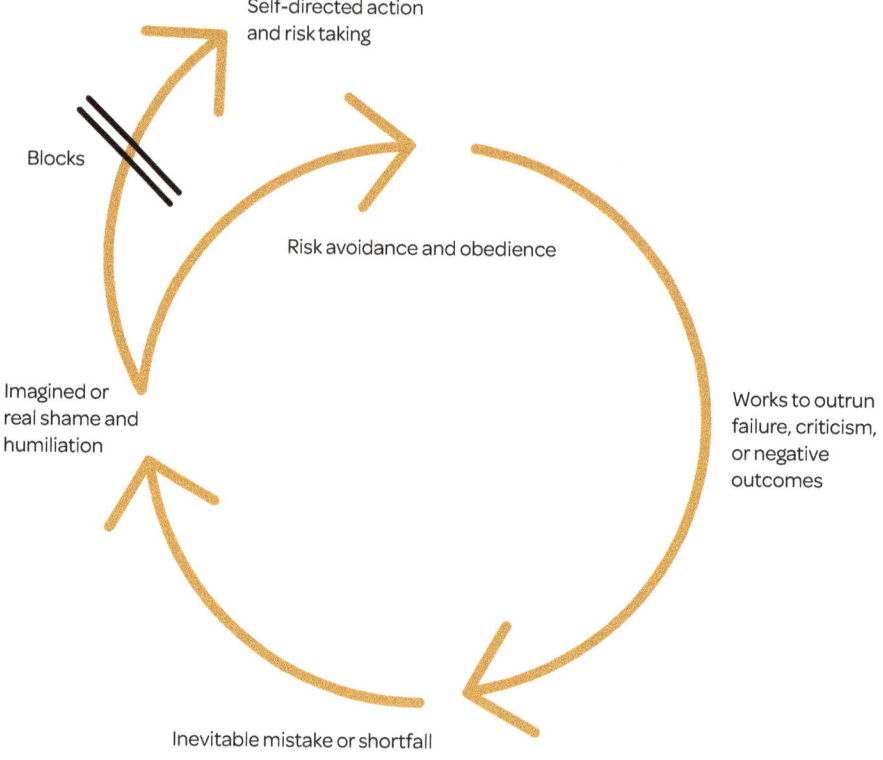

Figure 6.1: The Overachievement Cycle

A hallmark of the endurer is a sense of personal importance stoked by long, intense hours of work. It's often reminded that the boss ultimately holds the power, but believe it's the one who deserves it, so the endurer invests in elaborate calculus to arrive at the conclusion that it is, in fact, the real one in control and that it's their work that's responsible for the boss's success. Whether this is true or not, the endurer misses the point: power and leadership are obtained through greater capacity in all hubs, and overidentification and fixation on work lead to crowding out important facets of a fulfilling life, such as being able to feel deeply and to connect with family and friends.

RISK-TAKING

The shrinking hides from failure and the inflating runs from it; both adaptations are terrified that making mistakes invalidates them. Folks with a dynamic, relatively balanced sense of personal power and strong self-esteem can take responsibility for mistakes and have a healthy relationship with risk. Shrinking behavior is indecisive and seeks validation for even minor decisions; it's nervous about making a wrong move. These folks tend to hope someone will give them guidance or take responsibility if things go wrong. They may crave power (and/or resent it in others), yet the idea of taking responsibility for negative consequences is an overwhelming proposition for them. Risk aversion is common in shrinking and inflating adaptations. It's understandable to believe that risk aversion isn't a factor in the confident appearance of folks with inflating third-hub adaptations; keep in mind that in the overachievement cycle above, risk aversion is fear of negative consequences and outrunning failure, which is central to the inflating adaptation and is concealed in behavior that masquerades as confidence. Taking responsibility and withstanding criticism is an expression of authentic power.

INNER AND OUTER CRITICS

Most of us are familiar (and struggle) with internalized negative voices, either the ones in our own heads or the ones in the heads of people we love and care about. This inner voice is a continuation of someone who was harsh with us before it was physically or developmentally possible to protect ourselves. This inner critic shames, inspects for flaws, and levies judgment. The programming of this voice happened before conscious memories could form—anyone who deals with a critical internal narrative tends to be unable to imagine life without it. When there's adaptation in the third hub, there will be an internalized critic and its narrative *is an adaptation* (meaning that it's not an absolute truth). There are two predominant directions of operation for this adaptation: inward-facing and outward-facing. If you have an inward-facing internal critic, you'll tend to be hard on yourself and to take more than your share of responsibility for the actions of others while holding unrealistic and unfair expectations for yourself. The inward-facing critic is the more commonly discussed and understood, but the internalized critic can take another form, that of the outward-facing critic. It finds fault in everyone else, creating unrealistic standards for others and having little to no leniency for mistakes, which is an intolerance that is often labeled as "having high standards." This critic builds walls against genuine human connection to protect against disappointment and to defend against being hurt. Having been overly shamed early in life, it knows shame as overwhelming, so it protects itself and tends to cut people off rather than work through the disappointment or hurt. The outward-facing critic looks for flaws in others and often judges

them as unworthy—a projection stemming from the deep intolerance it has for its own mistakes and from an inability to see faults as part of a whole person. Shame, which is what it received as its third hub was growing and developing, engulfs the entire person, and feelings of unworthiness get triggered when the outward-facing inner critic sees people achieve goals it envies. As a protection from difficult feelings of low self-worth, it may discredit or target these folks. The outward-facing inner critic is a protection of diminished esteem that has been weakened, damaged, and underdeveloped due to shaming.

Alternatively, inward-facing critics tend to second-guess what they say and to be very careful about avoiding embarrassment; outward-facing critics tend to be more outspoken and to alienate others with their harsh delivery. Through socialization, folks may learn to consciously control the outward-facing criticism, but a few cruel words may slip out, shocking and hurting the recipient and even surprising the person with the adaptation who wishes to leave their alienating tendencies behind. Because of the intolerance for mistakes and isolating behaviors, the outward-facing critic will often abandon or block relationships over misunderstandings that could typically be cleared up with an honest (albeit uncomfortable) conversation.

Consequences for the Outward-Facing Critic

Criticism is a protective defense that keeps us separated from intimacy, esteem, and the things we truly desire. Initially it may seem like the solution for the outer critic is softening the judgment of other people, but the true solution is softening our judgment of ourselves. The deep-seated inner critic is a holding pattern that predates the development of the PFC and conscious thought—awareness and the somatic exercises below bring us back into physical connection with our power and ultimately with our worth, a process that continues in the fourth hub.

Talk Back to the Inward-Facing Critic

When we self-deprecate (as, say, labeling ourselves "idiotic"), we're ingesting small drops of poison that accumulate over time and can further damage our confidence and self-esteem. An inward-facing critic tends to be part of a shrinking third hub, and the outward-facing critic is more common with the inflating—but not always. When we don't know it's the internalized voice of an early criticizer *and that it can go*, this voice will conduct one-sided conversations of assertions that don't get questioned. These harsh assessments act as a vehicle for shame and once we start to notice, we see that there can often be a lack of specificity—shame thrives in nebulous conditions—so call this critic out and ask it to be more clear. Start a conversation with this voice the next time you hear it by saying, "I see you." When speaking to this internalized voice, ask for specifics and for direct experience instead of generalizations and abstractions. If you hear it say, *You're such a complete idiot*, or *That's disgusting*—put it on notice. Talk back to it. Ask it, "What exactly do you mean when you say I'm an idiot?" or "What exactly do you mean when you say I'm disgusting?" No one is a complete idiot—some actions and behaviors may fit the description but canceling an entire person over one bad move causes a lot of pain for everyone involved. There's always an opportunity and possibility for redemption.

JUDGMENT, CRITICISM, AND FEEDBACK

Harsh judgment of someone typically involves rushing to a conclusion or working off limited information—often based on early programming or the bias of previous experiences. Judgment and criticism levy sanctions by way of opinions that can range in severity from being told what we should or shouldn't have done, all the way to behavior that's overtly cruel and/or abusive. The internalized critic is an elaborate defense mechanism that has a magnetic relationship with criticism and judgment—both attracting it from others, and in its own reflexive fault-finding—they're inextricably linked as two sides of the same coin.

If we didn't have positive early experiences with a patient adult, we may perceive any feedback as critical; a hidden cost of defensiveness is the effect it has on our growth and development. Receiving feedback is important for ongoing progress, but when we have the need to protect ourselves even feedback from loved ones and trusted mentors is met with defense, and we may block reception and consideration of it. If we were criticized and diminished early in life, this protection is an understandable survival reflex. Folks who experienced considerate, constructive feedback early in life benefit from the ability to take and grow from feedback (and criticism) without recoiling or reflexively lashing back at a perceived threat. The amount of time we can remain open to what people are saying or doing without rushing to an opinion, judgment, or defense indicates our ability to accept folks as they are and our ability to accept ourselves as we are. This gives greater access to growth and development, both personal and professional. A practical example: if I'm working with someone and I can quickly offer advice or feedback without expecting the person to resist it or get upset, I will do it more often. But if the person needs buffered advice and additional time spent to be sure they don't feel attacked, there's the practical matter of a busy schedule and not having bandwidth to address an issue when additional time and energy are required. As a result, someone who can gracefully take feedback gets more development than the person who can't.

THE SHADOWS: ANGER AND SHAME
Anger

When anger is expressed it's not precise, and when it isn't given a voice or a constructive outlet, it becomes volatile and unpredictable, which can often lead to guilt and shame. Anger is a natural and powerful response to being shamed, belittled, undermined, and disrespected. Every human being should expect (and deserves) to be treated with dignity and respect—when these are denied, a natural corrective impulse of integrity arises first as irritation, then frustration, then anger, and eventually as rage. Emily Dickenson wrote, "Anger as soon as fed is dead, tis starving makes it fat." If anger doesn't get an opportunity to be expressed, it goes underground and can be triggered and explode over the light footfall of an unrelated minor incident.

Anger is a surge of energy that asserts itself in the service of our integrity. It can be used to push through tough tasks or to move out of inertia. Anger is a consequence, the energy to defend and correct. If we don't get angry and take action about being hurt, witnessing injustice toward others, or being poorly treated, we may allow it to keep happening. Just like fear and guilt, when used properly in moderation, anger can be a constructive and activating tool that supports us. Hopefully we learned some self-control during early third-hub development—a mature third hub can transform anger from a destructive impulse into constructive action.

Resentment is indignation over not being treated fairly and often contains trapped rage. When anger has been suppressed for too long it can become rage, which needs to be managed and given an outlet to discharge within safe boundaries. If we were not treated with dignity and respect, understandably, we can feel angry and cheated. This profound, natural impulse to correct for injustice may lack fineness or accuracy and may be directed at people unrelated to the original insult or abuse. The mantra of trapped rage is, *That's not fair*—say these words aloud with conviction and notice how your body responds. If you feel energy rising, move it out through stomping, hitting a soft object like a pillow, journaling, or talking with someone who can hold the space for you to process. Without anger there's inaction, when there's inaction, suffering expands and multiplies—in *The Parinama Method*, I seek to destigmatize anger and move it through safe and constructive actions.

There's a lot of fear around the power of anger. Sometimes it seems like controlling it is the only thing keeping us out of jail. Sometimes anger will express itself in ways that can either be as electric and scary as a live wire or it can create rigidity in the body as we attempt to control it—that is, until it inevitably lashes out with an outsized response to a stressor unrelated to the original offending event. But once it's been surfaced to our conscious awareness, we begin to have real choices about what to do with it.

Our frustrated infant cries were our first expressions of anger—we had needs and couldn't explain them to our caregivers, so we cried until they figured it out. As adults, the rising urgency when needs and feelings are not being understood, respected, or considered is reminiscent of our early irritations and frustrations. Any consistent or significant sense of lack in Daniel Brown's five essentials (see Chapter 5) will contribute to core frustration. When anger arises, it can feel overwhelming and scary, and as responsible adults we often need to conceal it—but eventually it needs a constructive outlet. When anger is suppressed, as Saul Bellow wrote in *The Adventures of Augie March*, "Everybody knows there is no fineness or accuracy of suppression; if you hold down one thing you hold down the adjoining."

Shame

Again, guilt is a bad feeling about a specific action and shame is the outsized, overwhelming sense of being fundamentally flawed (see Chapter 5). Shame places conditions on our self-acceptance, attracting others who share and validate these belief systems, and acts as a forcing function for adopting cultural norms even when they conflict with our integrity and authenticity. Men can feel undermined for having so-called feminine qualities, such as being gentle, small, or short, and women can be made to feel undesirable when they are labeled "masculine" and judged as too assertive, successful, and competent. In an interview with *The Atlantic*, Brené Brown, author and academic who researches shame, states that "Messages of shame are organized around gender," and discusses how women have "[W]hole constellations of often contradictory expectations that if not met are sources of shame, but that for men, "[T]he overarching message is that any weakness is shameful. And since vulnerability is often perceived as weakness, it is especially risky for men to practice vulnerability." In Brown's Netflix special she also says that shame is often expressed for women through their relationship with their body (its size and appearance) and men tend to have shame tied to their abilities, which can include athletic performance, professional stature, earning money, and in sexual power and prowess.

The Shame Cycle

When shame is overused to teach us lessons, it climbs onboard and goes along for the journey until it's discovered and made to leave. Shame makes shame possible—it's a vicious cycle of secrecy that's particularly effective because it creates a sense that there's something about us others can't know of, else, they would lose respect for us or reject us. The feeling that we'd face exile and despair if the truth were known can be carried for so long that we come to believe it's true. In the cycle of shame, what we protect and hide in our mind multiplies and expands.

We're all capable of doing hurtful and cruel things, but this does not make us unworthy of redemption or separate us from our humanity (although shame will certainly indicate otherwise). There's shame over things we've done and there's shame and regret for feeling helpless if we've watched another person suffer and didn't stop it. We often forget how small and powerless we were as children when we reflect back as adults. A child who could not come to the aid of a sibling or a parent when either needed help may not consider its own helplessness during the moment of an incident. There can be overwhelming survivors' guilt and shame, such as when soldiers survive an attack that wounds or kills nearby fellow soldiers. Soldiers with survivor's guilt and shame tend to forget that their life was also in danger.

As children we couldn't see the adults in our lives as fallible; even when we defied them, we considered their approval and perspective to be practically absolute, so feeling safe enough to confront them was a complex matter. I interviewed Julie, who grew up in a home with her brother Josh and their strict and unrelenting mother. While their mother was generally harsh with both of them, her penalties on Julie were relatively minor compared to those she imposed on Josh. He struggled as the frequent target of his mother's rage and over time, began to change from a sweet, goofy boy into an unpredictable recluse. Julie told me she remembers wanting to stand up for him but was too afraid, and now she feels shame and guilt as she watches Josh struggle in his adult life. As a child it was simply not possible for Julie to do anything—a notion she felt was both comforting and very sad.

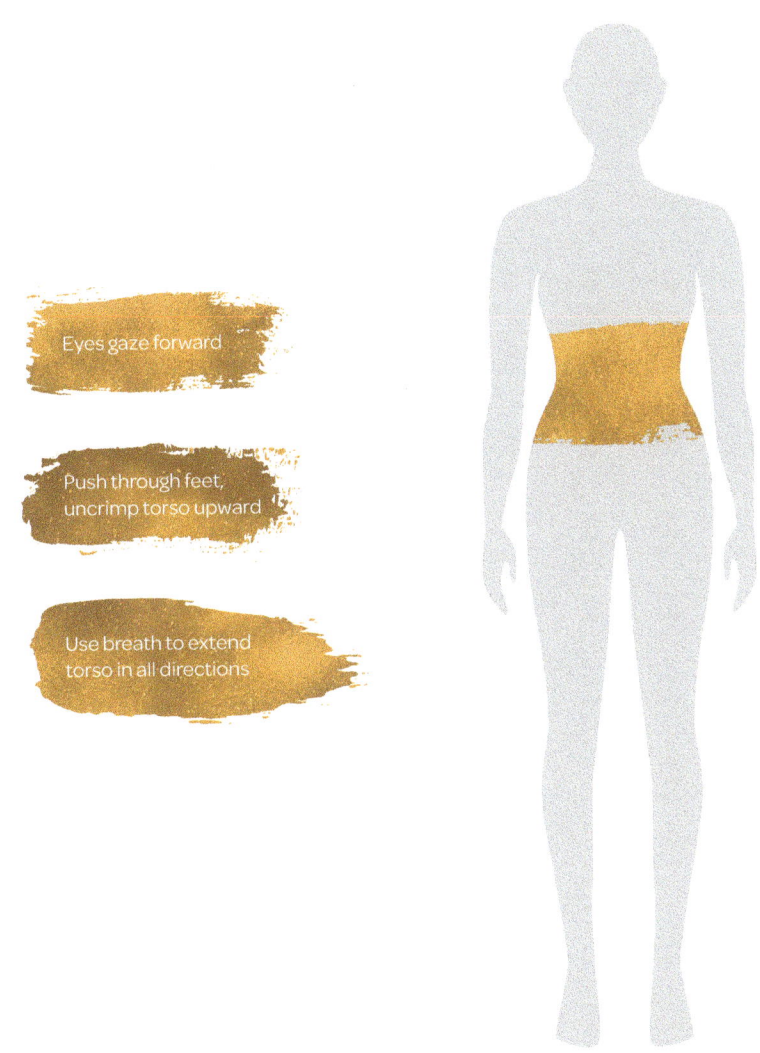

Eyes gaze forward

Push through feet, uncrimp torso upward

Use breath to extend torso in all directions

Figure 6.2: Third-Hub Body Prompts

THE PARINAMA METHOD THIRD-HUB FUNDAMENTALS

The physical domain of this hub is our torso, posture, and musculature. In the third hub we have a crucible in which transformation takes place: the digestive system, which converts food into energy. Building strength in our body gives us the capacity to stand up and stand tall for our integrity, even when the critics chime in (and if you're interesting, they always do). In the first hub we reclaim the relationship with resting and nourishing our body. The second hub introduces flowing movement, which along with emotional responsiveness and literacy, counterbalance the inertia of rest. The second hub moves for pleasure and curiosity, while third-hub movement is focused and purpose-driven in the service of results and transformation.

Reclaiming the third hub can be complex and difficult because a relationship with our power is so taboo that it runs laps around sexual and other stigmas. It's also the most challenging hub to reclaim because it contains aspects of ourselves that we've pushed into the shadows that can become suppressed and when activated: combustible. As toddlers—and throughout life—we're socialized to be manageable for others, and many potent insults involve slurs directed at third-hub attributes: *selfish, egotistical,* and *aggressive,* to cite a few. Your ability to stand on your own, consciously reclaiming some of that assertive toddler energy, makes you a more decisive leader and a better friend and partner.

Muscular holding patterns take energy to establish and maintain; the techniques and exercises in this hub open us to accessing blocked energy. There are often surprising outcomes from embodying power, such as taking self-advocacy action in relationships or delighting in uncovering our naturally occurring willpower. Some folks talk about having unprecedented confidence in job interviews and meetings after focusing on the practice of this hub. Shifts in it can be the fastest and most astonishing.

POWER AND POSTURE

The abdomen doesn't have bone structure for support or protection, and so relies entirely on the strength and musculature of posture. This (paradoxically) makes the physical location of our power the most vulnerable part of our body. Posture signals to others our confidence and conveys presence. When you embody the lighthouse of personal power by uncrimping your midsection, extending your torso, and expanding outward in all directions, you also send a signal to yourself. Anne Lamott writes in *Bird by Bird: Some Instructions on Writing and Life,* "Lighthouses don't go running all over an island looking for boats to save; they just stand there shining." We uncrimp the hose of our torso to unblock and unlock energy. Because your muscles may need to stretch and strengthen, don't wait until you need to walk tall for an important event or meeting—start strengthening your posture now.

THE POWER TRIO

This practice has three steps for preparing your body and stoking its power: first, uncrimp your midsection; second, discharge muscular tension; and third, stoke your power. You'll need a surface to lie down on, a yoga block or rolled bath towel, and a yoga strap with D rings (or a scarf).

Uncrimp the midsection

Lie on your back with your feet on the ground and knees up toward the ceiling. Place the heels of your hands in the creases of your hips; gently push into your thighs in the direction of your feet. Drop your shoulders and keep the sensation pleasant. As you push, feel the extension in your torso and breathe naturally.

Discharge muscular tension

Place a yoga block or a rolled-up towel on the ground and gently lower yourself to where the block sits comfortably between your shoulder blades under your spine. Lie over the block in a neutral position and allow a passive stretch to occur in your midsection and chest. If there's pain, start with a rolled towel that provides just enough lift and stretch so you can comfortably lie on it without strain or pinching. This is a strong practice inspired by Lowen's bioenergetic stool, so defer to a lesser intensity. Release and relax into the block or towel and on the exhale, make a sound *ahhh* to create some vibration in your chest. After about three *ahhh* breaths, lift your shoulders while keeping the bottom-most part of the block or towel in contact with your back, staying in contact with the ground while being able to look at your toes. Find a place where there's a slight muscular tremor and hold it for between one to five breaths. Release back over the block with another *ahhh*.

Stoke your power

Next, sit up, remove the block, and grab your yoga belt with D-rings (or a long scarf that you can loop around your midsection above your rib cage and below your pectorals). Make a slip knot in the yoga belt so the belt can expand against resistance. (If using a scarf, loosely tie it.) The purpose of the belt is to feel your breath extending your torso in all directions.

With your inhale, expand your torso outward from the front, back, and sides. On the exhale, contract inward. Repeat and notice any sensation that occurs.

Once you have completed these three exercises, take a walk, and focus on extension and expansion in the torso—notice how it feels and what it takes to maintain it without a strap or belt. (Below, I add planks and abdominal work to strengthen the third hub.) When standing in line at a store or even seated at home, you can extend upward along with the 360-degree inhale to expand the torso (focusing on expanding in all directions followed by a 360-degree contraction on the exhale). Also, notice the ergonomics of your desk or wherever you spend a lot of time during the day. A standing desk or a desk that's adjusted to avoid hunching is essential. Notice if there are places in your life where you spend time hunched over, such as your kitchen and your computer, and make adjustments.

PUSH DOWN, RISE UP

When we focus on posture, we often extend our backs upward to straighten our spines. But if you push into the ground, extending upward tends to happen naturally. If you're sitting in a chair or standing, push down using your bum or bottoms of your feet. Notice what happens: your body rises. When we connect to our ground, we grow.

Good posture sends a very strong signal as we operate in social hierarchies that use appearance to subconsciously clock people to determine the level of respect they command. Johnstone's exercises above are worth revisiting in concert with posture.

BOUNDARY AND THE PHYSICAL NO

Being clear about your time is a demonstration of both power and boundary. Because time is so closely related to power, a prevalent form of passive-aggressive behavior is being late, and a protection against time invasion is being physically present but mentally checking out. The ability for a person to take your time or your ability to take someone else's is an expression of power and is potentially a boundary invasion. A common example is an oblivious boss who distracts you with chitchat when you have work to do or a meeting that runs longer than scheduled without asking the participants for permission. People with power will say *no* when asked for more time than they intended to give; will communicate their reservations; and will perhaps even offer the opportunity for a response but will remain firm in their position.

The word *no* rings hollow when our body language and level of conviction transmit a nonverbal *yes* or an apologetic, *I'm sorry*. But finding the *no* in your body can feel more stabilizing than simply saying the word. Stand with both feet planted on the ground, knees unlocked, and bum unclenched. Hold your right hand at your waist in a fist with your elbow pointing to the back of the room. Draw your torso up on an inhale. Step your left foot forward and on the exhale raise your left arm parallel to the ground with your hand out to indicate *stop*. Move your left foot back to the starting position as you lower your arm and repeat; extend your torso up on an inhale, step left foot forward, arm extended, and say *no* on the exhale. Switch sides, repeat, and find any variations that strengthen the feeling of a physical *no*. Return to neutral standing. Place your hands on your heart. Notice if you feel physically or emotionally tired, activated, or something else entirely.

METABOLISM AND DIGESTION

Our nutrition fuels us—we only access a sliver of our capacity when working through the brain fog of a limited diet. Consciously reclaiming food is taking responsibility for our choices without criticism or judgment. The only must-do with food is to work toward self-advocacy without judgment and cruelty. Guilt and shame do not belong in a good relationship with food—a relationship which is a collaboration to serve your body-mind.

Healthy eating supports both how we feel right now and what we want to accomplish. A blood panel to check our nutrient levels and an allergy test for food and environmental sensitivities can jumpstart this process. Noticing how our body responds to sugars, salt, and hydration with nonjudgmental curiosity can provide helpful information for deciding what and when to eat. Pay attention to food that makes you feel good and use it as a tool.

As with gurus versus teachers, there will never be anyone who knows better than you how food makes you feel. You are the guru of your nutrition and using what you eat to serve you and your life supports your power. If you eat a cheeseburger combo and a pint of ice cream on occasion, enjoy the pleasure of filling a need to feel sedated, full, or comforted.

If we are restricting or disordered about food, we're using it to express power—and food and power are deeply connected. Again, the third hub contains the digestive system: the process of turning food into power. Eating issues are an outlet for demonstrating power and control when other avenues of expression are closed off. Restrictive and disordered eating attempts to control and overpower with ever-tightening conditions on self-worth that strangle the joy out of eating. If we can uncouple appearance from self-worth to understand that being attractive is more about power than it is about love and worthiness, perhaps the pressure placed on all beauty standards can relax its grip.

Draining Energy in Our Intestines

No discussion of the third hub is complete without a discussion of intestinal parasites. All of us host bacteria in our gut that support digestion, but certain strains of bacteria (and fungi) create abdominal bloating, chronic fatigue, anxiety, and joint pain. In addition, candida or any other bacterial or fungal overgrowth caused by pacifiers like refined carbs and alcohol can significantly impact mood and energy. I'm not a medical professional and have intentionally avoided addressing dietary material, but I am confident that getting blood and allergy tests can offer potentially life-changing information.

CHARGE AND DISCHARGE

Charging and discharging in the third hub is nuanced—we're working with energy at its source. The shrinking adaptation needs to access energy, so charging with intense and activating exercise can be particularly helpful—while an inflater needs to discharge and discover a more dynamic equilibrium between both charging and discharging. Vigorous exercise charges (and discharges) in the third hub, but exercise and fitness can also create rigidity through fixations on the achievement of punishing standards of appearance. Excessive and intense exercise can activate and exacerbate anger and aggression for an inflating adaptation, so dynamic balancing is an important consideration.

CHARGING

Charging can come in the form of spending time with people who energize you, eating good food, moving your body if you've been resting, or even with a cup of coffee. This is a sequence intended to stoke power in your body.

Plank

This exercise is technically both charging and discharging as it strengthens, energizes, and releases through tremoring. It's the perfect third-hub exercise with multiple variations—the plank, for readers unfamiliar with the term, is a static hold of the body (relatively) parallel to the floor on your toes, with your hands on the floor and arms extended. Begin with your knees on the floor and lean forward, placing your hands under shoulders slightly wider than shoulder width. Next, fully extend your legs back, toes on the floor, with legs parallel to the ground. Your legs should be working, too—be careful not to lock or hyperextend your knees. Neutralize your neck and spine by looking at a spot on the floor about 10 inches in front of your hands. Your head should be in line with your back. You're looking to find the point of tremor without straining your breath. Ideally, hold the position for 20 seconds—you can work up to this and then work toward extending the time. Hold your plank for as long as possible without compromising your form or breath; the goal is to achieve between five and 10 seconds of tremor. This is not an endurance exercise—you're looking to discharge and overdoing it will create the opposite of the desired effect. Watch out for collapsing your lower back, reaching your bum to the sky, dropping your head, or forgetting to breathe.

Other variations:

- **Forearms:** Place your forearms on the floor with elbows aligned below your shoulders with arms parallel at about shoulder width. This modification helps reduce stress on the shoulders and joints and can reduce intensity to help maintain the focus on discharging. Also, if flat palms bother your wrists, clasp your hands together and interlace your fingers while keeping the elbows parallel.

- **Knees:** Resting your knees on the ground puts less stress on your lower back. Place a rolled-up towel under your knees if they feel uncomfortable on the floor.

- **Side plank:** To increase intensity, lie down on your side with one leg stacked on top of the other, then prop your body up by pushing into the hand or elbow closest to the floor while keeping your feet and legs stacked. You can make the plank more difficult by raising the opposing arm or leg—or both—into the air.

Woodchopper

Start with your feet planted and knees slightly bent. On an exhale, bend forward gently and bring your hands to the ground (or as close as you can get). On the inhale, rise back up to standing. Repeat three to five times. Next, on an inhale, raise your hands over your head and then exhale as you bend forward bringing them down to the ground; on the inhale reach back up to the sky as you stand. Next, interlacing your fingers overhead, exhale while gently bending into a forward folding position, while bringing your hands down in a chopping motion like using an ax. On an inhale, come back up to standing as you raise your arms up to the sky, and on the next exhale fold forward again, bringing your arms back down with a bit more force as you chop. Repeat two more times, adding a little *ha!* sound on the exhale when you chop. Next, increase the force and increase the sound of *ha!* Imagine your hands are holding an ax, coming back down. *HA!* Again, *HA!* Again, *HA!* Again, *HA!* Once more with force: *HA!* Return to standing and feel that power in your body. It is yours. What are you going to do with this power and what does it serve?

DISCHARGING

An essential discharge in this hub is the conscious release of anger. It's worth noting that the shrinking and inflating adaptations often fail to recognize their anger because it gets expressed in the more diluted forms, such as irritation, frustration, and impatience. Anger may not be readily accessible or recognizable, but irritation and frustration are like hearing anger's muffled voice buried deep within us, trying to be heard.

The classic inflating adaptation will often believe that anger and impatience (sometimes redefined as "high standards") is an integral part of power. One indicator of suppressed anger is how activated you get in the presence of someone else's frustration or anger. Finding the dynamic equilibrium in this hub involves becoming responsive rather than reactive through exploration that doesn't detonate unexplored, undischarged anger and rage.

To discharge anger, you first need to find it. Unfortunately, it's been socialized out of our consciousness, so discharging it usually begins with some half-hearted movements. For example, hitting a pillow with your hands, a tennis racket, a plastic bat, or pushing into a wall can take a little encouragement before they build momentum. When releasing or discharging in the third hub, you can expect to feel some heat: heat and sweating are common. There are boxing lessons, vigorous exercise, stomping feet (pretty much anything that makes you sweat), along with journaling exercises and the fuck-you journal (see Chapter 11), that help surface consciousness around anger while expressing it in safe and responsible ways.

Abdominal contraction

Start by laying on your back with legs extended, lift both legs off the ground until you reach the point of trembling. Hold for two breaths, release, and repeat up to two times. Next, with your legs on the ground, lift your torso and find trembling for two breaths. Repeat up to two times.

The fostering and encouraging of the lighthouse relationship with our power supports self-worth and prepares us for fulfilling relationships in the fourth hub. In the third hub, if we don't fully individuate and have the capacity to stand alone, our relationships in the fourth hub, Chapter 7—CONNECT—may strain under the outsized demands of defining our identity. In relationships, we bring our own strength to make a greater contribution to them.

CONNECT: CHILDHOOD, SELF-ACCEPTANCE

Basics	Themes	Interruptions and Stressors	Adaptations and Holding Patterns	Techniques and Exercises
Give: Generosity	Family Belonging with Attachment Styles	Conditional Love and Acceptance	Characteristics of a Balanced and Out-of-Balance Fourth Hub	Receiving
Receive: Gratitude	Social Belonging with Personas and Projection	Perfectionism	Shrinking	Breathing Exercises
Balance		Parents Who Don't Know How to Love		Crying
Miserliness and Martyrdom versus Destructive Generosity	Organizations: Leaders versus Managers	Scorn	Inflating	Humanization
Devotion: Love Is a Verb	Cultural Belonging with Anima and Animus	Rejection and Loss	Ohm's Law	Charge and Discharge
Humanization	Intimate Belonging with Eros and Thanatos	Abuse	The Shadows: Grief, and Envy and Jealousy	
	Belonging to Yourself with Self-Acceptance and Self-Love			
	Belonging to the Natural Environment			
	Conflict			

Chapter 7

THE FOURTH HUB—CONNECT

CONNECTION AND BALANCE

*Love isn't a state of perfect caring. It is an active noun like struggle. To love someone
is to strive to accept that person exactly the way they are, right here and now.*
—*Fred Rogers*

RELATIONSHIP AND CONNECTION CAN obliterate perfectionism as they reveal and
reflect increasingly deeper layers of ourselves that are hard to face without the compelling power of
love. We are part of the natural world and although nature is magnificent, fluctuating, adaptive, and
cyclical, it's also imperfect and brutal in astonishing and sometimes epic ways. Perfection and purity
exist in imagination and in brief moments that come and go. Even a so-called perfect person poops,
sweats, gets sick, ages, and dies. Even if perfection and purity were possible, achieving them wouldn't
make us any more worthy of admiration, affection, and love than we already are. If we struggle with
self-worth, we likely have interruption or imbalance somewhere in the capacity to give or receive.
Here, I discuss this fourth hub and the natural world's homeostatic equilibrium—an innate balancing that's almost never completely centered, but that keeps things relatively even over time (a state
found within relationships). The strength of human connection is determined by our participation in
a dynamic balance of give-and- take.

The physical location of the fourth hub is in the chest, shoulders, arms, and hands. Our chest
contains our heart and lungs. We draw in oxygen as we inhale, and our heart's circulatory system
expands in concert, moving air into our bodies. Two by two, the arteries bifurcate into capillaries,
ever-expanding as they supply oxygen—the catalyst for unlocking energy from food—to our bodies.
On the return path, two by two, the capillaries converge into veins and return the waste byproduct
of respiration (carbon dioxide) to be released on the exhale. We're linked to the reverse-respiration
cycle of plants—they take in carbon dioxide and release oxygen—the complementary opposite to
human respiration.

Our heart beats and we breathe, regardless of how much attention we pay to it. Our beating heart
always shows up for us, doing the best it can with what's available. Throughout our lives we weather
disappointment, abandonment, and grief, and our heartbeat and breathing are always there for us. Let
them be a symbol of a connection to an aspect of yourself that has never given up, one that's essential
to our physical survival and deeply connected to our relationship with nature. It's always present and
always at its best. The inspiration for deep love and devotion is at the core of your body.

ORIENTATION

Physical location: Chest, upper back, shoulders, arms

First cycle: Between four and seven years of age

Task: Humanization: altruistic and empathetic connection with both self and others

Rights: The right to give love, the right to receive love, to belong

Identity: I am my relationships.

Reconciliation: How much of myself must I hide to belong?

Intimate relationships offer profound opportunities for our transformation. But transformational dynamics can also arise with bosses, friends, neighbors, and even in nature. We're in relationships with everything around us, and our need to connect and belong is a shared need and tendency we see in other beings. No one can exist in isolation, and even if we can live in relative seclusion, we need farmers, plumbers, medical-care providers, and myriad other people to make our lives possible. To be alive is to be in relationship. In adulthood, it's through connection—to ourselves, others, and nature—that we get the chance to repair and restore the first three hubs' trust, emotional literacy, and self-awareness. Through the multitude of ways our lives intersect with other people's, connections and relationships act like mirrors, reflecting and exposing hidden aspects of ourselves—if we're willing to see them.

In Chapters 4, 5, and 6, I discuss the importance of early caregivers' consistency and predictability. Here, the dynamic balance of give-and-take, which originates in the second hub with attunement, evolves with the creation of social identity through our interconnection with others—and our relationship with ourselves. We learn what matters most—both for ourselves and for others—by what we show up for (see Chapter 6). Even taking pills to manage health conditions or to relieve pain can be hard to do when we struggle to connect with our inherent worth. The Mayo Clinic reports that 50 percent of patients with chronic illness do not take medication as prescribed. The World Health Organization reports that as much as 40 percent of patients do not adhere to its treatment regimes, and another study showed that in the United States, 12 percent of people do not take their medication at all. Many of us know from personal experience that it can take a caring person to remind us to take medicine. It's not necessarily a matter of whether a treatment or solution is easy, it's a matter of showing up every day—and showing up can be hard to do.

New relationships bring the hope of positive change and the potential for transformation. A baby, a new friendship, a new job, or a new romantic partnership (or perhaps writing a book) all bring a sense that the future can be both different and better than the past. And in the beginning it almost always is. In the very early days of new love, holding patterns dissolve from the glowing gaze of a new partner—it's the idyllic period when new connections don't require work and feel incredible. Some meditation traditions call this "the beginner's taste," a short, early, effortless period when we temporarily experience the long-term benefits of a new relationship or practice without having to do work—but the work does eventually come. Eventually, we come back to the mundane reality of adaptations and holding patterns, except that now we want that feeling back (and we may be willing to work for it). In these moments, the glow dims a bit, and when we hit these first few bumps in the road, we find ourselves back in the familiarity of ourselves. This is when we can either turn away or continue to show up and bravely begin restoring or strengthening the dynamic, homeostatic balance in ourselves and with others through the transformative crucible of love.

INITIAL DEVELOPMENT

Starting at about four years old (the early years of the fourth hub), we naturally and effortlessly love—it's spontaneous. In these years the capability for thoughtful, altruistic acts begins to emerge: we start giving. Previously, we could give reflexively and respond to affection, but at the same time as we begin to socialize and to develop our social identity, we also develop the neurological capacity to connect the dots by doing things because they can make others feel good, and it feels nice to make other people feel nice. At this stage, we're completely open and receptive. This is the rosy era of kindergarten that transitions into early grade school as sweetness, and altruism often begins to emerge. When the third hub is coming online, there may be acts of kindness in the service of the will or in engineering an outcome that exclusively benefits the child. Now, as altruism begins to sprout, and parents can feel like they have a little buddy who demonstrates acts of kindness, revealing more of its unique personality in leaps and bounds. These years tend to be particularly golden for parents because a child moves out of the fierce individualism of the third hub and into the more loving fourth. The developmental capability for self-gratification and possession in the second and third hubs are captured here in the six so-called Toddler Property Laws:

1. If I want it, it's mine.

2. If I had it in my hand, it's mine.

3. If I had it a little while ago, it's mine.

4. If I'm building something, all the pieces are mine.

5. If it just looks like mine, it's mine.

6. If I think it's mine, it's mine.

Before the age of four, children are generally not very interested in friendships and in playing with others; their playing style tends to be in the form of so-called parallel play—they're in the same area as other children, doing different things. But in early fourth-hub development, connection and contribution begin to spark interest, and peer relationships emerge. Sometimes, the desire to learn effective socialization involves practice through creating imaginary friends for sorting out their experiences with other children. We often idealize early childhood as simple, but at this age children are navigating new and complicated dynamics all the time.

As children begin to form relationships outside the home, the transition into the fourth hub is a vulnerable time. Kids navigate the hurts of rejection and the occasional disappointment that come with making new friends and meeting new people. We respond to early hurts by hiding parts of ourselves and creating emotional defenses. Early social identity requires that children can moderate themselves to gain greater belonging; the fourth hub is where we learn to build social personas and identities so that we can be part of a group. It's also where we experience the heartache of grief, which can become a shadow in this hub as a protective holding pattern—avoiding the pain of loss by cutting connections and blocking the vulnerability of love. The work of the fourth hub is to remain dynamic as we balance our integrity with social belonging, the give-and-take of relationships, and the dichotomy and complexity of our inner selves—what we hide and what we show.

Kids operate with limited perspective and context at this age. Being teased and laughed at by other children feels devastating, so they may internalize the feelings, believing there's something they need to change about themselves. If other kids teased us about the clothing our parents picked out for us, perhaps we felt the bind of frustration toward our parents for embarrassing us while we are harboring a loving protectiveness toward them. This creates a conflict that children cannot effectively navigate, so they learn to conceal to restore peace, moving the conflict inward. In the service of harmony, they may hide pain, sadness, and even so-called weirdness. To the best of their ability, children will shape their personality into one that receives favor from others. Developmental psychologist Lawrence Kohlberg called this the "good girl/nice boy" moral development stage, which involves

- orientation to approval, to pleasing and helping others;
- conformity to stereotypical images of the majority through role behavior, such as gendered behaviors; and
- action evaluated in terms of intentions, so we can modify stories to fit an existing narrative, such as an aggressive boy showing promise and the same quality in a girl being flagged as problematic.

We learn how to be a good girl because mommy appears to love us more when we're helpful, and we learn how to be a nice boy because daddy loves and pays more attention to us when we play sports or behave with a competitive streak. Kohlberg organized three levels of moral development into preconventional, conventional, and postconventional:

- **preconventional/premorality**: primarily life before socialization—there's no morality.
- **conventional/role conformity**: early socialization of childhood—there's prescribed social morality that is accepted as fact.
- **postconventional/self-accepted moral principles**: there's conscious evaluation and auditing of the self and of the impacts of socialization, culture, and early family life.

Love acts through compassion and encouragement. Children raised with excessive judgment and punishment tied to conditional love and attention can have trouble with understanding connection with others. Being spanked, yelled at, or hurt in any way while being told it's done out of love will scramble important signals. This can initiate a search in the world outside our birth family to understand what love looks like, with attempts to learn the associated behaviors of loving connection. Through building a balanced capacity to both give and receive, we can feel how love is all around us and allow it in. As I continue to emphasize throughout *The Parinama Method*, everyone is deserving of love—perceived merit has nothing to do with it. As psychologist Eugene Kennedy said, "There would be no need for love if perfection were possible."

In the early years of fourth-hub development and into the fifth hub, the capacity for language is accelerating as children express new observations almost every day. At this out-of-the-mouths-of-babes stage, children speak their truth without awareness of stigma or social consequences. The reactions of others are an education for them that supports the formation of social masks (a.k.a. personas). Knowing what is appropriate and safe to say is learned through approval and rejection. In kindergarten and early grade school, a child begins to play different roles for different people. With friends, there may be explorations and conversations that are different from those held with parents and/or teachers. Navigating our social environment involves playing roles by amplifying some qualities and suppressing others. A little boy who likes to play dress up and/or play with dolls may engage in this play at a friend's house but not at home, where it's criticized. But a child's nature is arising spontaneously, and if family, social, or cultural standards crowd out too much of this natural expression, a child may either develop the shrinking response of low energy and sadness or the inflated response of overbearing behavior. The distress of concealing our true nature comes from sensing we cannot be loved for who we feel ourselves to be. The capacity for language is developing, but the more advanced skills of expression begin in the fifth hub. Therapist Pete Walker suggests in *The Tao of Fully Feeling* that nervousness or anxiety about public speaking may be a subconscious reflex resulting from the shock to the system of early shaming and punishment for speaking openly without knowing the social stigmas of what can and cannot be discussed.

Our parents are our first teachers (and, regardless of their parenting capacity, godlike to us). As adults, when we bring illuminating curiosity to this hub, sometimes sad and confusing feelings, thoughts, and memories can come up. It's understandable to seek reconciliation with our parents and people from our past, but expectations can cause a lot of hurt for everyone involved. Keep in mind that it's entirely within your power to build and restore your ability to connect and to love without a requirement of explanations and apologies from the people who hurt you. Everything you need to receive and to express love is within you, and I discuss tools to unlock greater capacity below.

The fourth hub is the in-between point for the physicality of lower hubs and the metaphysicality of upper hubs. The 13th-century poet Rumi wrote, "The angel is free because of his knowledge, the beast because of his ignorance. Between the two remains the son of man to struggle." The programming of the first three hubs remains behind what Jung called the locked door (the subconscious). The early development of the fourth hub is when conscious (episodic) memory begins. This is a very important inflection point to underscore—we began to remember things when our life was already in progress, and important programming about trust, emotions and power had already been set in motion. Because the first three hubs are subconscious and primarily preverbal, they're best explored and uncovered through somatic practice.

In the fourth hub, children begin to form conscious, episodic memories that they will be able to recall as adults. Episodic memory involves the hippocampus, a part of the brain found in the temporal lobe, which is not fully developed at birth. In an interview with *Parents Magazine*, cognitive neuroscience of memory expert Rachael Elward says, "The hippocampus should be ready at about the age of four, and this is usually when children start remembering things consistently. The older a child gets, the more stable their memories become." The memories from the initial development of this hub tend to be fuzzy, with pronounced specifics of seemingly random visuals: the hair braid of a new friend on the first day of kindergarten or the wallpaper in a room where someone was mean to us. Later, in the sixth hub, children can get more specific and focused about what they remember.

BASICS

This is the hub of give-and-take, of gratitude and generosity as a homeostatic dynamic like inhaling and exhaling, and between the two, sustainable relationships are possible. Inhaling is an activating intake of air and exhaling releases and softens. If we feel as if we're holding our breath, showing up and staying in a relationship is unsustainable. When we can love ourselves and others, our give-and-take is balanced, and our connections are sustainable. We can only pour ourselves into something without receiving or take without giving back for so long before the balance shifts and corrects itself. To build sustainable connection we must balance our needs and wants with the wants and needs of others. Showing up is easy when it feels good but showing up imperfect and even incapable is how we grow: it's how consistent devotion obliterates the soul-crushing notion of perfectionism. Showing up when it sucks? *That* is love. But there's nuance to consider, things shouldn't suck most of the time. Staying with someone or something when it gets hard is different from tolerating abuse or subpar treatment.

GIVE: GENEROSITY

If we don't have enough for ourselves, yet we give to people who can't receive or don't appreciate the offering, we're losing when giving. Organizational psychologist Adam Grant's *Give and Take* highlights multiple studies showing that givers are both the highest and lowest performing members of a sales organization. According to Grant, the difference between a giver who wins and a giver who loses comes down to three categories, which I call discernment, boundary, and connection to purpose. *Discernment* puts limits on the amount of giving to people who only intend to take. *Boundary* in giving assures that we're making time to focus on our own goals, in addition to supporting others in theirs. *Connection to purpose* aligns our giving with our integrity where it serves something or someone important to us.

When we evaluate our giving through the lens of these three categories, we may encounter reflexive cultural conditioning that emphasizes the so-called virtue of generosity. Giving is one side of the dynamic of give-and-take (generosity-and-gratitude), but generosity morphs into martyrdom and will express low self-worth when we support people who do not support us. Anaïs Nin noted, "I was always ashamed to take. So, I gave. It was not a virtue. It was a disguise."

There is an artistry, sensitivity, and curiosity in giving well, and unless we fear scarcity or feel discomfort with vulnerability, giving comes naturally. The fourth hub is one of altruism and the inclination to give, but some folks either conflate altruism, kindness, and compassion into attempts to win favor, pleasure, and rewards for themselves or they distrust the generosity of others because they sense real or imagined sinister motives. Maté (see Chapter 5) writes, "Our material culture tries to explain even unselfishness as arising from selfish motives. It's often asserted, cynically, that people who act in kindly ways, without any benefit to themselves, are doing so only to feel good. Neuroscience does not support that view." The neurobiology of altruism shows that the location in our brains that activates during a selfless act is in a different area from the pleasure- and reward-seeking behavior centers.

Our human dignity requires that we can give and contribute. Erikson called this psychosocial stage of development "industry versus inferiority." During my interviews for *The Parinama Method*, I met with people living in shelters and on the street, and was often offered food, drink, and other gifts. At first, taking was confronting for me, but eventually I came to understand that receiving the generosity built trust and was deeply humanizing for both of us—creating balance with the items I'd buy or relatively small amounts of money I gave.

RECEIVE: GRATITUDE

Receiving without expressing appreciation is appropriate in the earliest years of life. As we enter the developmental stage in the fourth hub, sharing through a balance of taking along with giving is now developmentally appropriate and part of successful socialization. In the earliest years of life, when it isn't possible for an infant or baby to express gratitude, mature parents must constantly quash the recoil from exhausting work that lacks appreciation. Attentive parents of a new baby will be attuning to signals and anticipating needs, asking for nothing in return except the health and safety of their infant. Adults who didn't experience this early in their lives may crave this proactive, intuitive attention by expecting other adults to anticipate their needs—even having tantrums or giving the silent treatment. As mature adults, we must use words to assist people to give us what we need. Once we've grown, having people guess is no longer reasonable or appropriate.

Many folks find receiving more difficult than giving. Even people who are chronic takers tend to lack capacity for gratitude, which is the core of receiving. Although giving can be an act of power, truly receiving requires strength in vulnerability. We may repeatedly give to people while they take and take without appreciation or the desire to reciprocate—takers have difficulty feeling when they are receiving. To receive means that we fully experience and embrace an act of generosity.

The issue at hand for folks who struggle with low self-worth or have experienced significant interruptions in the fourth hub isn't whether they are loveable or whether love exists (even though this may feel like a reasonable concern). Instead, the issue is the capability for allowing, receiving, and appreciating the love that surrounds you. Dissatisfaction with what is available or with what is being given is a protective adaptation that conceals a lack of trust in receiving. If we cannot tune in to the generosity of a kind word or a small act of service or gift, we're restricting what we can receive—it simply doesn't matter how much we're given if we cannot allow ourselves to feel that we're receiving it.

To have a direct experience with the energetic underpinnings of giving and receiving, try giving to someone who shows no appreciation and pay attention to the response in your body-mind. Then try giving to someone who is deeply appreciative and feel the natural response of wanting to provide more. When someone fails to receive and appreciate what you give, there is recoil and reflexive reluctance to give more. Appreciation and gratitude are universal signals for wanting more; lack of appreciation is the universal signal for wanting less. Pay attention to how you react and consider how this reflects what's happening around you all the time, in ways both large and small. If you want more love, money, and attention, get excited about the smallest possible signs of it in your life. Send the message of *more, please*.

This also works with generosity. Just like gratitude, there is an operating principle in which giving sends an activating signal. If you want money, find a way to give some—it doesn't need to be a lot, but enough to feel that tiny pinch of discomfort that's often an unspoken part of being generous. If it's attention you want, pay attention to someone else instead of waiting for it: send a note, a text, or make a call. If you want people to smile at you, smile at them—it's like transmitting a signal to the world. When you want love, you need to send a little bit out in your actions. Although this may feel a little unfair—especially because the people who need money and love the most tend to have so little—but it's a reminder that giving and receiving is like a wheel that sometimes needs a little push to get going.

BALANCE

Natural balance is not an accounting practice. If we need to repair an imbalance, we may need to engage in conscious acts that temporarily resemble keeping score; however, the goal is a naturally occurring, homeostatic-style dynamic balance that stays within a comfortable range and self-corrects to remain level. When giving and taking operate as a complementary opposite principle, they are healthy and relatively balanced (see Chapter 3). When we have a healthy, balanced capacity in our hubs, we can naturally feel when we need more or sense an arising impulse to contribute. Knowing we are worthy makes asking for what we need a graceful practice, and with boundaries, being asked for something we cannot give is not a threat—we simply say no.

MISERLINESS AND MARTYRDOM VERSUS DESTRUCTIVE GENEROSITY

Miserliness is on the opposite side of the spectrum to destructive generosity, which is giving when we don't have enough for ourselves. These two behavior patterns represent polarities in the adaptations of this hub and impact how we love and connect. Miserliness is the opposite and opposing expression of feeling worthy and loved; a fear that we don't have enough and that if we don't look out for ourselves, nobody else will. For some folks who are blocked in their ability to give, the act brings up paralyzing anxiety and defenses. The slight discomfort of loss that comes with giving can be emotionally overwhelming for someone with a shrinking adaptation in this hub, someone who will tend to avoid attachment to people (along with the vulnerabilities that attachments create), and so, excessive boundaries, protections, and rationalizations are erected.

There is a natural twinge of discomfort with giving that comes from our deep reflexes of safety and protection, which may register giving as loss. Donating stained hand-me-downs, used socks, or anything that needs repair is not the kind of giving I mean here. We *feel* when we give. The hesitation before hitting a donate button or the internal process and evaluation we do before offering money to a friend in need is part of giving. The admiration of giving is like commending another person's ability to tolerate that pinch of sacrifice. Yet there's another side to giving: the friend—the pinch masochist—who picks up the tab for the entire table but doesn't have the money to pay their rent. If giving makes you feel safe—even when it puts the safety and security of your basic needs at risk—it's worth noticing whether contribution is experienced as a conditional requirement for belonging.

DEVOTION: LOVE IS A VERB

I discuss the discipline of devotion in the third hub, but here we appreciate that love is a verb, and how consistently showing up is how we express it—and that perfectionism as the enemy. Aspiring to be our best is different from requiring perfection. By reducing or eliminating the pressure and shame of perfectionism, we show up as we are and give the best of what we have to offer. Each day of showing up builds momentum and equity—and the more equity we have, the greater the momentum and trust we earn with ourselves and others. As I discuss above, showing up on the shitty days is especially important. Every day we wake up and decide what we commit to, and because of this, love is new every day. We experience joy and sadness, pleasure and pain, good times and bad, but through them all, showing up demonstrates love as it increases our capacity.

The process of growing capacity for devotion doesn't necessarily require other people. Time spent with nature, plants, and animals provides a way back to the devotion and surrender found through connection. Connection will find us even if we try to avoid it: we find love with animals, nature, plants, and in art—and the deepening of self-awareness and acceptance is love in action.

HUMANIZATION

The awareness within this hub ties into the shared fabric of our humanity. Most of us know inherently that no human being is superior to another and that all people deserve love, dignity, respect, and safety. But the forces of dehumanization will have us convinced that folks put themselves in bad positions because they are characteristically bad or are paying the price of consequences; keep in mind that we all make plenty of terrible calls but some of us benefit from a significantly stronger and more fortified social safety net that keeps catching us and bouncing us back.

What I say next is an inconvenient truth: our limitations in love and self-worth are related to our ability to rationalize that other people have no worth or that they have lower worth than we have. By holding the position that it's *possible* to be worthless, we place ourselves in a choking bind that creates feelings of worthlessness within ourselves (and that we're only a few bad decisions away from lacking value).

There can be no complete restoration in the fourth hub without awareness of the unequal circumstances of others. Feelings of discomfort while reading and learning about racism and oppression are a symptom of the repressed self—shame, resistance, and defensiveness are all symptoms. We must learn to hear and to trust what oppressed people have to say about their lived experiences. Grief, activation, and reparative action for our fellow human beings are medicine and healing for all. Healing and repair hurt, but the alternative is a devastating slow burn of detachment from the connection to all of life. We can either defend, making a case for ourselves to continue a similar path to the one we've been on, or transcend by incorporating new information and finding new ways to do things.

Industrialization

The Industrial Revolution took many families away from their farms and moved them to cities, where the men labored in unsafe conditions as (overworked) machine operators—it was repetitive work that came with a tremendous cost to their human dignity. Philosopher Eric Hoffer wrote, "When you automate an industry, you modernize it; when you automate a life, you primitivize it." In the third hub, I discuss autonomy, purpose, and mastery as essentials for human dignity (see Chapter 6). The contemporary father who performs repetitive and meaningless work comes home and struggles to connect with his family as he bears the brunt of dehumanization and the growing sense of incompetence with age. Add to this the effects of war, cycles of persecution and oppression, addictions, trauma, and the result is that experience of our humanity seems like an indulgence. The notion of white-collar work may have led office employees to breathe a collective sigh of relief, imagining that they had escaped the assembly line and low-status manual labor. But long hours tethered to screens and the 24-hour cycle of electronic communication hardly put the modern office worker at an advantage over line workers. Similar to the addition of robotics on factory assembly lines, artificial intelligence is replacing white-collar jobs. Your humanity is a high price to pay to a system that will leave you behind; the resulting heartbreak can be seen in the faces and lives of many people as they grapple with difficult truths about loyalty, belonging, and compassion—and providing for their families.

THEMES

When we're comfortable with loved ones, we soften, relax, and express ourselves more freely. We can enjoy having our needs being met and can support the people who matter most to us. Belonging, along with how the need for it shapes and transforms us, is a central theme in this hub. Here, I discuss some of the fundamental entities of belonging that shape us, including family, society, culture, intimacy, the self, the environment, and the associated behavior patterns and paradoxes we navigate within each of them.

FAMILY BELONGING WITH ATTACHMENT STYLES

The foundation of our early programming was built through the familial conditions of love and acceptance that frame our worldview and shape our behavior patterns in adulthood. Our early experiences in our families taught us how to behave in relationships.

Again, we're born into families and communities full of people with lives already in progress. How we fit into these groups determines how we're treated, which we may perceive as objective and logical because it's the only way we know. Yet fitting in is entirely subjective. Our parents' ability to provide basic needs, have emotional bandwidth, and manage their own unrealized dreams and aspirations are just some of the factors they were juggling when we were born. Motivational author Louise Hay wrote in *You Can Heal Your Life* that we are all victims of victims, and if our mother was not taught to love, she would be unable to teach us to love.

Conditional love: Parents may have fantasies of their child continuing a legacy, of attending schools and joining organizations they consider important, and of gender—what it means to be a boy or a girl. There's also the (understandable) hope that a child will be agreeable, likable, and easy to raise. These dreams are fine, but the conditional love and support often showered on children as they follow these parental dreams and directions—many mapped before their births—can take a lifetime to reconcile. Children will contemplate and attempt to understand the difference between what's true for themselves as individuals and what's true for their family; in some places there will be overlap, but in others they will be forced to navigate conflict. There are many versions of ways that we behave to gain our parents' favor, and the reality is that families are composed of people from the general population, and their capacity to love was not a prerequisite for having children. They do the best they can, and even in the best-case scenarios, their parenting is always going to be less than perfect—and working through manageable struggles makes us strong. Even if we didn't learn to love, this is a capacity that can be nourished, supported, and grown when we give it conscious attention and work on it through somatic practices. It's through true belonging and connection that we can reconcile and heal maladaptation from interruptions in all our hubs. Our heartbeat and naturally occurring breath symbolize the enduring commitment our body and life have for us—and conscious breath plays a unique role in restoring dynamic balance and softening holding patterns.

Parents and the members of our childhood households shape how we experience early belonging. How we love ourselves now is how we were loved when we were children. How we were taught to love, and early family belonging, form attachment patterns that persist throughout adult life. *Attached: The New Science of Adult Attachment and How It Can Help You Find—and Keep—Love* authors Amir Levine and Rachel Heller examine three predominant attachment styles as secure, anxious, and avoidant:

Secure attachment: Are we attended to and seen for our unique needs, and is this attention and positive regard given to us without excessive conditions? Do we know that our mother may be frustrated when we make a mess but that she still loves us even when she's angry? If we do something embarrassing in public, do our caregivers attune to us and our needs, or does social embarrassment consume them? It's about being lovable and pleasing to our parents when we're good yet knowing we're loved even when we were misbehaving.

Anxious attachment: Children who believe that they deserve love only when their behavior is pleasing to their caregivers are excessively pleasing and highly attuned to a parent's needs, waking up every day believing they're starting with a clean slate, needing to earn love with every action. When love is experienced as highly conditional during childhood, our programming may have us migrate toward people with behavior similar to what we experienced early in life and may have us act out the pattern of needing to constantly prove ourselves to earn love.

Avoidant attachment: This attachment style will be highly protected yet will want to be saved by a perfect love that's offered without conditions. But because perfection is impossible and no adult relationship can exist without conditions, this is a defense that hides a deep feeling of inadequacy. A take-it-or-leave-it attitude hides the pain of loneliness and

deep disappointment. To create a sense of control, this leads to preemptive abandonment of relationships to avoid feeling abandoned again. This is a person who attempts perfection to win approval. This attachment style uses perfection and high achievement like a magnet to attract people without becoming vulnerable.

SOCIAL BELONGING WITH PERSONAS AND PROJECTION

Personas

For many of us, it was a motley crew that shaped our early social programming. Our first friends are cousins, children of our parents' friends, kids in the neighborhood and at school, or religious-community peers. We're so malleable and open in our early years that it only takes a few bizarre or mean comments from other kids to leave us fixated, and sometimes the desire to prove them wrong persists into adulthood. When kids have practically no authority to change their social environment, the primary coping mechanism is to change themselves.

In the early years of friendships, cliques play a significant role in socialization, sometimes with hurtful games of belonging and exclusion. As we grow older (and if our fourth hub grows its capacity for self-worth and considerate connection with others), these tribal games and their associated pressures tend to relax. But in the twilight of initial development, these games can get overwhelming for a child.

The agony and the ecstasy of a new social connection (or even the rebirth of an old one) is energizing and exciting. In kindergarten, the excitement of new friends filled us with emotion and energy, and when we'd return home and try to describe our new friend using our limited vocabulary, we'd struggle to do our adoration justice. In the glow of new love (platonic or otherwise), life is amplified. The sky looks bluer, the grass greener, and we wake up excited to meet the day. As social creatures, we want to hold on to these incredible connections, so we begin to adapt ourselves: we diminish and amplify parts of ourselves to make relationships work—we develop personas.

These personas are masks we wear to emphasize qualities and behaviors that our friends and family prefer. We learn through trial and error that a mask can conceal qualities and behaviors that have caused embarrassment or have led to criticism or even ostracism. For example, we may hide nerdy, babyish, or gendered interests around certain friends or disproving siblings, but when we spend time with friends who share these interests, we blossom and play our hearts out. There are different masks used with parents, teachers, and friends. In divorced families, the need to take sides and to develop conflicting personas can fracture a child's heart. I interviewed Imani, who remembered spending weekends with her dad feigning interest in motorcycles and even wearing clothing with his favorite motorcycle brand. "He loved it, and I learned things I didn't care about because he got so excited. I would bask in his happiness and attention." When she went home to her mother, she returned to her pink bedroom to happily play with her Bratz dolls. Her mother told her that she didn't have to pretend to like motorcycles. "I was nine years old and intuitively, I knew my dad would struggle to relate to me. It meant more to me to feel a connection with him, and I sensed that he would be challenged if he had to try and relate to my real interests." In the second hub, I discussed the rejected self, in which we hide certain spontaneously arising behaviors to reduce friction in our home life. The development of more advanced social masks in the fourth hub is a continuation of this natural tendency. Adapting to our environment is part of our human nature.

But personas can get in the way of building trust when we sense that something is being concealed. James, the CEO of a tech company, told me that when he interviews candidates for executive roles, "If someone is overly friendly and responds with safe and scripted answers, I wonder what they are hiding and why they don't feel comfortable showing more of themselves. I figure they either have skeletons in their closet or they lack self-awareness. Some companies may like excessively positive personalities, but in my experience, whatever is behind the facade is a mess I'll have to clean up."

The personas we adopt contain gender expectations, such as the unemotional big boy or the polite, sweet, nice little girl. For example, a five-year-old boy is told to *Stop crying, you're too old for that* when crying is a developmentally appropriate response to disappointment or nervousness. A girl of the same age may be allowed to cry—in fact, she may even be comforted. As adults, men who cry or who become openly sad or hurt can get accused of *Crying like a little girl* or are encouraged to stop by being told to put on their "big-boy pants."

This gendered ridicule doesn't just happen at home. Even if parents support the expression of emotions regardless of age and gender, peers may laugh at a tearful response and/or may genderize their ridicule. This can be both a painful embarrassment for the child and emotionally difficult for parents to navigate.

Projection

When we feel safe and our nervous system feels even keeled, we tend to be more accepting of others. Do you notice if your judgment of others tends to soften and relax when you feel good, happy, and at peace with yourself? Notice how compassion for others tends to correlate with the compassion we have for ourselves: it doesn't mean that we tolerate bad behavior, it means we can be understanding and uncritical as we maintain boundaries. As adults, we get the chance to shape our environment, choose our friends, and decide where we spend our time. We can begin the process of recovering the hidden self by watching where we have strong reactions to people who are minding their own business—often, people openly express some aspect of what we've concealed (even from ourselves). What harmless behavior in others makes you feel uncomfortable? The rejected self, relegated to the subconscious, will keep knocking on the door of our conscious mind through dreams and intense feelings of disgust, rejection, and fixation when we see our hidden qualities expressed in others. In Shakespeare's *Hamlet*, Queen Gertrude says, "The lady doth protest too much," referring to the play character's exaggerated reaction as an admission of guilt. *I know you are, but what am I?* as a response to an insult gets straight to the point of calling out insults as projections—how could this schoolyard defense persist, be passed down through generations, unless it spoke to a deeper truth?

When we see a stranger, what we choose to see is an expression of our own worldview—our observations and opinions are subjective. Remember my moon-gazing relativity analogy in the parallax discussion: looking at the moon with the naked eye, it can seem enormous; looking at it in a photograph, it can seem very small (see Chapter 3). What we focus on expands, and when we focus and fixate on things we don't like, perhaps it's a knock on the door from the hidden self attempting to reveal itself. And keep in mind that how others treat you also involves projection: people who cheat tend to accuse others of cheating, and liars accuse others of lying. Initially, how people treat you demonstrates who they are, not who you are, which is an important consideration for choosing the people we allow into our life. But eventually, because we're social and connected beings, the folks we surround ourselves with influence who we become.

ORGANIZATIONS: LEADERS VERSUS MANAGERS

Managers demand compliance, leaders inspire commitment. Leaders create a place for people to connect to their purpose and to develop mastery with the dignity of autonomy; managers create a place that conforms to their own comfort. Coaches, teachers, and others in positions of authority oversee the places where children interact outside the home—some act like managers and some act as leaders. Managers seek to standardize to the point of dehumanization and demoralization, standing in stark contrast to leaders who empower and can allow and appreciate individuality. It's often the leaders from our childhood who saw our authentic selves who provide a trail of breadcrumbs to follow when we excavate our authentic selves. Qualities that contribute to leadership are humility and curiosity, mixed with the courage and ability to stand one's ground. Managers who use authority to demand compliance tend to struggle with communication skills, and lack the fortitude to advocate for the people who depend on them—they're individuals in positions of authority who are primarily concerned with their own interests. Managers think they are supposed to have all the answers and believe they're supposed to be the most talented person on the team, so they're either highly defensive and/or hire mediocre talent. Author Simon Sinek writes in *Start with Why: How Great Leaders Inspire Everyone to Take Action*, "The role of a leader is not to come up with great ideas. The role of a leader is to create an environment where great ideas happen." The Parinama Method leadership style involves healthy, dynamic functioning in our hubs, specifically between the power of individuation in the third hub and communication skills in the fifth hub (see Chapter 8); it balances leaders' needs with the individual needs of their people, along with the long-term good of the entire group and organization.

CULTURAL BELONGING WITH ANIMA AND ANIMUS

The traditions of a culture—foods, music, holidays, and other customs and conventions—can be like a glue that holds people together. Belonging to a culture is the deep familiarity and comfort of home that can be shared and experienced anywhere. The food that was cooked for us as children connects us to the same meals shared by our ancestors, and the deeper we go into their traditions, the more connected we tend to feel with ourselves. Years ago, I was lonely and alone in Germany around Christmastime. The evergreen wreaths with candles, the advent calendars with little picture windows for each day of December, the sugar-coated Christmas fruit bread, along with the imagery and decoration, linked me to deep feelings of connection. The depth of my response surprised me as both soothing and joyful.

Yet culture, with its associated faith traditions, can also represent painful restrictions of personal integrity and self-expression. Gender, for example, is often reduced to simple roles that serve cultural order and assign duties and obligations. But gender identity reaches into profound aspects of how we experience ourselves. Jung described the anima as the unconscious feminine side of a man and the animus as the unconscious masculine side of a woman (see Chapter 6). This alludes to an inner paradox, one that transcends the traditionally binary view of gender. Some cultures' origin stories begin with the genders merged and aver that humans were created through separating this unification. Scholars examined translations of the origin of the Adam and Eve story and found that they were also separated from this merged state—not that Eve was grown from Adam's rib. Transgender activist Janet Mock's first memoir, *Redefining Realness: My Path to Womanhood, Identity, Love & So Much More*, states, "Gender and gender identity, sex and sexuality, are spheres of self-discovery that overlap and relate, but are not the same. Every one of us has a sexual orientation and a gender identity. Simply put, our sexual orientation has to do with whom we get into bed with, while our gender identity has to do with whom we get into bed as."

When I was seven years old, I stood at the end of the line for the Teacups ride at an amusement park. It was the final ride of the day, and I was nervous about my position being last in line. But my fears about missing the ride were eclipsed when the ride attendant gestured to me and said,

"There's room for one more—he can go." It felt like the wind got knocked out of me. For reasons I still don't fully understand, I was devastated and demoralized. I knew I was a girl and being mistaken as otherwise upset something deep inside me. As a child who felt very much that I was a girl, there was something profoundly upsetting to me about being mistaken for a boy that had nothing to do with sexuality, an aspect of myself that at the time was still many years away from emerging. There was something important about myself that had not been seen and the invalidation of it left me stunned and deflated.

INTIMATE BELONGING WITH EROS AND THANATOS

Falling in love feels like finding a place in the world where we truly belong. In the early stages of romantic love, we are lifted to new heights. Our partner sees us with what Perel calls "selective perception," and there is a sense of great possibility as we bask in this new, enhanced sense of self (see Chapter 5). We're shown how love can transform us into our best self. But we're given that first beginner's taste to see what's possible before the real work of transformation is presented to us—when the relationship gets tested, and it must either grow or die. Jung wrote in *Modern Man in Search of a Soul*, "The meeting of two personalities is like the contact of two chemical substances: if there is a reaction, both are transformed." A person, in the glow of a new relationship, is like a glimpse at what's possible seen through the transforming eyes of love. The power of connection keeps us in the crucible of transformation as we experience both pain and pleasure as catalysts of growth.

Couples' therapists Harville Hendricks and Helen LaKelly Hunt developed Imago Relationship Therapy (*imago* means a subconscious composite of unresolved parental characteristics). Hendricks and Hunt assert in *Getting the Love You Want* that we select for these qualities and behaviors that are subconsciously recognized in prospective partners. As a result, the people we fall in love with feel familiar, as if we have known them all our lives. The authors detail the process to resolve the dynamics from our childhood that hold us back from love, and explain that the initial, highly charged familiarity with a romantic interest arises from subconscious recognition of shared characteristics with our parents, specifically the unresolved dynamics we have with them. Although we may be drawn to attributes that are initially experienced as contrary to our parents, the more subtle, hidden dynamics tend to play out as a relationship evolves. And as the saying goes, what initially attracts us eventually repels us.

We find the imprints of interruptions from earlier hubs in our adaptive behavior patterns that carry into adulthood in our intimate relationships. The expectation to be understood without explicit explanation or the expression of specific needs (or mind reading), asks a partner to intuitively know what to do or to scramble to find the solution, which resembles the expectation placed on new parents attending to their distressed infant. If we expect our partner to guess our needs, we may recognize an opportunity to develop our second-hub emotional literacy, along with fifth-hub communication. If we have work to do in the second hub, we may sense but not understand our emotions. I discuss earlier another second-hub dynamic that can present itself in adult relationships—what psychologists call "emotional contagion"—or escalating an emotionally charged conversation and needing to see one's pain reflected on the other person's face (see Chapter 5). This is an adult attempt to attune, which is developmentally appropriate for young children, that is, learning our emotions through their mirrored reflection on a parent's responsive face. But even as an adult, being met with a blank face can be so distressing that the escalation becomes nuclear. This second-hub combination of being an emotional mystery to oneself with the hunger for attunement can result in an unfortunate aftermath following a conflict—one partner wonders who they are with shame, and the other wonders who its partner is with shock and fear. When the aggressing partner eventually de-escalates, this person usually returns to a calm state and sometimes is not fully able to remember fighting and feels remorseful and apologetic. An apology may lead to a sense of relief for the couple, but if partners don't work on the second-hub emotional literacy, they will repeat the escalating behavior whenever they're activated. As a result, a crossroads emerges for the other partner: walk on eggshells, walk away, or get help. (This can become increasingly complicated when there is a financial power imbalance or shared children in a relationship.)

Eros/Thanatos

"How can I miss you if you won't go away?" asks a smothered partner. In a relationship, a balance of absence and presence heightens the experience of the other person. If a couple spends every waking moment together the charge weakens, but if they never see each other, it's extinguished. A relationship needs its little separations to be continuously reborn—and the complementary opposites of togetherness and separation form a central paradox in all relationships. In absence, the spark of newness is refreshed. Perel says our intimate relationships are, "[A] paradox to be managed, not a problem to be solved."

The intimate relationship is energized and enlivened by a near-constant balancing of complementary opposites: the intense merging of eroticism (Eros), and the longing created through separation (Thanatos). The passion of Eros and separation of Thanatos cannot exist together, but each craves the other. Desire and security are never seen in the same room together. Love, when it's alive, dances and moves between one polarity and the other. This dynamic even plays out between the personalities of a couple: Perel says that every relationship has one person afraid of losing the relationship while the other fears losing itself. When a relationship gets stuck in gridlock, it may need a nudge of either separation or togetherness to keep it going.

BELONGING TO YOURSELF WITH SELF-ACCEPTANCE AND SELF-LOVE

There's a stigma of selfishness that will malign self-love, not understanding that our strength and ability to do more and to be of service comes from a full cup, not through being drained, diminished, and imbalanced by servitude. Whether we reflexively assume positive or negative intent in the actions of others is a good diagnostic for the relationship we have with ourselves. Our knee-jerk beliefs in other people's underlying intentions (and what motivates them) is a projection of our internal universe which is the result of adaptations and inclinations that subconsciously operate from the factory-installed programming of our earliest years. And although the people who programmed us can be held accountable, they are no longer responsible. If we want to update our programming, we must do the work.

Self-love is the experience of being you. The only person you belong to is yourself—you may share yourself, but you're the only one who's always there from start to finish, directly experiencing your life. The programming of our hubs creates filters and adaptations that can distort this relationship with chronic shame, guilt, and fear through an internalized critical voice. Do we make mistakes? Sure. Is there always room to grow and evolve? Of course. But there's nothing wrong with you. You solve problems, but *you* are not a problem. Treating your mistakes with the kindness and patience you'd offer a child, that is, assuming positive intent with yourself, is essential for self-love.

Again, how a person behaves toward us reveals more about who that person is than it does about who we are, and how we treat others reveals the same thing to them. How we treat others is a mirror of the relationship we have with ourselves. Our patience, kindness, boundaries, and self-respect radiate outward. How it feels to be you is a big part of what people experience when they spend time with you. The experience of self-love in another person is felt by basking in the glow of their self-acceptance. I received the following note from a client: "Through this process, I feel love in ways that I compared to putting on glasses for the first time. This was always here? It's so clear, bright, and beautiful. Before my 'glasses,' everything was fuzzy and now, the boundaries are clear, the colors brighter, and life feels good. Even on bad days I have compassion for myself. I allow myself to feel bad and give myself room to explore and respect my feelings."

BELONGING TO THE NATURAL ENVIRONMENT

The often-cited Chief Seattle statement, "The earth does not belong to us. We belong to the earth," may have unclear historical origin, but the sentiment is undeniable. In our modern homes and lives, the natural world is often viewed through a window as though it's distant and separate from us. Yet the relationship we have with the environment is profoundly intimate: it's in the cellular and atomic makeup of our bodies. We use modern conveniences to cook food, provide water to our homes, light our rooms, and cool the air in them, yet our bodies are part of (and depend on) the natural world and its condition determines our survival. We continue to see how modern life can't always keep us safe and separated from the harsher forces of the natural world—and anxiety and depression can come from feeling disconnected from ourselves and our true nature. We connect to a profound level of belonging, when we can feel ourselves in concert with the rhythms, phases, and cycles of nature.

CONFLICT

The crucible of transformation is experienced in conflict resolution; avoidance and peacekeeping are ways the intensity remains held at a distance. We may need to keep conflict at a distance when our emotional capacity becomes easily overwhelmed or we may seek it because the intensity feels energizing (even though over time, conflict is exhausting). Oppositely, a relationship in which conflict is not tolerated becomes frozen because unresolved, unspoken issues either get surfaced as irritation, frustration, and anger or they become internalized and require denial and ongoing tolerance of sub-par dynamics. The most profound work of our lives is frequently found in our repeating conflicts, the ones that follow us from relationship to relationship. These are the conflicts that have us wondering why we keep attracting the same types of people into our lives.

Being human involves conflict, regardless of whether we're willing to face it. Perel discusses couples wishing for their partner to be "fixed" so that the relationship can be "saved." When our conflicts feel like they're caused by external problems that would be solved if everyone else changed, both our power and self-awareness remain outside of us. Perel explains that conflicts are not about the subject matter; instead they deal with three predominant underlying themes:

1. Power and control (who in a relationship gets prioritized);

2. Care and closeness (Do you feel supported—does your partner have your back?); and

3. Respect and recognition (Do you feel valued?).

These are all matters of the lower hubs. The work needed to resolve our inner conflicts is the only way to resolve the outer ones and doing so makes us more patient with others and more confident in creating boundaries.

When we are in conflict, it's natural for protective feelings and emotions to get stirred up. When we feel safe, loved, and accepted, we can stop defending our bad behavior and take responsibility for it. Revealing ourselves through vulnerability is an opportunity to grow our capacity for the love of both ourselves and others. This hub's healing involves softening and allowing; we can simultaneously be in conflict while we soften and allow. If people don't feel safe because they feel judged or they're oppressed and experience gaslighting (being told it's all in their head), conflict may travel inward until it eventually erupts outward. The human spirit has integrity that may conceal conflict temporarily, but if it's suppressed for too long, it eventually reveals itself in some sort of corrective (albeit disorderly) eruption.

INTERRUPTIONS AND STRESSORS

Fourth-hub interruptions are primarily about what you trade so that you can belong. In this hub, you examine which parts of your authentic identity, that is, expressions of your integrity and your unique, distinctive quirks, need either to be diminished or completely hidden so you can enjoy the refuge of social belonging. Much of the hiding starts before we can remember, and it's in the initial development of this hub when conscious memories begin to form—but initially, these formations are sporadic. Memories are stored using images of distinct locations (I discuss memory further in the sixth hub, Chapter 9—SEE). All hubs have overlap, for example, memory and vision are the domains of the sixth hub, which is in the eyes and brow, while connection and belonging are the domains of this hub, located in the upper chest, shoulders, and hands; they're all connected but individually headquartered. As adults, our ability and willingness to remember through the sixth hub, links in with our first early memories starting primarily in the fourth hub—everything before will rely almost entirely on somatic practices.

Memories from our early days of socialization and bonding with peers are inconsistent and similar to the previous hubs; our present-day actions are more indicative of past programming and in many ways are more reliable than memories. Because this is the initial hub in which conscious memories are accessible, sometimes images can resurface, even though they tend to be scattered. Somatic practice and conscious reclamation are immensely valuable here—again, how we love now is how we were taught to love. The interruptions I discuss here look at some of the ways this was possibly affected by early experience. The primary interruptions in this hub involve conditions placed on love, acceptance, and belonging. The early experiences of scorn, exclusion, rejection, and abuse all interrupt the healthy functioning of this hub. Again, according to Hay, a repeating message throughout is that we are victims of victims; the reparative work of evaluating ourselves and finding the qualities of love through compassionate exploration and somatic practice is profoundly restorative and transformative. This is our work to do, and to do it requires courage and is the ultimate expression of self-love.

CONDITIONAL LOVE AND ACCEPTANCE

The experience of being entirely loved as a child becomes embodied in the adult. As children, having at least one person consistently see us as delightful, important, and interesting can shape the relationship we have with ourselves, and even change the way we experience our lives. To have this person as a grandparent is terrific, but to have in a parent is sublime (and to have more than one person is a great fortune). But even with adoration at home, we must face the outside

world. The idyllic version of childhood friendship and joy we remember often crowds out some of the more sinister experiences of early socialization. Kids can be mean, teasing, and labeling others as weirdos and punishing different kids through exclusion and/or bullying. Experiencing early child-on-child bigotry, misogyny, and/or gender binarism is hurtful to an openhearted child. Kids tell jokes to get laughs, with the shock of cruelty added for effect. The playground can be a place of joy and freedom, but it can also be a petri dish of children experimenting with the power of being mean.

Early in life we hide or obscure parts of ourselves, depending on the conditions of acceptance and belonging that are presented to us. If we were not taught to love in the home, as adults we become even more desperate for love and approval and become vulnerable to counterfeit representations of it. These can be parasitic, ranging from narcissistic partners to cult-like abuse practices in groups.

If we didn't have the safety to ask questions and to speak our mind or were indoctrinated with racist, misogynist, and/or anti-LGBTQ+ rhetoric, the programming below our consciousness becomes part of the rejected self. We are subconsciously aware that we're not fully loved when certain versions of being human are unacceptable to the people we love the most. Knowing that there are conditions required for belonging to our family creates an impossible choice for a young child: either believe and belong or face exile. Of course, for people who experience persecution and prejudice, the question of how much to hide to be culturally and socially accepted is impossible to gauge if there's something that cannot be hidden that affects social acceptance. To be mature and developed in this hub, we must have tolerance, curiosity, and compassion for the lived experiences of people who are different from us. We don't need to understand another's lifestyle to view it as valid.

PERFECTIONISM

Perfection, a theme throughout the hubs, is the epitome of conditional acceptance. If we inflict perfectionism on ourselves by hiding our flaws and bad days, we hurt ourselves and the ones we love by not offering the opportunity to be fully loved for who we are: the good, the bad, the ugly. Parents who feel pressure to be flawless, and so try to present themselves as perfect, positive ideals for their children, imprint these same unrealistic expectations on them when they hide tears, emotions, or deny and act defensive about their own mistakes.

Perfectionism becomes poisonous when it causes hiding or any striving that has us believing that our happiness, true belonging, and wholeness exist in the future—once we finally earn them. Again, for a child, having an adult who consistently shows up for you, pays attention without trying to change you, delights in who you are, and takes the time to see and appreciate you is essential for building self-worth. A little kick in the ass can be a good thing, but too many kicks and we're demoralized. If the connection to our importance, our uniqueness, and our worthiness is not established early in life, it's challenging to love ourselves in adulthood. Moziah, an interviewee in his early 30s, talked about evaluating his relationships: "I realized that I discredited kindness. When people treated me like I was special, I didn't trust them. I would migrate toward and respond to critical and difficult bosses and discount kind feedback. I was attracted to judgmental friends and boyfriends. I rationalized that I was tough and that the right people for me should be able to handle it." But when he started feeling connection within himself, he said, "I started looking at my relationships. I was unfamiliar with loving kindness, and the people who made me comfortable were the ones who were more like the critical family that turned away from me when they found me disagreeable. Simply becoming aware of this has caused a big change in me."

When self-worth and positive self-regard are unfamiliar, people who have it can be disturbing to be around, offending our sensibilities. If receiving is difficult because we don't feel worthy, we may defend ourselves against generosity. The devotion within love involves surrender, softening, and allowing, and perfectionism is the antithesis of this. Devotional discipline is the replacement for punishing perfectionism; you're remarkable right now, exactly as you are.

PARENTS WHO DON'T KNOW HOW TO LOVE

Physical and emotional absence and neglect happen on a spectrum from mild to severe. Because presence and consistency are pillars of love, abandonment and neglect are significant interruptions. Parents who are there for us when we need them—and who are available when we don't—demonstrate the devotion of love that's the opposite of loneliness and isolation.

Emotional maturity and capacity in the second hub play a significant role in a parent's ability to love and, as a result, in what they teach us about love. Caregivers who are inattentive or absent cause significant hurt in this hub. Neglect in early life results in protective adaptations in all hubs (but specifically in the fourth), and in the ability to enjoy connection and belonging. The adaptive protection is to either shrink the perceived need for love or to inflate with overcompensating behaviors to fill empty, loveless relationships with expressions of love.

Oppositely, caregivers who smother also cause interruption. As a child, Josh, now in his late 20s, was his mother's best friend. "She and my dad didn't have a good relationship. She called him 'the wallet.' My mom did everything for me and I loved the attention, but it came at a cost. I was always managing her loneliness by spending time with her. As I grew older, I wanted my freedom. The memory of her slumped shoulders and sad face when I'd leave the house still makes my chest ache. I haven't formed deep relationships with women, mostly because I feel so incapable of taking care of their needs, but I also fear being smothered by their expectations, so I get defensive." Even if he had wanted to, as a child, Josh couldn't fill the adult-size void left vacant by a father's inattention and by his mother's inability to make her own friends. He was left feeling guilty, inadequate, and responsible for his mother's unhappiness, in addition to feeling deeply conflicted as he pursued his own.

Children who feel responsible for either fulfilling household duties and the childrearing of siblings or who are expected to follow restrictive religious practices have unspoken expectations placed on them that require levels of responsibility far beyond what's developmentally appropriate and possible. Sometimes, taking responsibility is the only choice a child has when a parent dies or there's addiction in the home. Some children will attempt to rise to these impossible tasks, then feel inadequate in their ability to meet the challenges. In the third hub, imposed maturation causes interruption in a child's sense of personal power, and in the fourth it causes feelings of inadequacy in relationships.

These challenges are usually left unspoken, and naming the functions and responsibilities performed and the age they took place helps heal these hurts and feelings of inadequacy. Name the tasks and the age when they were placed on you—now think of a child in your adult life at this age and imagine placing the same expectations on it.

SCORN

Familiarity with scorn and criticism and the strong desire to avoid them carry the consequence of working to outrun disapproval—along with people pleasing—at the expense of your own needs and integrity. If you imagine standing up for what you believe in or accomplishing something that proves naysayers wrong, who is your imagined audience and, in this fantasy, how does it respond to you when you triumph? The protections and adaptations children use to support their survival in the fourth hub are complex and often involve pretending to be what other people want them to be—a behavior that can be met with scorn for being fake, creating a compounding effect of shame.

There's a Chilean saying: "Criticizing a musician is easy, but it's more difficult when you have a guitar in your hand." All the people we meet are on a continuum of who they have been, who they are now, and who they are becoming. Patience and faith in people are a vote for their potential—too much criticism so often leads to negative behavior and deeper defensive patterns. It's easy to point out flaws, but it requires significant effort to understand another person's perspective—a life experience that is different from your own—and hold space and offer constructive curiosity and support. Behavioral scientist Robert Cialdini, author of *Influence: The Psychology of Persuasion*, makes the case that encouraging people to live up to their best self is the more effective method of persuasion—more powerful than criticism. He spoke on a podcast about Anwar Sadat, the former president of Egypt, who successfully negotiated with the Israelis for the Sinai Peninsula. Sadat had started talks saying (I paraphrase): "I'm so glad I get you as a negotiation partner, because everyone knows how important fairness and equanimity is to the Jewish community."

There will always be people who are reflexively negative. Do you tend to focus on anticipating negativity or can you right size it as a normal consequence of any decisive action? In this hub we seek to resolve orientation around criticism and to shift focus from apprehension of negative responses to a focus on people who will be receptive to us. Consider Huber's words: "If a voice is not speaking compassionately to you, it has nothing worthwhile to tell you. Everything you need to know will come to you in compassion." There will always be critics, and some will offer perspectives worth considering—but don't take criticism too hard; it represents a single voice, and who you focus on is your choice.

REJECTION AND LOSS

Rejection, loss, betrayal, abandonment, and death are common and highly affecting interruptions in the fourth hub. Children can't help but love, and the size of the hurt of early loss and rejection relative to tiny bodies can be overwhelming, which can lead to immense grief getting perceived and internalized as personal shortcomings that can feel life-threatening without the support and tools for processing it. When we experience rejection as adults, these early pathways of overwhelming and unresolved loss can be activated by seemingly simple events. A slight loss or rejection, such as losing a social media follower or a friend not immediately returning a text message, can feel perplexingly amplified.

Children become disconnected from both inner and outer reality when they silence and distrust their true selves. The emotions are massive and without support to help understand them, children will be engulfed and may rely on the coping mechanism of *imagining* themselves capable, which can involve fantasy and even deception. This can also become part of the hidden self that benefits from the process of conscious reclamation.

For young children the experience of divorce creates complex dynamics with feelings of betrayal and abandonment that are confusing. Young children are only beginning to understand that people around them have lives that are separate from theirs. Kids take personal responsibility for loss because of their (developmentally appropriate) inability to comprehend the inner lives of others. Altruism emerges in this hub, but sympathy depends on our internal experience database, which will never contain the full complexity of every human experience (see Chapter 9). Initial sympathy connects us through experiences like our own, but if we continue to mature, this growth evolves to incorporate curiosity, becoming compassion for the unfamiliar lived experiences of others. Compassion and curiosity allow us to believe people and to respect experiences that are foreign to our own.

Psychologist and researcher John Gottman has done extensive work on divorce prediction and marital stability for over four decades and he can predict the future success of a marriage with 83 percent accuracy by how a couple communicates. Gottman identifies the Four Horsemen of the Apocalypse for a marriage: criticism, defensiveness, stonewalling, and the most revealing of all, contempt. Contempt is a pattern of attitudes and behaviors displaying characteristics of disgust and irritation. Words of contempt are his ultimate determination of a marriage's impending failure. Gottman observes the four-horsemen attributes within marriages—but what about when we express them in our relationship with ourselves? What happens when the voice of contempt is coming from inside? Perhaps we shake our head as we scorn ourselves for being forgetful or for making a mistake while distracted: "You're such an idiot," we may mutter. If we did this to a spouse, Gottman would predict a divorce.

ABUSE

Spanking, yelling, excessive punishment, or any other type of abuse causes interruption in all the hubs. But potent interruption is caused to the fourth hub when we're told that abuse is done out of love. The effect of abuse is magnified when we're told that it's done as an act of love. *This hurts me more than it hurts you* or *I'm doing this for your good* when spanking or excessively punishing are lies. Psychologist and child-development specialist Eileen Kennedy-Moore points out that children don't learn from suffering, but "by doing things right." Supporting children in growing their abilities rather than through punishment and hurt is how they develop.

I interviewed Cindy, who grew up in a home where her father told her, "Only the people who love you will be critical because they're taking the risk to help make you better." She believed this but found it to be painfully untrue when her first marriage fell apart under the weight of her endless judgment and criticism: "I thought I was helping my husband by pointing out all his flaws like my parents had done with me. It wasn't until it was too late that I could see what I was doing. Craig saw me as a monster, and in the end, I'd done so much damage that I couldn't rebuild the trust. I don't hold it against him. It's been many years and I still feel terrible about my behavior." Although Cindy had been in therapy for the past two decades, she told me, "I still feel the most comfortable with people who are judgmental and critical. But now it's conscious and I can manage this by identifying the red flags." Verbal and emotional abuse can also be in the form of mean teasing—hurtfully pointing out vulnerabilities and sensitivities as jokes and telling children (or adults) they're too sensitive when they respond with hurt or anger. Any mental or physical abuse that interferes with the personal boundaries of a child will cause interruptions. Physical, emotional, and excessive behavior modification are all damaging to the spirit and psyche. Essentially, consequences should be used for boundaries, and challenges and encouragement should be used for growth. Excessive punishment is a dirty fuel source for motivation that creates a lot of pollution.

ADAPTATIONS AND HOLDING PATTERNS

The fourth hub centers around the need to belong that's at the core of all human life. Our internal standard of who we believe we must be to deserve love is managed by the adaptations in this hub—although both inflating and shrinking feel unworthy of love in different ways and to varying extents. The interruptions in the fourth hub are deeply related to shame and interruptions in the lower hubs. It is the early interruptions that inform our ability to connect with others, and they are often the result of the same familial forces impacting personal power in the third hub. Although both shrinking and inflating adaptations affect feelings of self-worth, shrinking uses a defensive tactic of being inaccessible and inflating uses an offensive strategy of working tirelessly to be irreplaceable.

CHARACTERISTICS OF A BALANCED FOURTH HUB

- Is both receptive and generous—has gratitude and the ability to share while maintaining healthy boundaries

- Respects others and does not surrender inner calm to gossip or chaos

- Can be grateful for simple things

- Knows love is not a transaction yet it has practical aspects—knows love requires attention, effort, and parity

- Appreciates animals and has a relationship with the environment

- Has balanced and full breath

- Is mobile and pain free in the chest and shoulders

- Respects and accepts that people have separate lives outside of its relationships with them

- Feels—and is experienced by others as—authentic; its self-acceptance inspires others

- Actively engages in humanizing all people—is curious and open to people being themselves, aware of both the uniqueness and shared humanity in all people

CHARACTERISTICS OF AN OUT-OF-BALANCE FOURTH HUB

- Believes connections come from having the same experiences as others—*That's exactly like me*—in an attempt to connect; struggles with people who are different

- Has a hard time understanding anything that is not similar to its own direct experience, tends to orient around its own experience, invalidates the lived experiences of others when not matched

- Struggles with either giving or taking—will be very good at one over the other

- Operates from assumptions and generalizations about people

- Has difficulty taking deep breaths

- Has pain, aching, tightness in the chest, upper back, or shoulders

Both shrinking and inflating adaptations can coexist in the same person. A person may appear to be strong and highly guarded (shrinking) as a professional, but in a relationship may give to the point of exhaustion (inflating). There will usually be a dominant adaptation, but the central issue is ultimately a defense against the sense of unworthiness or feeling unlovable, experienced in both adaptation patterns.

SHRINKING

A shrinking fourth hub, like the avoidant attachment style I describe above, builds excessive walls and protections against intimacy and vulnerability, yet secretly dreams of a perfect love that will save it. Having been hurt deeply in the early years of the hub's development, the shrinking adaptation protects against experiencing overwhelming hurt and devastation again. Part of the fantasy is that perfect love doesn't cause pain, so that when difficulties in a relationship arise, the search to find the mythical ideal begins once more.

Shrinking Characteristics

- Defensive: *If I'm being honest, I don't really care.*

- Believes love shouldn't require effort

- Struggles with genuine connection to others; focuses on the measurable value of relationships

- Can be excessively generous in acute situations intending to impress, but is generally miserly and calculated when it comes to giving

- Struggles with gratitude—is only transiently grateful for big wins and significant gifts

- Takes without feeling grateful

- Can be antisocial, withdrawn, critical, and lacks empathy
- Lives by appearances with an inner world that is neglected and disregarded; tends toward narcissism

An interviewee, Malcolm—a perennial bachelor known for his perfectionism and relaxed charm—was admired by his college friends for having it all. But as his friend group shifted into middle age, the admiration had also shifted to a cautious sympathy as the group watched his revolving door of shallow relationships and his consistently last-minute social cancellations. A friend of Malcolm's had remained in contact with a couple of the ex-girlfriends. They all told the same story: a period of seduction and charm that would last eight or nine months, followed by Malcolm growing increasingly distant. He told me that his standards are too high: "I expect the best of myself and others. I realize this can feel unfair, but my team often tells me I drive excellent performance even though they hate my impossible standards [n.b., Malcolm had high staff turnover]. I know the board of directors at my company isn't complaining!" Malcolm, a textbook case of a shrinking fourth-hub adaptation, returned the serve of the sympathy his college friends had for him. "I have a girlfriend who's a model, I drive a Ferrari, and run the top division of my company. To be honest, I feel sorry for them."

During the interview he was at ease and slightly distracted until I asked, "Do you have any early memories of feeling like more was expected of you than was reasonable for your age?" And down the rabbit hole we went: Malcolm's father had been tough on him, yet with his sister he'd been affectionate and "without standards." When Malcolm cried after losing a little league game, his father was disgusted; when they got home, he told him he was far too old to be crying. His mother said nothing but after his dad left the room, she gave Malcolm a Popsicle and a pat on the shoulder. "I used to feel like I might be able to win his approval with my success, but now that I have surpassed him professionally, it's like we've entered into a new difficult dynamic. It feels unwinnable."

Malcolm opened up during our conversation, albeit on his terms: he swatted away any questions he sensed as me trying to push him. I quickly learned that it would go better if I showed respect and appreciation for what he had to say. Addressing flaws or faults was off-limits—except for one or two that he seemed to have rehearsed counters to. The shrinking fourth hub struggles to give or feel empathy because as children they didn't receive it from the people who mattered most. Criticism and judgment are sometimes positioned as care, such as when Malcolm pitched his impossible standards as good for his staff. He didn't seem to consider that his staff members, in light of his punishing conditions, could be telling him about high performance in the hope of minimizing the risk of his retribution or criticism.

In relationships, the shrinking fourth hub will expect to be saved by perfection, anticipating a partner to rescue them by pouring energy into the relationship while the shrinker risks almost nothing by remaining emotionally protected. In the initial phase of a relationship, a deep hope of being rescued from loneliness will elevate the shrinker, as it briefly believes it is finally being saved. A period of idealized romanticism will be followed by a shift into criticism and distance, which is often a shock to the partner because it seems to come out of nowhere.

In the early days of a relationship, the shrinking (avoidant) adaptation will tend to move fast, dazzling the would-be conquest with adoration as the thrill of the hunt is often mistaken for early love. But once effort and vulnerability are required, the shrinker becomes overwhelmed, frustrated, and bored. Having hoped that *this* time, love could cure the loneliness—this person may even become cruel, blindsiding the partner. It's difficult to understand that shrinking in this hub cannot be healed through surrogacy—adult partners can't fill in for parents who were unable to love. Building strength in this hub is like building physical fitness: a personal trainer can motivate you but can't lift the weights for you. Loving someone with this pattern gets distressing because there's a sense like hearing their cries for love from behind a wall; it's confusing and can be mistaken as encouragement. For someone trying to break through them, these walls of perfectionism, judgment, and impossible standards will punish persistence. Shrinking adaptations tend to avoid seeking the help of therapy. The fear of revealing imperfection—of being exposed as flawed—or a subconscious fear of being seen as fundamentally unworthy drives their avoidance of seeking help.

INFLATING

The inflated adaptation has also been hurt but is like an anxious attachment style, believing they must win love and connection by constantly proving themselves through exhausting, relentless labor. The feeling of being needed creates a sense of security and they often require near-constant validation that a relationship or connection needs them. This adaptation often tries to lock down relationships by becoming indispensable: it's incomprehensible to them that their presence and existence alone can be enough.

Inflating Characteristics

- Jealousy and possessive expectations and attachments with people
- Gives to ingratiate but excessive giving eventually leads to resentment
- Believes love is hard because it requires a near-constant fight to keep it alive
- Is a people pleaser: aware of who they think people want them to be; likely to conform
- Loses its sense of self in relationships, becomes clingy and anxious
- Has weak-to-nonexistent boundaries
- Struggles with receiving—needs to even the score and give back
- Tends toward codependency
- Believes one must constantly earn love through labor

The inflating adaptation expresses itself with a strategy resembling and offensive line, pushing relationships down the field, sometimes with demanding, possessive, and highly charged behavior that initially can be exciting for others. The inflating adaptation lacks boundaries, craves love, and struggles to understand why people are overwhelmed with the excessive acts of generosity.

Shayla, called the "mama bear" in her friend group, was fiercely protective and highly involved in her friends' lives. She often volunteered to take responsibilities off their plates, even when she felt like she was drowning in her already packed schedule. An inflating adaptation tends to believe if they become indispensable to others, people will not be able to live without them (this belief can lead to smothering). But because the inflated person generally isn't aware of the adaptation, eventually, they experience imbalance of effort as rejection and disrespect. This can lead to an emotional explosion and friends can feel blindsided by the generous friend who insists that nothing is needed in return suddenly going nuclear or distant. Shayla told me that she was embarrassed by how angry she became when a friend was unavailable to help with an urgent project: "I thought, 'I never ask for anything and the one time I need something nobody is there for me.'"

The inflating adaptation tends to give surprise gifts "just because," and feels slighted by connections friends share with others. This adaptation is the more likely of the two to seek therapy, because the hurt of giving and struggling to receive eventually leads to a hunger for greater self-discovery. After Shayla began therapy, she started asking her boyfriend to help around the house and learned that he had no intention of putting any effort into the relationship: he had signed up for Inflating Shayla, who did everything. The relationship did not survive.

HOLDING PATTERNS

OHM'S LAW

Opposites can attract, but when it comes to emotional voltage, along with the necessary emotional capacity to contain and work through it, the lower voltage will always pull the higher one down, that is, until or unless both voltage sources reach the same potential. It's a physics calculation—Ohm's Law: voltage equals current times resistance—and as much as we may elevate someone in an unbalanced relationship, by doing so we can get dragged down. Our closest relationships profoundly affect our lives—this includes professional relationships, the people we work with almost every day. The people we spend the most time with eventually affect our worldview and the way we see ourselves unless we actively maintain our fourth-hub boundary of being very clear with ourselves about who we allow to influence our sense of self.

As we do the work of restoration in the hubs, more energy becomes available in our bodies to enliven us and enhance our lives. A holding pattern—even if we are unaware of it—takes effort to maintain and absorbs energy. For example, physical rigidity is a sustained contraction and when released, the energy used to hold it is freed. And as we change, the world around us changes. At first, there can be significant disruption to old dynamics, including shifts that bring periods of loneliness, but eventually people who are better aligned with you start to show up. It's important to make note that personal dynamics that previously relied on adapted behavior patterns may struggle to adjust when we change. In principle, this can seem straightforward and simple, but in the short term it can be difficult and cause considerable pain.

We cannot perfectly time our growth with what works for the people around us. It's a natural and often painful consequence of transformation to lose people, activities, and things we're attached to as we can find they no longer fit. Like tearing down an old house to build a new one, there's a period between old and new when the lot is cleared and there is no home at all. This can be a very lonely experience (and take heart and be patient with yourself if you're not ready yet): new connections will come.

THE SHADOWS: GRIEF, AND ENVY AND JEALOUSY

Grief is an unavoidable part of loving because loss is inevitable. The fourth-hub shadows are conditions of being human. The other shadows I discuss here are envy and jealousy, which can also be both a price for the vulnerability of love and an accelerant that stokes passion, acting like an arrow pointing us to what we desire. Like all the shadows, there is a difference between wading in them (as part of the human experience) and drowning.

Grief

Grief can overwhelm us with distress, making our lived experience unbearable, but to be human is to grieve at some point. People we love die, leave us, and change. Grief makes our body and mind uncomfortable places to be as we struggle with loss, which undermines the sense of security and stability because we're made aware that although it's often imperceptible, the world around us constantly changes. Once we have experienced loss, we know something about life—we know that there is fallibility in all security. Nothing stays the same forever and directly experiencing this fact will change you. It's hard to stay with feelings of grief, and sometimes the only escape from the crushing sensation of unrelenting vulnerability and loss is escapism or dissociation. Grief is hard for others to watch because it's unsolvable and to sit in the presence of despair holding that space for someone can be challenging, particularly if we believe that providing support means fixing things. It takes strength that we may not have to tolerate sadness being expressed in our presence. Trying to distract someone from experiencing sadness with a brighter perspective or a small misdirection may be what the person needs, but an important distinction must be made about whom this distraction is helping in the moment. Is it for us to avoid being in the presence of suffering or does the grieving person want a break?

We experience the loss of people who are important to us, people who take some of our history, memories, and future with them when they go. When we can feel grief, truly allow it, we build fitness in our capacity to tolerate loss and so-called failures, and we can become stronger and braver with our ability to love. If we've never been allowed or taught to grieve, we will avoid risks in love or tap out early. The avoidance of the crushing suffocation of loss and heartbreak keep many people avoiding love and playing beneath their potential, which is like a death before death. It takes courage and bravery to love deeply because loss is always a risk.

Sometimes, the softening of sadness along with its jagged agony can feel like a betrayal and loss of the remaining memory and connection we have left—so we hold on to it. The time it takes to grieve will almost always be longer than anyone wants it to be. When possible, explore the sensation in your body with curiosity, find its location, and describe the feeling. Is it tight, burning, stinging, intense, or a dull ache? Gently ask it what it needs and wants. In grief, distractions give us a moment to take a break, rest, and catch our breath as we try to forget for a little while. As the acute pain softens and delivers us into the new world that exists in the wake of the loss, we may not feel the pain in paralyzing heaves, but we are changed forever by the experience. We can be more empathic, patient, and understanding with others and ourselves. If we deny our grief, it will live in the shadow and express itself in perplexing ways, such as anger and rage.

When we've lost people and things we love, one way to repair our broken heart is to help others by providing the empathic space and the support we know matters. We remind ourselves that we still have so much to give, we're not alone,

and strong connections form over shared experiences. A smile, a word of encouragement, listening, volunteering, mentoring, and donating can be life-affirming in the wake of loss. If we're not yet ready to be a help to others, as Mr. Rogers's mother advised, we can look for the helpers—the people who are, in the darkest moments and places, showing up to help. In this way, loss and grief can reveal simultaneously the best and the worst, showing us another paradox of being human.

Envy and Jealousy

Envy and jealousy are feelings of helplessness and vulnerability in the face of what we want. In *The State of Affairs: Rethinking Infidelity*, Perel writes, "Envy relates to something you want but do not have. On the one hand, jealousy relates to something you have but are afraid of losing." If someone flirts with our partner, we glimpse our inability to control the people we love, and perhaps we fear loss—this is jealousy.

Envy, on the other hand, can be awakened when we see our dreams realized by other people. The ability to exist in the discomfort of envy is an indicator of personal power. We may protectively minimize or criticize if we can't bear the pain of our powerlessness in the face of desire for something we do not have. Our confidence and self-esteem are required to manage the vulnerability of wanting things before we have them (see Chapter 6), and through sincere admiration we can look at what we want and soak it in. When we don't feel worthy, it's challenging to allow admiration, curiosity, and wonder. The bravery of the third hub powers our ability to remain open even when there's the threat of heartbreak and embarrassment. As a shadow, a little bit of envy is energizing; too much is devastating to the required openness necessary for love, and for achieving dreams and aspirations.

Success doesn't avoid envy and jealousy: it has a different relationship with it, extracting energy and inspiration through them. The spark of envy illuminates so that we can explore. This is how to draw what you want closer. However, envy as a shadow is a protection against the pain of rejection, disappointment, and failure through defensiveness. If envy is too intense, it sets a fire of fear and even rage, pushing what we admire away. If we criticize or minimize our desires, we place ourselves at a safe distance from them; so safe they can't get close to us. For anyone who's been hurt by deep disappointment, openhearted admiration is an act of bravery. If we can grieve embarrassments and failures and strengthen our sense of worthiness, we can admire beauty and inspiration. We can look with wide-open eyes at the people doing what we aspire to do, looking for clues and feelings to get a little contact high from their magic and as a result, draw what we want for ourselves just a little bit closer.

TECHNIQUES AND EXERCISES

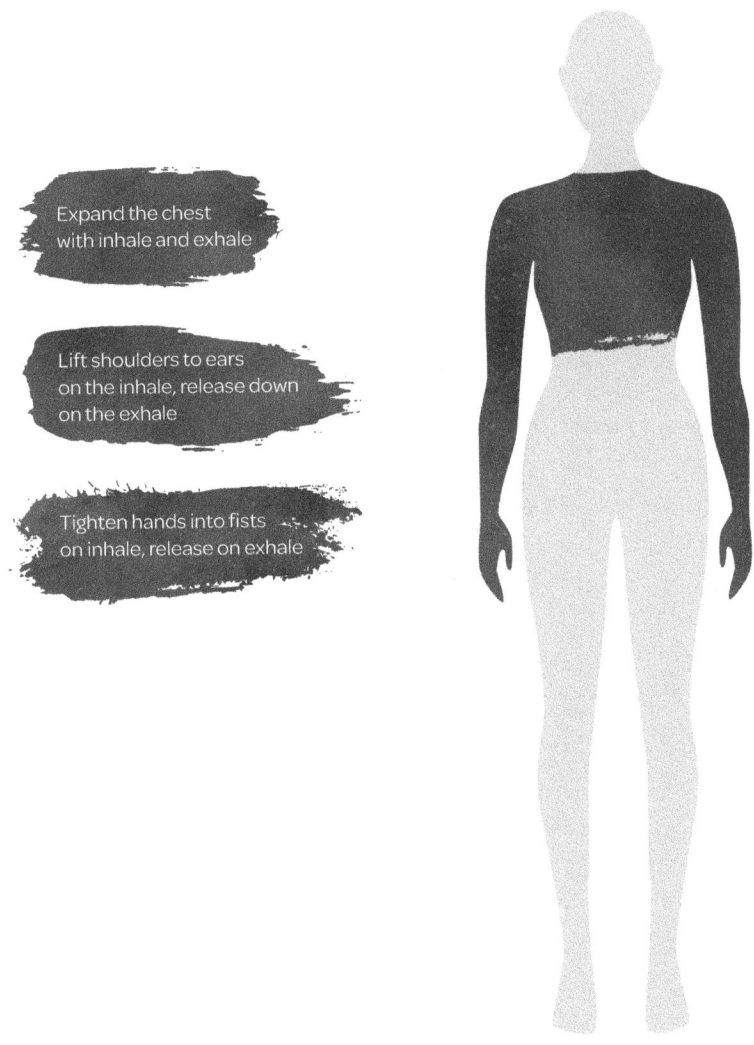

Expand the chest with inhale and exhale

Lift shoulders to ears on the inhale, release down on the exhale

Tighten hands into fists on inhale, release on exhale

Figure 7.1: Fourth-Hub Body Prompts

THE PARINAMA METHOD FOURTH-HUB FUNDAMENTALS

Fourth-hub practices focus on softening and balancing—relaxing rigidity in the chest to increase capacity for breathing, crying, and laughing to encourage a more balanced dynamic between receiving and giving. If you're reading these words, you've survived everything that's happened to you; through the good times and bad, your heart keeps beating and you've kept breathing. In this way, you've never given up on yourself. Like the simplicity of the previous hubs, the fourth hub involves conscious reclamation of everyday actions. In this hub, breathing and crying have often become restricted or buried in muscular rigidity. Your breath is a bridge between the conscious and unconscious management of your nervous system. An inhale activates the sympathetic nervous system, and an exhale recruits the parasympathetic functions that relax and release. A single, daily, deep, gentle inhale and exhale done consciously can begin to shift your life.

RECEIVING

If you feel lonely and have a specific idea of the kind of attention you want to receive, before looking for the specific version of care and attention you desire, take an inventory of the care that already surrounds you—a kind face on your commute, a coworker who genuinely asks about your weekend, or even people you know online who can bring good vibes into your life. We do this inventory to produce feelings that actively spark gratitude. Next, think of all the people who have helped you throughout your life: family members, neighbors, teachers, friends, bosses, and colleagues (include the love of pets and animals). Take five minutes and mentally walk through your day. Write down the names of the people who help and care for you. At first, this may go a little slow, but with time it will gather momentum. This is an exercise in receiving, not an exercise in appreciating. As you write down the names, bask in the glow of all the people who have loved and continue to love and appreciate you.

Then think of all the places where you have felt good: groups of friends, so-called happy places, maybe a class you took in which the students were especially excellent, a dorm you lived in, a team you worked with, a vacation spot, or a beach or mountain where you've spent time and felt great. Now close your eyes and breathe and feel all that love (even for the places that no longer exist) and remember how they felt before there was any sadness for their loss and soften. Receiving is recovering from loss and trusting that the same good feelings can exist again. Therefore, as counterintuitive as this will seem, we practice receiving on the exhale: to release into the trust that eventually there will be more, and to receive life as it is now—where the inhale will return to fill us again.

If you feel unsettled about your career, make a list of your accomplishments, not just job performance as measured by employers, but what you're personally proud of, and take a moment to soak them in. We cut off reception and experience deficiency when we focus on what we need to be, on how much farther we must go, or on other people we perceive to be more successful than us. Receiving your accomplishments is part of owning your narrative. Building momentum with any practice or habit involves getting increasingly better at it, and when we feel good about something, we want to do more of it. Favoring our inner criticism and blocking receptivity for appreciation is a fallacy about success that will hold us back from our potential.

The purpose of taking an inventory is not to moralize gratitude. If we haven't learned to experience the sensation of receiving without hypervigilance, we won't feel it. This hypervigilance comes from either not trusting or feeling the pressure to be polite and show appreciation before the gratitude is felt. And for children who are given a mountain of presents and rip through them only to ask what comes next, they will likely grow to be good at taking but struggle with the satisfaction of receiving. The feeling of receiving involves softening, allowing, and even savoring—and from this, gratitude naturally follows.

If you're not developing the feeling that comes before the intellectualization of gratitude, it doesn't matter how much you're given. Either you won't let it in, or you will require so much that people will become exhausted trying to spark the slightest feeling as they love and support you. Giving is fantastic, but we can't give our way to feeling love. We need to feel the reception of love and to cultivate the sensation to experience greater levels of connection.

If our chest and diaphragm are tight, taking in a deep breath will require discharging, releasing, and relaxing to make space so we can open them. The greater your sense of need, the emptier and more painful it will feel if your container (in this case your lungs and diaphragm) is obstructed or constricted—and breathwork is a very effective antidote.

BREATHING EXERCISES

Breath is a tool for activating, relaxing, diagnosing, and gaining deeper access to all hubs. As mentioned, an inhale activates the sympathetic nervous system (fight, freeze, or flight), and an exhale activates the parasympathetic nervous system (rest and restore). Different results occur by emphasizing the inhale or the exhale; for example, if you're feeling anxious, exhales that are slow and gentle will release tension. Oppositely, when feeling tired, inhales that are deep or rapid are energizing.

Tightness in the chest and diaphragm interfere with how deeply we can laugh, cry, and orgasm. Opening the chest and expanding lung capacity has benefits in many layers of life. Doctors have long noticed that depressed patients present with shallow breathing and hunched upper backs with shoulders reaching forward (as if to protect the heart). Grief and sadness literally can take our breath away, and without expressing these feelings they can get trapped in our bodies. Breathing, like all conscious reclamations, uses something familiar to gain greater access to deeper layers of ourselves. Breathing is an activity that loses its spectacularness because we do it all the time. The profound revelation that our breath has persisted through every hardship of our life is evidence

of our inherent worthiness and that the love we seek always surrounds and fills us. If we increase our activity, heavier breathing happens without conscious effort. Unconscious breathing activates and relaxes the body in response to our activity. With every breath, we balance between charging and discharging, energizing and relaxing. When we make our breathing conscious, we have a chance to take control and shift excitation and relaxation out of autopilot.

Our programming from early in life informs our reflexes that over time may have become maladaptive as fear, guilt, and shame become shadows and influence our unconscious and subconsciously generated behaviors. If you want to relax, inhale to the count of two and exhale to the count of four. If you want energy, reverse it and inhale for a count of four and exhale for two. To enhance relaxation with soothing, lightly pat your heart area with the pads of your fingers, then gently rub the heart area with an open palm in circles both clockwise and counterclockwise. To enhance excitation, tap your solar plexus (found at the center of the top of your abdomen, just beneath your rib cage) with the tops of your fingers.

As a yoga student in India, I *tolerated* the pranayama (breathing) classes, secretly watching the clock, waiting for the gymnastics-like asana (yoga) classes that build physical strength and flexibility. At the time, the value of meditation, scripture study, and breathwork helped me justify my excessive, high-intensity physical training as spiritual. As an inflated third hub, I had wanted to exercise constantly but needed to imagine it as superior and more special than simple exercise. I sustained many, many, many repetitive-stress injuries before I even considered softening my practices. Like many people, the natural balance of softening came to me even when I would not go to it.

Reception and Gratitude Breath

Begin with your arms extended outward like you're receiving applause from a standing ovation. Inhale and exhale from this position without moving your arms. Next, as you inhale, bring your hands inward and place them on your heart. Briefly pause to feel, then exhale as you extend your hands and arms back out to the starting position and pause again briefly to feel. When your arms are extended, think, or say, *Thank you* after the inhale, and when you bring your hands in after the exhale, think or say, *This means the world to me.*

Breath Ball

The link between breath and the unconscious functioning of reflexes and adaptations offers a bridge for nervous-system transformation. Synchronizing movement with breath is the central principle of the vinyasa yoga style. Vinyasa links movement with breath to synchronize the mind with the body. This linking and its benefits can also be achieved with simple movements, especially considering that the intensity of physical exertion in a yoga class or of a teacher's pace can distract from concentrating on this union. In Sanskrit, yoga means *yoke* (as in two oxen walking in synchronization). In this exercise, we are yoking the mind and the body through breath and simple movement.

Imagine holding a ball and hold your hands in front of you at chest level, palms facing each other. Expand your hands out, growing the size of the ball, and coordinating this movement with your breath on an inhale. On the exhale, move your hands together, shrinking the size of the ball. Do this for up to 10 breaths, at least until you feel your hands are coordinated with your breath. Once you have synchronized the movement of your hands with your breath, pause and return to breathing naturally for a moment and feel any sensations that are arising.

Next, with your hands in the same position, turn your wrists and slightly shift your fingers to face the front of the room. Imagine them representing your ribcage and your thumbs as the back of your body. First, expand the space between your fingers (the "ribs") moving them outward, holding your thumbs (your "back") steady, and synchronize the expansion of your fingers and ribs on the inhale. On the exhale, the fingers coordinate and return. Repeat three times. Next, synchronize the movement of the thumbs with breathing into the back body, anchoring your ribs and fingers. Repeat three times. Now bring it all together as you did with the ball and expand the fingers and thumbs and ribs and back, and coordinate breathing with your body. After three full breaths (inhale and exhale) pause and notice any sensations.

Resonance Breath

Resonance breathing helps to relax the nervous system by activating the parasympathetic functions through extending the exhale and adding holds on each side of the breath. This practice also helps to expand breathing capacity: the count is: 6:3:9:3; if you need to build some momentum, start with 2:1:3:1. Inhale as you count to six. Hold for a count of three. Exhale for a count of nine. Hold for a count of three—repeat.

According to the sacred yoga text Hatha Yoga Pradipika, "Both the mind and the breath are united together like milk and water, and both of them are equal in their activities." If you slow down your breathing, your thoughts and physical activation will correspondingly slow down, too.

CRYING

We are socialized very early to suppress the urge to cry. Tears are often stifled or hidden out of embarrassment, and sobbing and any associated noise are considered dramatic, childish, and only suitable for the absolute worst moments of life. But even then, crying is mostly muffled sound and moisture coming out of our eyes with minimal movement. Some people cry only when they see beautiful and poignant things, but not for grief or sadness. During one interview, a spouse told me that it concerned him that his wife quietly sobbed during sweet Pixar movies but appeared unmoved at the funeral of a beloved friend. The fact is most of us have forgotten how to cry as a release and discharge of grief and sadness. As a result, we have the tightness of trapped grief in our chest and diaphragm. Some clients told me they didn't want to cry because they feared that if they started, they would never stop. The first few cries can be significant, exhausting releases, but eventually things calm down, and a quick little sob keeps a sad moment from lingering—but it takes some practice.

The three primary factors of crying are sound, movement, and, of course, tears. When you feel the sting in your eyes, try to find a private place (or a supportive person) and allow the feelings to arise. To get things going, try to make sounds or repeat words like *no* or *I can't* or even *this is too much*, which can help with the release. Now bring movement into your chest, perhaps adding a *haaa* or *uhhh* to the mix. If you have a soft surface like a bed or a couch, you can smack the palms of your hands on the surface for additional release. When you feel like the crying has passed, and it always does, let yourself settle and relax before making any sudden moves. If it feels nice, splash some cool water on your face and take a few sips of water—you did a fantastic job!

HUMANIZATION

Giving and Altruism

The impulse to give is part of human nature and human dignity. Altruism is giving without the expectation of reciprocity. Like an inhale or exhale, giving naturally provokes a reciprocal response. Say hello to someone and most of the time you're likely to get a *hello* back. But it's hard to give when we're in physical or emotional pain and when we feel that we don't even have enough for ourselves: pain can make us "selfish." It's a demand for attention, and it won't go away until it is comforted, discharged, or it passes on its own schedule. Noticing and effectively supporting another person requires your own pain be cared for and managed. When our pain and neediness require support, seeing pain and neediness in others may provoke feelings of disgust coming from the hidden self, especially when we deeply crave mercy and kindness that we don't believe we'll receive. Statements like *They need to pull themselves together* or a cavalier *That's life, so toughen up* are protections and reflections of hurt over unmet needs. Give yourself a break for having your own needs.

When there's a social hierarchy in giving, some folks can be deprived of their sense of contribution. When I was interviewing unhoused folks, I experienced firsthand how declining their offers of food or kindness interfered with the dignity of our connection. Human dignity involves contribution and reciprocity.

Activism

It's impossible to reach the full potential in our personal connections when we deny another person's humanity or lived experience. In *Team Human,* media theorist and professor Douglas Rushkoff writes about "recalibrating" our humanity by looking into the eyes of another human being. Be mindful of invasive eye contact, which can interfere with the psychic boundaries of the sixth hub but notice if you can sense the shared presence in the eyes of all other human beings.

Evaluating your beliefs, speaking up, and making donations are vital to working in this hub. Fourth-hub activism involves action: standing up and fighting for humanization and the conservation of the natural world—we're fighting for ourselves.

Fourth-hub interruption to connection causes inner harm that allows us to detach and not feel when other people (and the environment) are being degraded and in pain. But we can act at any moment, and a single action on behalf of another can shift a lifetime of inaction as we build momentum and feel connection to each other. The shared network of humanity is interconnected, and denial of this connection requires physical constriction and rigidity. This work also involves hearing lived experiences of others in their own words and accepting them without the requirement of understanding them—all that's needed is tolerance and acceptance. Psychotherapist and trauma specialist Resmaa Menakem's *My Grandmother's Hands: Racialized Trauma and the Pathway to Mending Our Hearts and Bodies* is essential reading for this fourth-hub work. Someone else's lived experience doesn't need to make sense to you for it to be true, and the same goes for you when it comes to feeling the need to explain yourself—you shouldn't have to. Your life is not validated because it makes sense to other people. Indigenous Australian artist and Murri activist Lilla Watson says, "If you have come here to help me, you are wasting your time, but if you have come because your liberation is bound up with mine, then let us work together."

Nature and Forest Bathing

Scientific studies have measured and demonstrated the effect of spending time around trees (forest bathing) on mental health, healing, immune function, creativity, and general well-being (see Chapter 4): trees make us feel more connected and boost our mood. But despite the scientific literature supporting the positive effect of time spent outside, many of us find it hard to do. Sometimes when we're tired or stressed, the relative calm of nature feels out of sync with the speed of our thoughts and the tension in our bodies. When we're out of sync, the frustration of this dissonance can initially feel aggravating (for the first five to 10 minutes). That initial tension is at the center of much anxiety—but the payoff is worth it. One study uncovered that people were more helpful and caring after watching nature videos or looking at pictures of trees. If you can't get excited about going outside, there are other options. Having plants in your home and natural materials for both furniture and decoration have also been shown to be supportive. Simply adding photographs of trees to your home can also support happiness. Keep in mind, that until we synchronize with the pace, watching nature programs can have that itchy, out-of-sync, too-slow feeling like initially being out in nature. Try to approach watching them with the same awareness of attempting to sync up.

Several studies cited in forest-medicine expert Qing Li's book, *Forest Bathing: How Trees Can Help You Find Health and Happiness*, tracked the increase in altruism, spontaneous gratitude, and connection that occurs when we spend time in nature. It's hard to feel alone when you're surrounded by earth, sky, sun, plants, water, and animals. If you work from home, try looking out a window before you begin your morning meetings, stepping outside to get some air, or going for a walk at lunch. Notice the sights and sounds of the world that surrounds you.

CHARGE AND DISCHARGE

This hub connects the nonverbal lower hubs with the increased cognition of the upper hubs. Rigidity in this hub blocks the expression and connection of the body with the mind, so we focus on softening and melting with the intention of reception and release.

CHARGE

You can directly experience the energizing side of the breath—the inhale—by taking a few sharp inhales through your nose, followed by passive exhaling through your mouth; it's called the "breath of fire." This technique can be used when you're feeling sluggish and need to sharpen your focus and energize.

Breath of Joy

This technique uses coordinated breath and the movement of your arms and shoulders to charge and stoke the sense of joy in the body. Stand with feet slightly wider than shoulder-width apart, knees slightly bent to keep them from locking. Inhale hands up in front of you, parallel to the floor, exhale before making the next movement. Inhale arms to the side, making a "T" shape (parallel to the floor), exhale before making the next movement. Inhale arms up overhead. Last—exhale your arms down past your sides in a quick, swinging motion. Repeat this sequence three to five times then stand still and notice how you feel.

DISCHARGING

Discharging in the fourth hub focuses on finding tremors in the shoulders and arms, with opening and release in the chest.

Inhale, hold, and melt

Start by making your shoulders a little energized with a slight shrug. Turn your hands slightly outward or rest the tops of your hands on your legs with palms facing out. Next, squeeze your shoulders up toward your ears on an inhale, squeeze and find a slight tremor. Then, on an extra slow and soft exhale, *slowly* release your shoulders down and stretch them slightly down past where they naturally land. Repeat up to two times.

Chest release

Lie on a block or rolled towel, placing it between your shoulder blades down the length of your spine. There should be no pain or discomfort as you allow the chest to passively open as your shoulder blades relax toward the floor. Use your breath to expand and soften your chest. The extension over the block is particularly beneficial because it focuses on release without the distraction of physical exertion.

Cactus arms

Start with a yoga strap or a scarf, holding it above your head with both hands, and extend your elbows to 90-degree angles like a cactus. Introduce some tension by pulling on the strap with both hands until you feel a tremor. Finding the tremor can take a little time and exploration—be patient and avoid straining. Hold for two to three breaths, repeat up to three times.

In Chapter 8, the fifth hub—SPEAK, the balance of give-and-take and the paradox of belonging and independence will continue to develop and evolve. We learn to find personal expression and validation which supports both being known as who we truly are and supporting others in their expression of integrity. The voice in this hub can connect us with increasingly sophisticated use of language.

SPEAK: EARLY ADOLESCENCE, SELF-EXPRESSION

Basics	Themes	Interruptions and Stressors	Adaptations and Holding Patterns	Techniques and Exercises
Talking and Speaking	Discussion and Conflict	Seen but not Heard	Characteristics of a Balanced and Out-of-Balance Fifth Hub	Communication
Hearing and Listening	The Three V's	Abuse of Trust	Shrinking	Setting Up
Auditory Boundaries	Positive and Negative Words	Verbal Abuse and Bullying	Inflating	Listening and Validation
A Good Listener	Creative Expression	Secrets and Dissonance	The Shadow: Lies	Speaking
Truth		Shame and Unspoken Standards		Elevator Pitch
Sound and Silence				Voice
				Tone
				Pitch
				Pattern Interrupting and Tone
				Harmony versus Discord
				Creating
				Journaling
				Affirmation
				Charge and Discharge

Chapter 8

THE FIFTH HUB—SPEAK

EXPRESSION AND COMMUNICATION

*Loneliness does not come from having no people about one, but from
being unable to communicate the things that seem important to oneself
or from holding certain views which others find inadmissible.*
—Carl Jung

WORDS HAVE THE POWER to both build and destroy. The Hebrew word *abracadabra* means *I create as I speak*, and according to the Bible, all of creation began as a single word: *In the beginning was the Word.* The Gospel of John says, "Jesus is the Word because through him all things are made." The fifth hub is the center for our words, creations, self-expression, and the collaborative aspects of communication that involve listening. Many paradoxes collide within the balance of talking and listening: the give-and-take of second-hub attunement along with the fourth-hub exchange of gratitude and generosity. But there's a particularly profound paradox of third-hub individuality and fourth-hub belonging that's experienced when we express ourselves—we speak and create so that our individual perspective can be understood while simultaneously seeking validation and belonging. To be understood and to feel seen, we need other people to hear us. The absence of people is not the singular cause of loneliness: loneliness can be caused by either unresponsive or critical people who have no interest in what you have to say or by people who attempt (or succeed) to censor you.

Although powerful, words are subject to interpretation by a listener. We hear parts of what is being communicated and we construe other parts based on our experiences. Words are not impartial for a listener: they are subject to how they are perceived. If you're trying to make a point, it's important to be aware of the perspective and mindset of your audience, and to know there's the potential for disappointment and distress if you desire to be understood exactly as you are. When we're on the same wavelength—have similar thoughts—talking and listening can amplify who we are through the pleasure of harmonious communication. Oppositely, dissonance and discord can be unsettling and agitating because we struggle to find common ground with people who have different beliefs than us. Without conscious awareness, most of what we hear moves passively through the filters of our early programming—our adaptations and belief systems—and affects what we perceive and how we understand. The ease and pleasure of communication with people who share our views is without a doubt satisfying, but if we avoid and/or block out other perspectives because we find them disagreeable, we risk strengthening our limiting beliefs and biases and becoming narrow-minded.

ORIENTATION

Physical location: Neck, jaw, mouth, ears, vocal cords, the base of the skull, sinuses, tops of arms, and hands

First cycle: Approximately seven to 13 years old

Task: To find your voice, to express your truth, to be heard

Rights: To speak truth, to be told the truth, to be heard

Identity: I am my word. I am what I create and express.

Reconciliation: How much of my truth can I speak without punishment or retaliation? How much of another's truth am I willing to hear?

To *find your voice* means to be able to express yourself as you are—to find yourself. We come to know ourselves through processing our thoughts and emotions with words and artistic expression. The fifth hub is an inflection point dedicated to making our inner world known to the outer world so we can connect with people who will understand us. We also become known to others by sharing ourselves: if we don't express ourselves, the people who can truly know us will have difficulty finding us. During the early years of lower-hub development, we communicated through behavior. For example, if we became sick, we used opaque or nonverbal language, such as crying, losing our appetite, or becoming unusually quiet or inactive. The fifth hub is when children begin to effectively advocate for themselves with words: *Hey Mom, I have a stomachache.* Or instead of just throwing a tantrum, they make an impassioned case: *That's not fair, my sister gets to have that—why can't I?*

Some people will like it when we speak our mind and will gravitate toward us; others will want to create distance. When we can be explicit about what we want, we become better at selecting for it and making choices to support its existence. What we choose to hear, along with how we speak and express ourselves—for better or for worse—helps to create our experience of the world. Words are the most direct, effective, and specific form of communication we have. They help us process, organize, and communicate our thoughts and feelings. Learning to use them to be transparent and honest makes us more effective in our relationships and aspirations, both with ourselves and others—yet words are only one component of communication, as I discuss below.

Honesty transmits a feeling. There's magnetism and charisma in someone capable of telling and holding space for the truth. Yet, as we've seen in interruptions and adaptations of the early hubs, there are many reasons why we may not tell the truth or may struggle with the ability to hear it from others. An example of this is being subjected to excessive criticism in childhood, which can lead to understandable sensitivities with direct or unbuffered feedback. The work in this hub holds understanding and compassion for our suppression or repression for survival—there should be no shame in what we had to hide to survive as we shift into integrity with our words and all types of expression. We become simultaneously more powerful and more at peace after the dust has settled from the work of this hub. In the yoga sutras there is a Sanskrit word, *Satya,* for speaking truth. Satya contains a basic understanding that it's important to tell the truth, but there are deeper implications: people committed to the truth create the truth when they speak. Sri Swami Satchidananda, the guru who opened the Woodstock festival, said, "All nature loves an honest person. He need not run after things; they will run after him."

When we use the framework of our hubs to make dreams and ideas real (see Chapter 12), the transition of an idea from our mind into words that communicate with others supports the process of building and manifesting things. But for now, we continue traveling upward on the bottom-up path of greater self-actualization.

INITIAL DEVELOPMENT

Human babies are born with their larynx placed high in the mouth, similar to animals. This makes breathing and feeding easier. Anatomically, an infant's larynx gradually lowers into position, allowing for the sound production that makes human language uniquely possible. The initial high placement of the larynx is why a baby's early speech is so muddled. Anthropologist Meredith F. Small writes in *Our Babies, Ourselves: How Biology and Culture Shape the Way We Parent*, "What makes human speech different is that we are able to produce a range of noises with greater subtlety, and we have the cognitive ability to both hear and interpret those sounds." She also notes, "Kids not only have to talk, they also have to listen and understand." Children learn to talk by listening. Before they can speak the word for it, a child can correctly point out a location on their body when asked. For example, before children can say the word *hand*, they can show you their hand.

In the early months of life, nonverbal communication happens through emotional attunement, but when a baby begins to talk, its inner world begins to be revealed. The skills and abilities for language and writing grow throughout initial development of the hubs, but at about age seven, there's an increase in logical thinking and progressively, an emerging ability to write stories and to use advanced imagination that incorporates metaphors and symbols.

How the family and surrounding social environment responds to children as they learn to express themselves impacts their developing communication and may result in adaptations of either a meek (shrinking) or an overbearing (inflating) communication style that carries into adulthood. Developmental biologists point out that early emotional attunement (the second hub) will affect communication style in adulthood; the mirroring and responsiveness of emotional attunement are found in the sophisticated verbal communication and creative expression of the fifth hub. The hallmark of second-hub attunement is body language, which includes facial expressions that get blended into our communication style. In this chapter, I discuss how vocal tone, inflection, and body language play significant roles in how others receive and perceive our words. For example, *I love the rain* can mean that the speaker either does or does not love rain, depending on the tone, inflection, and body language that accompany it.

During childhood, as we began the process of finding our voice and using words, we made mistakes. Being corrected after saying the wrong thing was how we learned about forbidden topics, stigmas, and what constitutes polite conversation. Kids say the darndest things when they communicate what they see, and how they learn to filter what they say is a process that can either interrupt (and cause adaptations) or can support healthy social sensitivities. Try to remember a time when you unknowingly spoke of a forbidden topic and how the adults around you responded. Were they angry and were you confused and embarrassed, or did you receive a patient explanation for why what you said wasn't appropriate? Or did you experience another option, such as being ignored and sensing the adults in the room had grown uncomfortable?

The fifth hub starts in primary school and transitions into our sixth hub for high school.

Every year brings an increased ability to manage the paradox between belonging and individuality: most children experience a considerable shift as they transition from middle school into high school. In the sixth hub, the child who enters high school will leave as a young adult. These hubs incorporate all the previous stages of childhood development as mature adult levels of consciousness begin to emerge.

BASICS

The basics of this hub are simple paradoxes that on the surface are relatively straightforward, but under examination go deep: speaking and listening, truth and lies, and sound and silence.

TALKING AND SPEAKING

About 80 percent of people experience *glossophobia* (fear of public speaking). Several intersecting fears are cited as contributing to this, such as a fear of being exposed as incompetent, causing oneself embarrassment, or being judged for making a mistake. Many people tend to be quieter with people they don't know and louder with family, friends, and trusted colleagues. Considering that we tend to speak freely with people who make us feel safe and that we protect ourselves in unfamiliar situations, standing in front of an audience can be unsettling. It's worth noting that when it comes to public speaking, feeling settled and centered, that is, feeling safe within ourselves in the four lower hubs, can change our relationship with external validation and safety. One of the challenges of public speaking is figuring out how to engage and connect with an audience.

The people we click with are on the same wavelength as we are: a study conducted using FMRI scans by UCLA and Dartmouth College showed similar brainwave patterns between people who perceive and respond to the world in the same way. Like-minded listeners and speakers are more likely to become friends. A sense of harmony and amplification of one's beliefs are characteristic of enjoyable communication. This syncing is attributed to easy transmission of thoughts, feelings, and memories between people, and was observed to be a result of brainwave overlaps. Conversely, when people are out of sync, the feeling is like discordant noise and can lead to discomfort and agitation.

Rather than change minds, harsh words tend to strengthen people's positions and are more prone to cause folks to defend themselves, to double down on their convictions. Studies have shown that bridging communication gaps is easier when we find some commonalities with the people we disagree with and show we're willing to acknowledge we sometimes make mistakes and get things wrong. Hating other people for their hate will not shift their hate. Bravely speaking up for what you believe in, living with integrity combined with having respect for others can change hearts and minds—but your mind needs to be open, too. Genuine curiosity is an effective catalyst for bridge-building—try asking *When did you learn to feel that way?* when you encounter an opinion you disagree with. People often spend energy trying to convert others instead of investing in the enrichment of their own understanding of another point of view. Talking is about expressing truth and being heard. To be heard, we need to appreciate our audience. And if our audience senses an effort to connect when we're speaking, it's more apt to listen. If we wish to be understood, speaking should involve the use of specific language and analogies that resonate with our intended audience. When we speak to a child or a peer or an elder, we use different slang, speed, volume, and sometimes even different languages.

We may attempt to change someone's mind with facts and assertions, but we have a better chance of changing a heart by speaking our truth and giving it a chance to resonate with another person's humanity. If someone is absolutely committed to not believing you, when possible, leave the conversation—there's no better way to teach someone about humanization and boundaries than to enact them. When a person is actively ignoring your perspective or disrespecting what you have to say, whenever it's possible, activate boundaries and create distance. When it's not possible to leave, find a private place and use your hands to form an invisible forcefield around your body—and decide who's allowed in. As a person is addressing you, you can feel yourself safely inside your created space. It may sound kooky but try it—it's effective. The importance of this fifth-hub boundary is often underappreciated; invasion by words and loud noise can be dangerous and harmful.

Dynamic flow between speaking and listening creates health in this hub. If we tend to talk and not listen, we fail to learn new things and wall ourselves off from curiosity and the transformational potential of new information. If we only listen and do not disclose, we're blocking the vulnerability and revelation that is a hallmark of connection—our own comfort with personal disclosure can be like granting permission for others to speak freely. Virginia Woolf wrote in *The Years,* "If you do not tell the truth about yourself, you cannot tell it about other people."

HEARING AND LISTENING

We are legitimized and lifted when we're listened to by someone seeking to understand us and looking to see the best in us. When we don't feel listened to by someone, the experience can range from slightly annoying to very distressing; perhaps there's a nod and a murmur of agreement that's slightly out of sync with what's being said, or the person doesn't appear to be present. This links to early attunement and a distress similar to what infants experienced in the so-called still-face experiment, a procedure developed by child-development researcher Edward Tronick in which a mother faces her baby and is asked to maintain a still face and does not react to the baby's behavior (the mother stops mirroring the baby). In general, the baby becomes agitated by failed attempts to get a reaction from its mother.

Actively seeking to understand someone is a powerful experience for everyone involved, whether it's with a child, a family member, a professional relationship, or a stranger. Active interest is so rare that showing genuine curiosity can result in a sense of bonding that can occur very quickly. Journalist Kate Murphy writes in *You're Not Listening: What You're Missing and Why It Matters,* "Hearing is passive. Listening is active." She goes on to explain the goal of listening is to understand. Murphy describes listening as "*[T]he experience of being experienced* [author's emphasis]." Buddha was described as "listening with his entire body," and that experience was said to be astonishing by those who experienced it. Listening requires sustained attention—often in short supply—and the ability to drop your internal narrative to be present for someone else's. When done well, we resist the urge to provide unsolicited advice, personal anecdote, and strategy, and we support the glorious process of providing space for another person to work something out and/or to feel attended to and understood.

AUDITORY BOUNDARIES

It takes extraordinary skill and energy to hold space that allows people to process and express their truth without interjecting and projecting our own. Listening is not a passive process—it's skillful and demanding work. Listening is active, and sometimes we just don't have the energy to do it. Being inactively listened to can be extraordinarily frustrating, so part of being a good listener is being able to communicate when we can't do it: "It's important to me to be honest with you and I don't have the capacity to listen right now, based on other things that happened today. I wish I did, and this is not a reflection on you." If we're not used to upholding fifth-hub boundaries, initially it can be difficult, but with some practice we become empowered. Learning to respect our own needs when it comes to absorbing charge is essential for management of this hub—and with any boundary, it starts with the awareness of our right to uphold it. Awareness and enforcement of our sonic boundary is often second-guessed, and we can be accused of being too sensitive. We find ourselves in the position of being easily invaded and vampirized when we let other people decide when a conversation is over or if it has crossed a line. Perhaps we're used to staying in a conversation with an energy sucker—and as the vampire goes on, more and more of our energy gets drained and the longer we stay, the harder it is to leave.

Excessive talking can be an inexplicit way of creating a boundary against hearing what others have to say. It can be used to prevent further exhaustion when we can't take in any more information. Filibustering (excessive talk that blocks others from speaking) is used in legislative procedures to delay or prevent others from speaking or taking action and is sometimes used in everyday interpersonal interactions. Sometimes the best way to get someone to stop talking is to use silence, showing that you're not going to start talking when they stop. But sometimes, when folks are too spun up and oblivious, we need to have the fortitude to put our hand up and say, "I'm so sorry to interrupt, but I have to go."

A GOOD LISTENER

As kids, people who listened to us and took an interest in what we had to say without interrupting or correcting were treasured—grandparents, teachers, or anyone who would just listen with complete attention. Something special happens when we're listened to: we feel seen, accepted, and validated. When we're not heard, we feel invisible and lonely, and when we don't express and process our experiences and thoughts, our shame, grief, guilt, and fear can fester and grow. Take a moment and think of the people in your life who listen to you and make you feel understood. Do you actively honor them and let them know how much they mean to you? Growing up, were your parents too busy or were they able to give you the time and listen to you—did you have to fight to be heard? One interviewee told me, "My mother loved me very much, but she could not slow down to listen, so my aunt became my sounding board. Looking back, in many ways it feels like my aunt saved my life."

TRUTH

Our truth is like a single thread containing many small fibers of experience, belief, family, and culture surrounding the embloom, all of which are uniquely our own—both the lived experience combined with our inner depths, longing to be expressed. This thread is woven into the fabric of our shared humanity, our lives incorporated into the lives of others. But there is always a distinction between our personal truth and the larger truth of the shared fabric: we are all unique, separate, yet woven together. Each thread is infinitely complex, and the only truth we can come even close to fully understanding is our own. Unfortunately, instead of sharing one's own lived experience, there's a practice of using facts, figures, and so-called evidence in attempts to override and disregard the opinions and perspectives of others. When there's no personal disclosure, we use the truths and materials of others to make a case for us, tossing articles and memes over the fence of our self-protection and feeling surprised when the response is correspondingly guarded and unreceptive.

The only person we can change is ourselves—and why would we want it any other way? If we can change others against their will to fit our worldviews and preferences, it means it would be possible for others to do the same to us. When expressing our truth, it's important to remember that what we reveal is the axis-mundi of our own lives, not of the entire world. Again, our perspective is a unique formation, different from every other human life on Earth, yet part of a shared experience. Aversion, disrespect, and censorship are ways to avoid experiences that deviate from our own. When we try to stop the expression of lives that make us uncomfortable, we act in violence against life itself and sacrifice a piece of our truth in doing so. By denying another's humanity, we lose a piece of ourselves. The parallax effect of our perspective and relationship to an issue can lead us to believe that we know what is best for everyone (see Chapter 3). If your truth interferes with another's ability to be free, then it's dishonest. There's no absolute truth that requires the subjugation, denial, or dehumanization of others. Everyone we meet is on a continuum of their past, present, and potential. This doesn't mean that we need to invite them all into our lives, but it does ask that we demonstrate compassion for our shared humanity to the best of our ability (except in the case of oppressed and abused people: survival and preservation of their own human dignity come first).

SOUND AND SILENCE

The sound of our voice is an indicator of adaptation in this hub. Baby voices, vocal fry, and other constrictions indicate an inability to be entirely centered and comfortable. Trying to sound younger, sweeter, and less threatening is a social condition (usually for women) that's absorbed unconsciously through the subtle influences of social approval and disproval. Oppositely, an overbearing, loud, tone-deaf voice that fills a room tends to crowd out other voices. If you tend to speak with any of these affects, experiment with releasing the constriction in your throat and talking in a more natural, relaxed register. See how it feels and notice how people respond. One client I interviewed told me she thought she sounded butch and unfeminine when she tried this; another told me he initially thought he sounded too quiet—until his boss said he seemed calmer and more confident. It can take some practice and getting used to, but notice how people respond to an unrestricted, authentic voice.

Silence allows us to connect with ourselves and to hear our inner voice, but it's often avoided if we fear what the voice has to say. Sometimes we're afraid of what we know, but when we feel safe and grounded, we may feel ready to begin the process of uncovering deeper truths. When we're ready, in hubs five, six, and seven, we receive: for the fifth hub—*I'm ready to hear;* for the sixth—*I'm ready to see;* and for the seventh hub—*I'm ready to know.*

THEMES
DISCUSSION AND CONFLICT

We don't choose the people at work, in public, our families, or neighbors, but we need to figure out how to live with them. Interfacing with people on different wavelengths from the one we're on is part of life. A significant contributor to our quality of life is our effectiveness in connecting and dealing with different people. Many conflicts and disagreements can be more like slap fights than actual discourse. For an observer, an online-comment war can be funny to watch, but even if there's a so-called winner, everyone involved loses when they attempt to overpower the truths of other people instead of having curiosity, and all involved are left with red faces. How can we develop our own personal truth if we're unwilling to respect those of others? When two or more truths collide on different wavelengths (as they often do), conflicts arise, so we all need to strap on our BRAs (boundaries, respect, and self-advocacy).

Boundaries

All boundaries require awareness before they can be effectively enforced—be clear about what you will and will not tolerate. If you're being devalued, disrespected, or screamed or yelled at, you cannot expect the invading person to be responsible for deciding what's enough or too much. If a boundary is crossed or invaded, be aware of what you're absorbing, such as intensity or abusive language, and when possible, wait to leave the interaction before actively discharging. Give the intensity space to move through and out (the exercises at the end of this chapter are helpful). Discharging into a situation where there's excess charge will amplify it, often resulting in a blowback of further invasion. Whenever it's possible and responsible, shut it down and allow for emotions to pass before you consider reengaging. For an infant or young child, agitation and upset need to be handled in the moment, but mature adults can know how intense emotions pass and how nothing is gained by instigating conflict with people when they're at high intensity.

Another aspect of a fifth-hub boundary is sound. Noise overload can overwhelm this hub with unwanted comments, loud ambient noise, or unwanted music other people are listening to. Some folks walk around wearing earbuds or headphones without playing music to protect this boundary. Some people won't leave the house without wearing headphones as a subconscious protection against environmental noise.

Respect

The lives of others are different from your own, even when some aspects are similar. It can be healthy to have a heated, passionate argument in which both parties remain respectful of the other, energized, and excited by the other's perspective. Healthy conflict should involve both speaking and listening and transmitting and receiving. But if the perspective of your lived experience is not being respected, you should carefully consider how and to what extent you should continue the interaction—perhaps an attempt or two to make your case (although arguing for human dignity with someone committed to denying it can cause damage and trauma). Rarely, if ever, has a heart or mind been changed through defenses in an argument, but if a fight does change a heart or mind, it's usually the softening that occurs after the heat of conflict. In personal interactions, the best way to send a message is not to tolerate dehumanizing language and delusions: if the softening is going to happen, let it begin sooner by leaving the conflict earlier, and stand up for yourself by demonstrating the standard for what you're willing to tolerate—and what you will not.

Advocacy

Respectfully practicing self-advocacy involves making the big asks in life—weathering the moments before the response, and when the actual response comes, being able to stand your ground one way or the other. The excruciating time between asking for a raise and receiving an answer is what we train for when practicing self-advocacy. It's not always comfortable in the short term but ultimately, it's preferable to accepting less than we should. Advocating for yourself with small things prepares you to do it for big ones. Don't wait for the big game: practice firm-but-polite advocacy with the little things, such as asking for small favors: *Would you get that for me?* and *Could I have some extra [whatever you want]?* When we go too big with an ask before we're ready, our discomfort can unintentionally transmit as irritation or even hostility and turn a benign interaction into a conflict. Conflicts come in an array of intensities, and the dynamic we anticipate can become the one we create—so expect the best but be prepared for the worst. When we expect the world to be hostile, we'll be spring-loaded to respond, but if we expect it to be entirely kind, we may not be prepared to enforce boundaries and advocate for ourselves when hostile situations do arise. When we practice with smaller interactions, we learn to handle disappointment and further prepare ourselves for the realization that knowing rather than stewing over an unasked question usually puts us in a position to make better decisions. There are plenty of conversations that take place inside people's heads blaming others for disappointments that have never been directly addressed. Developing a self-advocacy practice is life-changing because it increases our personal power by resolving the loose ends of unspoken grievances, reducing situations that make us feel victimized, and lessening the emotional load of carrying around unasked questions. Self-advocacy changes our relationship with the world.

We want to be capable of standing for what we believe in and standing up for others. For those of you who don't have a problem asking for more for yourself, put your powers to use and try advocating for someone else who could use your support.

THE THREE V'S

Body-language researcher Albert Mehrabian finds that only a small percent of the total effect of a message is in the words. His research reveals that the "big three" for the effect of communication are verbal (what we say) for 7 percent (!); vocal (how we sound) for 38 percent; and visual (body language and other visual cues) for 55 percent. Thus, the words we use to communicate are framed by sound and physical expression, so the more we can consciously reclaim our voice and body language, the more effective we are as communicators. I'm a staunch believer in the idea that the best way to boost the effectiveness of your communication is to become increasingly comfortable with who you are, no matter what that looks like: quiet/loud, silly/serious—it doesn't matter. Authenticity has a compelling quality felt by everyone who encounters it.

I discuss how adaptations can shape the tone, modulation, and volume of a voice later in this chapter. A shrinking voice adapts so it can sound small, quiet, and unthreatening. Lilting the ends of sentences—so-called upspeak—is also a shrinking adaptation to diminish any threatening interpretation of statements by making them sound like questions. The inflating and overcompensating adaptation is interrupting, overbearing, and loud. Balanced expression in this hub is a resonant voice with a range that can either be loud or quiet as a situation calls for it. As with any adaptation, we're not trying to change ourselves. Instead, we're restoring dynamism to the hub to have access to more expression within it. A vocal adaptation is noticeable because the affects and constrictions don't adjust to the situation they're in, but instead tend to amplify when under stress. When uncomfortable, a shrinking adaptation becomes quieter and an inflating becomes louder.

POSITIVE AND NEGATIVE WORDS

Some developmental psychologists say that negative words are five times more impactful than positive ones and that neutralizing any negative comment requires five positive ones: one cruel word requires a lot of repairs. As adults, we seek out and respond (often without being aware of it) to the voices and tones like the ones we first heard in our early lives, and as our biology conflates safety with familiarity, without conscious reclamation we'll migrate toward familiar-sounding voices and tones even when they are in fact not safe at all. We both internalize the early voices and seek them out. If we had critical parents, we would likely find critical people to be more credible than people who are kind to us. If we grew up with kind and encouraging voices, we would find harsh and critical words and tones especially overwhelming and difficult to tolerate.

In the third hub I discussed how internalized criticism can be directed inward or outward (see Chapter 6). The inward-directed critical voice tends to take inappropriate responsibility for others while holding unrealistic, unfair expectations for itself. Conversely, the outward-facing inner critic finds fault in everyone else and creates unrealistic standards that judge others as unworthy or not good enough. This forms a (subconscious) protection against connection, which can often result in the marriage-destroying scorn and contempt of Gottman's work (see Chapter 7). When people with an inward-facing critic speak, they tend to second-guess what they say and be very careful about avoiding embarrassment. Folks with outward-facing critics tend to be more outspoken but are alienating because of their harsh delivery. Through socialization, outward critics may learn to behave when consciously controlled, but eventually they will let slip a few cruel words that may shock or disturb the recipient. Consciously surfacing and ousting the critical inner voice changes our relationship within ourselves and the ones we have with other people.

CREATIVE EXPRESSION

We communicate to be understood, to build bridges, and to unify—but ultimately, every human experience is unique and cannot be duplicated. This introduces the relationship between a creator and a recipient as simultaneously universal and uniquely one's own. Music, cinema, written and spoken language all transmit part of another human's lived experience to our own. Someone else's self-expression will be seen, interpreted, and experienced through the lens of our own perception—the same words spoken to 20 different people will create 20 distinct experiences.

We use language when we attempt to describe an experience. Still, most of the description will remain in interstices, a mystery that psychoanalyst Otto Rank described when he wrote, "The artwork presents a unity, alike in its efforts and in its creation, and this implies a spiritual unity between the artist and recipient. Although temporary and symbolic only." In our experiences with art and creative expression, we crave the paradox of a shared experience that is unifying while also being completely our own—and it is both. Rank continued by saying that artwork "[P]roduces a satisfaction that suggests that it is more than a matter of passing identification of two individuals, that it is the potential restoration of a union with the cosmos which once existed and was then lost." Perhaps the goal is to be understood, but the result is that observers come to better understand themselves.

INTERRUPTIONS AND STRESSORS

Interruptions in this hub happen both early and throughout our lives, but it's the early environment and development that are particularly potent, forming patterns with long-lasting implications unless we consciously reclaim and actively develop our communication and creativity in adulthood. Murphy writes that "[P]eople spend their lives seeking and creating circumstances that match what they knew in childhood. They selectively listen to people who sound like who they heard first and thus reinforce old neural pathways; they're trying to sync in a way that feels familiar." As I discuss in previous hubs and above, the early experiences coded into our biology and psyche create the sense of familiarity that signals that something is safe, regardless of whether it actually is.

In the fifth, sixth, and seventh hubs, we see the ripple effect of early interruptions, such as fear, guilt, and shame, which interfere with our ability both to feel safe enough to speak freely and to listen without being excessively self-protective and guarded. Physical security, emotional capacity, personal power, and worthiness are all involved in how safe and free we feel in expressing our opinions, talking about our personal experiences, and in our ability to hear difficult things without becoming emotionally flooded: to understand that one person's opinion is exactly that, a single person's opinion.

SEEN BUT NOT HEARD

Communication is a skill, and like any it needs to be developed—our first teachers are usually our parents, and we have them to thank (either in earnest or sarcastically) for our early programming. Judith writes, "To give children the gift of clear communication is to give them a key that will unlock the majority of impasses and difficulties they will face in the future." Children develop confidence by practicing at home. Also, according to Judith, "Without discussion, there is no practice ground for the child to learn communication skills." If the rule of the house for children was *Don't talk back,* this often meant that strong thoughts and feelings were not tolerated, and perhaps were even met with punishment. For a child raised in an environment in which being respectful required obedience and silence, speaking up can have harsh and sometimes scary consequences.

Children have complex emotional lives, and they learn from listening and participating in conversations with adults. Like the early attunement of feelings and emotions in the second hub, talking with parents and family is how the inner voice synchronizes with others and learns to trust itself. A child who's told *You have no right to feel that way* by a parent is apt to feel that this is both untrue and unjust, yet will also believe the parent, creating an inner conflict that undermines the child's self-esteem and self-confidence. Communication skills need development in the home, and if children are shut down when they try to speak, they grow to be adults missing skills that will need to be developed, a process that can require a lot of patience and effort.

Being ignored, neglected, and isolated is also interrupting to this hub. As I discuss throughout this chapter, by talking through our thoughts and feelings in a meaningful way, we process experiences while learning to use language to effectively express ourselves.

Fear of public speaking is common and often mystifyingly intense but consider that if a small body's early experiments with speaking up are met with high-voltage backlash from adults, it's easy to see how a strong physical aversion could be programmed into a body's reflexes. After all, the nervous system activation of an increased heart rate, shaking or trembling, sweating, and anxiety over an objectively harmless activity must have deeper roots in early experiences.

Blocking out harsh, loud, or cruel words can be a protective defense (an adaptation) against high-voltage words coming from adults. As a result, listening can also suffer the consequences of intense early experiences. Trusting and instating the ability to listen involves feeling safe, having a commitment to growth, and working patiently with an atrophied function.

ABUSE OF TRUST

When a respected teacher, coach, family, or community member pays attention to a child, the child is excited to feel important. If the need to be heard (and even delighted in) is met in primary, loving relationships, this vulnerability is decreased or even eliminated. Tragically, many predators sense when children (and adults) are starving to be listened to and understood. Grooming for abuse often involves taking advantage of the naturally occurring trust that tends to arise when we feel that someone wants to understand us; a child who's ignored or undermined at home is particularly vulnerable—sometimes to someone within the home. A predatory adult (or in some cases another child) will sense this need and create loyalty and attachment by building a trust trap. The starvation for attention and the fear of losing the affirmation

are already expanding when predators begin to place their conditions on the attention. When the abuse of this trust occurs, it is an interruption that teaches children that trust and opening up harms them. When this happens, it's understandable that they become self-protective and distrustful as a practical defense against future abuse, perhaps even feeling guilty or ashamed for needing and appreciating the attention and the fulfillment it provides.

Abuse of trust can also happen as a betrayal by peers or siblings. The comfort of feeling close to a friend and disclosing secrets and truths is destroyed if the trusted person broadcasts our vulnerabilities and embarrasses us, causing shame and invoking self-protection. For example, my interviewee Sasha told me that when she was 11 years old, her best friend, Lise, betrayed her by telling the so-called popular girls in school her secrets. She remembers knowing that Lise had used their intimacy and her most personal information to gain short-lived status with girls who didn't like either of them. Sasha told me that the shaming and teasing left a mark that she carries today as an adult: "I felt like I lost so much when it happened. My trust in my best friend, some of my innocence and openness—and school became a terrible place for a while. I would hide and walk on eggshells to avoid the teasing even though the surprise attacks were unavoidable."

VERBAL ABUSE AND BULLYING

Criticizing is a hard habit to break and telling people they're not enough or explaining to them who they are—delivered as a so-called fact—is a terrible practice, especially if the words are intended to hurt. However, telling people how their behavior affects us and what you believe is possible for them can be part of the process of transformation. Sometimes critical attention is a necessary wake-up call, but when it's done by diminishing or degrading people, it can be destructive. You have every right to tell people how their behavior has affected you, but you have no right to tell people who they are. You have every right to enforce a personal boundary, but you do not have the right to tell someone who they are (for example, "a bad person") because they invaded it.

The bullies we encountered as kids on the playground hurt our feelings and sometimes, we adapted our personas, but there is simply no hurt greater than that caused by the cruel words of a parent. When our parents tell us who we are, we tend to believe them. I interviewed Yvonne, who said that even though her father left when she was 10 years old, his kind words had made it possible for her to build her self-esteem as an adult after recovering from the verbal abuse she experienced from her mother. "Remembering my dad telling me at five and six years old how smart, kind, and generous I was has helped me as an adult to connect dots about my true nature and to heal."

The act of so-called setting people straight can be violence on self-image, especially while that self-image is forming. Accusations that tell people who they are or point out negative or sensitive characteristics can be especially distressing—and adaptations are inevitable when verbal abuse, such as yelling, demeaning, or intimidation occur in the home. When there's a bully at home or at school, a child will have to learn to navigate the complex waters of difficult people, and an adaptive pattern will emerge, shrinking to hide or inflating and fighting back. The options on the farthest ends of this spectrum are running away or becoming a bully and somewhere in between we stand up for ourselves.

The inclination to notice negative things about people can be consciously shifted into looking for positive ones. If you're going to look, why not focus on the good stuff? We can fine-tune our compliments: instead of asserting so-called facts about who or what people are, tell them how you experience them. *You're so pretty* becoming a first-person experience is *I admire and appreciate your style and beauty.* Or *You're a rockstar* becomes *You inspire me with your charisma and bravery.* The idea is to shift a subjective assessment to one that is oriented from your direct experience, not general—often impersonal—platitudes stated as facts.

SECRETS AND DISSONANCE

If we keep a secret, we can't be completely at ease and spontaneously respond to people—almost everything must pass through a filter and, to a greater or lesser extent, a secret keeper must always be vigilant. Judith writes that when we keep a secret, "We have to guard against talking about the things that matter most." For people threatened with terrifying consequences if they tell, keeping a secret cuts off the ability to feel fully alive and connected to important people in their lives.

Growing up in a home with secrets is confusing for a child. On the one hand, we're being told to tell the truth and be honest and on the other hand, we're seeing and experiencing our family do the opposite. Worse yet, pointing out secrets before we knew they were forbidden topics can lead to being snapped at, yelled at, or even punished or abused. Siblings often secretly convene to compare information about and to decode their parents. Secrets and incomplete information result in fixations on topics like sex and parental dynamics. Children will sometimes covertly inspect the rooms and belongings of their parents. This exploration and fascination can feel illicit. Still, the urge that compels the behavior is the deep curiosity to really know our parents, possibly based on the dissonance we experience between what they say and what we sense and see. We notice the difference usually when their words lie, but their body language and tone continue to tell the truth. If a mother hangs up the phone and her shoulders slump with a look of hopelessness on her face as she says to her children, "Daddy has an exciting work dinner and won't be coming home," the children will question this dissonance initially and reflexively. Although eventually, with repetition, children will likely surrender their inner knowing so they do not increase their mother's pain and to restore harmony to the best of their ability. The reflex to harmonize the dissonance in our home by changing ourselves is a survival mechanism.

As children we were sponges absorbing everything around us. When we're developing our intuition and learning to trust our instincts, being told what we suspect is wrong (when it isn't) or being given incomplete information affects this calibration process between the outside world and our inner knowing. As adults, we may become agitated and activated when we sense that what we are being told conflicts with what is happening, or worse, we may accept it because we are familiar with disregarding our intuition and instincts. Secrets require ongoing management, and the expenditure of subconscious energy leads to stress and tight muscles. Although it can be difficult, when we unburden ourselves of a secret we tend to experience relief, softening, and more energy.

Body language is perhaps the more reliable communicator of truth—after all, it's over 50 percent of what we communicate. Body language–expert Jeanine Driver teaches in *You Say More Than You Think* that shrugging (even slightly) is a tell of uncertainty, regardless of what the person says. In addition, she writes, "When we don't like what we see or hear, our lips disappear," referring to the mannerism of folding lips inward. Some of her tells for untruthfulness are pointing the torso and naval away from the person you are deceiving; using the body to block or hide an object associated with a deception (for example, standing in front of a pack of cigarettes); behaving *differently* (prolonged or shortened eye contact, slowing or speeding up speech); and in some cases, scratching the nose.

SHAME AND UNSPOKEN STANDARDS

We usually learn of unspeakable cultural and family expectations and beliefs by accidentally stumbling onto them and speaking of them without knowledge of their meaning. If a family has addiction, mental illness, financial problems, or other emotionally loaded issues that are not discussed, this hub can be deeply affected. Perhaps we noticed and mentioned a parent or family member's drinking or pointed out the absence of someone. Maybe we spoke of a deceased family member or someone's body weight or a physical difference we observed. Adults may react with shaming, which is a shock to a child making an innocent observation. Young children who mean no harm and are unsure of what is acceptable and what is not may begin walking on eggshells and attempting to avoid the seeming randomness of punishment or embarrassment for their observations. Being punished or reprimanded when we tell the truth is confusing, especially when we're given little to no explanation and this can lead to adapted behavior patterns. Leadership and organizational-behavior researcher Amy Edmondson writes in *The Fearless Organization: Creating Psychological Safety* of behavior modifications she calls "impression management": If you don't want to look ignorant—*don't ask questions*; if you don't want to look incompetent—*don't admit weakness or mistakes*; if you don't want to appear intrusive—*don't offer ideas*; and if you don't want to appear negative—*don't critique the status quo*.

ADAPTATIONS AND HOLDING PATTERNS

This hub isn't just about the act of talking: it's about the integrity of self-expression through speaking, listening, being heard, and creativity. In the fifth hub, truth exerts its force and wants to be expressed; it can require significant effort to control what we say, and the truth can feel stuck in our throat. Perhaps we adopt a quiet voice, a vocal effect of pitch or cadence, use excessive small talk, or a voice so loud it's unsettling for others to hear. As we open our throat and stretch the neck and shoulders, speaking can feel like water through a rusty pipe. Sometimes emotions surface, sometimes there's discomfort, tickling, and coughing that start when we begin to physically release tightness in the neck and throat and to speak with integrity and authenticity. We may be articulate and capable of commanding an audience in a professional setting, but when disclosing personal truths our voice may constrict, and we may struggle to find the right words or may have greater ease and comfort at home but struggle with communication at work.

The holding patterns in this hub are relatively straightforward—inflating adaptations get louder and attempt to control through excessive talking; shrinking adaptations speak less and tend to be quieter when they talk. Keep in mind that our behavior tends to be more moderate within a given hub when we feel safe, but when we get stressed, we amplify the expression of our adaptations. This can mean that people who are already quiet become imperceptible when under stress and usually, loud people start to sound like they're using a megaphone.

Being loud isn't necessarily an adaptation unless it's used to crowd people out of conversations; being quiet or soft-spoken isn't necessarily an adaptation either unless accompanied by an inability to speak up for oneself. There are plenty of powerful people who speak quietly and carry a big stick and plenty of naturally loud people capable of listening.

Talking can be used to vent low-voltage nervous chatter (small talk) or it can overwhelm a listener with high-voltage blasts that contain intense topics at high volume. Small talk and nervous chatter serve to discharge energy rather than communicate, often leaving listeners feeling drained. Oppositely, yelling and intensity will shock, exhaust, and overwhelm listeners because they tend to either blow out or scramble listeners' circuits. In balance, or at least in a dynamic flow, communication is authentic, brave, and magnetic without being overbearing. If you're not being authentic—deciding to play it safe—you have your reasons, but you can't be surprised if people don't find you interesting. When there's integrity in this hub, we speak with a resonant, centered voice, with the ability to either be quiet or to speak up (and even yell) when a situation calls for it. When we hold back, common physical symptoms are tension in the throat, neck, and trapezius muscles (tops of shoulders closest to the neck).

CHARACTERISTICS OF A BALANCED FIFTH HUB

- A resonant, clear voice that's pleasant to listen to with situationally appropriate tonality and volume
- Clear and considerate verbal communication
- Good listening with balance between talking and listening
- Written communication is both concise and expressive
- Effortlessly and naturally creative
- Smooth and graceful physical movement acts in concert with verbal communication
- Feels heard and therefore can make space for others to feel heard

- Respects others' different perspectives; is calm and does not reflexively feel attacked
- Confident of its opinion, unafraid to (respectfully) voice dissent
- Feels in the loop and keeps others aware of what's going on; able to stay in touch with friends, family, and colleagues over time
- Feels safe to say what it believes—not excessively fearful of being rejected
- Has good timing, grace, and rhythm, can "read the room" and project or speak quietly based on what is needed

CHARACTERISTICS OF AN OUT-OF-BALANCE FIFTH HUB

- Tightness or stiffness in throat, neck, and tops of shoulders, awkward, agitated or shifting physical movements that nonverbally express discomfort
- Doesn't read the room—defensive, self-conscious, and out of sync with what others are saying
- Voice can either be inaudible (shrinking) or booming (inflating)
- Avoids difficult conversations, talks about everything except what truly matters—often behind people's backs
- Written communication is hard to follow, contains syntax, punctuation, and word-choice errors
- Gossips and complains excessively
- Insecure and cut off from creativity, copies the work of others either as so-called flattery or outright plagiarism
- Protects against disapproval by lying or deceiving
- Feels out of the loop and is paranoid (nervous about what others might be saying)
- Doesn't believe or respect other people's lived experiences when they're too different

- Assumes negative intent or discounts people as only trying to get attention when what they have to say is overwhelming or difficult news

- Incessant talking—quietly for shrinking, loud for inflating

- Can use embarrassing detail oversharing to gain trust, but does not disclose anything with real vulnerability

- Tone-deafness

SHRINKING

The shrinking adaptation is nervous about exposing thoughts and feelings, afraid of accidentally revealing flaws that could result in rejection or embarrassment. This adaptation is adept in Edmundson's behaviors of impression management: don't ask questions, don't admit weaknesses or mistakes, don't offer ideas, and don't critique the status quo. But taking risks is a component of authenticity that's difficult when we don't feel psychologically safe enough to speak up. The characteristics in the shrinking adaptation tend to be likable to friends, colleagues, and peers, but not necessarily admired or even respected. For someone with a shrinking adaptation, it can be challenging to find the right words; writing an email or a social media post can be excruciating, so the person goes with the simplest, least-revealing option. There can be a lot of discomfort in having a lot to express but fearing the consequences of doing so.

Characteristics of Fifth-Hub Shrinking Adaptation

- Fear of public speaking

- Awkward conversationalist (difficulty putting things into words)

- Remains silent to avoid the discomfort of confrontation

- Feels awkward about standing up for what it believes

- When speaking, is afraid of mistakes, judgment, and being wrong

- Wonders what people will say and often chooses to remain silent until it can gossip or judge from a safe distance

- Quiet or constricted, high-pitch voice

- Overly concerned about embarrassment and humiliation, worried about appearing stupid

- Feels like nobody listens to it, often frustrated and complaining about this to people who cannot help it

- Can be secretive or gossiping

- Susceptible to flattery and excessively loyal toward people who listen to them, which can lead to mistakes in discernment. Likes when people tell them who they are—telling them their strengths and weaknesses feels safer to them than self-awareness and self-confidence.

Under stress (when an adaptation tends to become heightened), a common shrinking response is giving the silent treatment. The shrinking adaptation will likely complain to almost everyone except the person directly related to the issue. When it experiences unfavorable behavior, instead of directly communicating to the person perpetrating it, the shrinking adaptation is more likely to ask others *What kind of person does that?* There's often overlap between a shrinking second hub that struggles to understand and process emotions without second-guessing them.

I interviewed Loren, in whose childhood home speaking clearly and with composure was respected. She would be admonished as being sloppy and weak when she would become emotional, expressing thoughts and feelings before she had processed, polished, and organized them. As a result, Loren learned to restrain what she would say until it was sanitized and could be said without emotion. Now, this means that a lot of time passes—days and sometimes weeks—between an event and Loren's ability to talk about it; when she does speak, a lot of important things are left unsaid. Loren talked about feeling blocked from living up to her full potential and sensed that her career was affected by her inability to speak with leaders and to effectively communicate ideas in meetings. This also led to significant strain during arguments or conflicts with her husband, who told Loren he feels iced out as she processes her feelings while he starts to imagine the worst and becomes increasingly agitated in the loaded silence. When Loren finally speaks, he explodes from the built-up tension, further pushing her into her shrinking pattern.

INFLATING

An inflated adaptation may encourage a lively conversation, but it quickly becomes evident that contradicting or outshining is not welcomed. The adaptation may even scoff, undermine, or ignore attempts of others to contribute, using loudness and excessive talking to control people and situations.

This adaptation can be a chatterbox, charismatic, and commanding, or a blowhard energy vampire crowding others out (overpowering them in conversations). A characteristic of all adaptations in this hub is that substantive discussions are avoided in exchange for gossip, complaining about people who aren't present, or topics discussed using rehearsed talking points. The inflating adaptation can be particularly difficult because attempts to make communication more collaborative and interesting can be met with resistance.

Characteristics of Fifth-Hub Inflating Adaptation

- Frequently interrupts—excessive talking as a defense mechanism
- Doesn't want to share the mic, is entertaining and charming but discourages input or participation from others
- Tends to be loud
- Fears losing audience's attention, resents and punishes anyone who undermines or steals their spotlight
- Promotes censorship of others when it conflicts with its position
- Out of rhythm, struggles to synchronize in a conversation or to read a room, leading to awkward moments
- Tells people who they are through overbearing assessments or flattery
- Has a hard time allowing others to complete what they're saying without weighing in
- Is a poor listener—fidgets, avoids eye contact, looks at their phone

During my interviews for *The Parinama Method*, I didn't want to reinforce what I already believed or to control the conversations. I was looking for my own blind spots, so I developed a practice: I thought of five questions to ask and placed two conditions on myself: I could not control or interfere with the responses as they came (which I found very challenging); and the questions had to be about topics unfamiliar to me. Before the interview, I would spend 10 to 15 minutes meditating on which questions to ask. For example, when I asked a question about excellent life advice the interviewee had received, the initial answer may have been a platitude, but when asked about the most important money advice the person received as a child (a more specific version of the question), I was silent as the person thought about it. That's when the magic would happen. I would count a full five to 10 seconds after the person had stopped talking before I'd say anything. This silence would usually prompt further reflection, and the most profound answers came in the additional time provided for the thoughts to arrive.

HOLDING PATTERNS
THE SHADOW: LIES

According to Galileo, "All truths are easy to understand once they are discovered; the point is to discover them." He was convicted of heresy by the Catholic Church for his heliocentrism in 1633 and placed under house arrest until his death. The Church's position against Galileo was reversed in 1992. It's rumored that during his trial Galileo mumbled *"E pur si muove"* ("and yet it moves," referring to the Earth's relationship to the Sun). Speaking truth to power is rarely well received, but the truth will never stay hidden forever.

Lies and deception are in the shadows of both the fifth and sixth hubs. Lies are what we speak and hear (fifth hub); deception is what we conceal and intentionally hide from others (sixth hub).

We're often taught a black-and-white morality about lying, but practical reality tends to be a bit grayer. When I was a kid in the 1980s, I learned from a friend's father, a long-haul trucker, that he kept two logbooks to record his mileage: one for the cops and one for his boss. He told us that the cops enforced truck driver–fatigue laws while the bosses paid more if truck drivers drove farther faster, which meant sleeping less. Furthermore, the trucker said that both the cops and the bosses knew about this practice but pretended to be unaware of it because each party was getting the information it wanted. At the time, I was fascinated. While it's universally agreed that lying is wrong, I remember thinking that if I wanted to be in good favor with everyone, it seemed impossible to avoid telling a few fibs. I also asked my friend's father which log was the correct one, and he told me the truth was always somewhere in between.

When we have so many different facets that we show to different people, who sees the truth? Experimenting with deception and lying starts early as we try to shift ourselves to fit into our home, perhaps by testing a boundary or trying to get something we want. We may attempt to avoid blame and punishment by telling a little fib. However, deception builds momentum as we begin to operate in different environments, fulfilling various roles and shaping ourselves to fit them. For example, when friends and family from different parts of our life meet, we may wonder what will happen when two versions of ourselves collide—will they like each other? Do we fear disclosure of embarrassing facts, or worse yet, secrets? Often this friction is reduced throughout each of the four life cycles (see Chapter 3), and our personas fall away. As we age, our insides begin to match more closely who we consistently present to the world. As a result, mature adults don't change very much when they migrate between different parts of their lives.

Deception can be a temporary relief from discomfort and pain if we feel unsafe, unworthy, or ashamed of ourselves. But a painkiller doesn't heal a broken bone—if we don't find a safe place to receive medical help, we can become addicted to painkillers as the injury fails to heal properly. Lying is like pain relief that temporarily relieves the discomfort of the truth. Covering the pain will not reset and heal a broken bone, and what it grows into can become poorly formed and maladapted, eventually requiring deeper reconstructive work.

Being able to tell your truth is powerful. It can also be hard work, especially when it's not pleasant. It's often a risk that we cannot afford to take, like telling our bosses that they infuriate us—it's often overlooked how luxurious and privileged telling the truth can be. When I was putting myself through college—without health insurance or family support, driving a car without functioning brakes, and four dollars in my checking account—I lied to everybody and hustled them for money, food, and rent. When I finally made money, lying was a hard habit to break, but breaking it provided some of the most significant relief within the freedom of financial stability. Lying may reduce pain or shift an outcome in our favor, but it robs us and others of rightful accomplishments and wins. Lying deprives us of the satisfaction and calm of integrity and being lied to doesn't allow others to make decisions with all the available information, which can lead to serious outcomes. Telling the truth involves courage, integrity, and energy. We lie when we don't have power and when we don't feel strong enough, that is, when we don't have the freedom and safety to manage the consequences.

TECHNIQUES AND EXERCISES

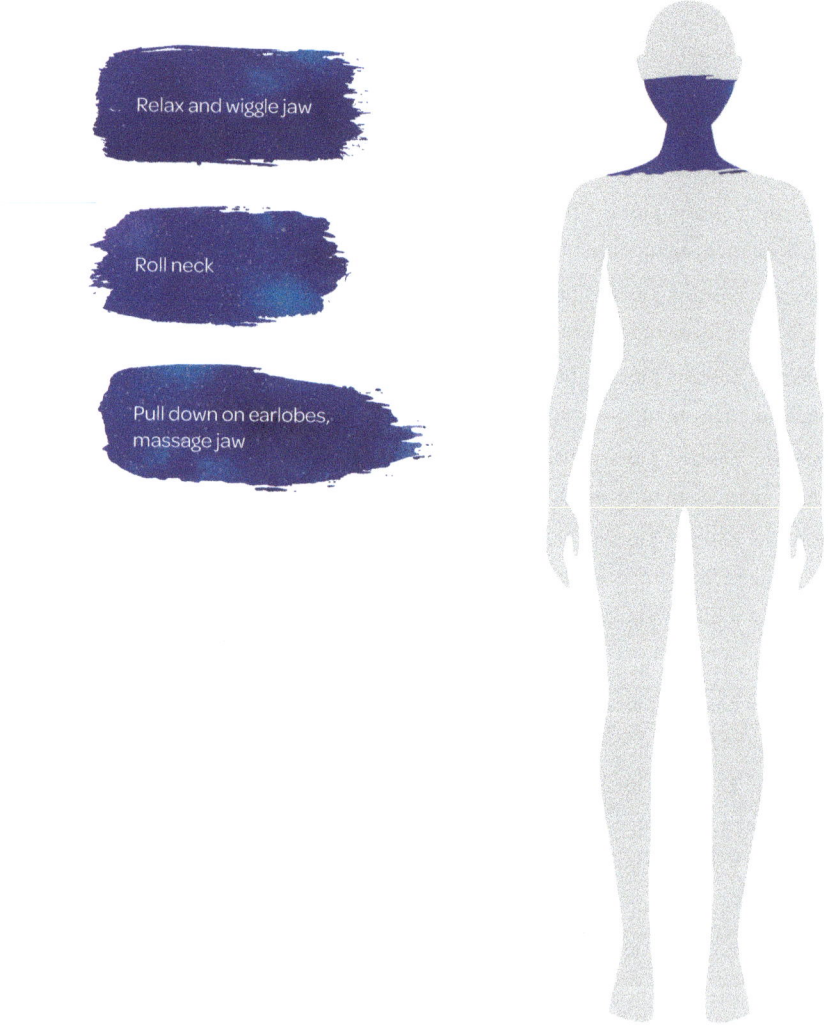

Relax and wiggle jaw

Roll neck

Pull down on earlobes, massage jaw

Figure 8.1: Fifth-Hub Body Prompts

THE PARINAMA METHOD FIFTH-HUB FUNDAMENTALS

The physical location of the fifth hub is in the neck, jaw, chin, lips, tongue, roof of mouth, ears, and in the use of the shoulders and hands. Hands are instruments of communication and creative expression and are used to enhance verbal communication—some studies have shown that gesticulating can help us think. Sign languages are profoundly somatic styles of communication that yoke physical movement and inner expression. Writing, building, and creating with your hands or playing an instrument are all further enhanced when the dynamic equilibrium of this hub is restored (during the writing of this part of *The Parinama Method*, a ride-service driver told me that he finds it difficult when passengers don't talk to him and so, he restores himself by playing guitar).

To consciously reclaim our voice and the ability to create, we explore the early behaviors programmed into us. Cultural, social, familial, and personal values collide as we seek to express our identity in the early years of fifth-hub development. Now that we're adults, we examine these factors and consciously reclaim their influences to decide what serves us and what we want to let go of. When we hold back or conceal what we have to say, our vocal cords become tight and can be experienced as tension in the shoulders, neck, and jaw, which can become a chronic holding pattern. Flow in this hub is speaking your truth without talking over the truth of another or invading that person's boundary with the overwhelming intensity of noise. The balance we seek to restore is listening to and validating others, and of expressing ourselves without invading or causing harm.

This hub has much power and voltage; words are potent with regard to causing intentional and unintentional harm. Yelling and harsh words are used when emotions are overwhelming and using the shock value of words and their delivery can feel validating and satisfying when they get a response. When this hub is interrupted, the attunement of conversation struggles to synchronize—a continuation of interruptions and adaptations in the second hub. Communication requires a dynamic balance of expression and validation, and if we experience an interruption, we may develop an adaptation that blocks one or the other, and sometimes both.

The boundary and human-right interruptions in this hub are often similar to the second hub's: blame is placed on others for not being tough enough and for being too sensitive. Still, words and sound invade and can cause harm. Parents who constantly criticize their children as they begin to express themselves in their early teens interrupt their right to self-expression. As a result, children may protect themselves from listening because they know it can hurt them when they do. A good place to look for interruption is in your behavior patterns that you don't understand—especially those that get labeled as moral shortcomings. Being a bad listener is a good example of this. We can't shut our ears, so we develop other adaptations—like not paying attention.

COMMUNICATION

Communicating effectively involves a dynamic balance of speaking, being heard, listening, and clarifying to validate others. Your voice and hands provide you a uniquely human capacity to express yourself. Language is particularly effective for communicating facts that lead to action, such as *My stomach hurts* or *I want that cookie*. But while poetry and prose can express greater nuance of experience and feeling, the fact remains that we can never fully know how other people feel. The closest we can get is active curiosity: to seek to understand. The following are some pointers and practices to help balance communication and conversation, to allow them to be more fulfilling and to encourage better connection.

A few overall considerations:

- Look for the best in people and even if you don't speak it, the sense of admiration and respect will transmit itself through your eyes and body language.

- Take notes with pen and paper. Signal that you're giving your full attention by asking if they mind if you take notes. Writing down what people say allows you to remain present in a conversation. (Using tech devices to take notes, even after saying, "I'm just taking notes," creates disconnection because the sound of typing is distracting.)

- Eliminate distractions. Try to meet in a quiet place outside or in your home or office. Use noise-canceling headphones for calls.

- Admit when you don't know something. If you pretend to know, covering your tracks will take away from your focus for the rest of the conversation, possibly affecting future interactions. The lowered focus and even a slight suspicion of deception will diminish the level of respect the listener can have for you. It's a distraction to both the speaker and the listener.

- If you want to demonstrate that an interaction matters to you, close your laptop or tablet and put down your phone. When you're on a video call with another person or a group of people, close tabs, and apps on your laptop—people can feel how much attention they receive. You know what it feels like to have someone pay complete attention to you; it's magnetic, engaging, and validating.

- If you control conversations, the magic of new information and unexpected insights gets crowded out. Instead, allow people to speak freely by asking open-ended questions to increase your capacity to withstand uncertainty in a conversation.

- Distracting thoughts can affect your ability to listen. Journaling helps to process and releases cycling thoughts; writing down a cycling thought helps to ground it and seeing it in writing reduces the anxiety of forgetting to take care of it. Cycling thoughts can get stuck as a question or concern or by having the same issue be considered in an infinite number of ways. By writing it down you can begin the process of forming an answer and resolving it.

SETTING UP

Containing a conversation helps to reduce anxiety and overwhelm while it creates connections and grows a relationship. Containment begins with understanding the purpose of the discussion. Start by considering a reasonable outcome, such as getting contact information, setting the next date, or simply making the other person feel validated. Then, make it something that can be reasonably determined. When someone comes to you with a problem, relationship educator Kate Kenfield suggests asking, "Do you want empathy or a strategy?" Large-scale surveys show that most people (about 70 percent), want to be heard and the minority want advice (about 30 percent).

In a professional conversation, such as a sales meeting, start with the end in mind. Imagine what a good outcome looks like and use it to steer the conversation. A good result from a meeting is a next step that supports making progress toward the bigger picture. When you start with your purpose as a destination in mind and the conversation begins to go off-topic, you can steer it back on course. Most discussions have a time limit, and it helps to be aware of what it is by asking, "Do we have the full 30 minutes for our conversation?" or by setting it yourself: "I have to wrap up at 3:00, which is about 20 minutes from now. Does that work for you?" This creates containment (and if you're going to run over, ask if this is okay).

Being clear about who you are also supports the containment, not only for other people but also to remind yourself of who you are in the conversation. For example, "I'm your friend, and I'm here to listen," or "I'm your partner, and today I need someone who will listen to me."

LISTENING AND VALIDATION

Active listening involves engaging in a conversation without taking it over. Don't offer advice unless specifically asked for it. This is particularly difficult if you feel that you add value by providing solutions. Instead, consider your value as giving people the space to think aloud and to do their processing while you support and validate them. Satisfy the reflex to participate by asking questions that help the speaker think and show engagement with body language, such as nodding and turning your body in the speaker's direction. One hack for better listening is to ask questions that interest you. If you don't care to hear the answers to canned interview questions like

What are your strengths and weaknesses? ask questions that arise spontaneously, such as "What is the most interesting thing to happen with a customer this week?" or anything appropriate that may spontaneously occur during a conversation.

While listening, encourage sharing with statements like *Yes, I hear you,* and *I understand,* and *Tell me more about that.* If you're feeling courageous, try to paraphrase what you heard with *What I hear you saying is* and then ask, *Did I miss or misunderstand anything?* If you have the capacity, hold space for people to process and have their feelings without interruption. It can be uncomfortable but ultimately, most people tend to release negative emotions and arrive at a neutral or positive place if they can talk them through—similar to writing down a cycling thought, people need to ground the issue or concern and work it through in the space of a page or in the space created within a conversation. Suppose you interrupt with a well-meaning, positive perspective—you may be serving your own need to keep people positive, which can be a sign of needing a discharge of your own if taking on someone else's intense emotions can take you past your current capacity.

Boundary awareness is essential for listening. If you're feeling emotionally overwhelmed, tell the person, "This is really important stuff you're saying, but I'm not sure I'm the right person to talk to about this right now." Helping someone release frustration isn't your responsibility, especially if doing it overwhelms and exhausts you. This can be a tough one and requires some practice. People who have previously benefited from overstepping boundaries will be the most offended when they are enforced. If people are offended by the suggestion of journaling or seeking therapy, keep in mind that they may prefer talking to you because it's easier for them—this is not a privilege for you, regardless of how it may be positioned. You may also notice that when people target you for their need to vent, the relationship can become limited to this type of interaction.

SPEAKING

I've learned from a career in sales that an effective way to get someone interested in you is to listen to them long enough that they think you have something to say about them. You've probably heard the joke about this: someone who has been talking nonstop says, "Enough about me—what do *you* think about me?" If you do have something to say and you've followed the above steps, now is your time. Think of people who only occasionally speak in meetings and when they do, everyone stops and listens, and they get the full attention of the room. Usually, the only thing anyone can remember from the discussion is Strong Silent's comment or statement. There's a reward for active listening and setting boundaries: being listened to when you speak. When it's your time to speak you will have attention, and the vacuum formed by your silence and awareness will amplify anything you say or ask for. If you need some time to be heard and don't receive it, this is a good indication that you need to create a boundary.

There are cases in which remaining silent may feel frustrating but that ultimately can be the stronger position. If you must fight for a chance to speak in a conversation, it's unlikely the other person will be listening when you do (exceptions to this are if there's an audience like at a debate or meeting). However, keep in mind that some folks may listen just to collect what you say and use it against you. When used effectively, silence is a powerful tool.

ELEVATOR PITCH

No matter who you are or what you do in your life, explaining who you are succinctly is an important skill. Not only does it help you figure out who you are, but it also helps you effectively frame and shift conversations so they're more enjoyable for everyone involved. The point is to be brief, be bright, and move the conversation forward. In Chapter 12, the fifth hub descending elevator-pitch exercise goes more deeply than I do here. For conversation, an introduction such as *Hi, I'm Katie, what is your name?* can be replaced with *Hi, I'm writing a book about transformation. My name is Katie—what's yours?* It may seem awkward, but you're extending a conversational lifeline to the person and doing some work to invest in a conversation you're interested in having. Choose a personal descriptor that opens possible doors of opportunity and for talking about a topic that interests you. Sometimes conversations can feel like fumbles and the small talk can be polite but not particularly engaging or memorable; offering a descriptor gives people something to hook into for a conversation.

Use probing questions that begin with *what* and *how* (asking questions that start with *why, when, where,* or *who* can make a person feel interrogated).

For example:

- What's the best way for someone to get to know you?
- What's your favorite place in the entire world?
- Do you have any nicknames?
- What do you think every visitor to your city/town absolutely has to do or try?

When people finish talking, encourage them to say more if they want to:

- I'd love to know more about that.
- Please tell me more.

VOICE

Earlier, I discussed Mehrabian's three Vs of communication (verbal, vocal, visual)—and vocal tone, modulation, and cadence are 38 percent of what a listener perceives. The trick is to have self-awareness and to shift communication into conscious control. When we carefully choose our words to be effective, we can strengthen the message even more by using our voice.

TONE

The five primary factors that inform our vocal tone are speed, volume, enthusiasm, prosody, and the use of silence. When we are conscious of these factors we can use them to increase the effectiveness and impact of our verbal communication.

Exercise: Remove the Content

Listen to people talking (preferably in another language). Instead of focusing on the words, tune in to the tone along with the variation of pitch and cadence:

- Do they seem energized or exhausted? Do they sound frustrated, happy, or something else? (Being just 10 percent more energized than the person you speak to is a rule of thumb for infusing energy into a conversation.)
- Are they talking fast or slow? High or low? What does their tone tell you about them right now?

- Are they dominating the conversation or letting other people speak?
- What is your impression? Do you find them likable? What is it that you like or dislike about their tone and cadence?
- Without knowing them, how do you reflexively feel about them? Are they annoying? Funny? Scary? What else about them are you noticing about how they sound that's contributing to your impression?

Exercise: Awareness of Tone

This is an exercise I did in small groups with my sales teams over the years; you can do this alone by recording your voice. First, write down two or three descriptive words you'd like people to use when they characterize you (examples: confident, smart, charming). Next, record yourself—either making the introduction from the above exercise or giving a simple opinion of your favorite restaurant and why you recommend it. Take a short break—then listen. What are the two or three words you would use to describe the voice you hear? Are they different from the descriptors you first wrote down? This can be cringe-inducing, as many of us avoid hearing our voices at any cost, but shifting the power and impact of your spoken voice requires awareness of it. Try to identify where your tone and modulation affect the impression you give with your voice.

PITCH

Talking in a high-pitched voice is unthreatening and signals youth. Notice how a heightened tone involves the restriction of the throat and breathing. To establish more command with your voice, reduce the constriction in the throat and back of the mouth and drop your tone. Relaxing the chest and throat and speaking in a natural voice helps us to sound in control and mature. Using upspeak signals a lack of power. It registers as apologetic because the speaker is trying to be nonthreatening (when they're already not a threat). Ending a sentence with a neutral tone indicates confidence and comfort. And to demonstrate power, *drop* your tone at the end of a sentence. However, the point here is that if you *do* want to sound cute and unthreatening, make it a conscious choice—bring awareness and intention to all facets of your communication.

PATTERN INTERRUPTING AND TONE

If you must talk for a long time, people will tune you out. One way to tune them back in is to shift your tone and volume and to pause in unexpected places, and to emphasize, elongate, or shorten words in unexpected ways.

HARMONY VERSUS DISCORD

Masao Watanabe, professor emeritus at the University of Tokyo, wrote about the cultural differences between East and West in an article published in *Science* titled, "The Conception of Nature in Japanese Culture." He explains how conversation creates either discord or harmony. The example he used starts with the statement, "A whale is not a fish." A standard Western response is to the statement itself; "No, a whale is not a fish" is an attempt to agree, but ultimately is discordant. According to Watanabe, a Japanese response to the speaker creates harmonious agreement: "Yes, of course, it is not a fish." Both responses say the same thing, but one response creates harmony while the other introduces subtle opposition even though there is agreement. Creating greater harmony in conversations makes us more likeable and in general lends itself to people being more agreeable with us.

CREATING

Creativity isn't only expressed through activities like art and music—the scope of what is creative is vast: it's all the work you do with your hands and voice, such as gardening, woodworking, car restoration and repair, home decorating and interior design, fixing things around the house, landscaping, cooking, crafting, telling a story, and singing in church. Technologist and author Kevin Ashton asserts in *How to Fly a Horse: The Secret History of Creation, Innovation, and Discovery* that creation is at the very core of what it means to be human. He writes, "What makes our species different and dominant is innovation. What is special about us is not the size of our brains, speech, or the mere fact that we use tools. It is that each of us is in our own way driven to make things better. We occupy the evolutionary niche of new. The niche of new is not the property of a privileged few. It is what makes humans human." Anything you do that creates and builds the world you want to live in and that communicates your values and perspective expresses your unique self and is an act of creation.

JOURNALING

Writing and journaling are particularly effective tools of expression because they take free-floating ideas and concerns and land them on a page where they can be seen, addressed, and processed. E. M. Forster asked in *Aspects of the Novel*, "How can I tell what I think until I see what I say?" Practicing emotional hygiene by releasing feelings and emotions from the previous day clears our heads. If emotions are not processed, they will recycle and resurface as misplaced frustration, fixations, and obsessions or even erupt as anger or become physical discomfort or pain. Other journaling practices also involve inquiry and exploration with free writing to clear the emotional pipes to allow for creative expression, specifically, Julia Cameron's process of morning pages from *The Artist's Way: A Spiritual Path to Higher Creativity* (see Chapter 11 for all the Parinama Method's journaling practices).

AFFIRMATION

The word *mantra* is of Sanskrit origin meaning mystical formulas spoken and chanted to be cast like magic spells. You can use words and phrases to soothe, to encourage, and to begin the process of making something real. Again, *abracadabra* means *I create as I speak*. Affirmations set the process in motion by strengthening an idea with sound and specificity, coaxing a new belief into our subconscious. Writing them repeatedly is good; saying them out loud is great and recording them and listening to them is excellent. To turbocharge this practice, add a timeframe with a word like *now*.

First Hub
- My body deserves to take up space.
- I trust my body.
- I know my limits and uphold them.

Second Hub
- I express and respect my emotions.
- I move easily and effortlessly.

Third Hub
- I decide for myself what is best for me.
- I feel the power and confidence in my abilities, my courage, and my individuality.

Fourth Hub
- I feel love, belonging, and connection.
- I see a fellow human being in the eyes of everyone I meet.

Fifth Hub
- Now and forever, my truth is mine and deserves respect.
- Now and forever, my truth and integrity are important.

CHARGE AND DISCHARGE

Talking can be a release and listening can fill us with charge (which can get overwhelming). Listening involves feeling safe enough to hear what's being said, but it can be blocked when we're already overcharged and in need of an outlet to discharge. For example, suppose you're still holding a charge that didn't get an outlet: the act of blocking out what you hear can be a defense against taking on more.

CHARGING

When we listen, we receive stimulation and take in charge. This can range from pleasant to excruciating depending on the content and voltage of the delivery. To positively charge this hub we can look to music, make the therapeutic humming sound of *Vu*, and gently stimulate the face, neck, and shoulders with massage (see the *Vu* entry below for how to do this). Most of the adaptations in this hub need discharge because auditory overstimulation (along with restriction of personal expression) exists in enormous proportions.

Music

Listening to music that feels good is a positive charge for all hubs and gets special mention here because it's stimulation that occurs as vibration in our ears. Take the time to find or make a playlist to express moods like *relax* and *energize* and put it on when you need it. Music without lyrics can be particularly soothing, and music with lyrics can help with finding validation. To charge, listen; to discharge, sing along. Again, to block charging wear headphones without sound or with noise cancellation to help reduce stimulation from unwanted ambient noise.

Massage and Movement

Rub your jaw with circular motions, gently pull on your earlobes and sides of your ears, rub the back of your neck with both hands, followed by gently rubbing your chin and the front of your neck. To bring the extension to the neck and spine, start from a standing position, bend forward using your thighs for support. Cup your hands over your ears and allow the weight of your arms to passively extend the spine and neck for three to five breaths. Return to standing and place your hands on the back of your head, intertwining your fingers. Press downward with your hands to stretch your neck, letting the head yield under pressure. Keep your knees slightly bent and your back straight but not rigid. Release your hands and roll your head in a circle from left to right, breathing slowly and easily, keeping your eyes open and blinking often. Do this three times and then reverse direction.

Vu

With your lips closed, make a humming sound, and place the index and middle fingers of each hand on the sides of your nose to feel the subtle vibration and connect with the physical vibration that is part of your voice. Next—and you don't need to keep your fingers on your nose for this—make the sound *Vu* on an extended exhale; this is a particularly soothing central practice for nervous-system regulation in Steven Porges's *The Polyvagal Theory: Neurophysiological Foundations of Emotions, Attachment, Communication, and Self-Regulation.*

There are two channels when making noise: charging and discharging—smooth vowel sounds are charging and the sharper vibration of consonant noises in the throat, face, and chest are discharging.

DISCHARGE

Biting can release tension in the jaw, but any accordion (tensing and releasing) with the jaw and neck muscles can damage your teeth and strain your neck. The discharge we explore here comes from making noise and movement.

Making Noise: Opening the throat

- Drop your chin to your chest extending the back of your neck and inhale.
- Exhale as you lift your head back up with a light *ha*—eyes go from the floor to the ceiling.
- Repeat five to eight times with a slight increase in the intensity.

Other Discharging Exercises

Do what makes sense for you and consider that breaking the seal on this release can feel awkward, but once you get some momentum going, it feels good. An added benefit is that this release can give you more patience in conversation when jaw and neck tension are no longer causing stress.

Go for a drive alone down a highway and scream-sing along to music. Allow the vocal sounds to become whatever they need to be. Doing this to music that was meaningful to you at the initial age (seven to 13) of this hub is particularly cathartic. Screaming into a pillow is hard at first, but once you get going it feels good (a more subtle release can be reading aloud to yourself).

The healing effect of being able to talk to someone without being judged or interrupted is profound. Having someone listen to you as you speak your truth is an intense release in this hub. Therapy is effective for this. It's also good to ask someone to just listen. In the words of a friend, being heard and being allowed to speak feels like a drink of cool water after a two-hour hike.

Throwing hands

Lowen (see Chapter 2) created this process for releasing. Start by lying on your back on a bed or any soft surface where you can freely move both of your arms. Next, ball your hands into fists and start pounding on the bed, five times with your right hand and then five with your left. Hit as hard as you can. Now just lie back and allow the feeling of energy to flow and observe. Next, do five pounds with both hands at the same time. Rest, allow and observe, and repeat. Add words if it helps: *enough* or even *no* work well.

Get off my back.

Start in a standing position with your knees slightly bent. Next, bend your elbows and then raise them to shoulder height like wings with your hands at your armpits. Then, forcibly thrust both elbows backward and say, "Get. Off. My. Back." Repeat several times, giving vocal expression to a feeling of anger. This can be done with both arms at once or by alternating between left and right.

Get away from me.

Make two fists with your thumbs on the outside. Drive both fists strongly forward and say, "Get away from me." Repeat multiple times. A variation of this can be placing hands on (not punching) a wall and pushing against it.

The fifth hub transitions into the sixth in Chapter 9—SEE, with its complementary self-reflection and imagination that support self-expression. The power of mythology and symbols emerge as we begin to imagine and sense ourselves in a much larger context within the world and acts of creation become inspired and driven by the vision of imagination, ideation, and curiosity.

Basics	Themes	Interruptions and Stressors	Adaptations and Holding Patterns	Techniques and Exercises
Intuition and Pattern Recognition	Myth and Meaning	Invalidation of Intuition, Ideation, and Curiosity	Characteristics of a Balanced and Out-of-Balance Sixth Hub	Intuition, Insight, and Imagination
Ideation: Capturing Inspiration	Rite of Passage: The Hero's Journey	Bad Data: Garbage In, Garbage Out	Shrinking	Decision-Making
Curiosity	Dreams		Inflating	Ideation and Dreams
Looking	Memory		Imaginary Audience	Curiosity and Looking
Being Seen	Decision-Making		Pattern Recognition versus Emotional Literacy	Assume Positive Intent
	Overwhelm—Too Much Information		The Shadows: Denial, Illusion, Delusion, and Bias	Visual Boundary
			Cognitive Bias Organized by Hub	Charge and Discharge
			Tips for Critical Thinking	

Chapter 9

THE SIXTH HUB—SEE

INSIGHT AND CURIOSITY

The only thing worse than being blind is having sight but no vision.
—Helen Keller

THE SIXTH HUB SUPPORTS decision-making, clarity, ideas, and the vision required for playing an active role in creating your life and the world you live in. This hub can see patterns and truths in our families, cultures, and communities, including some that don't get discussed and some we may wish not to see. Both the sixth and seventh hub do not fully develop for many adults. If we don't develop in this hub, we strengthen reflexive biases, slowly decrease our curiosity over time, and become increasingly oblivious and unable to introspect and iterate, which result in becoming easier to control. The capabilities of this hub are often described using expansive language, with words that connote mysticism like *intuition* and *insight*, so much so that we often overlook their practicality. Vision involves both how we see ourselves right now and what we believe is ultimately possible for ourselves—our potential. The sixth and seventh hubs offer the keys to unlock the ability to see yourself with ever-increasing capability and capacity, yet they also contain the early programming and influence of limiting beliefs. They're where we find the cognitive tools for conscious reclamation supporting the entire Parinama Method process, including the ability to see ourselves and others as products of circumstances that shape us and to know that we can get involved in the process to create change. New beliefs require space that can be filled with our imagination and vision (see Chapter 10). While you've been reading *The Parinama Method*, your sixth and seventh hubs have been activated and are expanding in capacity because consciously reclaiming the lower hubs increases upper-hub capacity.

Intuition, ideation, and curiosity all thrive with the counterbalance of strength in our lower hubs. Something must be imagined and believed in (seen with the mind's eye) before it can become grounded in reality—strong embodied lower-hubs support our full potential by creating a foundation. In this hub, we can begin to see the transpersonal interconnectedness of everything, starting with how we affect our family and the people around us, which eventually extends farther into a vision for bringing change into the world. But keep in mind there's no requirement that your vision changes the whole wide world—the notion that we should want to help others more than we want to help ourselves can be sanctimonious and shaming. Just by changing your own life, you change the world around you; you're participating in changing the world by affecting all the lives you touch.

It doesn't need to be grandiose: your capacity to believe and imagine only requires that you see the potential of the most fulfilling life imaginable for you.

In the sixth hub, we access inner vision and memory, which can involve seeing things we may not want or be ready to see. When we envision and perceive, we're using a mixture of insights, a patchwork of images and ideas reimagined and reorganized from previous experiences to make sense of new ones. Perception is prediction based on what we've already seen and experienced, combined with the internal force of our unique embloom. To see more and to gain access to greater visionary capability, we must tolerate discomfort and increase our capacity to withstand the dissonance of encountering the unfamiliar without negating or defending against it as foreign (and therefore reflexively interpreting it as hostile). The more facts and input our inner database contain, the more we have to build with—but beware: not all previous experiences are quality building materials. In earlier chapters I discuss how familiarity is conflated with safety for better or worse. Biases and negative beliefs are also filed away in our database, so we must proceed with caution and awareness as we explore this hub.

When we work to expand our capabilities here, we know to expect the crosscurrents of limiting beliefs and to see them as signs that we're doing the work to press forward into new horizons and possibilities. When the crosswinds start blowing—often rattling our resolve—we will feel the gale-force winds of *Who am I to do this?* or perhaps, *I'm not smart or talented enough*, and other effective forms of resistance used to test our fortitude. When you want to grow, you can expect resistance to knock on your door—and if you're prepared for its company, you can let it in and play with it to expose it for what it is: early programming (see the exercise in Chapter 12). Try to be ready, try not to let it take you by surprise—you can even be encouraged by the kind of discomfort that signals imminent transformation.

When we can't conceive of a future we want for ourselves, we risk being hijacked to serve the creation of another's vision. When we lack awareness, the sense of safety and familiarity programmed into our limiting belief systems makes us vulnerable to people who can manipulate our deeper wants and desires: they paint a picture of a future before we can consider what we want for ourselves. And if we're not careful, we wind up chasing dreams that aren't even ours—like careers, lifestyles, and monetary goals. There are plenty of people who pour their lives and careers into chasing a life they've never consciously evaluated, tending to assume that *everyone wants this*. Steve Jobs said, "People don't know what they want until you show it to them. That's why I never rely on market research. Our task is to read things that are not yet on the page." Jobs likely meant that preference relies on a choice between known options, and that he was bringing forward things previously unknown to the world. He was also said to be acutely aware of the paradox in human psychology: the desire to be different while remaining safe. If we don't actively envision and seek to fill our inner database with new experiences (exposing ourselves to more options and alternatives), we may believe that the only options are the ones we know—and important differentiating aspects of our humanity and potential are at risk of being hidden in a blind spot and possibly missed entirely.

ORIENTATION

Physical location: The eyes, the third eye (between your eyebrows), memory, and smell

First cycle: Approximately 12 years old into adolescence

Task: To see and be seen

Rights: The right to be seen as who you are without punishment or cruelty

Identity: I am my ideas. I am what you see—my image.

Reconciliation: Intuition versus bias, and what we allow ourselves to see

This is the hub of all kinds of vision: it's in the eyes and the space between the brows (a.k.a. the third eye, and in Sanskrit called *Ajna*, meaning to perceive and command). Here, I demystify intuition for what it is: the use of pattern recognition for prediction. I explain how to conceive of ideas using the different states of your brain and discuss decision-making and memory. Because the brain is first come, first served, your physical survival will reflexively prioritize over the more mystical destiny of your embloom. I discuss the practical components of vision and the tools you can use to unlock your unique genius at whatever level you feel comfortable accessing.

Lower-hub-dominant folks tend to borrow from the upper-hub-dominant—the intrepid visionaries who comfortably experience the field of curiosity without grabbing for the anchor of what already exists. Lower-hub-dominant folks are more prone to be builders without strong vision (and so, they look to creators for ideas) while some visionaries struggle to build because they're disconnected from the lower-hub drive and practicality required to build (see Chapter 11). An intrepid visionary needs the fortitude to withstand the projections and insecurities of people who have underdeveloped imaginations, along with the strength and courage to proceed before there's precedent or evidence. Watching the process of groundbreaking ideation and imagination can be uncomfortable for some folks because it requires taking risks and standing alone with confidence. Many industries get crowded with competitors that only offer mild differentiation from each other—and many style-and-design trends replicate visionary work with slight tweaks and revisions while massive swaths of creative terrain remain unexplored. So, if you seek to access your vision and genius, it is here that you will find it.

INITIAL DEVELOPMENT

There's a shift from literal into symbolic thinking during the early development of the sixth hub. Piaget called this the "formal operational" stage of human development, beginning around 12 years old and lasting into adulthood. In this stage teenagers start to grow their ability for abstract thinking by playing around with ideas. Erikson called this stage "identity versus role confusion," referring to the strengthening of the authentic self. The process of differentiating and shedding personas within the social identity formed in the fourth hub begins in early adolescence as self-expression becomes increasingly more authentic and unadapted. Teenagers begin to actively rebel against social identities prescribed for them and seek out the people and the places where they feel they truly belong. They also wonder who they are in the context of society and the larger world, which can lead to stress and overwhelm as they think about what will happen when they become adults. This tension is activating, and teens rely on the relative strengths of their lower hubs as they navigate the paradoxes of being safe yet brave, and unique yet connected.

It's natural to be self-conscious during the pre- and early-teen years; teenagers often feel like everyone is watching them and fear social embarrassment. Most of us can remember this challenging transition between childhood and adolescence in seventh and eighth grades—we can look back now and remember crossing the turbulent waters of social belonging while seeking greater autonomy from a mandated family identity. It's an awkward and often emotional time because rejection, belonging, joy, and grief continuously collide. And adolescents often lean on their peers, who are just as clueless as they are. In early adolescence, we began to make friends outside of our immediate childhood community as early childhood friend groups experienced shifts and changes. We rapidly developed intense, magnetic bonds with new friends over shared interests like music and dating. Trying out different clothing styles can cause a stir, and spending time with new relationships can leave childhood friends feeling abandoned. Friends from earlier years can feel tricked—having thought they knew a peer who then changes—and may express despair as the friendship begins to weaken and sometimes dissolve completely. This hub is about creating a personal and social image, seeking to have our outsides more closely match our insides—often involving rebellion with the natural impulse to push parents away and/or challenge them during a growth phase as they hunger for independence yet need the protections of home and safe adults to turn to when things go wrong—as they often do.

The sense of destiny in these years is dramatic and expansive; we need our life and creations to be more significant than those of others. Characters and heroes in movies and books help us understand our experiences as we learn from their sagas. Myths and archetypes are used to organize and to explore different roles people can play. Campbell's hero's journey, which I discuss more below, is the mythology found in the quest of the embloom (see Chapter 4). Quest stories and images transcend cultures and geography as a universal call to achieve our unique purpose.

Again, appearance is very important in this initial development. Attention to physical beauty and appearance can wind up as a holding pattern if we do not balance it through our continued development. Vanity becomes a trapped adaptation in adults, sometimes causing delusion and denial—and an inconvenient fact about denial and illusion is that the truth is visible to everyone except ourselves.

One of the questions we ask in this hub is, *What are we willing to see?* Figuring out how to appropriately honor and appreciate our parents without participating in the suppression of our truth can be a substantial undertaking. One of our initial heartbreaks is seeing our parents as fellow humans not universally recognized as gods and heroes. In adulthood, sixth-hub work allows us to see what was too difficult to face in our younger years, holding us back from fully living our adult lives—over time, repressing awareness requires significant energy. If parents' control is still in effect during the teen years (blocking the natural assertion of independence and individuality), children will likely go off the rails when they eventually go to college or leave the home. Jung referred to this phenomenon as *enantiodromia*, meaning that an equilibrium of counterbalance shifts anything extreme to its opposite polarity. Another common course correction for the interrupted sixth hub is a midlife crisis—asserting independence in adulthood through behavior that was not permitted for a teenager and child.

BASICS

Imagination and intuition are often associated with mystical qualities that distance us from trusting them, yet they have practical applications that support decision-making and the organizing and understanding of information.

INTUITION AND PATTERN RECOGNITION

Intuition

We use our experiences to predict the future. Intuition is pattern recognition using subconscious memories pulled from our inner image-and-information library—the gut feel of intuition is the subconscious within our body expressed through reflexes and responses. We use intuition to make decisions, yet not all the information we've collected is constructive (I discuss the influence and effect of bias on intuition below).

We're born into bodies that grow into all shapes and sizes with differing abilities. As we progress through our development, we have experiences that program our perception, resulting in adaptations and holding patterns that often become belief systems. This is combined with coded reflexes from hundreds of thousands of years of human evolution and survival—reflexes that inform us where to look, what to look for, and what to expect. We consume astonishing amounts of information from our environment and over time, learn to choose what we focus on. We assign meanings to these things and build our lived experiences around those meanings. One way to influence the quality of your library is to take an active role in choosing what goes into it, which involves seeing images of people, bodies, and lives that push against bias and retrain our brains and bodies with humanized reflexes.

How far back does this library go? Plato considered intuition to be the capacity of a rational mind to understand the true nature of reality; his philosophy of anamnesis asserts that humans possess innate knowledge, perhaps acquired before birth. He described this preexisting knowledge as residing in the "soul of eternity," and posited that intuition happens when we become aware of this knowledge. He provided the example of mathematical truths and posited that they're not arrived at through reason. Instead, he argued that these truths are accessed using knowledge present in a dormant form and obtained through our intuitive capacity. Is it impossible to imagine bodies, comprising material from the cosmos, containing codes from the DNA of our ancestors?

Again, we are hardwired to view familiarity as safe. Intuition and instinct are felt in the body, but whenever possible we should consciously explore our impulses before we act—fear can masquerade as intuition. As an example, what some companies call "culture fit" is an undefined metric indicating that people feel safe with a candidate who is similar to an already existing team. The so-called sixth sense of culture fit that many hiring managers apply to building teams is where bias can hide in plain sight. We internalize prejudice because in our daily lives we're subjected to a drip campaign of subtle and not-so-subtle racism, misogyny, ageism, and dehumanization. Since our pattern recognition is subconscious, it's worth noting the quality and content of the information going into your database—consumption of social media, advertisements, the words and terms we hear, the preferences and beliefs of the people we spend time with, all go into forming the world that we recognize as familiar and "correct." Beliefs that we may consciously disagree with can slip in and exert influence from behind the veil of the subconscious.

Pattern Recognition

We see cycles of repeating themes and patterns when we look back on our lives. When we resolve a conflict or solve a problem, it can be surprising when the underlying theme reappears in our life, but this time a little more complex and a little more intense. As I'll discuss in Chapter 10, nature is filled with repeating patterns; the golden ratio (Fibonacci's sequence) we observe in Nautilus shells, which steadily expand and grow larger, is also seen in flower petals, pineapples, and countless other examples in the natural world. Jackson Pollock's so-called drip paintings of the late 1940s and early 1950s were likened to what appeared to be the artistic skill of toddlers. But a 2002 *Scientific American* article by Richard P. Taylor, "Order in Pollock's Chaos," reports that computer analysis revealed Pollock was creating fractal patterns "similar to those formed in nature by trees, clouds, and coastline." The subliminal appeal Pollack had accessed was the appeal of the patterns in the rhythms of nature.

IDEATION: CAPTURING INSPIRATION

We don't know where ideas come from or how to predict them, but we can actively cultivate space for ideas and inspiration. In *On Writing: A Memoir of the Craft*, Stephen King states that ideas for stories come "[S]ailing at you right out of the empty sky: two previously unrelated ideas come together and make something new under the sun. Your job isn't to find these ideas but to recognize them when they show up." Ideas can land in our minds as images and feelings, and sometimes as a tangle of words or sounds that require combing and coaxing. The larger our database of experience, the greater the scope of our potential for creativity; traveling, meeting new people, seeing new things, working, attending cultural events, taking different routes than the ones we typically take, and any other new experiences all show us a larger world outside the one we typically inhabit. Creation is a mystical mashup of different things coming together to form new ones—and once we start to see or envision something, it begins the process of becoming possible for us. When we're curious and open, we look to expose ourselves to new ideas and people as often as possible.

Most people can recall having an idea, not acting on it, and then seeing it come to life through someone else. Ideation is fickle, lighthearted, and behaves like a mirthful wood sprite that wakes you up at three a.m. to play, and then hides when daylight comes. Ideas flirt, seduce, and evade in their game of hide-and-seek. This muse of creativity waits to be found, and if you give up the search, it looks for someone else who wants to play.

As adults, we can be out of practice and inclined to crowd out the liminal, open space—the receptivity and time—needed to allow for new ideas. Inspiration tends to strike when we clear our minds and ask a question; in almost every example of a culture-changing dream, the dreamer spent waking hours asking a question that a dream answered—the conscious mind works in concert with this process. The delta brainwaves of deep, dreamless sleep are experienced in the first sleepy moments of the morning, before you shift into the brief period of theta wavelengths that support the ideal state for ideation. Theta waves are between the alpha, beta, and gamma waves of different states of wakefulness. The theta-wave state is when you have one foot in awakened consciousness and the other in the subconscious; it happens when you're waking up, falling asleep, relaxed, or sleepy. Preparing for this brief, potent transition between being awake and in deep sleep increases your chances of capturing inspiration. This is when our brain delivers ideas from the subconscious (and perhaps the great beyond) and knowing this is important for being able to take full advantage of it.

According to Bellow, "You never have to change anything you got up in the middle of the night to write." Da Vinci and Einstein maintained extensive journals throughout their lives; the experience of everyday life inspired them to fill their diaries with imagination, dreams, musings, and questions. The range of questions was absurd and fascinating. Da Vinci and Einstein's 21st-century biographer, Walter Isaacson, used these journals for his research, and noted that both men had asked the same question: Why is the sky blue?

The ability to use the states of our brain to take advantage of our full potential can involve tackling analytical problems at the beginning of the day (when we're most awake) and taking on problems that require insight and creative thinking later in the day (when we may be a little sleepier and a bit more theta). Keep a bedside journal devoted to capturing ideas (using a phone or other device will shift the brain out of theta and into a different state of wakefulness). Some of your ideas are good, perhaps even great. The notion that genius is IQ (logical problem-solving) or only the capability of particular people is a modern construct. We're indoctrinated with belief in separatist individualism in modern Western culture, but our ancient predecessors, the Greeks and Romans, knew that creative genius was too much pressure for an individual and in this context, creativity and genius are available to everyone, including you.

CURIOSITY

In the sixth hub, we foster curiosity, and in the seventh that curiosity expands and becomes awe and wonder. Curiosity is essential for the actualization of all the hubs. The ability to regard ourselves with interest and delight, one of the fundamental psychological needs from early childhood, is something we can do for ourselves. It becomes a transcendent behavior when we can simultaneously experience and observe our discomfort, pain, and pleasure with interest and relative equanimity. This equanimity is an ability to create enough distance between yourself and an experience so that you don't become completely absorbed in it—creating some perspective to become a curious observer. As we balance between both awareness and acceptance of ourselves exactly as we are, we enter the space of transformation. It's another paradox. Our ability to experience our life as it arises requires active interest while simultaneously benefiting from just the tiniest bit of distancing so we can have perspective.

LOOKING

Absolute certainty is a trap that cuts off exploration and leaves us stuck in a time that's already passed. There's a freshness in wonder and curiosity and in experiencing a moment as if it's brand new (because it is). Curiosity is a field we enter, an acknowledgment that taking interest offers limitless possibility in any given moment. People tend to dress like and/or listen to music from the time period when they stopped being curious, and to retell tales. Folks who repeat stories can lack awareness of their audience and can get stuck in the past. A side effect of this becomes fear of both the unfamiliar and the new (sometimes manifesting as fear of teenagers and young adults—without curiosity, they seem terrifying; with curiosity, they're fascinating).

The extent to which we create reality is affected by the filters we look through and the intensity with which we look. In this hub, we reclaim our eyes and become aware of the filters on our perception. We can choose to remove the filters that no longer serve us and consciously evaluate the interference of our biases.

Children sometimes ask, *How do I know that what I call red is the same red that you see?* It's a question that can't really be answered—the fact is that we can never know. There is no objective reality; what we see is influenced by our programming, level of development, and adaptations from lower hubs, in addition to our innate inclinations.

BEING SEEN

Anyone who has ever felt invisible understands just how destructive this can be to a psyche. We get overlooked for promotion; our raised hand is ignored in a classroom; or we work at a service job where customers look through us, not at us. Paying attention to the human beings around us can be a wake-up call for anyone who sees retail workers, support staff, cleaners, delivery, or service people as machines that only perform functions. Looking just briefly into the eyes of someone we may typically overlook can be the jolt that activates our compassion and connection, and it begins to shake the foundation of biases that limit the full capacity of our humanity.

THEMES
MYTH AND MEANING

Stories connect us with transcendent, unifying, and humanizing concepts. When we laugh at a movie, we laugh with millions of other people who respond to the same film and its universal subject matter of love, grief, and joy. The themes that unify us are told through myth and metaphor. In *The Wizard of Oz* (a story told within a dream), Dorothy and her friends learn that the things they want are already within them ("You had the power all along"), and they just needed to make the journey to reveal their capabilities so they could know and understand them. You already are everything you want to be, and your trials and tribulations help you to grow by showing you who you are and what you're capable of.

A paradox of human life is that we're minuscule in comparison to the size of the Universe, yet astonishing in our rarity, remarkable in our uniqueness. According to Campbell, myths and stories are our subconscious communicating with our conscious mind. His four functions of myth are mystical, cosmological, sociological, and pedagogical. Taste in movies and books can differ, but the themes all remain the same: love, loss, betrayal, overcoming adversity, personal growth, and the hero's journey. Every person you meet was once a child who got scared, was teased, and experienced loss and/or alienation at one point or another. If we enhance the lens of our curiosity and look, we see ourselves as interwoven with each other by the shared themes of the human experience.

RITE OF PASSAGE: THE HERO'S JOURNEY

The hero's journey or vision quest beckons to us by speaking to our embloom from the pages of books and movie screens; we can experience exploration and adventure from relative safety while we feel a stirring of our unique sense of purpose. In *Hero with a Thousand Faces*, Campbell outlined the stages and themes of the personal saga. The journey is widely recognized as a universal set of stages in a rite of passage. See if you recognize any of the stages in your own life in the list below and look to Campbell's signposts as a guide to what to expect if you heed the call.

Ordinary Life (limited awareness)

- Call to adventure (increased awareness)
- Refuse the call (reluctance to change)
- Meet the mentor
- Cross the threshold and begin the quest alone (commitment)

The Special World

- Tests, allies, and enemies (experimenting)
- Approach the innermost cave (preparing)
- The ordeal (big change)
- The reward (outcome and consequences)

Return to Ordinary World

- The road back (redirection)

- Resurrection (final attempt) is a final battle; failure can have drastic consequences in the ordinary world. The hero uses new skills to overcome old obstacles.

- Return to society with the merits achieved through the journey (mastery); the hero returns in a changed state. Any issues with ordinary-world characters are resolved. The hero uses newly acquired knowledge to great effect.

HERO'S JOURNEY

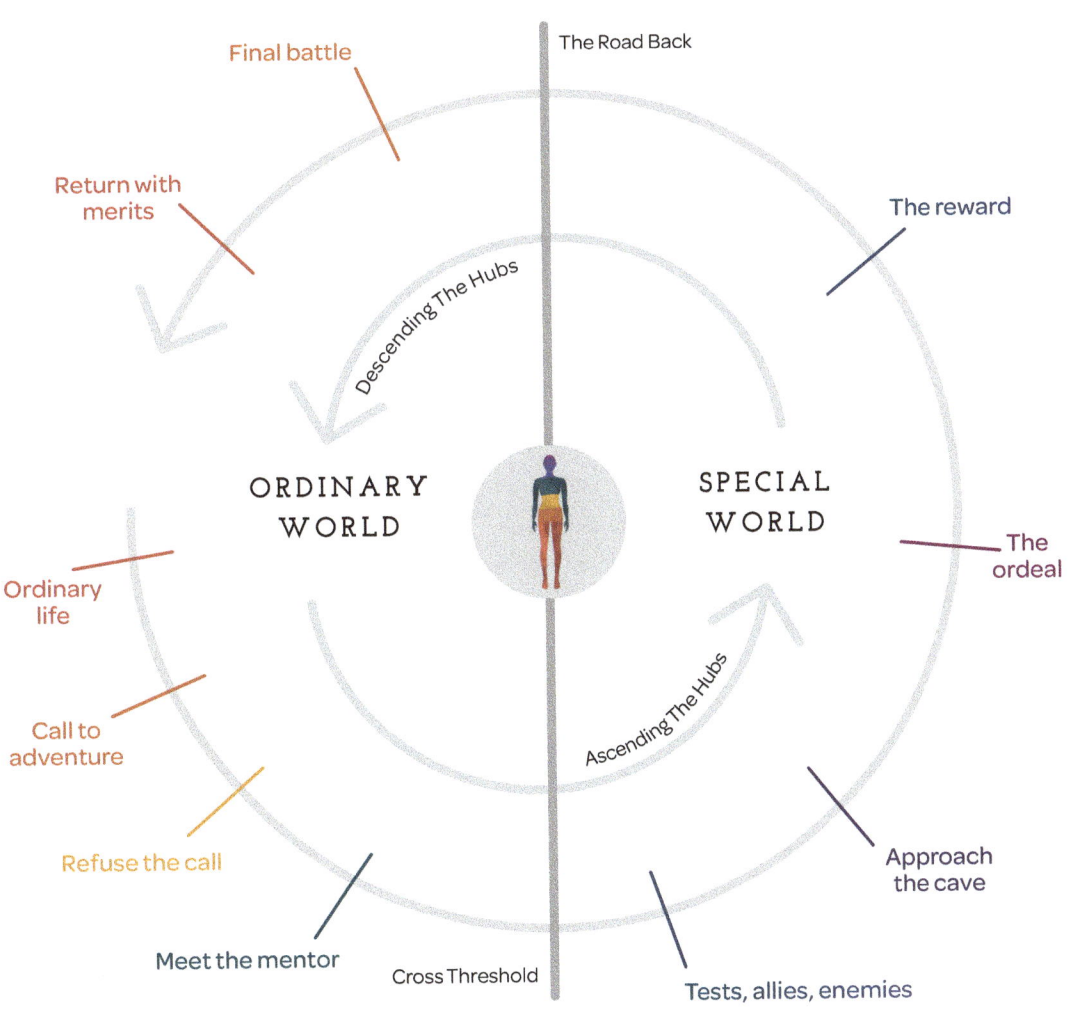

Figure 9.1: Hero's Journey

DREAMS

All progress comes from inspiration, and there's no richer, more surreal, or more creative world we occupy than the one of our dreams—and many ideas that have shaped our modern world came from them. Everyone dreams, but their recall, frequency, and even whether they're in color differs from person to person. An astonishing paradox is that many discoveries that drive us toward so-called logical thinking first emerged in the liminal space of dreams. In *The Wizard of Oz*, it's after Dorothy's dream of her trip to Oz that she awakens with a newfound perspective. From Google to E = mc², the practices and tools of modern science and its discoveries, such as the periodic table, medicinal insulin, the shape of DNA, and the theory of evolution by natural selection, are just a few examples of ideas that came from dreams. Even literary themes like human duality in *The Strange Case of Dr. Jekyll and Mr. Hyde* and the plot of *Frankenstein or, The Modern Prometheus*, were initially conceived in dreams.

Math prodigy Srinivasa Ramanujan explained how he discovered the infinity of Pi: "While asleep, I had an unusual experience. There was a red screen formed by flowing blood, as it were. I was observing it. Suddenly a hand began to write on the screen. I became all attention. That hand wrote several elliptic integrals. They stuck to my mind. As soon as I woke up, I committed them to writing." Ramanujan made use of after-sleep notation, and according to mathematician G. H. Hardy, relied on a "mingled argument, intuition, and induction" for the many math solutions he would produce throughout his (short) life. Following are more examples of dream-inspired work in technology, science, and popular art that have shaped our shared reality.

Technology

The idea for Google began as an anxiety dream about a clerical error. In 1996, Larry Page had an irrational fear that he'd been admitted to university because of an error and so, believed he'd be kicked out at any moment when the mistake was discovered. That anxiety fueled a dream Page had about downloading and storing the entire internet on individual (personal) computers. When he woke up, he was curious to see if it was possible, so he did the math. Given the amount of data, it wasn't—but he figured he could save all the data as individual links. That gave him the idea of creating a searchable database of links to what are now webpages, leading to Google's creation.

Science and Math

Ramanujan reported that throughout his life, he repeatedly dreamed of a Hindu goddess known as Namakkal. She presented him with complex mathematical formulas, which he could then test and verify upon waking. One example was the infinite series for Pi, cited above. Ramanujan produced almost 4,000 proofs, identities, conjectures, and equations in pure mathematics in his 33-year lifetime. The richness of his ideas and conjectures in fields like elliptic function and number theory was ahead of its time (and almost all correct) and continues to inspire and direct mathematical research.

Einstein's conception of the speed of light came from a dream in which he was sledding down a steep mountainside, going so fast that eventually he approached the speed of light. At this moment, the stars in his dream changed their appearance in relation to him. He awoke and ruminated on this idea, soon formulating what would become one of the most famous scientific theories in history. The theory of relativity also came to him in a dream—one about cows. He dreamed he was walking through a farm when he came upon some cows by an electric fence. He then saw the cows jump at the same time as the fence gave them an electric shock, but a farmer, who had been standing at the other end of the field saw them jump one by one, like a Mexican wave. Einstein realized their views of the same event had been different, which led to the theory of relativity, the idea that events look different depending on where we're standing because of the time it takes light to reach our eyes.

James Watson and his colleagues discovered the shape of DNA. In one account, Watson had a dream of a double-sided staircase and in another he dreamed of two snakes coiled around each other with their heads at opposite ends. Niels Bohr discovered the structure of the atom by dreaming of horses on a racetrack—Bohr was later awarded a Nobel Prize in Physics due to this leap in creative thinking. Frederick Banting dreamt about a diabetic dog, which led to a breakthrough relating to the understanding of the disproportionate balance between sugar and insulin for a diabetic. And this led to another dream indicating how insulin could be used to treat diabetes. Dmitri Mendeleev dreamt of the organizing principle for the periodic table of elements after he had spent many waking hours struggling with how to organize atomic matter.

Music and Literature

Mary Shelley had the idea for *Frankenstein,* which many consider the first sci-fi novel, after having a vivid nightmare. Robert Louis Stevenson described the inspiration for *The Strange Case of Dr. Jekyll and Mr. Hyde*'s premise as a man who could hide in plain sight with his two distinct personalities: "For two days I went about racking my brains for a plot of any sort, and on the second night I dreamed the scene at the window, and a scene afterward split in two, in which Hyde, pursued for some crime, took the powder and underwent the change in the presence of his pursuers." And according to Paul McCartney, the melody for "Yesterday" came to him fully formed in a dream. When he woke up, he found what key it was in and played it in full. But it sounded so familiar that he worried he was copying someone else's work. He played it for friends and family and asked them if they'd ever heard it before, which of course they had not.

MEMORY

Memory is stored using visual locations—when recalling an event from the past we think, "It's as if I'm back there." When I relisten to an interesting podcast or audiobook, I can often remember my surroundings from the first time I listened to it. A memory (in our mind's eye) involves something we saw or heard and is enriched through other senses like smell, taste, and touch, and becomes indelible as the charge of emotion sears the experience into our mind.

It's often the unusual or the absurd that makes something easy to remember. If you have a pizza delivered you may not remember much about it the next day, but if the delivery person is wearing a clown nose and balancing the pizza on their head, it will be hard to forget. Days can come and go, but a jolt out of monotony can form a memory, not because it's positive or negative but because it gets our full attention in the moment.

Greek and Roman orators used a visual method of imagined places (loci) to remember their complex, nuanced speeches. Sometimes called "memory palaces," the orators relied on how our brain remembers: by location and the

unique form of attention that comes from being surprised. If you want to try this exercise inspired by the work of memory expert Jim Kwik—pick four locations on your body:

1. Top of head
2. Nose
3. Mouth
4. Ears

Make a grocery list with four items: bananas, milk, butter, and spinach. Travel one more time over the body areas and say them out loud—top of head, nose, mouth, ears—to cement the locations. Next, imagine an odd placement for each grocery item:

1. Bananas on top of your head
2. Getting a milk mustache
3. Using butter as lip balm
4. Spinach growing out of your ears

Now close your eyes and repeat your grocery list using the four points on your body: top of head, nose, mouth, and ears with the absurd images. The locations on the body will be the anchoring point and the oddity of the placement will create the memory.

DECISION-MAKING

When we're faced with making an important choice, the decision-making process usually begins with some struggle, strain, uncertainty, and cyclical thinking due to worry that there's information we're missing and fear of doing the wrong thing. "Thinking" and only using conscious thought is like basing our understanding of an iceberg by what we can see above the waterline—there's deeper (gut) knowing within us we'll want to access. Before a decision is made, do the work to explore and determine the known options. When folks ask for advice, I've come to believe that most people don't have the express intention of taking what's offered, rather, they wish to enrich their understanding of the options and bounce different ideas off their subconscious, collecting information from both the external world and from their internal library.

So, even if I happen to help someone unearth an underlying truth, the fact remains that it's the person's process of discovery and recognition, not mine—I only had the opportunity to participate. Any missing information is either within you or will resonant when you hear it; the task at hand is how to access this insight—and before a decision is made—to understand your choices and work from there.

After information gathering—this includes conversations with people—the time eventually comes when it's just you and the decision that needs to be made. Once you've gathered information there will usually be two predominant paths: the choices that feel comfortable and the ones that feel exciting (and perhaps scary). When you find yourself at the crossroads, set aside some time to visualize each option separately. Close your eyes and envision yourself having made each choice with as much detail as possible, then imagine what it feels like to live with each version. Notice how your body feels, notice if what you see in your mind's eye is bright and colorful or fuzzy and bland. Notice if you feel energized, happy, and hopeful or if you feel bored and disappointed. Take yourself past the initial point of decision and imagine your day-to-day life one month or year later, living with the choice. What do you see and what does it feel like? The act of deciding is a short-lived but potent point of inflection, and the fear of the initial difficulty in a choice can interfere with our ability to make the better, long-term one.

OVERWHELM–TOO MUCH INFORMATION

The approach to overwhelm and anxiety in the earlier hubs focuses on embodiment—with the containment of expansive feelings within the boundary of our physical bodies (see chapters 4 and 5). Here in the sixth hub, we can manage overwhelm by using cognitive awareness. Feeling that there's too much information to process and having our peace of mind hijacked are aspects of feeling loss of control in a situation. Overwhelm happens when we lose our place in a pattern: we lose our perspective and find ourselves in either unfamiliar territory or a situation that requires greater capacity than what we may believe we currently have. Or, perhaps we bite off more than we can chew and feel overwhelmed by not knowing what to do next; when this is the case, just take the next step. Sometimes we think we need to know the entire plan when all we really need to do is take a single next action. Sometimes this means slowing down and not doing anything so that we can regain our footing—especially if things become overwhelming because they're moving too quickly. We can only see patterns when we have perspective. For example, look back at your personal history and you're more likely to see that you always pick the same kind of partner, repeat the same mistakes, or consistently excel in certain areas.

Losing our place often starts when we encounter something unfamiliar. When we read a book and run across a word we don't know, studies show that reading comprehension for everything that follows declines. We live inside patterns, and when we get overwhelmed and feel lost, we can resolve the anxiety of uncertainty by looking back to discover the exact moment when the feelings began, investing in the effort to understand the unfamiliar, and then moving forward. Sometimes, we need to catch our breath before we can look back: *This too shall pass* is a beneficial mantra when we lose our place in a pattern in our life, getting overwhelmed by thoughts and emotion. If you think about it, we always find our way back, and if while lost we can remain relatively calm, we tend to get back on track faster. The ability to tolerate uncertainty can help reveal insights when we can watch our downturns into overwhelm, sadness, and low energy with interest and compassion. All rhythms and patterns pass through downbeats, descending before they rise again. The knowledge of cycles helps to instill some peace, knowing that although we will likely lose our position again, we can also return. It's always darkest before the dawn, and after daylight, darkness returns—a pattern that repeats itself indefinitely.

INTERRUPTIONS AND STRESSORS

The primary interruptions and stressors in this hub involve the invalidation of intuition, ideas, and curiosity. Being told we ask too many questions or that what we see isn't real or correct or having our ideas laughed off leads to an interruption in the development of this hub. In the following section on adaptations and holding patterns, I discuss how we adapt, either by overinvesting in our imagination or by shutting it down. Again, throughout life we build an inner library, and we receive subconscious input through advertisements, pictures, and cultural standards. For even the most well-adjusted kids, cultural stressors alone can cause interruptions when they try to figure out who they are in the larger world. With adaptations from the first four hubs relating to worthiness, self-doubt, powerlessness, emotional regulation, and physical trust and safety, body dysmorphia and impossible beauty-and-appearance standards get heightened as outcomes of the (subconscious) intake of cultural imagery. How we feel about ourselves can contort what we see when we look in the mirror. The passage of time can allow a clearer retrospective view when we look at pictures from our past: we can see our beauty and vulnerability, and perhaps the same distortion that hid the truth from view then may still be at work—and this may provide us the opportunity to question these distortions and reclaim ourselves.

How we were taught to view differences in other people and ourselves has profound and long-lasting effects on our relationship with our bodies. If we were singled out for our unique appearance when we were little, the effect can last a lifetime unless we explore and untangle the snarled psychological damage caused by ignorance and cruelty from others.

Our (lizard) brain stem has us fearing the unfamiliar, yet our higher consciousness sees variability and difference as interesting, unique, and a vital contribution to the world. It's a common misconception that we need to understand the differences in other people to accept them and embrace our shared humanity. In *The Body Is Not an Apology*, author and activist Sonya Renee Taylor outlines three steps to radical self-love: the first is to make peace with not always understanding other people; the second is to make peace with differences; and the third is to make peace with your body. Judgment and shaming aren't about what we objectively see, they're subjective—and the reasons we judge and shame are related to early interruptions. The restorative process involves lifting any illusion that there can be anything objectively wrong with a body—*there's nothing wrong with you.*

INVALIDATION OF INTUITION, IDEATION, AND CURIOSITY

Recall the importance of the presence and mentorship of someone who is consistent and who believes in you (see Chapter 8). Someone who fills this role supports development by strengthening our curiosity, interest, and delight in ourselves, and without the early practice of having someone see you as remarkable, it may feel awkward and uncomfortable in adulthood. As children (and sometimes as adults), we need someone to reflect with, validate our experiences, and provide space for us to process what we see and go through. Being seen is how we feel validated and connected, and without someone to do this with, we risk becoming delusional and disconnected. If we take in information without a sounding board, we can create distorted perceptions, struggle to sync with others, and can even mistake biases and shadows for arising intuition.

As children, when we learned about the world, we took in new information like sponges—this includes forbidden topics that we learned of by experiencing the adults' reactions. Having an adult shame and label curiosity as impolite is a type of erasure, and it interferes with development in this hub. Ideally, a child is taught that differences are part of life and to appreciate and tolerate them in others. Being taught to ignore differences interferes with our ability to see and can lead to behaviors that range from being dehumanizing to dangerous for the well-being of others. Think of someone who declares to have color blindness about race or someone who ignores people in wheelchairs. It's understandable to want to avoid offending someone who's differently abled or neurologically atypical, but if our response is to deny or ignore, we potentially cause the stress and harm of erasure.

Interruption here is caused by invalidating what is seen or experienced, such as children whose parents are chronic substance abusers or who abuse them physically and/or psychologically. When children are told they're wrong about what they see and experience, for example, being told *It's nothing* (which is similar to interruption in emotional attunement), their internal calibration with the outside world is affected and they can lose trust in believing what they see or in knowing that what they perceive is a valid interpretation. When people have survived their own disappointments by adapting with protective cynicism (primarily, the domain of the seventh hub) they may diminish and discourage the dreams and imagination of other people to justify their own interrupted capacity.

Invalidating Intuition

We're often protected from the complex and sometimes harsh realities that surrounded us as children. It's challenging terrain for a parent to navigate; on the one hand, a young child needs to be protected from issues that are too complex for them, and on the other hand, children are highly intuitive and can sense when things don't add up. Parents often do the best they can; for example, a mother crying because she feels alienated or abandoned by her husband tells her child she has allergies. The child can sense that something is not right about this, but if the mother is trying to come to terms with growing challenges in her marriage, she may not be ready to provide teachable moments to a young child. If she does tell the child what's going on, the child may shoulder a portion of the burden and potentially add conflict into its sense of safety at home. Taking this one step farther, perhaps at dinner with dad, the child mentions that mommy was crying earlier. The mother quickly dismisses this, saying the child has an overactive imagination—as a result, the child may second-guess what it saw and question its ability to effectively judge a situation.

Invalidated Ideas and Curiosity

People often wonder why adults lose their imagination, but it doesn't take many experiences of being told your imagination is weird or stupid to shut it down. When children are told their ideas are foolish and get laughed off, they experience shame and embarrassment and begin to stop fostering their imagination. Our ideas are vulnerable: they have the delicate quality of anything newborn and require protection and careful treatment. When we're in the process of ideation as adults, we need to be selective about who we share with because other people's projections can be like a lawn mower ripping up the new grass of emerging ideas before it has had a chance to take root.

Children are naturally curious, and it can be a hassle for a busy adult to field endless questions that may feel boring or irritating to answer. When children are shamed or embarrassed about the questions they ask, they may begin to suppress and divest from their curiosity. Again, there are no stupid questions—both Einstein and Da Vinci wondered why the sky is blue.

BAD DATA: GARBAGE IN, GARBAGE OUT

Censorship is often intended to keep bad information away from children. Restricting high-voltage images of violence, pornography, and explicit language support children's healthy development. However, keeping them from seeing people who hold different views or who lead different lives from theirs is not helpful for sixth-hub development. For adults, censorship effectively eliminates the introduction of information into our conscious and subconscious library and supports limited thinking and biases, stifling creative capacity. Here, I discuss the interruptions that occur when our ability to add information to our internal library is controlled and blocked. We can also be inundated with bad information that sneaks in and resides below the subconscious layer of our psyche, controlling our perception from just slightly beyond our conscious grasp.

Social Programming: Ads, Images, and Power

In the 1910s, American advertising pioneer Claude Hopkins said of the industry, "We're not known, but we control what people all across America want and do." Over the next 100 years or so, marketers perfected the craft of creating needs that require their products. For example, Listerine® influenced the public about the so-called stigma of bad breath (halitosis). It worked: a medicinal tasting mouthwash seemed like the only suitable option to combat the newly imagined horror. Likewise, the early success of selling cigarettes to women came from ad campaigns touting the product's support in maintaining a so-called healthy weight.

Social media is essentially an advertising platform that gained astronomical stock market valuations by effectively harvesting human attention. Companies want your eyeballs on their messages. When advertising targets our subconscious biases and pushes the buttons of our adaptations, it can shift our feelings, thoughts, and behavior. For most people, social beauty standards like body size and shape, skin tone, and hair are bound up in an emotionally loaded tangle with worthiness of love and acceptance. Cultural beauty standards tend to make our appearance an asset that depreciates over time, reducing our lives to a constant competition as a commodity in a market full of options. But you are not a commodity: there is only one of you, and you are priceless. Lining up for the societal meat market will take your power away and distort your relationship with yourself. Conventional beauty and attractiveness are not related to worthiness of love and acceptance—they are related to power, and we often conflate the attention attractiveness receives with worthiness. Again, our appearance and the social judgment applied to it is about power, not love. When we can recognize the lunacy of beauty and attractiveness being a depreciating asset and identify it instead as power that tends to diminish as our insight and wisdom grow, we can treat it accordingly and use it rather than be used by it.

When women on my teams have relied on their looks and the power of their flirtation skills to win deals, I advise them that learning how to negotiate masterfully to occupy personal power and to build connections is essential for career longevity. Although attractiveness opens doors easily and creates initial interest, it doesn't build long-term business relationships. Unfortunately, the same appeal that opens doors often blocks the elevator for anyone who doesn't know how to transition charm and appeal into credibility and respect. Decoupling appearance and worthiness is a good first step toward loosening this inner bind.

ADAPTATIONS AND HOLDING PATTERNS

Discernment—and the distance and perspective it provides—is the ability to take in new information and evaluate it consciously, which allows us to remain open and receptive while maintaining a boundary against runaway emotion, illusion, and fantasy. Dynamic balance in this hub is comfortable with imagination, ideation, and curiosity, and can rein in and contain insight and creativity when a situation calls for it or can expand to greater capacity when needed.

CHARACTERISTICS OF A BALANCED SIXTH HUB

- Relaxed forehead and space between eyebrows
- Penetrating insight
- Alert, relaxed, and observant
- Intuition supported with conscious evaluation
- Able to consider that intuition and opinions may contain biases
- Good memory
- Ability to vividly imagine potential in people and things
- Creative imagination
- Sees potential for beauty and inspiration in many things
- Good dream recall
- Has a personal vision, can envision new possibilities
- Uses the inspiration of heroes and archetypes to move forward with confidence
- Discernment—can implement emotional distance to see more clearly

CHARACTERISTICS OF AN OUT-OF-BALANCE SIXTH HUB

- Memory issues
- Obliviousness and lacking in curiosity
- Vanity
- Very susceptible to biases and exploitation
- Body dysmorphia
- Limited definition of beauty
- Can't remember dreams
- Feels stuck in current life, feels obligation to someone else's vision
- Insensitive and uncoordinated—may break things or make a mess without noticing
- Delusion about self—without realizing, often complains about people doing the same things they do

SHRINKING

The sixth hub shrinking adaptation has difficulty with imagination, memory, vision, and trusting its intuition or anything outside a narrow, restricted range of perception. This protection is likely the result of being embarrassed for being creative or curious, but that's not always the case: sometimes we just don't have people in our lives who encourage the development of this hub. One of the behaviors of this adaptation is obliviousness to nonverbal cues, such as a host clearing a table or all the other guests leaving a party—someone who shrinks in this hub will overstay. This adaptation has a tough time imagining and appreciating the different realities and experiences of others and tends to attribute its lack of imagination and curiosity to being logical. Also, it will likely think dreams and intuition are silly and/or childish—that adulthood is a so-called reality that leaves imagination and creativity behind along with its toys and games.

A shrinking adaptation may fear being too creative and may overcorrect by having a low tolerance for anything considered weird, but as I discuss above, creativity and imagination unlock fulfillment and enjoyment in life. It's not a matter of anyone else's taste: when making something sparks delight and comes from inside, it's a process of creation.

Characteristics of a Shrinking Sixth Hub

- Struggles with maintaining eye contact
- Poor memory
- Blurry vision, sometimes a furrowed brow
- Has a hard time imagining things
- Obliviousness
- Says *I don't dream*
- Skeptical and believes itself to be logical when it is in fact rigid with confirmation bias
- Denial, both personal and collective
- Can't imagine other perspectives, and so denies their validity
- Believes its reality is the only truth
- Acts aloof or distant as a protection

On one end of the spectrum, the eyes and face of a shrinking adaptation can be frozen in a squint, sneer, or retraction. Hiding one's eyes can also be a sign of trying to hide in shame. Driver discusses eye shielding as a way people attempt to hide deception through physical behavior (see Chapter 8). For example, if people have difficulty showing their eyes and evade eye contact either by covering them with a hat brim or closing them, it's a tell for attempting concealment: they may be lying, but they also may be experiencing shame. On the other end of the spectrum, an inflating adaptation can have eyes that are invasively penetrating, shifting, or have an unsettling quality to them, which signals being ungrounded and out of touch with reality. Next time you're passing people on the street, notice how some folks can have fixed, frozen expressions in their eyes and on their faces unrelated to their current activity. Balance in this hub is evident in a relaxed face with attentive eyes that are dynamic and not frozen.

INFLATING

Creativity and intuition (especially from a shrinking perspective) are often associated with the inflated, expansive adaptation's tendency to place complete faith in unexamined, unproven ideas. The inflated adaptation rejects boundaries and struggles to understand that its perspective is its own—not representative of how everyone should think. Incongruously, if people disagree with the inflated adaptations' expansive views and beliefs, they will often find themselves being accused of closed-mindedness. Delusional and disconnected behavior has given creativity and intuition a bad name, especially when the examples we see are terrifyingly ungrounded, such as artists who swing into destructive volatility and grandiosity or cult followers who scorn discernment as lack of faith. There's a tendency to associate visionaries with disconnection from life and reality because in extreme cases, this is what happens. The balanced visionary has both the ideation and the bravery to bring an idea into existence (see Chapter 12). Many folks with inflated adaptations in this hub are dreamers who have plenty of ideas but lack follow-through, often blaming outside forces. Healthy creativity is activated by solving challenges that require work. The inflated adaptation can blur the lines between the sense of reality through unquestioning participation in self-help, psychics, new-age practices, and belief systems that strengthen biases and the narrow tolerance for other perspectives. According to Bellow, "A great deal of intelligence can be invested in ignorance when the need for illusion is deep."

Characteristics of an Inflating Sixth Hub

- Dreams big, lacks practical application (example: talks about buying a big house when it can't pay the bills for a small apartment)

- Imagines a future without considering the present (example: starts planning the wedding after a first date)

- Extremely revisionist memory

- Struggles to concentrate

- Prone to lucid nightmares

- Susceptible to self-help, cult mentality, and spiritual bypassing (a tendency to use spiritual ideas and practices to sidestep or avoid unresolved emotional issues, unhealed trauma, and unfinished developmental tasks, see Chapter 10)

- Projects onto others by telling them who and what they are (see Chapter 8)

- Impaired ability to tell truth from fantasy (example: gives power over to psychics)

- Exceptionalism: overcompensation for low self-worth, needs to believe itself is more special than other people

- Equates uniqueness with superiority

- In delusion: bloated sense of importance, can be glib with nonbelievers

- Prone to obsession

- Thinks other people talk about it, maintains an imaginary audience well into adulthood

HOLDING PATTERNS
IMAGINARY AUDIENCE

In 1967, child psychologist David Elkind coined the term "imaginary audience," referring to individuals (usually early adolescents) who believe that most people are listening to or watching them with great interest. The spell of this developmental stage is usually broken with maturation by the realization that almost nobody is watching, and those who are looking are doing it through their own projections and perceptions. Any self-consciousness outside of actual celebrity will involve an outsized sense of other people's interest in us. When we examine our own repeating thoughts about other people, we can see how we're working through projections of our own inner issues.

The self-consciousness of an imaginary audience feels real during early adolescence. Comparing our appearance to others surges in this hub. Few people outside our inner circle have the bandwidth to pay attention to us, and even the people in our lives don't do it nearly as much as we think—they're too busy thinking about themselves. The only thing more unsettling than feeling constantly watched is knowing that almost nobody is actually doing it. There's a breakthrough when we realize we're not really being watched and that one opinion out of the nearly eight billion souls on Earth is not a final and complete assessment of anything about us.

The gravitational pull of the need for social belonging can yank us out of our orbits, especially in the early teen years. Again, appearance confirms belonging, and kids in this stage will beg parents for clothing and shoes with urgency, afraid of being singled out as the only one not following an important style trend or being unable to signal to the so-called right people that they belong with them. Parents may punish or recoil at a child's personal style experimentation. The approval within a family can create inner conflict in children who wish to express a style that either clashes with the family's or reveals something they must hide to be accepted.

PATTERN RECOGNITION VERSUS EMOTIONAL LITERACY

I discuss in Chapter 5 how the interruption and underdevelopment of emotional literacy in the second hub can lead to enhanced pattern recognition (intuition). An infant or young child trying to make sense of an unstable environment can develop heightened pattern recognition at the cost of connection to bodily sensation and gut feel. In early years, the energy that could be supporting lower-hub development gets repurposed into higher hubs before the nervous system is developmentally ready. The notion of an unusually perceptive child as a so-called old soul is a rationalization often used to make sense of a survival adaptation.

We may learn at an early age to detect minute movements and changes in our environment as precursors to behavior of our parent or other people in our home. For example, a slow, deep inhale from our mother may signal that she is about to get angry, and it gives us a head's up that it's time to leave the room. These behaviors can register in the subconscious and can signal to a child that something is about to happen before it does. As we grow older, this capability becomes increasingly sophisticated. Because intuition relies on the experience library we've built, some junk from the cultural programming that surrounds us has also been captured. Part of our so-called gut feel about a person can (and often does) include

dehumanizing cultural standards. Awareness is a powerful tool against this fallibility.

The following section reviews cognitive biases and how together, intuition *and* conscious intellectual capacity are necessary to avoid causing harm unintentionally. Cognitive dissonance is the intensity that occurs from the collision between subconsciously held reflexes and who we consciously believe ourselves to be. Many social conditions we consider dangerous or distasteful are (to a considerable extent) subjective, with elaborate rationalizations going into justifying the associated reflexes we have about them.

To help us survive, our brains evolved to make strong impressions of what puts us in danger. Our primitive predecessors, who were good at remembering which plants tasted delicious, were outlived by our ancestors who could remember to avoid the poisonous ones. The pessimistic inclination to magnify attention on the poisonous plants led to survival, and eventually became passed-down information. In the spirit of paradox, the hypervigilance for survival that made our current physical existence possible is now killing us with maladaptive chronic-stress responses. And in the sixth hub, where we create meaning, the wires can cross to rationalize maladaptive socialization as a survival reflex.

THE SHADOWS: DENIAL, ILLUSION, DELUSION, AND BIAS

The shadows of the sixth hub are denial, illusion, delusion, and bias, which can be found in all types of behaviors and adaptations. Unlike imagination and vision, which also see things that don't exist, denial, illusion, delusion, and bias are fixed, lack dynamism, and can get mistaken and/or lauded as so-called values (or even integrity) because of their inflexibility and defense against change. On the one hand, "thin-slicing," a term used by Malcolm Gladwell in *Blink* to describe rapid cognition and intuition, can be a superpower; on the other hand, there's always the risk of unknowingly granting entry to the cognitive-bias shadow. Our subconscious takes in all sorts of information from our surrounding environment: the good, the ugly, and the downright toxic. Because biases function from the subconscious, their force and influence exert power from below readily accessible self-awareness.

Biases are like shortcuts: they are reflex-level thinking efficiencies. We don't like unfamiliar things—they represent change, and they conflict with our deep desire for the comfort of things that fit into familiar patterns. Challenging an unconscious bias can raise a lot of intense charge because it can feel like a challenge to our sense of safety. Becoming heatedly defensive about something that requires leaps of rationalization to make personal is usually a good indicator that bias could be involved. Also, getting intensely fixated and fearful can signal that we're dealing with bias. Menakem's work is uniquely positioned to support the process of examining the depth of racial bias, along with highly effective somatic practices (see Chapter 7).

When bias gets reinforced by remaining unseen and unexamined (for example, so-called culture fits in companies), intuition and the sense we get about a person can be a dangerously dehumanizing disguise for expressing prejudices. If we cannot define a workplace culture, it will be a danger zone of racism, ageism, and sexism, along with any other homogenous standards that a company subconsciously maintains through rationalization. Using clearly defined principles for what it means to be a so-called culture fit requires greater thinking about what makes someone a good or bad fit and can help eliminate blind spots.

We must grapple with paradox and ambiguity when we go deeper into our self-awareness and understanding of others. The more we know, the more we realize how fundamentally impossible it is to be certain about almost anything except change—it's constant and there is always new information to learn.

COGNITIVE BIAS ORGANIZED BY HUB

Human thinking is fallible and as a result, is particularly vulnerable to influences outside conscious control. We all struggle with biases, and we should be able to recognize a few of them in our own behavior. In this section I organize biases into five primary categories that correspond with the first five hubs: (1) risk and loss aversion; (2) change and ambiguity; (3) avoidance and self-centering; (4) herd mentality; and (5) information bias—accepting information when it's told as a story.

First-Hub Bias: Risk and Loss Aversion

We needed to remain hypervigilant for danger at one point in our evolutionary history. As a survival reflex, our memory for threats needed to be at least five times more pronounced than that for remembering positive, pleasant things. These reflexes are now maladaptive and benefit from conscious oversight so that we don't live our lives in fear.

Negativity bias comes into play when we irrationally value the potential for a negative outcome as more important than a positive one. It reflects a deep aversion to losing—we like to win, but we hate to lose even more. Being more activated by the thought of losing than by the thought of gaining is likely to lead to protective actions being prioritized over attempts to make gains. Winning is intellectually more appealing but reflexively less activating.

Pessimism bias is related to but different from negativity bias; it's the tendency to *overestimate* the likelihood of negative events while *underestimating* the probability of positive events.

Sunk cost–fallacy bias is when we believe that when we put in effort, time, or money, we should get something back; the reality is that nothing is guaranteed and sometimes we lose and get nothing in return. *Sunk cost* refers to something lost that cannot be recovered: the illusion is that a next move after losing is tied to recouping the loss, not the reality of continuing to invest in something that doesn't work—throwing good money after bad. Examples of this are staying in a relationship that doesn't work because of time invested or making an expensive repair when buying a new item would be a more cost-effective choice.

Anchoring bias is the sense that we're getting a deal when a merchant leads with an original price before presenting a reduced price (determining the deal by its price relative to other offers). The suggested retail price is rarely paid but leads many of us to feel triumphant when we compare it to the so-called reduced price.

Second-Hub Bias: Change and Ambiguity

Avoiding change and ambiguity restricts expression in the second hub. Movement, change, and managing paradox all reflect the nature of life while these biases attempt to keep our lives simple and static—and in this (over)simplification we eliminate the nuanced realities of other people and limit our own capacity to experience life's fullness.

Confirmation bias is the tendency to interpret any new evidence as verification of one's existing beliefs or theories. We prefer ideas that conform to our existing beliefs, and if new information does not conform to them, it's either ignored or reimagined to fit. This bias also subconsciously seeks the comfort of information that validates our existing beliefs and ideas.

Cognitive dissonance is the inability to tolerate nuance, that is, stress is caused by simultaneously holding conflicting beliefs. The stress and tension of having two or more contradictory beliefs, ideas, or values create an internal struggle, and hence, a divided mind. Different aspects of ourselves—sometimes our subconscious versus our conscious mind—enter a battle in which there can only be one winner. The internal struggle will seek the path of least resistance to restore harmony (even if this means returning to nonsensical behavior).

The backfire effect is the strengthening of a belief after it's been challenged with factual, contradictory information. Because our mind decides how to assign meaning, it can interpret information and rationalize it in whatever way suits its interests. In concert with cognitive dissonance, this seemingly perplexing response to new information is that it actually strengthens the initially held belief.

The decline bias (a.k.a. diclinism) favors the past. We like patterns that we understand and when things change in ways that may feel unsettling, we change how we perceive them to fit existing beliefs rather than being changed by new information. We're not inclined to invest in the energetically expensive work of cognition, so we try our best to avoid changing our thought processes by resisting change.

Third-Hub Bias: Avoidance and Self-Centering

This hub's biases position us as central to everything, often making us the protagonist of any narrative, which includes reimagining our good luck retrospectively into well-thought-out strategies that yielded great outcomes and our bad luck as the interference of outside forces.

Self-serving bias is the repurposing of any narrative to make ourselves heroic and central—attributing positive outcomes to skill and negative outcomes to bad luck. In other words, we attribute the cause of anything that happens to whatever best serves our own narrative. Many of us can relate to having determined that if everything is going according to plan it's due to skill, but if things go the other way, then it's just bad luck or someone else's fault.

Desirability bias is the belief that something will happen because we want it to, including the illusion of controlling timing. For example, those with wealth and privilege may believe they've activated a grandiose (possibly spiritual) personal power by wishing for something to come true—and then receiving it—blissfully unaware of the impact of their privilege and good fortune.

The Forer (or Barnum) Effect is the tendency for people to accept vague, general personality descriptions as uniquely applicable to themselves, without realizing that the same description could be applied to just about everyone else (think: horoscopes). When we process vague information and interpret it in a manner that makes it seem personal and specific, we hold on to what we deem is meaningful to us and discard what is not. Information we believe to be personally tailored to us is perceived as better, regardless of its ambiguity.

Representativeness heuristic is the false belief that if two objects are similar, they are also correlated.

Fundamental-attribution error (or correspondence bias) is holding a double standard and using stereotypes to assume negative intent when things don't go our way. An example is judging colleagues as lazy or incompetent if they're late without having considered that they may have extenuating circumstances, such as having a sick child at home. This bias would have us consider our reasons for lateness as different and justified from those of our colleagues. The tendency of this bias is to underemphasize situational and environmental reasons for other people's behavior while overemphasizing personality-based explanations for our own.

Optimism/pessimism bias (not directly related to first-hub pessimism bias) is our tendency to overestimate the likelihood of a positive outcome if we are in a good mood and to overestimate the likelihood of a negative outcome if we're in a bad mood. It's the emotional nature of optimism or pessimism that makes it irrational. Folks without clear, objective performance expectations from their boss may experience their performance assessment as subjectively tied to the boss's emotional state—a state tied to factors outside of their control. As a result, they may experience an underlying sense of instability about their job security.

Hindsight bias is the common tendency for people to recall past events as having been more predictable than they actually were when they were happening. Nostalgia sanitizes the memory of the past, which at the time always involved uncertainty when it was happening because the outcomes were unknown. Sometimes called "revisionist history," this is a bias that allows us to center ourselves as confident heroes in the retelling of an event that at the time actually involved a lot of uncertainty and doubt.

Fourth-Hub Bias: Herd Mentality

These biases involve the subconscious influence of wanting to belong and feeling safe when others do the same things we do, regardless of whether the behavior is in fact wise or safe.

Herd mentality and social proof biases create a false sense of safety in a decision because we see other people doing it. Herd mentality can be the fear of missing out as we see our friends and family partake in a behavior, such as buying into a particular trend or investment and feeling compelled to join in. Social proof is the sense that other people liking something makes it a safe choice, and we trust that we're more likely to like it, too. If social proof is provided by people we perceive as aspirational or admirable, it can be particularly potent. An example is the comfort of buying a product with hundreds of ratings from strangers versus the discomfort of

buying a product with no reviews. Social media marketing also uses social proof. The illusion that influencers you feel you know like a product overrides the obvious fact that they are being paid to tell you they like it.

In-group and out-group biases refer to favoring people we believe we belong with, folks we perceive to be like us who are in the same social groupings as we are. These are very impactful biases with far-reaching consequences: groups that share identities tend to feel protective of each other, going to great lengths to protect people they see as being like themselves. The opposite side of this is dehumanizing people and perceiving them as outsiders when they are not part of the group.

Implicit bias (or implicit stereotype) is the reflexive attribution of stereotypical qualities to all members of an out-group.

Fifth-Hub Bias: Information Bias

The fifth-hub biases relate to our inclination to trust and to incorporate information that's told in the format of a story.

Narrative-fallacy bias is storytelling bias: we like stories and find them easy to make sense of and to relate to. This bias makes us more susceptible to anecdotes told in story form than to the bigger, more accurate picture related through data. Telling someone that out of 5,000 patients, 70 percent taking a certain medication didn't experience any negative side effects is less likely to influence them than if they learn their neighbor wound up in the emergency room after taking the medication.

Framing bias occurs when people make a decision based on how information is presented to them instead of focusing on the facts alone to make the decision. It's a hard one to avoid. A person may be recruited into a multilevel marketing program by getting excited about the details of a single success story versus considering research showing that 90 to 99 percent of people who get involved lose thousands of dollars.

TIPS FOR CRITICAL THINKING

Biases thrive by remaining in our unconscious, but they can be obliterated through working on them in the light of conscious attention. Below I list five critical-thinking tips:

- **Two-handed thinking (or playing devil's advocate).** Practice considering another opinion that counters a strongly held belief of yours (see Chapter 5).

- **Pause, and take a step back.** Remember that biases are usually unconscious and subconscious reflexes. When we pause and give ourselves time to think before making a snap judgment, we give ourselves the time to incorporate conscious functions.

- **Reduce emotional contamination (see Chapter 6).** Emotions can escalate and can act as an accelerant; the effect of acting reflexively from bias can be unpredictable and dangerous.

- **Do it in the morning.** Again, our logical thinking is primed after we wake up and start our day; we tend to get sleepier (and more influenced by) our subconscious later in the day.

- **Discernment.** Discernment is the practice of giving ourselves just enough intellectual distance to create perspective, allowing us to make more conscious decisions about the things that go through our minds. Critical thinking and confronting biases can be disruptive to a sense of inner calm and as a result, we can avoid doing it. When it comes to confronting biases, focus on the issues that matter—specifically the ones that negatively affect other people—and accept that there are relatively harmless biases that don't necessarily need to be tackled in the short term.

Many industries try to make sense of human behavior, attempting to make markets predictable and to take advantage of illogical reflexes. Business academics have been particularly interested in biases in attempts to forecast and predict the buying behaviors of a market and to help explain the actual behavior we observe versus the logical behavior we expect.

Nin wrote, "We don't see things as they are; we see things as we are." Our beliefs are not facts, they are interpretations of events deeply connected to our early programming, cultural conditioning, and natural inclinations. It's naive to expect a fact to change someone's mind. To believe that a piece of information can override the complex network of sensations and experiences contained and stored in a human body-mind is not only naive, but it's also arrogant and assumes that our relative position is the absolutely correct one.

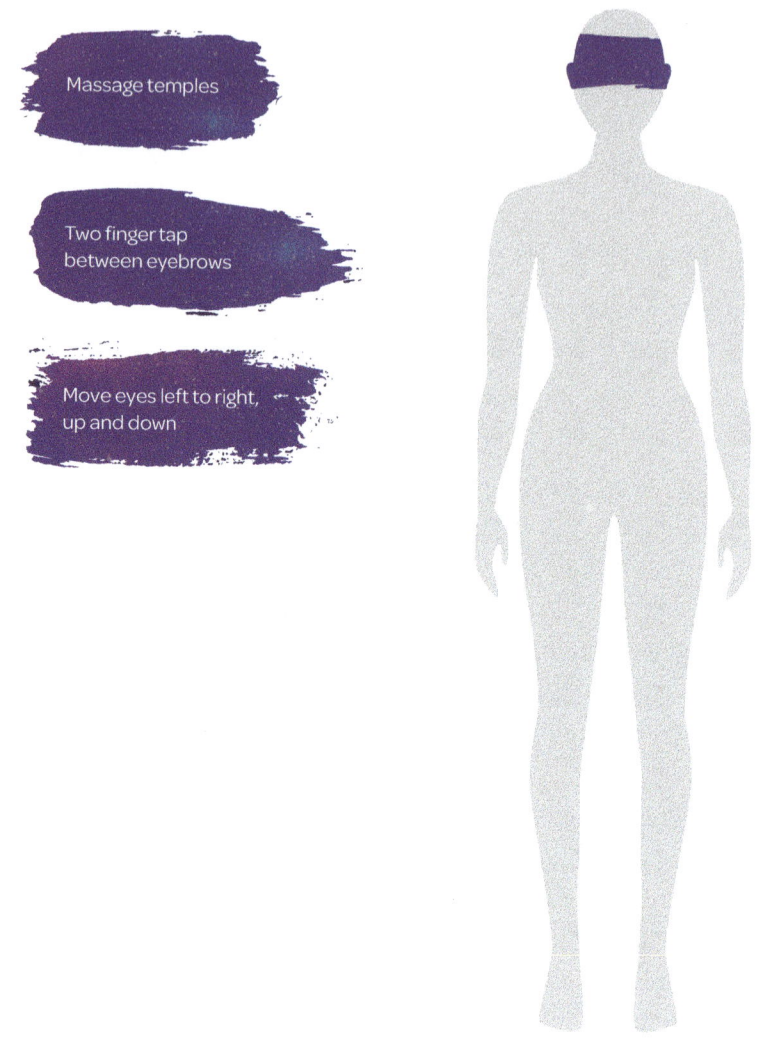

Massage temples

Two finger tap
between eyebrows

Move eyes left to right,
up and down

Figure 9.2: Sixth-Hub Body Prompts

THE PARINAMA METHOD SIXTH-HUB FUNDAMENTALS

Imagination, insight, and curiosity are the domain of this hub, located primarily in the forehead, brow, temple, and eyes. Your attention is like a flashlight that illuminates wherever you choose to point it. Restoration in this hub involves allowing insights and deeper patterns to reveal themselves to us. Dynamic flow in this hub is ready to see the truth from the past and have insight into the future. The sixth hub is about expanding the aperture to see more while cultivating awareness of the biases and blockers that limit us. E. E. Cummings wrote, "[N]ow the ears of my ears awake, and now the eyes of my eyes are opened."

Seeing is believing—and our beliefs dictate what we see. The sixth hub views subconscious information stored in our body-mind through the attention of our conscious mind. Your subconscious is a deep archive of everything that has ever happened to you, both externally and internally. Restoration and further development involve broadening your worldview through a wider perspective via exposure to people, places, and things unfamiliar to you.

INTUITION, INSIGHT, AND IMAGINATION

Intuition and Imagination: Building the Library

To paraphrase King's quote from earlier, imagination combines things we already know or have seen to create new things. Like Lego bricks, the volume and variety in our inner library determines what we can build. The more variety you have in what you've seen and experienced, the more material you have to work with for creation. If your days are spent with the same people, surroundings, entertainment, roads, buildings, and meals, there's a greater chance of feeling creatively limited—and perhaps uneasy about new things. But it doesn't take much to grow and stimulate the capacity of your nervous system: try brushing your teeth with your nondominant hand; sleeping on the opposite side of the bed (get your partner involved); taking a different route to work; or trying a different recipe or new restaurant. Activities like a day trip to a new place, visiting a museum, reading a new book, watching a new show, and vacationing in a new place all expand our horizons—and are extra effective when body movement is involved. Try noticing new things—where is the first bird you see today: outside, in a painting, in a decorative detail?

Social media can be used as a tool to either expand or limit horizons. If you're scrolling and something makes you feel less-than, put yourself in the driver's seat and either unfollow or mute. Just because you know a person or choose to follow strangers, it doesn't mean you're obligated to see whatever they decide to post. Part of a boundary in the sixth hub is getting involved with what you will tolerate seeing. Addition to a feed can be subtraction: stop tolerating and participating in other people's battles with perfectionism and instead, fill your eyes with empowering, engaging, enlightening, aspirational images—also, try following people who challenge the status quo of your current perspective in ways that are unfamiliar to you. This will constantly change, so keep it alive by unfollowing and then following others to keep your feed a place you go to enrich and grow. Seeing friends' pictures of their happy families when you're going through a separation can feel painful. But notice the difference between this and seeing lives unfamiliar to yours that push against your comfort zones and create dissonance and discomfort; when we're mindful of where we direct our attention, we can reprogram ourselves and unlearn biases. You can build a social media feed full of images of other human beings and do daily consciousness expansion through exposure therapy. Work through discomfort with differentness and scroll your way to greater humanization and creativity. And when you're in the spaces created by the people you're seeking to understand, don't comment—just observe and learn (and perhaps notice the urge to comment and explore where it's coming from).

Imagination and Insight: Seeing Potential

You also have unique, visionary capabilities, and whether you're in touch with them or not, there are versions of the future that you can see before they exist. A teacher sees the potential in a student. An entrepreneur sees a business opportunity when presented with a problem. An architect sees a structure before it's built. If you struggle to identify your purpose and talent, pay special attention to where you can see potential. Your embloom, your unique capability to create the future, wants to express itself wherever you envision potential—be patient and pay attention to this inclination.

Don't look to where you naturally criticize and point out flaws. Criticism has no vision because it cuts down an existing creation and lacks the curiosity to imagine a positive alternative—usually with a sentiment like *Things need to be changed* but without the intention to take responsibility to make the change. Making judgments without the intention of fixing anything is a bad habit that robs us of our potential. Instead, see if you can shift criticism and judgment to an inclination to imagine positive solutions. The distinct feeling is of vision and inspiration. This can be tending to imagine new melodies or new harmonies to existing songs or seeing an outfit and imagining an accessory for it—having respect for the original creator as you add your vision. Being critical can be transitioned by using the energy to imagine how something could be better while considering why something is the way it is to begin with and respecting that no matter how flawed something is, it represents inspiration and action of an initial creation.

DECISION-MAKING

Intuition doesn't work particularly well when we're anxious or stressed. Clear decision-making gets hijacked when our nervous system isn't calm. Activation of unconscious survival reflexes interferes with accessing deeper layers of the subconscious. Before you turn to intuition to help decide, evaluate how physically and mentally safe you feel and if necessary, calm your nervous system with first-hub exercises like grounding. Intuition often provides inconvenient information and following it can push us outside of our comfort zone and leave us second-guessing ourselves about leaving a relationship, taking a new job, moving to a new city—or taking any kind of risk. The right choice may be a little uncomfortable: it feels right but can also introduce short-term difficulty into our lives. Alternately, acting on biases and old patterns makes us feel safer almost immediately—when cognitive dissonance is triggered, eliminating the conflict provides instant relief. Change can be tricky and relying completely on cognitive reasoning for decision-making can lead us to overwhelm or to make safe, short-term choices that take us off a better, long-term course. Naturally, there's plenty of nuance, and in cases where your immediate physical safety is concerned, acting reflexively is your best protection, such as entering a room that doesn't feel right or getting the sense that someone is a creep.

Somatic Pendulum

The sway test, as described in chiropractor Bradley Nelson's *The Emotion Code*, uses your body to answer questions. It's a simple technique using the subconscious and can offer surprisingly accurate answers to your questions. First, make sure you're hydrated and feeling relatively calm and stable, then stand with both feet planted on the ground (this can also be done while sitting at the edge of your seat and giving your body the range of motion to lean forward and backward).

Calibrate

Begin with a sincere request, asking your personal source for truth—a higher power, the universe, or however you connect with your deepest integrity—to support you in seeking insight. Start by noticing the subtle body movements of your postural muscles as they constantly work through microcorrections to create balance. Like a plant reacting to light, we lean toward positive answers and lean back from negative ones. Leaning forward is *yes*, and leaning back is *no*. Try saying, "My name is [insert your name]," and observe how you lean, and then use a name that is not yours, saying, "My name is [insert another name]" and observe how your body responds. Be patient, as it can take 10 to 20 seconds to tune into this. Increase the strength of the exercise by increasing the negativity and the positivity of the words. For example, try the word *war* and consider its horrors and then notice any sway in your body. Try thinking of someone or something you love and fill your heart with gratitude, and then test for sway with a stronger positive. Your subconscious mind will communicate by swaying your body like a pendulum in a *yes* (forward leaning) or *no* (backward leaning).

Questions

Once you have calibrated, ask yourself questions and allow the sway to respond. How you ask a question makes a difference. For example, you could ask, "Is this job okay for right now?" and get a *yes* or you could ask, "Is this the best job for me right now?" and get a *no*. Greater specificity can change the answer: oftentimes *Is this okay?* versus *Is this the best?* produce different answers.

IDEATION AND DREAMS

Everyone dreams—it's a matter of remembering them. As our conscious mind sleeps, a door is opened into the subconscious, allowing for a visual, emotional tour of what's occurring within us. We can see how past events have affected us, although the message is communicated in symbol and emotion—dreams also help us process events. We can see ideas and visions through a mashup of visualization and emotion using our inner library and an archive of feelings and emotions from our experience.

I discuss above that the best time to catch insights from dreams is when we're waking up. It helps to not move your body too much. Again, have a journal by your bed and write down what you can remember. Explore the messages and meaning. (Consuming alcohol and cannabis suppress dreams, so be aware of the trade-offs for what you may use to wind down at the end of a day.)

Also, write down your ideas as they arise throughout the day. If you already have a journal for general note-taking, try putting a star next to every idea you have so that you can look back through your pages to see if patterns appear (they usually do). Before going to bed, think about where you seek clarity and state it to yourself, for example, *How should I address this [name a concern] with my friend?* or *How do I solve [insert the problem]?* Or you can take a mental walk through the previous day to allow for the events to be processed in your sleep. Allow and accept that the answers to these questions can come to you without effort if you become receptive.

CURIOSITY AND LOOKING

There's perhaps no better way to sharpen the capacity to see things than to draw them. Drawing something increases our level of attention, making us better observers. Don't worry about skill level—this is a sketch. When we try to draw something, we pay attention to how it exists in its environment, how light affects it, the facets, and the details of the object. Sketching brings your attention to details and provides enough activity to help tune out distractions—in the morning, it can clear the lens of our mind and enhance focus for the rest of the day.

Exercise: Quick Draw 8

It takes only a few minutes to shift from scattered to focused. A great way to do this is the Quick Draw 8. Start with paper and a pen or pencil. Pick an object like a plant, a decorative item, or a piece of fruit—of course, something natural is ideal, but any simple object works. Set a timer for eight minutes and draw without interruption. When time is up, stop and get a sense of how your focus has shifted.

ASSUME POSITIVE INTENT

We create the world we live in through our perception, but if we allow our early programming to shape our lives without evaluation, the scope of our experience can get contracted, limited, and unpleasant. It doesn't need to. When we reflexively assume people have bad intentions, a lot of work goes into shifting to a neutral perspective or disguising disdain. Also, there's significant risk of encouraging defensiveness or even escalation when the starting point of an interaction is negative. Notice whether you reflexively assume positive or negative intent in other people's actions. Try to assume that people do things for reasons that support their needs, needs that are very similar to yours yet also different. It's the cognitive bias of fundamental-attribution error that assumes other people are thoughtless or inconsiderate yet justifies and excuses the same behavior as reasonable for ourselves. Assuming positive intent is knowing that people have their reasons when they don't show up at their full capacity. Instead of knowing the reasons, consider that people are dealing with factors they may not be able to articulate, such as personal stressors, traumas, or circumstances disrupting their lives.

This doesn't mean that you lower your standards or your healthy boundaries. You can see the good in people and still have them not meet your standards. You just don't need to add insult to injury by judging people as they struggle. For example, if people never learned time management, it doesn't mean they're assholes—though they may be acting like one in a particular instance. Still, you can decide they're not respecting you and draw a boundary without holistically accessing them to be a terrible person. Most people are trying their best, and a healthy boundary in the sixth hub sees this while maintaining a level of distance that best supports you.

If we feel safe within ourselves, every interaction won't need to be about gaining or losing the yardage of respect. A regulated nervous system can handle bad behavior without taking it personally. This is not about justifying terrible behavior. For example, if you're in traffic, imagine the other driver is nervous about being late and had a problem at home or was somehow distracted and now is embarrassed. We tend to think that assholes are idiots—except when we're being the asshole. When you're thinking about what an idiot someone is, take comfort in knowing someone, somewhere, is thinking the same way about you.

Choose someone at random to observe and look for something beautiful about the person and imagine the person's story with curiosity and positive intent, noticing how it feels to assume the best for a stranger.

VISUAL BOUNDARY

Kids know when the visual boundary is being invaded and ask, "What are you looking at?" or say, "Take a picture, it will last longer," as spring-loaded defenses. But as adults, this boundary begins to feel more subjective—perhaps we second guess ourselves and wonder *Am I being too sensitive?* or have concerns about being rude when encountering a leering look or violence in entertainment. If your boundary feels invaded, trust yourself and either politely remove yourself from the situation— or be rude if you must be.

The visual boundary includes both what we see and how we're seen. When folks say that representation matters, they're referring to the importance of seeing aspects of oneself in popular culture (and other spheres) because seeing yourself represented as part of the larger world and being seen as part of society by others is validating and humanizing. What we see shapes our reality, and when it comes to appearance standards that cause hurt and harm, the visual boundaries between ourselves and the world can benefit from (protective) gatekeeping.

CHARGE AND DISCHARGE

This hub gets charged when we diversify our inner library by actively choosing to enrich ourselves and to shift our worldview to one that assumes positive intent until proven differently. A shrinking adaptation can charge its capacity by using practices that include light and stimulation. Discharging releases muscular tension through movement, which supports both inflating and shrinking adaptations. Discharging comes through movement, self-acceptance, and allowing truths to arise and be seen.

CHARGING

Light

Awareness of the seasonal cycles of light is important for this hub. Charge by using seasonal-affective-disorder lamps during the shorter photoperiods of winter; by supporting the natural day-night light cycles by using softer light in evenings; by being aware of exposure to screens (using blue light–filtering glasses). Also, consider taking vitamin D supplements. All are ways to support and charge this hub.

Massage

Using your fingers, gently massage your temples, brow, and forehead. Using a staccato-style tapping motion of your index and middle fingers (see Chapter 5) and tap on your brow and around your eyes.

Palms on eyes

Rub your palms together until your hands become warm, close your eyes, and place your warmed palms over your eyelids with the heels of your hands resting gently in your eye sockets and tips of fingers in your hairline. Let your eyes savor the darkness and warmth.

DISCHARGING

Accordion

Squeeze your eyes closed as tight as you can, contract the muscles of your face, pucker, and squeeze your lips without clenching your jaw. Try to achieve a tremor, and then slowly release while keeping your eyes closed. Using the fingers of both hands, sweep them over your closed eyes toward the sides of your face as though you're drawing curtains open (starting position: index fingers on the forehead and middle, ring, and pinky on the bridge of your nose) and slowly open your eyes as wide as possible, taking in as much of your surroundings as you can. Hold for two breaths.

Brow release

Using the edge of a yoga block or padding the side of a table with a towel, place your eyebrows in line with the edge. Gently roll your brow back and forth to help release and relax tension.

The transition from the sixth to the seventh hub is from curiosity to awe as we open ourselves to access our most profound aspects and face mind-bending paradoxes that require the solid ground and self-awareness from all the preceding hubs.

KNOW: YOUNG ADULT, SELF-AWARE

Basics	Themes	Interruptions and Stressors	Adaptations and Holding Patterns	Techniques and Exercises
Direct Experience	Meaning and Belief Systems	Standards of Purity and Perfectionism in Spiritual Abuse	Characteristics of a Balanced and Out-of-Balance Seventh Hub	Inquiry
Consciousness and Science	Inquiry: Questions and Answers	Rigid Belief Systems	Shrinking	Limiting Beliefs
Parallax	Stillness and Space	Censorship and Suppression of Curiosity	Inflating	Stillness and Silence
Ambiguity	Patterns and Fractals		Assumptions	Take an Awe Walk
Paradox	Wonder and Awe		Spiritual Bypassing/ Denial	Meditation: Focus and Concentration
Embloom (The Witness)	Sense of Humor		The Shadow: Absolute Certainty	Charge and Discharge
Hub Identities	Amazing Grace and a Higher Power			

Chapter 10

THE SEVENTH HUB—KNOW

KNOWLEDGE AND AWE

The nitrogen in our DNA, the calcium in our teeth, the iron in our blood, the carbon in our apple pies were made in the interiors of collapsing stars. We are made of star stuff.
—Carl Sagan

.

THE DENSE SOLIDITY OF the first hub of the Parinama Method, HAVE, is the complementary paradox to the lightness and space that we explore here in the seventh hub. The first hub is where our feet meet the ground and we find consistency, and it is also where we have the containment of a physical boundary. Now, for the seventh hub, KNOW, I discuss the seemingly limitless (and even cosmic) counterbalance along with the consciousness that makes transformation possible. Remember that transformation involves change, and change isn't possible if our lower hubs consider it a security threat and reflexively block it from happening. But here I discuss a different kind of security: being part of something much larger than ourselves. Our relatively limited cognition makes comprehension of our cosmic origins something too immense to fully understand, but in the seventh hub we try to through contemplation and inquiry, wondering what part we play in the Universe. If we're receptive, we may catch transcendent connection through the natural world, exposure to art, creation, love, and inspiration from the actions of other people—or simply through the inexplicable awe of what is sometimes described as grace. We access the mystery and invite its wisdom through our curiosity, inquiry, and the creation of inner space, quiet, and stillness. The vast and the profound communicate through subtle sensation—you've probably felt it, perhaps in silent moments of peace shared with family and/or in moments of sheer awe experienced while in nature, during the birth of a child, or in an astonishing act of mercy and compassion. There's a transcendent peace when standing in a forest or having our feet in the sand while looking out on the ocean. The body's felt senses developed throughout each hub open us to the possibility of a direct relationship with the greater force that unifies the natural world through shared rhythms, cycles, and patterns. Knowledge, art, and wisdom conspire to support your process of knowing. Again, when the student is ready, the teacher appears (see Chapter 2). When we open ourselves to knowing, serendipitous people, books, music, and numerous other signals keep pointing us toward the path, a convergence of forces and synchronicity that previously may have eluded our attention.

ORIENTATION

Physical location: Top of head, and the subtly felt sense of body

First cycle: Approximately late adolescence and into adulthood

Task: Inquiry—to navigate paradox and ambiguity

Rights: The right to ask questions, the right to receive answers

Identity: I am what I know, I am what I believe.

Reconciliation: Transformation through consciousness

This hub is often highly adapted from the intellectual restrictions of punishing perfectionism, rigid certainty, and limiting belief systems (beliefs that feel very real). The three predominant experiential layers of our body are experienced through conscious awareness in this hub:

1. The grosse: sensory stimuli with stiffness, injury, discomfort, and pain; these are typically felt as pain and/or blank spaces on the body. People don't say things like, "My hips are stiff, but my arms feel really good." They usually say, "My hips hurt, and my arms are fine."

2. The subtle: body processes like heartbeat, breath, digestion, and circulation; these can be sensed if we pay attention to them.

3. The sublime: the embloom—the full-body presence and essence that can feel twinkly, transcendent, and calm. Sometimes we can feel this when we're tired and lie down to rest; when we wake up well-rested; after a massage or intimacy—it's a blissful, subtle full-body sensation.

When we let go of intellectual restrictions, we can experience a greater sense of freedom and become more joyful and prosperous with greater clarity. The seventh hub is the locus of inquiry where we expand the electrifying capacity to tolerate the tension of nuance and paradox, and in which transformation and transcendence are made possible. As the connection to conscious creation, this hub makes us uniquely human: it's where we wonder and ask about alternatives, optimizations, and creation. It makes the Method possible through conscious reclamation of and intervention in the nervous system programming that has already been set in motion. One of the many paradoxes of this hub is to fully accept yourself *and* engage in a process of evolution, growth, and change. In *On Becoming a Person,* psychologist Carl Rogers wrote, "The curious paradox is that when I accept myself just as I am, then I can change."

Interruptions in this hub cause feelings of fundamental unworthiness, such as believing yourself to be flawed or full of sin. You are not changing to correct for any perceived imperfection and/or impurity (you're not flawed or broken): you change like a flower that continues to blossom—it changes in a process of evolution and growth. The belief that you're not worthy of love and attention, that your ideas and thoughts are not interesting, that you can only enjoy pleasure once you have earned it are all examples of adaptations from lower hubs that are emphasized and expressed as belief systems in the seventh hub. This is how transcendence and redemption can happen—in the seventh hub we find hope in the consciousness that allows us to imagine, to know new options, and to expand and evolve—it's where change becomes possible.

INITIAL DEVELOPMENT

Your capacity for critical thinking is not complete until around the age of 25 (also, your eyes and vision don't reach full development until your early 20s). The physicality of the seventh hub is your PFC, which completes its full development in early adulthood, meaning that the reassessment and revision and second phase of life are made possible with the maturation of cognitive development (see Chapter 3). Through high school and college, teenagers have intensity and confidence due to the dominant influence of the emotional limbic system relative to the higher executive brain functions of the PFC, which is still baking in the oven. The Supreme Court's ruling that 14- and 15-year-olds cannot be tried as adults was determined using scientific evidence highlighting a teenager's *biological* incapacity for adult-level critical thinking and impulse control.

Piaget's final stage of cognitive development—formal operational (see Chapter 9)—is characterized by abstract thought, the ability to form a hypothesis (that is, to ask a question), and to systematically test it to arrive at an answer. He believed this process begins around the age of 12 and continues into adulthood, and that once we reach this final stage, we build on existing knowledge rather than change how we understand things. This is a sobering concept: our intellect and biases are based on earlier brain development (again, much of it from before we have episodic memory)—unless we consciously engage in change. Modern neurogenesis research provides some uplifting findings, such as that the brain can continue to grow its capacity if exposed to new things. Some of the things researchers suggest for promoting growth are as simple as those referenced in Chapter 9: changing the route you take to work and switching the hand that you use to brush your teeth. Anything that disrupts reflexive behavior causes the recruitment of conscious attention, even if it's on a relatively minor scale. But what if processes of conscious intervention and change don't occur? In those cases, we remain stuck in the patterns from early life, and the reduction of cognitive function will likely follow a traditional path of decline.

In the seventh hub we develop truly differentiating human technology: the PFC capable of inquiry, contemplation, and self-awareness. We can see an animal's ability to sustain conscious awareness—just watch a dog enjoying every nook and cranny in its path. Our uniquely human capacity is for consciousness to contemplate itself: awareness of awareness. Sagan said, "We are a way for the cosmos to know itself."

This hub can be underdeveloped because many parents encourage obedient behavior and require children to follow—without questioning—traditional family religious practices that can restrict and interrupt curiosity. Perhaps it's by design or perhaps it's just good fortune that we need to find this hub on our own. Nonetheless, it's essential to activate our interest in the world or else we accept preset limitations.

BASICS

Exploration in this hub benefits from physical anchoring because contemplating larger themes, reducing distractions, and being physically still can stir up agitation. The original intention of the physical yoga practice was to settle this agitation by using movement to release energy; the challenging physical postures were intended to calm and tire the body to decrease distraction, creating optimal conditions for entering inner calm in meditation.

If the physical reality of our body is bypassed, the inquiry and exploration of this hub can generate a surprising amount of reflexive agitation and distraction. Even with a complementary lower-hub practice, when we try to be still, the inclination to indulge the arising resistance of distraction becomes strong—you're standing on the threshold of profound and transcendent stuff. I discuss the fact that resistance gets stronger the closer we get to something that will change us (see Chapter 6). Resistance in this hub can be astonishing, so using physical practices becomes essential, as does noticing the impulse to crowd inner space with the stimulation of music, media, texting, talking, shopping, or whatever form of distraction we prefer.

All the previous hubs have paradoxes of ambiguity that ultimately prepare us, and the seventh hub is the pinnacle of paradox. Instead of allowing programmed reflexes to steer us with reactivity, paradox and ambiguity require us to tolerate the knowledge that things change constantly and to aspire to remain dynamic, responsive, and aware. Subconscious and unconscious reflexes operate without nuance: they are yes/no reactions, and conscious thought is a legitimate threat to the status quo.

If we're receptive, persistent, and sincere, the questions we ask in the seventh hub receive very real and undistorted answers—again, *if we're receptive*. Much of what holds us back involves attachments and certainties involving beliefs that no longer serve us. This doesn't mean that release and surrender are easy, and in fact, being willing and able to change your mind and to let go is profoundly difficult, so only you know when you're ready—and only you know when you know. There's a trap of mistaking rigid belief systems and reflexive bias for conviction, which interferes with the ability to grow and change—and keep in mind that earnestly exploring other perspectives can allow us to strengthen our opinions and positions, but to do it with more compassion and context. We can never fully know what's best for anyone other than ourselves. But seeking to understand other positions and perspectives gets us closer to our humanity and to others.

DIRECT EXPERIENCE

Awe and wonder are often cut short by the impulse to put them into thoughts, words, or images, categorizing what we see and experience or clouding it with a fuzzy overlay of thoughts. It's a natural, understandable response to take a moment of wonder and awe and drop into our other hubs with words or a desire to connect. Sharing experiences with others can feel validating and can create a sense of connection, but this can also evaporate the nectar of the transcendent qualities they contain. The challenge we face with reflexive sharing is that we may begin to look to others to tell us what we see and to guide us in thinking about what we're experiencing. It's an organic impulse in social beings, but part of accessing higher states of our existence is found when we can resist this impulse and stay with the direct experience.

Sitting in silence with another person is deeply intimate and requires security within both the individuals and in the connection. To experience awe and wonder together without speaking is a level of unity that requires development and practice, a demonstration of simultaneously belonging and remaining individual. The reflex to validate that you've had the same experience as someone else is fruitless anyway—you did not. But you did both experience awe in the same moment, and to understand this together is a profound experience not all people get to have in their lifetime. When we look at art, hear music or a story, there can be a sense of connection and enlightenment that eludes explanation and unites us in the immensity of shared awe. We try to explain, but all we can do is point in a general direction with insight—perhaps frustrated by an inability to communicate the direct experience that has lifted (and maybe even transformed) a part of us.

CONSCIOUSNESS AND SCIENCE

Consciousness is hard work: thinking can double the energetic demands of the brain, demands already disproportionate to those of the rest of the body. The brain is only about 2 percent of our body weight yet accounts for 20 percent of a body's energy expenditure. During a typical day, a human brain alone uses around 320 calories. Add a cognitively demanding task to the day, and the energy consumption jumps by at least 100 additional calories; spend time learning something new and that additional demand can double. According to scientists, we operate from automatic reactions and reflexes for an astonishing 90 to 95 percent of our lives. We're adapted toward the efficiency of reflexes—as much as we may like the idea of burning calories, we've biologically evolved to conserve them. There are different kinds of energy expenditure: there's being mentally tired (the exhaustion we can feel after a first day at a new job when everything we're doing is new) versus the physical exhaustion after a day of physical labor. It's my experience that mental exhaustion feels like more of a depletion than physical fatigue, which is often satisfying.

Because thoughts predominantly are repetitive, tedious, and negative, they tend to get a bad rap. We have about 6,000 of them a day, and most of them have a tendency toward problem identification. Feeling relaxed was not an evolutionary advantage until recently: we now live in hyperstimulating environments that slowly kill us with stress. Long before there was language (or Post-It Notes) to help us remember, fixation on negativity helped our ancestors survive by assisting in the memory of dangerous plants and other hazardous things by repeatedly emphasizing them. Most worry is repetition of a piece of information our nervous system doesn't want us to forget. To reduce worry, write thoughts down, make time on your calendar (or use an organization system you trust), and consistently follow through: break a concern down into actionable items and put a plan in place. If you have trouble following through, this may be why you worry too much—your brain doesn't trust you yet. Procrastination and worry are linked fundamentally, but you can change this.

Just as blood circulates in our bodies, thoughts flow through our minds—and we need them. If you tell your thoughts that they have guaranteed lifetime employment and that you intend to respect them, a more cooperative relationship with them can begin. Consider looking at thinking as a bodily function, such as a kidney processing blood or the digestive system moving food: your brain is reflexively processing sensory information, including feelings and emotions, to manage your physical survival. Thoughts are important, but not necessarily accurate or factual; they're pieces of information seen through the lens of a belief system. The best way to tell if something is important or valid is to give it a little time to separate it from reflexive reaction. When we become reactive, obsessive, and consumed by our thoughts, we merge into identification with them. Repetitive thoughts are not necessarily bad—they've just outlived their usefulness as a mechanism for keeping us safe, which is now vestigial and maladaptive.

PARALLAX

Every perspective is both correct and relative, and where we stand informs our perspective. Parallax represents the uniqueness of our perspective and incorporates the direction and speed of travel relative to what we observe (see Chapter 3). As adults, when we rewatch a movie or reread a book, we relate to different characters and different aspects of the story. When we are absolutely certain of our opinion, it helps to remember that our perspective has changed throughout our lives and will likely change again. In *Star Wars: Return of the Jedi*, Obi-Wan counsels Luke that he's "[G]oing to find that many of the truths we cling to depend greatly on our own point of view."

AMBIGUITY

You've done wonderful things and you've done terrible things—just like everyone else. Before you understand that other people can't fit into narrow categorizations, you first need to understand this about yourself. Ambiguity is in the massive space between two seemingly polarized opposites, and the moving and shifting of nuance within this space is where life occurs. There is very little—arguably, nothing—that is fixed and absolute, because life is dynamic and always changing. If binary classification worked, we could simply file away our judgments and be done with them and they would be self-evident to all. But we cannot, even though some folks become flustered and frustrated as they try to push others into categories that fit bigoted, dehumanized narratives, finding themselves in a futile struggle of trying to make people static and unchanging. Nothing can be pure, and nothing can be perfect; these hyperbolic descriptors elude us, taunt us, and destroy the experience of grace and joy. A so-called perfect rose grows out of mold and compost; it prefers worms in its soil and can draw blood with its thorns. Perfection and purity are not real—we are dynamic and living, and so much lusher and more prosperous than any notion of purity could ever allow.

PARADOX

A paradox is logic that cannot be true and cannot be false—it's self-contradictory. Instead of thinking in terms of this or that—black or white—paradox is an ampersand of this *and* that, black *and* white, with possibilities and opposites existing together as they both challenge and strengthen the existence of their opposite. A paradox does not negate opposition, but highlights how one truth can simultaneously oppose, contradict, and amplify its opposite. As with black and white, a paradox cannot exist in exactly the same place without becoming gray, but when juxtaposed, each makes the visibility of the other possible. It would be hard to understand or see white clearly without having seen black—and when placed beside each other, we can better see each of them because of their contrast. This is the phenomenon of complementary opposites (see Chapter 3), and to be capable of simultaneously contemplating and comprehending them, we must loosen our grip on absolute certainty, which is the shadow of the seventh hub. This is an overwhelming and outrageous proposition for many people, contributing to why so many struggle within this hub. If intellectual paradox is initially unappealing, practice it physically or experientially: push down into the ground to rise up and achieve posture, spend time away from someone to strengthen the connection, or experience the astonishing loudness of the silent treatment.

EMBLOOM (The Witness)

The embloom (see Chapters 1, 3, and 4) is a constant, observing presence within you, watching with nonintervening equanimity and able to perceive thoughts, which provides us with evidence that thoughts are not who we are. If we can be aware of them, what is the awareness that is observing them? And although this presence does not directly intervene, it exists as an integrity so central to our being that it makes denial of it increasingly uncomfortable over time. Still, the embloom does not acquiesce, and life can become quite painful when we deny its expression as we live through our adaptations, biases, and beliefs instead of through our core inner truth. A lot of our pain is a form of course correction driving our lives to integrity. Our adaptations and holding patterns, in their attempts to keep us physically safe, have protected us—but eventually, they became maladaptive, and we become protected from the embloom's expression. Our adaptations are not malevolent; their genesis was in the service of our safety and survival. They're a deep and profound expression of self-love and self-protection but they don't know how or when to let go, so only you can assist them to

do it. You have two loving forces within you that have different beliefs about what it means to be alive: one keeps you safe and the other is for your ultimate fulfillment—and in a quintessential paradox, both are correct. The inquiry and the work of consciousness involve appreciating and loving these aspects of ourselves; we release or relax our adaptations and holding patterns with love and appreciation when they no longer serve us, being patient in the process so that they, too, may be free—they have done important work and will always be part of us, but their service can wind down now.

The embloom is eternal, and the seventh hub is where we attempt to comprehend the scope and magnitude of our existence. We are dynamic and multidimensional in ways that are nuanced and paradoxical, contained within a larger pattern just beyond the edge of our intellectual grasp. This cannot be understood rationally—it can only be felt and experienced. As soon as we start trying to put the expansive, astonishing nature of this experience through the filters of observation and verbalization, the essence we touched begins to disintegrate and becomes another object viewed through the influence of our relative beliefs. This hub is where we do our most advanced, logical thinking, but it's also the frontier where we sense what is just beyond the horizon of our logical comprehension and practice advanced forms of surrender to access it.

The embloom is the enlivening, eternal aspect of yourself that observes and can be experienced as the sense within you that looks outward with complete equanimity. We're a phenomenon of consciousness becoming aware of itself. In contemplation or meditation, two questions you can ask are, *How can I be aware of my thoughts if they are who I am?* and *What is this aspect of myself that can see my thoughts?* Any arising responses are more senses of revelation than answers.

When we meditate, we can practice exploring three predominant layers, as I discuss above. The first layer is usually the sensations of pain and discomfort in the body, sometimes referred to as the "grosse body," a term referring to the most immediately accessible aspect of our physical experience. This is a difficult layer to penetrate because it's the loudest and most distracting. If you're not used to an observation practice, you may reflexively try to resolve the pain and discomfort. This often leads to directing focus entirely on the sensations or to addressing the sensation by stopping the observation to fix the discomfort and, therefore, ending the practice. If our early hubs were interrupted by neglect and inattention from caregivers, ignoring our pain can be highly distressing. Therefore, the order of operations for actualization is from the bottom up. Bypassing our interruptions and holding patterns is possible for short periods but cannot be sustained. When we sit with our bodies, we notice things that need to be addressed right *now*, which is an experience we all have when initially exploring stillness. But notice how a hangnail, an unshaved leg, or any other distraction requiring so-called urgent attention is no longer urgent as soon as the practice stops. Leave the practice and the agitation is resolved, so the random fixation is forgotten.

The second layer is the more subtle functioning of the body: the awareness of your breath, the feeling of your heartbeat or digestion, or maybe the sense of your circulatory system or the sensation of the air on your skin. In these first two layers, we can learn to accept what we are experiencing without intervening, and in the third layer, there's a more sublime, more exquisite twinkling of the entire body: the simple, subtle energy body that presents a paradox to the hardline boundary of the physical body. How this layer is experienced is individual, but the unifying fundamental is that it's a state in which we can sense the outer reaches of our consciousness and can experience universality within our bodies.

HUB IDENTITIES

Each hub contains components of our identity, and most folks tend to identify with one or two of them. Diversifying our identity across all our hubs has benefits similar to diversifying a financial portfolio—our overall growth is more likely, and we're better protected from the vicissitudes of life. Each of our hubs has a natural inclination to burn brightly, gently, or somewhere between. When they are relatively balanced and without adaptation, our hubs are uniquely expressed, dynamic, and responsive. Our adaptations are often regarded as personality traits and considered part of our identity, similar to having limiting belief systems about ourselves. However, over-identifying with any aspect of ourselves can cause rigidity and can interfere with growth when we mistake and even idealize (for example) stubbornness or fixation as conviction.

Below is an overview of the hub identities; notice which ones feel more important to you than others. Everybody will have a slightly different take on which aspects of identity are the most important, revealing one's own inclinations.

The First Hub: Physical Identity—I am what I have. I am my body. The condition of our home, health, possessions, and reliable income forms this layer of our identity and like any foundation, everything built on it relies on its stability. *This is the hub of self-preservation.*

The Second Hub: Emotional Identity—I am what I feel. I am what I want. How we feel and what we want are important parts of our identity. But overidentification makes us believe our feelings are inflexible facts, either turning want into irrefutable need or flooding us with emotion so we can't think clearly. This can cause tunnel vision (loss of perspective), which puts us out of sync with others. This is developmentally appropriate for babies: their feelings and wants are fused with their identity and tantrums can erupt when the feelings and needs of others take precedence over their own. *This is the hub of self-gratification.*

The Third Hub: Individual Identity—I am what I do. Career, achievement, and goals are central to the identity of this hub. It's the work we do and its relationship to our sense of purpose, growth, and development and how it aligns with our contribution and purpose in the world. In this facet of identity, our career, full-time parenting, or whatever work fills our days is central to our sense of self. Our level of responsibility, our title, and awareness of whether these represent our values are central considerations for this hub. Overidentification with work is a common, dominant identity in which the search for life's purpose orients almost entirely around career, sometimes causing us to overlook the dimensions of self in the other hubs. *This is the hub of self-direction.*

The Fourth Hub: Social Identity—I am my relationships. I am my connections. Family, culture, and professional, religious, and other social groups and affiliations are central to the identity of this hub. The people in our lives and our relationships with them define it: a *husband*, a *mother*, a *son*, a *colleague*, a *friend* refer to our relationships with people. When indicating who we are by belonging (or not belonging) with them, this facet of identity can include the community of people in the company we work for, our alma mater, or where we grew up. The primary caution with this identity is how much our identity becomes the roles we play with others. In some cases, overidentification in this hub can create an attachment to a specific dynamic within a relationship, and when the person or people in the relationship change, we can feel lost. *This is the hub of self-acceptance.*

The Fifth Hub: Creative Identity—I am my word. I am what I create and express. What we say, write, and create form the identity of this hub. If I say I'm writing a book, I become a writer. When we commit to marriage, there are vows that change us into a husband or wife. We sign our name when we commit to starting a new job, buying a house, or writing a letter expressing our innermost thoughts and feelings. But when we read letters or journal entries from earlier times in our lives, our words express who we were at a point in time when we made a commitment. This identity and the commitments we make evolve and change. *This is the hub of self-expression.*

The Sixth Hub: Symbolic Identity—I am what I see. I am my ideas. The identity of this hub is our vision of how we see ourselves and the world, and what we believe is possible. The aspirations for who we want to be in the world—often connected to archetypes—are expressed in our outward appearance, that is, our image. How we dress, style our hair, and even how we decorate our home expresses the identity of inner vision expressed as outer appearance. We can be inspired by people we see in our own lives (and in the surrounding culture) and can feel connected to how they're expressing themselves. Myths, archetypes, and metaphors are found and connected within this hub. Expression and aspiration transcend words and connect us to a larger, shared experience. We use our image to signal to the world who we are and where we wish to belong. *This is the hub of self-reflection.*

The Seventh Hub: Transcendent Identity—I am part of something bigger than myself. We are on a small blue dot in a massive, majestic cosmos so enormous that it defies comprehension—this hub extends into a spiritual life if we choose to have one. When we remain open to learning, we can always find deeper levels of understanding—again, to know anything with unwavering certainty blocks new knowledge. We can become attached to something we learn, having forgotten that it was once something we didn't know, and so, resist the continuous unfolding of revelation. Although this is the hub that connects us to worldly knowledge, the ability to remain open and receptive requires that we release overidentification with the idea of our intelligence, trading it for inquiry and wonder. When there's identification with this hub, we experience ourselves as intelligent and wise and are often certain of what we know. But to overidentify with this hub is to interfere with its ability to assimilate and process new insights and deeper layers of information. We can know for certain that we're looking at a rock, but deeper exploration contemplates its origin, composition, and relationship with its environment. *This is the hub of inquiry and transcendence.*

MEANING AND BELIEF SYSTEMS

We use meaning to organize and prioritize information. There are countless sensory inputs surrounding you in this very moment. What you choose to focus on and assign meaning to is filtered through your beliefs, which have been shaped by the circumstances of your development, and we tend to consider this interpretation to be fact. We react to our interpretations with our behavior, which further reinforces our viewpoint. Thus, our beliefs inform meaning and meaning informs our beliefs. Without conscious intervention, it's a cycle of self-fulfilling prophecy.

Limiting beliefs like *That's impossible* or *I can't do that* make decisions about outcomes before they've happened. Meaning and belief function in both conception and interpretation. Judith writes, "When the egg and sperm come together in biological conception, there is very little material substance but a great deal of information. Likewise, our beliefs and concepts are *ordering principles* for information. They allow us to organize our data and give us guidance on how to behave." The early programming of our hubs built within us a worldview factory that turns raw sensory material into predictable widgets. We're in the business of meaning-making, and business is good.

When beliefs are unexamined, we look through tinted glasses and believe that the world as we see it is how it exists for everyone. This can also include believing in our limitations and ferociously defending them with *I'm stuck in this job forever, I don't have time to go back to school,* or *I'll never have enough money.* Our beliefs feel real because they were programmed by family and culture long before we could play an active role in deciding what they are. Remember, their early formation predates episodic memory. The challenge is that they are now so familiar that they get mistaken for identity and examining and changing them is often disruptive to the relative peace achieved by maintaining the status quo.

In earlier hubs, interruptions involved invalidation and shaming that, combined with an education that limits (or even forbids) questioning, blocks access to our potential within this hub. Your curiosity is a muscle that can atrophy under the withering gaze of other people who have underdeveloped curiosity themselves—and like the fourth hub with love (victims of victims), in this hub if children are not taught to inquire and be curious, they will not know how to teach their children. The seventh hub offers the opportunity to transcend and evolve through consciously reclaiming and evaluating our early programming and to use these advanced functions to expand our capacity in all the hubs. But keep in mind this is hard work and requires patience and understanding—otherwise, it just becomes another stressor.

INQUIRY: QUESTIONS AND ANSWERS

Our inclination to expand our intellectual capacity will be more developed if our parents and early teachers respected and honored our questions and answered them with genuine engagement. Gaining knowledge from asking questions is an entirely different process than gaining knowledge through having it told to us, regardless of our level of interest.

Our questions guide the quality of the answers we receive. Throughout our lives, the type of responses and answers we get are shaped by the questions we ask, how we ask them, and our level of authentic curiosity. Curiosity can be activated by letting yourself attend to your naturally arising questions—the things you pay attention to because they interest you. Be patient; this impulse may be shy and may hide because it's afraid of being shamed. If you've internalized the shaming voices of others, your curiosity will need you to be kind. Telling yourself that you ask dumb questions and that what you want to know is stupid or embarrassing will send your innate curiosity into hiding, where it will wait until it's safe to come out—a time that may never come unless conscious inquiry and compassion are fostered and encouraged.

Curiosity looks to uncover and examine the intersections of self-knowledge and knowledge of the world, and we benefit from having a running start. Those who came before us left us wisdom in the written word. Their life's work gained yardage in the advancement of human consciousness and so, gives us the chance to pick up the ball and run with it. Any advancement we produce becomes a new frontier, a jumping-off point for those who will come after us.

Many of us were taught that intelligent people know all the answers (or that smart people think like computers). This is an interrupting notion that can distance folks from their own intelligence. Your intellect is expressed in your ability to ask questions and to listen with openness and discernment. Intelligence is a field of curiosity, inquiry, wonder, and awe—and the byproduct of this is insight, knowledge, and wisdom.

Critical thinking is the act of holding and inspecting an idea that you disagree with while intending to understand it (see Chapters 6 and 9), knowing that your values are not at risk of contamination (see Chapter 3). When questioning has a so-called gotcha agenda, that is, intended to prove someone wrong by using their words against them, it's not inquiry, it's battling to convert or overtake another's position. You're not running for mayor (trying to collect votes), nor are you trying to sell something to someone who doesn't want to buy. If you need to defend yourself (rather than explain yourself), don't waste the time. If you find yourself engaging in this behavior—trying to convert someone to your worldview—instead, try to see how deeply you can understand the other person's perspective. Studies have shown that people are more willing to change their minds when we show that we're open to doing the same.

STILLNESS AND SPACE

This hub's physical presence is at the top of the head and extends out and above like the area above the top of a funnel. The seventh chakra, often called "the crown," sits atop our

head, too. For the most part, it's vast and empty. Atomic matter and the universe are mostly made of space; the building block of all matter, an atom, is 99.9999999999996% empty space. If a single hydrogen atom were expanded to the size of the Earth, the proton at its center would be only slightly larger than $\frac{1}{10}$th of a mile.

We make room for physical new things by clearing clutter in the first hub. In the seventh hub, we make room for grace and inspiration with space and silence—a blank canvas of calm that requires stillness. You cannot hear a new piece of music over one that's already playing. When our minds are full of work fixations, repetitive thoughts, images from our screens, and noise in our ears, there's no room for grace and inspiration. But empty space can create anxiety if the first hub is not grounded. If open space is allowed, ask a question into it and eventually, it will fill up with answers. Eckhart Tolle, author of *A New Earth: Awakening to Your Life's Purpose*, writes, "Some changes look negative on the surface, but you will soon realize that space is being created in your life for something new to emerge."

PATTERNS AND FRACTALS

Feeling lonely, anxious, or overwhelmed is synonymous with feeling disconnected and lost. Turning to people and pets can help to restore a sense of connection—and for people who don't feel like being around others (and don't have access to animals) this connection can be restored through the natural world. No matter how hard we work to build the boundary between our relationship with nature, we are born, we live, and we die by it: our bodies are made of the same organic material as all living matter. Yet we're often encouraged to politely hide or dissociate from the corporal realities of our bodies. Our bodies are a temporary phenomenon that go through phases, cycles, and stages (similar to everything else in nature). We're linked in these patterns and cycles by the food we eat, the air we breathe, the seasonal changes of temperature, weather patterns, and the 29.5-day cycle of the moon. The complete cycle of our life is birth through death, which has a specific directionality that isn't necessarily linear, but fits in and synchronizes with the patterns and cycles of our ancestors. If you feel disconnected, anxious, and overwhelmed, reconnect by creating inner space with time spent in nature, recognizing the patterns of your life reflected in the phenomenon surrounding you—and feel how deeply connected and immersed you are in all of it.

As I discussed in Chapter 9, there are specific patterns in nature that repeat: branching, spirals, waves, packing (repeating geometric shapes like a honeycomb), and explosion. The explosion pattern is seen in flowers, snowflakes, and starbursts. Our own branching circulatory system extends into the outer reaches of our body. We see similar patterns in the roots of trees, in the vasculature of leaves, and even in the bifurcated branches extending from a trunk. Nature not only reflects our bodies, but also our minds. Like a spiral and the ever-expanding chambers of a Nautilus shell, we regularly encounter similar challenges throughout life that increase in magnitude as we continue to solve them (often, after thinking we've resolved the issue forever, we get a similar challenge with increased complexity). This is very frustrating if we're inclined toward polarity and believing that once a problem gets solved, it goes away forever. They so rarely do, and we can get perplexed by the Whac-A-Mole nature of life as things constantly arise. There is no changing this, but we can change our expectations and relationship with it.

Fractals are a series of simple patterns that repeat and magnify to create a magnificent, larger arrangement that looks like a big version of the small pieces it contains (see Chapter 9). A fractal is never-ending and infinitely complex: the configuration is self-similar across different scales. When we look closely at the more prominent pattern, we discover the smaller patterns within. When you feel overwhelmed, know that you're in a pattern, and instead of focusing on the feeling of being lost, allow it to unfold and show itself. Hindsight always reveals the existence of this familiarity, so while you're overwhelmed, trust the process—you have been here with this feeling before, and it ended—it will happen again. Challenges simply increase in size as you grow, so wait for it; the clarity will come. If you feel disconnected and anxious, again, try to get yourself into nature and give yourself a little time.

WONDER AND AWE

The curiosity from the sixth hub transitions and expands into wonder and awe in the seventh hub. Our ability to sustain wonder and awe is tied to our capacity to stay present in a moment and to take it in without attempting to categorize it as it ascends beyond definition, words, and images. If only for a few moments, we experience that we are part of a greatness and grandness that defies explanation. Rumi wrote, "Sell your cleverness and buy bewilderment."

Perceiving an experience without processing it into information is, for example, found in the ability to look at a sunrise and extend the awe of its initial effect by not feeling the need for naming its colors, pointing out specific areas, or capturing it with a photograph. It's surrender to the extraordinary moments (which eventually leads to finding similar delight in the so-called ordinary ones)—to be inquisitive, to comfortably withstand the tension of not knowing while delaying the impulse of filing an experience away with others that are similar, into our existing belief system.

In all the hubs, the Method encourages us to listen to ourselves without controlling the narrative. When we ask our bodies what they want to tell us, we must listen for the answer without rushing to fill in the blank with what we'd be comfortable hearing. We betray our bodies by not listening to them and by engaging in things that we sense are unhealthy: too much work, foods that hurt us, exposure to people and experiences our gut tries to warn us about, and media consumption that can fill us with self-doubt and self-loathing. This listening and attending is the essential yoke for reunifying our disembodiment and bringing our body-mind back into harmony.

Our sincere inquiry with wonder and awe allows the hesitant voice to speak and the voice we hear is our own—one that often wasn't listened to as a child. And now, as an adult, you have the chance to give it care and the space to be heard. As you have developed each of the hubs, you have prepared your body like an instrument for more profound levels of communication and experience.

SENSE OF HUMOR

Remaining lighthearted and receptive to absurdity opens the gates of heaven in everyday life. There is heavier energy in the first hub, but up here in the seventh there's a sparkly-eyed wit (something that's particularly annoying to people with shrinking adaptations in this hub). An essential distinction exists between being mindful of others and not taking ourselves too seriously. Like the somatic release that crying creates in the fourth hub, the laughter of the second hub accesses and activates the buoyancy of the seventh (the delight in surprise and absurdity also stimulates it). Laughter releases physical tension, stimulates organs, increases oxygen intake, soothes tension, and releases immune-boosting neuropeptides and endorphins.

The movement of laughter is considered to originate from the second hub—but our sense of humor is movement and joy in concert with the intellect. It's a whole-body experience that supports transcendence. When we remain grounded yet lighthearted, we experience a transcendent quality because humor loosens rigidity and helps us access deeper states of joy and understanding.

AMAZING GRACE AND A HIGHER POWER

Many people have had their relationship with divinity interrupted by the severe practices in organized religions. Our relationship with God is profoundly personal and the contemplation and inquiry is accessed through the seventh hub. Organized religion can form communities that gather to achieve greater connection and contribution. But religion can also act as a broker for your relationship with God, defending its perceived superiority with violence and subjugation. This can lead to dehumanizing and destructive practices. It's ludicrous that any practice that devalues a human could be considered holy.

Because religion has been associated with alienation and spiritual abuse, many people feel very resistant to investigating their connection to something greater than themselves and turn to alternative spiritual practices, which can be just as abusive as some traditional religions can be. There are no all-knowing gurus who know more about your relationship with God than you do—though there are some excellent teachers—and people who profess otherwise are potentially dangerous because of their ignorance and arrogance. Your feet will always be the ones walking your path; those who expect you to follow their advice yet don't equally share in the consequences should be viewed with discernment. We are each a thread in the fabric of a shared existence, and although others may have your perspective and connection, ultimately, your experience is uniquely yours. There's an enlivening force within you that is somehow united with everything, and it is your work to find the relationship you wish to have with it.

INTERRUPTIONS AND STRESSORS

This hub is where we develop a relationship with our thoughts, belief systems, self-knowledge, knowledge of the larger world, and the cosmos. The awakening of intellectual curiosity in a teenager can create strain within a family, especially if parents want their children to adhere to specific belief systems (due to the mistaken notion that their beliefs are correct for everyone). Attempting to save children from making so-called mistakes is well-intentioned but misguided, often leading to a child's fear, guilt, shame, grief, or denial about feeling like they're in opposition to their family. Parents' memories of their own mistakes get erased or repurposed as cautionary tales. There are many complex justifications that all share the same sentiment: *Don't make the same mistakes I made.* Children often need to learn by trial and error to understand things for themselves, just like their parents did.

The apex of this hub is our personal connection to our higher power, which can get severely interrupted when God is introduced as an angry man who sees our very being as consumed with the cancer of sin. When he was in his 70s, my father, who had never been a religious man, told me a story about drawing a picture of God for school when he was about seven or eight years old. He had filled his paper with dots of every color in the crayon box and when he joyfully showed his teacher, he was punished severely. He recalled the reprimand from almost seven decades earlier as he told me, "It was confusing; I was ashamed. I felt a genuine connection to God and in that moment, it felt cut off." As an adult, it was a profound moment for me to hear my father, whom I'd never seen attend church and had never heard speak of faith, explain to me how he experienced God as being in everything.

STANDARDS OF PURITY AND PERFECTIONISM IN SPIRITUAL ABUSE

This hub is interrupted and traumatized by the severity and intensity of age-inappropriate voltage found in some religious and spiritual practices. Telling children, they're full of sin at a young age when they're still developing the neurological capacity to understand what this could even mean imposes fear, guilt, and shame without a good outlet for its release. If you are fundamentally flawed, how can you be a creation of God? Understandably, the futile practice of attempting perfection can and does become an outlet of relentlessly attempting to earn the value and worth you already have. It's a wicked scheme to get people to believe that something they own is not theirs, and then sell them on the notion that if they work hard enough, they can get it from you.

When severe restriction and austerity are taught as being noble—and when restrictive practices are moralized—the interruption of perfectionism and aspiring to attain purity becomes destructive. Practices that require deprivation and unquestioning, blind obedience are trained into children at ages before they have the cognitive capacity to understand them. The intensity and severity create a relationship with obedience and punishment avoidance, not with the sincere devotion of a personal relationship with divinity.

Enlightenment is not charisma, it's not being an effective communicator, appearing happy, wise, peaceful, somber, or any other popular notion about the appearance of an actualized person. It's the quality of watching without correcting, watching *before* correcting, and a state of radical acceptance that's embodied within us as the embloom (and not to be

mistaken for inaction). Achieving this state is interrupted by fear, guilt, shame, and envy, along with the so-called virtuous behaviors that insidiously feast on us through notions of imperfection and impurity.

Purity

Purity is another interruption that can be part of spiritual abuse. Babies and children are very tactile, self-serving, and naturally free of guilt and shame. They perform seemingly endless examples of behavior that can be labeled as impure, which helps form a narrative around the so-called sinful nature found within babies and children. This furthers the disconnection from knowledge of developmentally appropriate behavior and denial of the depth of our interconnection with the natural world.

Practicing faith in community is another paradox to be managed because the connection to others within it is so important. But when belonging becomes an identity of in-group/out-group tribalism with restrictive rules striving toward perfection and purity, this hub is either getting interrupted or stuck in a holding pattern. All communities have standards and boundaries to protect, but when a community justifies oppressive action done to others, it has become distorted and maladapted in its pursuit of knowing God.

Perfectionism

Perfectionism is a mental construct and an interruption of the seventh hub (although it can be imposed throughout all stages of a child's development). The interruption is debilitating and restricts the ability to love and to accept ourselves and others. It interferes with allowing, accepting, and surrendering to the awe and magnificence of being a remarkable part of the Universe. If accepting yourself as you are right now is too painful or difficult because of past hurts of shaming, neglect, or any other interruption that creates feelings of worthlessness, it often leads to the protection of dissociation and disembodiment, which is the detachment from feeling, and a struggle to stay in the present moment. Parents with unhealed interruptions of perfectionism try to teach their children how to be the perfect child, student, community member, spouse, parent, and employee. But perfection is a mirage—even if its pursuit begins with great optimism—and it eventually becomes joyless. Feeling unworthy is a profound disturbance and perfectionism, trying to prove oneself worthy, is a punishing practice.

There isn't anyone who is undeserving of love and mercy, but that doesn't mean you have to be the person providing it. Instead, you must be able to receive love and mercy. A common theme during my interviews for *The Parinama Method* was parents who gave their children advice but were incapable of following it themselves. I would ask, "Was the advice a behavior or action that they demonstrated for you?" and in most cases this was the first time the interviewees had realized that their parents had not been able to follow their own advice (although they hoped their children could). On further exploration, the advice was very often about the unrealized achievements parents blamed for their own disappointments.

RIGID BELIEF SYSTEMS

Unsurprisingly, parents are pleased when their children agree with them. But if questioning children are met with ridicule, punishment, or rejection, they find themselves at an impasse: should they suppress their differences or take a stand and rebel? This choice forces either the loss of an important parental bond or the loss of oneself. Conditions for receiving parental approval can require children to claim falsely that they agree. Children who suppress their beliefs to please their parents may not/probably don't realize that a decision was made to do this, and children who rebel can activate their parents' rejected selves, which can trigger disdain for and rejection of these children.

A parent's rigid beliefs can be political, religious, or so-called lifestyle positions related to human rights and human dignity, in addition to numerous other ethical considerations. Rigid beliefs are found on both sides of the political aisle, in both conventional religion and new-age spirituality—in mansions and trailer parks. As a projection, the rigidity is almost always blamed on whoever has the opposing viewpoint. A common, shared activity of rigid communities is complaining about how inflexible everyone else is and/or targeting specific people and groups and labeling them as ignorant because they disagree. An earnest and open inquiry, such as, "I wonder what contributes to creating that belief?" is instead reduced to name-calling and reductive assumptions. According to 19th-century physiologist Claude Bernard, an early advocate of the blinded testing method, "It is what we know already that often prevents us from learning."

CENSORSHIP AND SUPPRESSION OF CURIOSITY

A parent's role in intellectual and spiritual development is massive. When parents are highly inter-rupted with their own adaptations and holding patterns in this hub, they can genuinely believe that teaching a rigid belief system is for the good of their child. Parents can unintentionally limit their child's intellectual capacity—often in the name of safety and protection—and when they suppress curiosity, they limit options and/or censor information.

Children need mental stimulation, and when deprived of mental nourishment they experience cognitive starvation that interrupts intellectual development. Parents who intentionally control and withhold information, not allowing for or not supporting the exploration of different ideas, attempt to prune their children into their own image.

Some parents believe they must have all the answers and become defensive when they don't, and either laugh at or shame so-called stupid questions. This blocks the future leadership capacity for the growing child; leading is a daunting proposition when it requires being better and more intelligent than everyone else. Many bosses will reenact this interrupted behavior pattern and build teams that they are confident they can dominate. These are work environments in which questioning is restricted, and misinformation and lies are provided to protect leadership against the threat of being exposed as fallible, having strengths and weaknesses just like everyone else.

ADAPTATIONS AND HOLDING PATTERNS

In the legend of the Gordian Knot, a rope bound a chariot with an impossibly tangled knot. It was believed that the rightful ruler could release the chariot. The knot remained in place for hundreds of years, until Alexander the Great rode into town and, after inspecting the knot, simply cut it in half, releasing the chariot. Imagine how many people, from kings to commoners, contemplated that knot while it remained tangled for nearly a thousand years.

Much of our education system attempts to shape our minds rather than teach us how to think for ourselves, so it's easy to get tied up in the impossible binds of what we learn. The interruptions in this seventh hub freeze our thinking and bind us with attachment to old ideas. The sharp blades of inquiry cut through the ancient knots that were tied long before we were born. To release ourselves from holding patterns, we slice through beliefs that seemed true for many generations.

CHARACTERISTICS OF A BALANCED SEVENTH HUB

- Discerning
- Curious
- Thoughtful
- Wise—understands consequences
- Questions—respects traditions but sees how they evolve over time
- Quickly analyzes and assimilates new information
- Respects differences
- Open-minded
- Aware—both alert and calm
- Knows it's not possible to know everything

As we've seen in the other hubs, the inflating and shrinking adaptations share the central underdevelopment within the hub but express this in different ways. Balance in the seventh hub relates to inquiry and discernment, and the ability to grasp and comprehend what is obscure. Imbalance and holding patterns range from the shrinking cynic who avoids broader contemplation to the inflating believer who lacks discernment and accepts information without using the filter of judgment.

CHARACTERISTICS OF AN OUT-OF-BALANCE SEVENTH HUB

- Perfectionism
- Denial and avoidance
- Certainty—a belief system that does not change
- Controlling to avoid
- Believes in one right way
- Tendency to generalize, distort, and erase to support their current worldview

SHRINKING

Our relationship with what we believe in can become enmeshed with our sense of who we think we are, who we think we belong with, and our sense of conviction or principle. When we adapt by shrinking, we can be protecting ourselves from what we perceive to be hostile and threatening information, or even the fear of being alienated by people we love if we have dissenting viewpoints.

The shrinking adaptation tends to discredit alternative viewpoints rapidly through dismissal, generalization, or even ridicule and distortion. This adaptation often adopts a position of certainty or expertise and will end or discourage further discussion, claiming to have already examined alternative perspectives. This is a protective defense, so it's not interested in feedback and/or others' thoughts unless they fall within narrow criteria; being considered intelligent by someone with this adaptation has the single requirement of being in agreement. Both inflating and shrinking adaptations restrict their social access to only like-minded people. This is how extreme conservatives and new-age spiritualists find common ground in conspiracy theories. Insular thinking leads to paranoia, self-absorption, and alarming urgency in defending and validating existing beliefs. Shrinking intellectuals invest so much of themselves in proving a particular hypothesis or in strengthening a case that when faced with new information, they can't let go of the old. In some cases, these folks are initially delightful and intriguing, but eventually reveal they have a fixed catalog of thoughts and ideas that do not grow or change.

Characteristics of a Shrinking Seventh Hub

- Unimpressed, cynical, and guarded
- Belief in limitations
- Either doesn't believe in God or practices a religion with excessive rigidity
- Serious personality; limited or absent sense of humor
- In general, not interested in learning new things outside of specific interests
- Vapid, dismissive, and controlling
- Know-it-all
- Weak attention span with anything other than its specific interests
- Excessive skepticism
- Afraid of looking stupid
- Cannot tolerate being wrong
- "Intelligent" and knows a lot about a specific subject matter within a particular parameter

INFLATING

The intellectual certainty of the inflated adaptation can be both magnetic and a bit of a booby trap for folks seeking to grow in the seventh hub. The confident conviction exhibited in this adaptation can be fascinating and can draw people in, especially those struggling with some of the big seventh-hub topics like divinity and transcendent purpose. Even when inflated people are not particularly charismatic, they can have a mesmerizing effect on someone with underdeveloped intellectual confidence and capacity. There's an understandable temptation to bypass the hard work of inquiry—sidestepping nuance in exchange for easy answers that don't exist. Knowledge exists within paradox, and navigating this ambiguity is essential for a strong and dynamic seventh hub.

Often obsessed and fixated and either building a following or acting as followers to a cultlike leader for all types of obsessions (religious, dietary, lifestyle), seventh-hub inflators may even go no-contact with nonbelievers because they represent a threat that can't be tolerated. Strength in this hub involves intellectual tolerance for different perspectives and beliefs. This adaptation is the same regardless of how it's expressed, that is, expansive and unreceptive to new ideas. Think of a vegan who cannot tolerate the nutritional choices of others or of cult members who refuse their nonparticipating children. And yet, there is nuance here, too: when someone disregards your perspective (and the inherent humanity of living a non-harmful lifestyle different from its own), reducing exposure and enacting boundaries with it can be necessary.

Some folks with the inflating adaptation will retell conspiracy theories with jaw-dropping conviction, discussing an issue as an exercise in dominating so-called opponents with no intention of hearing what they have to say. They are highly influenced by emotionally charged content and place an unrealistic emphasis on something feeling right and, therefore, don't require investigation or inquiry to become enthusiastic believers. Research outside their bubble can be viewed as lack of faith because they tend to become frustrated with details. In general, this adaptation is disconnected from its body even though they may be fixated and obsessed with physical disciplines like yoga or fitness. They don't tend to feel a lot and gravitate toward extremes, intellectually bypassing the importance of the body by ignoring it altogether or becoming obsessed with it.

Late 20th-century Indian mystic Osho, arguably a cult leader himself, said, "The believer does not want to seek; that's why he believes . . . he needs a savior . . . somebody who can eat for him, chew for him, digest for him. But if I eat, your hunger is not going to be satisfied. Nobody can save you except yourself."

Characteristics of an Inflated Seventh Hub

- Enjoys being right and dominating people with opinions stated as facts
- Employs subjugation and domination of others when it's easy, yet their beliefs have surprising fragility and are defended by blocking or cutting off nonbelievers
- Obsessive, expansive, and fixated with manic excitement masquerading as wonder and awe
- "Understands" with suspiciously little information—doesn't require credentials
- Considers discernment and research a lack of faith
- Can be so lighthearted that they detach from reality, including the suffering they cause others
- Oblivious to their obliviousness
- Dissociated from the body, despite being obsessed with it
- Often becomes manic when challenged
- Expansive and hyperbolic—immediately buys into a new belief without requiring evidence or extensive information

HOLDING PATTERNS

ASSUMPTIONS

Assumptions are antithetical to inquiry. When we assume things about people, we don't ask questions because we believe we already know. Processing new information requires work and energy expenditure, so reflexively, we tend to do as little of it as possible. When we're not continuously curious about the people in our lives, we cut ourselves off from their growth and evolution, which has an erosive quality on relationships over time; if we expect others to stay the same, they may feel restricted within this limited perspective.

SPIRITUAL BYPASSING/DENIAL

Recall my discussion of spiritual bypassing in Chapter 9: it's the tendency to use spiritual ideas and practices to sidestep or avoid unresolved emotional issues, unhealed trauma, and unfinished developmental tasks. If we are spiritual beings having a human experience, don't you think we should learn from our physical embodiment? The transcendence in the seventh hub isn't a denial of the other hubs: it should be a dynamic, integrative acceptance that is rich with nuance and incorporates all aspects of ourselves. Transformation is a process and requires effort and the ability to handle both dark and light subject matter—excessive positive thinking is a form of denial that avoids the hard work—think of Dabrowski's Theory of Positive Disintegration: breakdown leads to the breakthrough (see Chapter 1).

Spiritual bypassing is avoidance and turns transformation into a consumer product (along with the expectation that deep work feels good all the time). This puts students in the position of deciding what they will buy, with the unspoken threat that they will stop buying when the process becomes too challenging or unpalatable. Just looking at the pretty things of life and focusing on positivity is regressive and a resignation from the work of humanization; it can lead to the most privileged folks turning their backs on those who suffer.

THE SHADOW: ABSOLUTE CERTAINTY

If you have absolute certainty (without tolerance or consideration of nuance), it's a protection and an adaptation. Theoretical physicist Stephen Hawking said, "The greatest enemy of knowledge is not ignorance; it is the illusion of knowledge." The shadows of previous hubs have the same quality as certainty does: a little is good, a lot is destructive. As an example, dehumanizing people is wrong, but how and why people become adapted to dehumanize others is nuanced, which deserves consideration. To dehumanize a person for dehumanizing can't possibly be the solution.

The conditions of our lives constantly change and as a result, so does our perspective: health and longevity are not guaranteed; children grow up and go on to build their own lives; money is subject to inflation; and jobs that feel important can become irrelevant if the company changes direction or needs to downsize. Certainty is false protection against the unsettling truth that nothing can remain unchanged. If our lower hubs are not at least somewhat developed, we may grasp at intellectual certainty for stability and use assumptions to block and defend against information that feels threatening to the illusion of control. We can exchange absolute certainty for what technology forecaster Paul Saffo calls "strong opinions, weakly held," allowing for increased intellectual expansion.

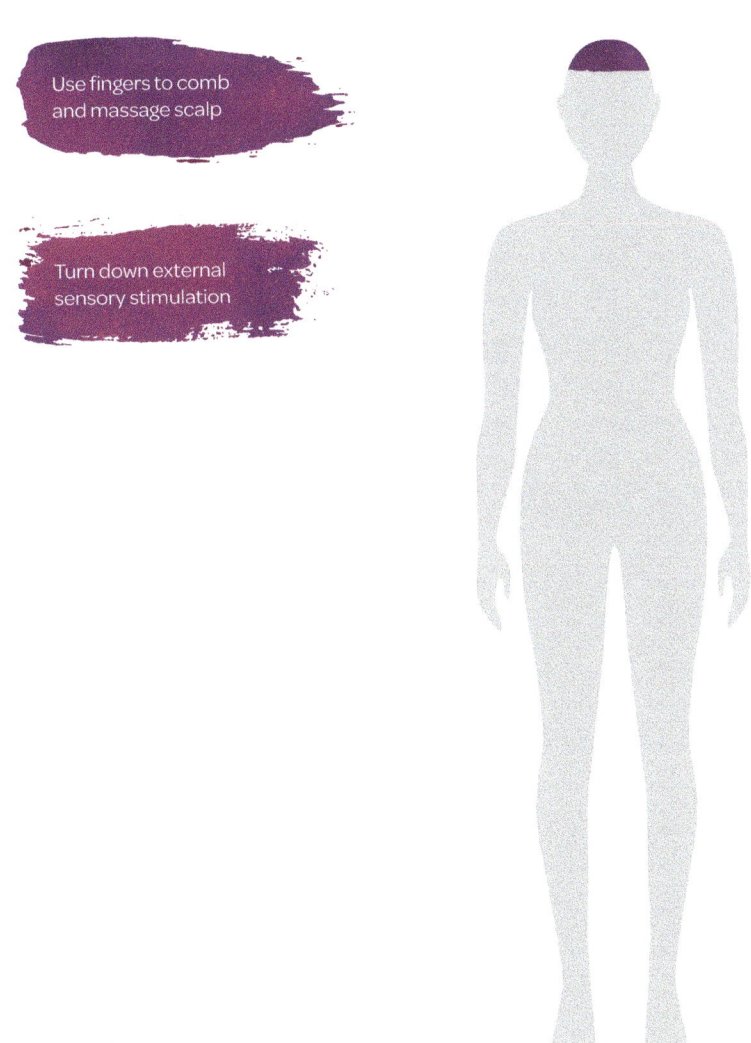

Use fingers to comb
and massage scalp

Turn down external
sensory stimulation

Figure 10.1: Seventh-Hub Body Prompts

© 2022 Parinama LLC. All rights reserved.

THE PARINAMA METHOD SEVENTH-HUB FUNDAMENTALS

The seventh hub can practice awareness of itself and is self-referential. The uniquely human capability of self-awareness is possible because of the PFC: we can choose what we focus on and evaluate reflexes and responses. Again, the physical practice of yoga was intended to prepare the body for stillness so the mind could engage in contemplation, inward focus, concentration, and transcendence without the restlessness of the body causing distraction. The final stage of Erikson's Psychosocial

Development Theory is integrity versus despair (see Chapter 13): forming a sense of identity (integrity) strong enough to withstand physical disintegration (despair). In his model, this stage starts at age 65, but we can begin building toward this integrity at any time.

Our tolerance for the unknown and the questions we ask determine our capacity in this hub. The more we learn, the more we realize how little we know. How could we possibly know everything and put ourselves in the position of being absolutely certain? The pattern recognition associated with intuition in the sixth hub becomes conscious wisdom when we consider outcomes and their consequences. We see how our life involves a series of increasingly complex challenges like fractal patterns that are both mathematical and naturally occurring (see above and Chapter 9). We encounter the same issues in life but at an increasingly larger size and scale in a natural pattern—somehow linked to our unique embloom.

INQUIRY

Our questions inform the answers we receive. You may wonder about your purpose and perhaps even feel forsaken by not knowing, but have you asked, "What's my life purpose?" in earnest and been receptive to incoming insights and inspiration? If you ask a question and pay attention, you eventually get an answer, which is a process that can be immediate but more often takes a little while and requires patience. But be prepared: before you can surf the big wave, you must first ask the question, paddle around, and wait to catch it. I discuss stillness, silence, and concentrated focus (a.k.a. meditation) below, but first, consider inquiry as if it were prayer. In the Christian traditions this involves talking to God, but the practice is powerful even without religion. You may feel desperate and ask, "What should I do?" or fear for the well-being of a loved one and find yourself on your knees. This type of inquiry is for desperate moments; there's no shame in asking for help when you need it and accessing profound truths in your darkest times. Again, a lot of pain functions as course correction, pointing us into our integrity. However, inquiry (and prayer) can be used for nonurgent, larger questions, too.

How you ask questions matters. A famous example: King Croesus asked the Delphic Oracle if he should go to war against the Persians. The Oracle confirmed that if Croesus went to war, he would destroy a great empire. Unfortunately for the king, the empire was his. We get better answers from better questions, and there can be a process of iteration as we work to figure out what the question is. A good place to start is to become aware of what you want to know. The next step is to get more specific. Below are four examples of how to fine-tune the nuance of your inquiry from self-help author Laura Day's *Practical Intuition:*

1. Will I have enough money?
Enough is a slippery word. A good first question would be, "How much money do I want?" which can lead to other lines of inquiry. Once you have determined a specific number, pick a more specific time and ask, "Will I have $_____ [amount] by [specific date]?

2. Will I be happy?
First, ask yourself, *What does it mean to be happy?* and when you get clearer about specifics, ask about them.

3. Should I take the new job?
Using the word *should* introduces biases that are beyond conscious comprehension. As Day writes, add the specificity of *If security is my primary goal . . .* or *If experience rather compensation is my primary criteria . . .* or *If I want to spend more time with my family . . .* to your question.

4. Should I end this relationship and move to a new city?
Compound questions have compound answers. Separate the one question into two and explore each of them.

If this feels onerous, keep in mind the implication of cutting corners with the inquiries that shape our lives. If you feel pressure to provide answers before you're clear about the question, it can force your hand. An example: when we're young, adults may ask about our plans before we have them. The answers we provide can be like casting spells for future states you don't even want. If someone asks, "What are your plans?" the reflex can be to come up with something that sounds intelligent and responsible—but now, an idea has been planted in your head that you must come to terms with not doing. I suggest that the answer to the question is a redirect, such as, "When you were my age, how did you approach figuring this out?"

LIMITING BELIEFS

Our belief systems shape how we experience life. The lower hubs support the confidence and self-worth required to overcome early programming that taught us we are limited. I discuss throughout this chapter how curiosity is an important indicator of intellectual capacity. The ability to see patterns and to imagine a future, and the capacity to explore new avenues of interest determine intellectual capacity. Everyone has a unique parallax of perspective. Everyone has something important to contribute. Reflect on your limiting beliefs about yourself by thinking about what you believe is holding you back. Trace this back to the source and ask yourself if this belief is based on your direct experience or on something someone told you (so often a projection of *others'* limitations). There are many ways to be talented and intelligent (see Chapter 3). You and your embloom contain a unique seed of brilliance.

STILLNESS AND SILENCE

Consciously reclaiming your human rights and dignity through rest, pleasure, power, connection, expression, and creation reduces agitation and allows for the cultivation of stillness. Constant vigilance of the threats and challenges in life is an ongoing interruption that leads to adaptation, and eventually to holding patterns. In peace and silence, we can surrender and access limitless possibilities and transcendence.

Visionaries speak of stillness and space as the origination of their creation. In a 1934 *New York Times* interview, Nikola Tesla said, "Be alone; that is the secret of invention; be alone; that is when ideas are born." Unfortunately, this vital concept hides in plain sight because it's in dissonance with the commonly held belief that hard work is the singular origin of creation. We tend to see a quietly contemplative student as inferior to one who is furiously banging away on a keyboard. Cultivating the capacity to observe and contemplate allows the mind to open its aperture and capture a greater spectrum of information and pattern recognition. Once you've asked your questions, make space for the download. Identify time when you can have uninterrupted space. Set the stopwatch on your phone to one minute (or more) to sit in silence, ask your questions, and then allow for stillness.

TAKE AN AWE WALK

Awe expands our focus, extending it into the greater world and allowing us to experience wonder and appreciation for the surroundings that may otherwise feel distant or go unnoticed. Slow down or even stop what you're doing and appreciate things like how nice the air feels on your face or the beauty of everyday nature in your life. If nature is not available, focus on the simple miracle of your physical mobility as you walk. If going outside and walking is not an option, try meditation.

MEDITATION: FOCUS AND CONCENTRATION

Although meditation has many spiritual implications, it's actually pretty simple: you're training your concentration. This can be as practical or as spiritual as you want it to be. Meditation is a celebration of the PFC, the uniquely human ability to choose where we focus and concentrate (versus having focus driven by reflex). Again, the physical practice of yoga as explained in the yoga sutras prepares the body to be still. If your body is restless or stiff, it will cause distraction. Likewise, if your thoughts are excessively preoccupied in adaptation and holding patterns in other hubs, they will reflexively steer your focus. The eightfold path of yoga is built sequentially, with the first and second branches as ethical practices; the third branch is the physical practice most often associated with yoga (asana); and the fourth limb is breathing practice (pranayama). The topmost four branches (the most advanced practices) are introspection (pratyāhāra); concentration (dhāraṇā); drawing awareness inward (dhyāna); and transcendence (samādhi), which is the experiential realization that everything is connected.

All of yoga orbits meditation, which can seem kind of boring, especially if you're in the process of resolving imbalance in lower hubs. But none of the upper four branches requires sitting still or having requirements for what meditation should look like. While sitting for long periods works for some people, any practice of prolonged conscious concentration and focus is meditation. For example, gardening can be a meditation if it involves sustained concentration, focus, and awareness of our body.

The underlying cause of much everyday misery is overwhelmed and distracted attention. When we can slow our breath and focus, there's an immediate shift into peace of mind. Training our mental focus is like taking a multivitamin that supports mental and physical health, and makes us better at almost everything we do, including work and relationships. But meditation also can be unbearable and can surface anxiety if your lower hubs are highly adapted, so don't be too hard on yourself if you're not ready yet. When the time is right, a concentration practice will be a good fit. It can start with a few simple moments when you first wake up. The key to forming a lasting habit is to yoke it to something you already do every day, such as sitting for a minute before pouring your coffee. Starting small relieves the pressure around the amount of time required for meditation to count. Mediation is not a contest: a single deep breath of gratitude with five seconds of meditative focus can shift and soften the intensity of your day. A simple practice can have a magnetic quality that organically grows over time. Just like consciousness, it happens little by little in fits and starts, and only requires the devotional discipline of love—showing up for yourself. When people confess that they haven't been practicing, I encourage them to explore why without judgment and to seek a deeper, noncritical understanding of themselves.

There are different ways to meditate and most involve a single point of focus: walking silently and mindfully (preferably with bare feet in nature (first hub); allowing free-flowing, gentle movement of your body (second hub); following your breath (fourth hub); repeating an affirmation or a mantra (fifth hub); gazing at an image (sixth hub) or a flame (third hub)). The seventh-hub form of meditation releases focus on an object and surrenders into an all-absorbing presence. Judith uses the analogy of the illumination of an overhead light instead of a flashlight. Regardless of the style, mediation is choosing your focus, observing it with attention, and firmly and patiently returning your attention when the mind wanders.

CHARGE AND DISCHARGE

In the seventh hub, we charge ourselves through learning, new experiences, and cultivating awareness of how we're part of something bigger than ourselves. To discharge we laugh—because taking ourselves too seriously is the antithesis of intellect.

Whenever I travel, I get itchy about all the other places I want to go. Getting out into the world reminds me how ample it is and how much there is to see. We live in unprecedented times: travel and knowledge are accessible at a level unimaginable to previous generations. If there's something we want to know, there's a good chance that people have already devoted their lives to studying and contemplating it. The yardage that has been gained through human curiosity is remarkable: if we explore, we can find the marker where we start running the ball into new territory. Exploring what has been studied is magical and connects us to those who came before.

Diving into the waters of intellectual curiosity reveals depth and expansiveness in an ocean of knowledge. There's so much to know and experience and like traveling, it's in the pursuit and action of learning that we become aware of how we're living within something big and infinite—its size and scope are beyond comprehension. To stand at the shore and look out is to believe we know what we see; to dive in and experience the ocean changes everything.

CHARGING

Learning

When we read new books that show us different perspectives, we fill ourselves with the knowledge that life can be experienced in an infinite number of ways, yet it contains shared themes. When books fill us with new ideas and possibilities, we expand our capacity to live. We broaden and charge this hub when we allow ourselves to experience new things without immediately minimizing, comparing, and categorizing them. Openness to learning and new information charges us up: read a book, go somewhere you've never been, or take a class and learn about something entirely new to you.

New experiences

Traveling, meeting new people, and trying new things feeds intellectual curiosity. However, when we try new things, we risk having bad experiences. The lowering of one's threshold and tolerance for disappointment and discomfort are sneaky ways we become rigid, stuck in old ways, and avoid trying new things. But negative experiences are just that—experiences—and we can learn from them in ways that can be positive, becoming more patient, compassionate, and even self-reflective—or we just need to try not to shut down our willingness to try new things because of a few negative experiences.

Relationship with a higher power

A personal relationship with a higher power or a sense of being part of something larger than ourselves can be a hard sell for folks who had early interruption caused by religious practices that were either developmentally inappropriate or abusive. Reclaiming this aspect of life on your own terms can be tremendously energizing and fulfilling.

DISCHARGING

Laughter

The release and discharge of laughter clears us out. Laugh at all the ridiculous things people told you while growing up, laugh at the silliness of people who misunderstand you, laugh at bad ideas, and clear the way for new ones. Laughter is the discharge in this hub because it releases intellectual rigidity. Remember, discharging and charging are connected: the afterglow of laughter can feel like a charge as it opens the body and allows for greater sensation.

It's important to be open to laughter because like crying, if we have muscular rigidity in our chest and diaphragm, we can get out a few chuckles, but a good belly laugh is elusive. Open the chest and diaphragm with a few deep breaths, put a slight smile on your lips, and say to yourself, *There's nothing funny about this, don't laugh.*

Next, in Part 3 of *The Parinama Method*, all the hubs come together for collective evaluation and work in concert, and in Chapter 12, they're explored in reverse order in the downward direction for the purpose of turning dreams into reality through conscious building and creation.

Part 3

UP, DOWN, AND THIS IS IT

Chapter 11

FROM THE BOTTOM UP—ACTUALIZE

It takes courage to grow up and become who you really are.
—E. E. Cummings

THIS CHAPTER OFFERS THE most straightforward and accessible practices that can be easily incorporated into a busy day. Your practice is an ode to the devotional discipline of showing up for yourself every day. It doesn't have to take a lot of time, but it does require consistency. The process is cumulative. Ideally, the Method is practiced actively at least five times a week and considered daily with the tune-ins and diagnostics. Here, I present an accessible daily routine that supports ongoing evolution and transformation. This practice is pragmatic, but it's just theory if it's not incorporated into your life in a way that works for you. A short-form morning practice done with consistency on weekdays can change your life.

The evening discharge practice can be done as needed, and for folks working a nine-to-five job, it works particularly well on Sunday through Thursday evenings—any time after work or even before bed. To turbocharge transformation, add in a monthly (or semimonthly) long-form practice that incorporates the journal prompts at the end of this chapter. It can be tempting to just think about these prompts but putting the words to paper is vital.

People often experience the beginner's taste of shifts within a single practice, but without consistent devotion, old reflexive patterns will return. The practices in this chapter are specifically chosen to be done from between one and 20 minutes, almost anywhere—and they need to be done. Find a time that already has consistency and structure and add it into your routine (after working out or before you shower and get ready for work in the morning). You can even do the tune-in with children as you give them the prompts.

The nine practices:

1. *The body-mind tune-in* can be done almost anywhere in less than a minute.

2. *The classic diagnostic* is a mental scan to rapidly access overwhelming situations and to support decision-making for taking action.

3. *The body-mind diagnostic* is a body scan used to cultivate hub awareness using body sensation to process stressors of daily life.

4. *The morning sequence* is a foundation of the Parinama Method. Five to 20 minutes to gently charge the body and release from the previous day. This practice increases capacity for dealing with the challenging situations of everyday life by both releasing and charging; it

prepares you to start your day and supports enlivening your body-mind before a short but impactful morning journaling, stillness, and concentration practice.

5. *The daily journal prompts* are for the emotional hygiene of clearing out residual emotions, so they don't interfere with clear thinking and peace of mind.

6. *The evening sequence* is a discharging practice that can be done at the end of the day to release tension.

7. *The interruption assessment* explores the human rights of each hub and their impact on the overall distribution and relative strength and weakness when looked at together.

8. *The overall hub patterns: playing to your strengths* is an overview of the different distributions of hub development.

9. *The long-form journal prompts* are intended for monthly or semimonthly practice.

The tools of the trade are

- a journal or something to write in or on;

- a block or rolled towel (though the back of a chair or couch can work for the discharging practice); and

- a carpet or nonslip floor surface—a yoga mat is not necessary but can be good if you have one.

THE BODY-MIND TUNE-IN

There are 17 actions for the tune-in, which take about a minute to do, and if done with concentration and focus, it can bring an immediate shift to your body-mind. You can do the tune-in whenever you feel disconnected or overwhelmed.

1. K1 grounding (see Chapter 4): establish the connection in both feet with the ground. Slightly bend your knees to unlock them. Squeeze glutes (bum) to a tremor followed by a slow, gentle release.

2. Make a Hula-Hoop movement with your hips twice in each direction.

3. Push feet into the ground and extend posture upward, eyes facing directly forward.

4. On an inhale, expand your torso simultaneously in all directions (360 degrees), followed by a single sharp exhale through the nose, using the diaphragm if you can.

5. Take a natural, slow inhale with hands at your sides. Exhale extending arms out, inhale hands to heart.

6. Hold hands on the heart for one breath and connect to yourself.

7. A single, gentle neck role clockwise and one counterclockwise.

8. Inhale chin to the sky (optional: unlock jaw and open mouth wide, stick out tongue).

9. Exhale chin down to chest.

10. A quick tug on your earlobes and massage ears.

11. Say, "Even as challenges come my way, I love and accept myself."

12. Place the heels of your hands on your eyes, inhale, and visualize the day ahead: *imagine how you want to feel* and one specific thing you want to happen. Take a couple of breaths if necessary to see and feel this.

13. On an exhale, remove palms and widen eyes into bug eyes, taking in as much as possible.

14. With your nose facing forward, lift your eyes to the sky; then lower your eyes to look forward.

15. Comb fingers on your scalp.

16. Give your hair a slight tug upward.

17. Shake out your hands, do a little body wiggle, and stomp/tap your feet on the ground.

Take a moment to tune into the sensations of your body.

THE CLASSIC DIAGNOSTIC

You can use awareness of your hubs to get to the bottom of how you feel and quickly prioritize how to handle a situation.

For a specific situation, rate each hub on a scale of one to 10, one being *this isn't important* and 10 being *this is very important*. Don't overthink this: the first answer is the best, but once you've rated all seven hubs, look to see if anything needs a tweak. Multiple hubs are always affected when we face a challenge but choosing the one with the highest score supports our ability to take the most effective initial action. The worksheet on the following page can be used for the exercise; begin by explaining or writing down the basics of the specific situation you wish to explore.

The primary purpose of this exercise is triage, which allows you to prioritize to take effective action when multiple stressful factors get tangled up, as they often do in an intense situation. This exercise can reduce the sense of overwhelm and lack of clarity about how to proceed and replace it with greater certainty about what to do next. In many cases, emotions (the second hub) can crowd out a more significant aspect of the issue. For example, if in a particular situation you give yourself a relatively low rating in the second hub because enjoyment and satisfaction are not being affected, yet there are strong emotions (like anger) about the primary concern in the moment in the fourth hub (for example, losing social credibility). A lack of process can prioritize the anger over the predominant concern of losing social standing. Compartmentalizing the emotion (anger) as you first address your fourth-hub concerns with the appropriate people makes it possible to process the effect experienced on each hub in descending order. Eventually, find a constructive outlet for the anger. There's a difference between feeling disrespected in a single instance and being concerned that there's a pattern developing. A single instance can be activating, but if it's an isolated incident, acting on it will probably compound the greater concern of having social credibility threatened.

You can use this exercise for both personal and professional situations. As a boss and advisor, I've used this to help a staff member get to the bottom of a conflict, prepare for a conversation, or decide whether to take a new job. As a friend, I've used this to help figure out quickly how to address conflicts with partners and others. Rather than offering advice based on the vignettes of information provided when they're upset, using this exercise helps people figure out how to solve their problems for themselves. They can access the fuller context of their knowledge of a situation as they consider it hub by hub. Once the primary issue has been identified and diagnosed, the next step is to figure out how to communicate or to take specific, constructive action. This is when advice can be helpful, so constructive steps are taken to get to a resolution.

The Hub	The Consideration	The Rating
First	Is my physical safety feeling threatened? Does this situation make me afraid that I can't pay my bills or take care of my body and/or put my physical health and safety at risk?	
Second	Is my ability to find enjoyment and satisfaction being affected? Name your predominant emotion:_____	
Third	Is my power being threatened? Is my ability to act on my own behalf, to be appreciated, or to be respected being interfered with?	
Fourth	Are my relationships and/or social credibility being threatened?	
Fifth	Is my ability to express myself with integrity being interfered with? Is the truth being kept from me?	
Sixth	Are my perspective and insight being respected and validated? Are things being hidden from me?	
Seventh	Am I being censored, or is the information I'm receiving being censored?	

Table 11.1: The Classic Diagnostic Chart

THE BODY-MIND DIAGNOSTIC

Sometimes it can be challenging to identify exactly how we feel about something or to figure out the cause of a change in mood. As we run from meeting to meeting, juggling commitments and responsibilities, we may suddenly notice ourselves feeling tense, frustrated, or being in a foul mood. Of course, we may attribute this to the catchall of a stressful day, but by using our body we can track the source of the feeling and identify specific issues through sensation. The benefit of addressing the source is that you attend to it directly and so, avoid misattributing it to general stress as just a part of everyday aggravations or misdirecting it at a random person who crosses your path when you're about to burst. There can be multiple contributing factors, but you can only address them one at a time; start with the most pressing one.

Begin by noticing where you feel sensation in your body, specifically stiffness, discomfort, tension, or pain. First, note the physical location and its associated hub. Then, reflect on what has happened in recent days and weeks that may have affected the hub. To name a few examples, some folks experience lower back pain when they have unacknowledged and unprocessed emotions; some have tightness in the chest when feeling disconnected in a significant relationship; some feel jaw tension after being demoralized by a boss or client and not being able to say anything; some have upset stomachs when they're not being appreciated or respected; some have stiffness in the feet or plantar fasciitis when feeling anxious about losing a job or about their health.

Give that physical area attention with the charge or discharge it needs by reviewing the techniques and exercises for the associated hub. Listen to what the sensation has to tell you without forcing a narrative to fit a more convenient (but inaccurate) worldview. Keep in mind that sometimes pain wants to be babied and simply allowed to hurt for a little while. When this is the case, just acknowledge it and contain it with patience and compassion. This is a good cue for journaling: a repeating thought can be a blockage, so merely writing it down or journaling on it can help release its bind.

THE MORNING SEQUENCE

A morning sequence can begin with the simple tune-in above or with the sun-salutation sequence here, which incorporates some charging and strength building.

Sun salutation to begin movement (do one or two times):

- Inhale and extend your arms above your head, exhale them down to palms together (in prayer position) in front of your heart. Repeat.

- Inhale while in a standing position and exhale while folding your torso forward over slightly bent knees; inhale a slight lift and bring your torso parallel to the floor, and then exhale your hands to the floor (or as close as they get).

- On your next exhale, transition into a plank position, lowering all the way to the ground. Leave the fronts of your legs on the floor, and place your palms under your shoulders, pushing into your hands, extend your arms as you inhale your chest up into the cobra position by lifting your chest up to face the front of the room. Try breathing to expand your chest and gently rotate your shoulder blades in the direction of your upper back. Take a deep inhale.

- On the exhale, push back into a downward-facing dog with your knees slightly bent and take care not to lock the shoulders by slightly rotating them inward.

- Stay for five breaths, then step your feet to your hands on an exhale and inhale up to standing.

FIRST HUB

- If you have bare feet, rub your soles on the carpet for gentle stimulation.
- Plug your K1 (see Chapter 4) into the ground keeping your knees slightly bent, squeeze, and then release your glutes.
- Sumo squat: bend knees, drop bum, keep toes visible for two rounds of five breaths—try to achieve a discharging tremor by exploring the different depths of the squat.
- Come down to seated.
- Rub and pat the body parameter: *This is mine* and *I'm in here*. Massage the bottoms of your feet.

SECOND HUB

- Roll onto your back with your feet planted on the floor and knees pointing to the ceiling.
- On an inhale, push into the soles of your feet and lift your hips to the sky—lower on the exhale, pump up and down with the breath four times, and lift and hold for eight counts.
- Rub your tummy with hands in clockwise and counterclockwise motions, say something sweet to yourself (*hello baby, hello sweetie*)
- Transition onto hands and knees and prepare for plank.

THIRD HUB

- Plank (see Chapter 6): Start with your knees on the floor if a full plank puts strain on your back or can't be held for at least 10 breaths. You can also do a plank with your elbows on the floor under your shoulders. Then, using a timer, hold your plank for as long as you can—start by trying for 10 breaths—and write the number of seconds (eventually minutes) in your journal next to the date, or mark it on your calendar.
- Come up to standing.

- March your feet in place 20 times and return to standing still.
- Breath of fire (see Chapter 7): 10 sharp exhales incorporating your diaphragm—out through the nose with passive inhale (you can use this during the day to increase energy).

FOURTH HUB

- Coordinating your breath with the movement of your shoulders, hands, and arms, inhale your hands up to your heart, and on the exhale, outstretch your arms wide in any direction, and then inhale them back to your heart.
- Stand still for a moment and breathe with long, slow exhales through pursed lips (like blowing out a candle).
- Bring your hands behind your back (using a towel or a scarf if your hands don't connect or if clasping them causes any kind of pain) and open your chest, shoulders moving down away from your ears, with each exhale for three breaths.

FIFTH HUB

- On an inhale (through your nose), extend your head back to look up as you extend the front of your neck; on the exhale bring your head forward touching your chin to your chest while making the sound *ha*. Repeat two times.
- Gently place your right ear to your right shoulder for a neck stretch, hold for one or two breaths. Repeat on the left side.
- Unlock your jaw and open your mouth wide, massage your jaw, and stick out your tongue with a gentle *haaa* or *ahhh*. Try to get the sound to create vibration in your throat and chest.

SIXTH HUB

- Raise your eyes to the ceiling while keeping your nose pointed forward (you may feel a slight stretch in your eyes).
- Bring your eyes back down and place the heels of your hands over eyes (see the tune-in above) and imagine your ideal day ahead: how do you want to feel and if you can, bring some of those feelings into your body right now.
- Tap between eyebrows, massage temples, gently massage brow, and use bottoms of palms to gently massage your cheekbones.

SEVENTH HUB

- Massage your scalp, combing your fingers through your hair.
- Tug your hair upward for a gentle stimulation.

Shake out your hands, wiggle your body, and tap or stomp your feet. Bring attention and movement to anywhere else on your body that calls for it. Come to a comfortable seated position on the floor or in a chair. Rub legs and bottoms of feet. Sit quietly and count five breaths. Pick a daily journal prompt.

USING COLOR THROUGHOUT THE DAY

Colors correspond to the hubs and help with symbolism and organization. Like light through a prism, red is closest to the earth with a wavelength that's the slowest frequency of all the colors on the visible light spectrum. Violet, the color of the uppermost hub, is the shortest frequency light wave and has the lightest energy on the visible spectrum. If you're focusing on the embodiment of safety, security, and trust of the first hub, wearing a red bracelet or carrying something red can help with periodic reminders to tune into grounding into this hub throughout the day using body prompts. After your morning practice you can pick the color(s) representing the day you want to have or the area you want to tune into throughout the day. Then, throughout the day when looking at the color, tune into your intention by doing a physical prompt. Three examples are a red bracelet to remind yourself that you're safe and to plant your feet on the floor; a yellow bracelet to remind yourself that you are powerful and to push down, rise, and expand your torso in all directions; and a green bracelet can be used to remember to receive and to breathe.

DAILY JOURNAL PROMPTS

When left unexplored and unprocessed, emotional contamination is the creep of residual emotions from earlier experiences into new ones. The morning journaling practice is like taking a shower or brushing your teeth, helping to clear the way and make room for the day ahead—it's emotional hygiene. You are removing emotional obstructions, addressing cynicism, frustration, and disillusionment, and allowing for flow—starting a new day without carrying over the previous day's residue.

Ideally, a morning practice takes five minutes for a physical sequence, 10 minutes for emotional-hygiene journaling, and the last few minutes for stillness. The stillness can be any of the concentration practices from the techniques and exercises in Chapter 10; popular options are observing a candle flame or following your breath and tuning into subtle sensations in your body.

Daily morning journaling is specifically about flushing the pipes, processing, and moving thoughts and emotions out: we surface negative thoughts, feelings, and emotions and let them go. Morning journaling is not for rereading (these pages can be thrown away or deleted); the sense of an audience (even when it's you) can introduce subtle pressures to say the right thing and to be polite, and this can make the exercise feel performative. This journaling is for dropping the masks of persona and letting it all out. You're working toward the resulting fitness, which in this case is increased emotional and creative capacity.

Cameron suggests a practice of what she calls "morning pages," using free writing to surface and process whatever is on or in your mind (see Chapter 8). The key is to do it daily, freehand, unedited, and to keep it to yourself. This isn't a diary, blog, or notes for your memoir—it's clearing emotional residue. A simple journal prompt can be *Tell me how you're feeling today*, followed by, *Is there anything more you want to say about that?*

EMOTIONAL HYGIENE: DAILY PROCESSING PROMPTS

- Use the emotion wheel and rate the intensity of your current mood on a scale of one to 10 (see Chapter 5).

- Is there predominant emotion(s)? Use the wheel if you need help naming.

- Can you make a connection between this feeling and something that happened recently? Explain the specifics. Imagine that your journal is saying *I want to hear every detail* and allow yourself to decide when you've said enough.

- Now think about how you'd like to feel right now. What needs to happen to make that possible? If that surfaces more emotions, process them too.

JOURNALING: DECONSTRUCTING AN EVENT

Interview yourself with the five journalistic W questions: *who, what, when, where, and why*. Processing emotions involves containing them and defining what is happening; a single inflamed and minor issue can fill up all the space available with repetitive thoughts. By nailing it down, it can stop banging around in your head and hijacking your peace.

Who's involved?

What's happening?

When's it happening?

Where's it happening?

Why is it happening?

THE EVENING SEQUENCE

Use the following sequence as needed. For support, roll up a towel or use a yoga block. Lie down and place your support between your shoulder blades (behind your heart). Release your body into the block or towel with a long exhale, allowing your chest to expand. Once you feel settled, lift your shoulders off the support so that only the bottom of it is in contact with your back. Find the tremor in your abdomen and try to move it out through your legs or up and out through your breathing. Lie back down on the towel or block and say *ahhhh* to get some vibration and release in your neck and vocal cords. Allow for the release and then come back up for another discharge. Optimally, this is done two or three times and is followed by a period of release into the block. Tap or slap the bottoms of your feet on the floor to release any remaining tension, then come up to a seated position and massage your thighs, legs, and feet. You can also sit in a chair with four stable legs or on a couch. Plant your feet on the ground and lean back to extend and open your chest.

Orgasm is a particularly effective discharge, especially when recruiting deep breathing, spontaneous physical movement, and sound. The more hubs you can incorporate, the greater the sensation and the greater the release.

INTERRUPTION ASSESSMENT

Everyone has a different overall pattern of hubs, depending on a combination of our natural-born biological inclinations, life circumstances, and experiences. What we seek in this process is to cultivate awareness, play to our strengths, and to try collaborations with others where we're not strong. The Method isn't about building the perfect human; it's about fully becoming who you already are, making the most of your miraculous life, and working in concert with others and the world around you. As the Serenity Prayer adopted by 12-step programs puts it, "[G]rant me the serenity to accept the things I cannot change, the courage to change the things I can, and the wisdom to know the difference." Which human rights do you struggle with, and which boundaries could use the most attention (see Chapter 2)? Using the All Human Rights worksheet below, rate the amount of importance you currently place on each hub from one to 10. A lower rating represents an area you don't think about often, and a higher rating represents a greater level of focus—the hubs with lower scores need more attention, and those with higher scores may benefit from some release and discharge.

The Hub and the Right	The Scale of 1 to 10
1. Physical security	
2. Feeling and enjoyment	
3. Freedom, power, and taking action	
4. Connections, relationships, and love	
5. Telling the truth or being lied to	
6. Vision and validation of being seen	
7. Knowledge and concentration	

Table 11.2: All Human Rights

HUB PATTERNS: PLAYING TO STRENGTHS

There are distribution patterns within our hubs. Conscious reclamation allows us to bring attention to the hubs that will enhance and expand the overall quality of our lives. Through conscious reclaiming, we can play a more active role in the programming that shapes us. Here, I review the most common patterns, the compelling events that drive change, and some general thoughts on balancing.

LOWER-HUB DOMINANT
(Higher numbers in Hubs 1 to 3 relative to other hubs)

The lower-hub dominants tends to prefer to keep things steady, not wanting to rock the boat. This work-hard, play-hard inclination doesn't overthink and tends to have simple expectations; usually following rules and routines, they experience work as virtuous, essential, satisfying, and often physical. Rather than overthinking and intellectualizing, they're usually guided by instinct and emotion (but recoil at the notion of being "emotional") and are primarily focused on self-preservation and self-gratification. This pattern may consider creative and intellectual work weird, elitist, or nerdy. But when a meaningful relationship calls for deeper self-awareness or they face a crisis like heartbreak, illness, or injury, they may be motivated to contemplate, to reflect, to turn to art and music for comfort, and to yearn for more effective communication—all the domain of upper hubs. This pattern can be supported by expanding social horizons through meeting new people, reading, trying new things, and exploring new ideas (using boundaries in a way that supports feeling safe).

UPPER-HUB DOMINANT
(Higher numbers in Hubs 5 to 7 relative to other hubs)

The upper-hub dominants tends to be self-reflective and expressive. These thinking-intuitive types struggle with spontaneity and *decide* how they feel before they take action, sometimes getting stuck in patterns of overthinking that lead to inaction. This pattern is taken advantage of when their talents are used without credit or consideration because they can be seen as people who will not fight back. The compelling events that drive their desire for change come from feeling a lack of power and stability. This pattern may be good at intellectually understanding others' emotions, but their own feelings often remain a mystery. Focusing on grounding, embodiment, and *feeling* emotion in the lower hubs will support balance. Getting a massage or walking in nature and just taking things a little less seriously can be especially therapeutic.

MIDDLE-HUB DOMINANT
(A higher number in the third hub relative to other hubs)

The middle-hub dominants finds their identity in activity. They use their bodies and intellect in the service of productivity but often lose sight of the big picture, not fully aware of why they work so hard or why they choose work over life's enjoyments. The compelling events that drive this pattern to seek change must be self-directed; pleas from loved ones to work less are met with impatience and defensiveness. Change tends to involve becoming aware that the rewards for working are neither linear nor fair, and that there's more to life in the other hubs. Burnout, being laid off or passed over for a promotion, or having a health or personal crisis can cause shifts into embodiment and introspection.

Unfortunately, since this pattern is third-hub dominant change usually comes from extremes and rock bottoms.

MIDDLE GAP (Lower number in the fourth hub relative to other hubs)

Folks with the middle-gap pattern are aware of head and body but are disconnected from them both. This is usually the result of significant interruption to relationship and connection in the fourth hub. They're typically intelligent, intuitive, and creative in the upper hubs, but physically challenged by allergies and chronic pain, or are obsessed with diet and exercise (and are sometimes hypochondriacal). There is often a desire to stand up for underdogs and to advocate for others (often more effectively than they can for themselves). This pattern tends to be introverted and to struggle with intimacy (though outward appearances can indicate otherwise). The compelling event that causes shifts can be a growing sense that their isolation is not resolving itself. Shifts can occur through relationships with animals and nature (they don't always need to involve people). The techniques and exercises can support this pattern in the second hub with emphasis on attunement and emotion and in the fourth hub with emphasis on receiving and self-worth, specifically expanding the capacity to receive and deepen connections.

BALANCED (Numbers are fairly consistent throughout all the hubs)

Some folks have been blessed with minimal interruptions, some have been taught healthy boundaries, and some were born with a natural inclination toward balance. The balanced pattern usually has good health and vitality; awareness of feelings without being overwhelmed by them; confidence and power without needing to dominate others; secure attachments in relationships; clear communication and listening; and imagination, wisdom, and a connection with awe, wonder, and inquiry. But when they're interested, balanced folks can benefit from fine-tuning their awareness and growing their capacity.

In professional settings there are dynamics that play out between different hub patterns. The upper-dominants are inspiring, have ideas, are exceptional at communication, and often have excellent one-on-one relationships with people inside and outside the company. Nonetheless, they often struggle with authority, organization, focus, and follow-through. Also complicating matters is their tendency to behave in rigid, overly formal ways when meeting with executives: upper-dominants lack swagger and confidence because they overthink their behavior, causing them to be viewed as more junior than they are. Conversely, lower-hub dominants typically exhibit focus, fun, and the brute force of a strong third hub, and are often regarded as top performers even when they are not—a dynamic that can be like apex lions and APDs (see Chapters 2 and 6):

Lions—The lower dominants are successful as individual contributors. Still, their lack of imagination and intense individualism sometimes make them difficult fits for leadership of people, and they can be prone to using others' ideas and taking credit. Remember, the lions in the jungle are apex predators not just because they can hunt but also because they scavenge off smaller predators.

APDs—The upper dominants, with their 85 percent kill rate, keep having their ideas stolen by the lions. Upper dominants often get robbed and struggle as lions keep overtaking them for career advancement and recognition. It's a sign of a healthy culture when the lower-dominant lions make sure the upper-dominant APDs gets the credit they deserve. Despite appearances, the lions are in an unfavorable position: they rely on the ideas of others, and without talented, upper-dominant people in the organization, they starve. The lower dominants sense their own potential for greatness but will struggle to find it, so they either need to cultivate champions in an organization or develop their upper hubs. When they work together, incredible things are possible.

LONG-FORM JOURNAL PROMPTS

Pillars of a Parinama Method practice, the long-form journal prompts are to be used monthly or semimonthly—not daily—when you have time, such as on evenings and weekends. These practices complement the techniques and exercises for each hub in Part 2.

FIRST HUB: SAFE PLACE

Describe in detail where you feel physically safe. It's most effective if this is a physical place you can create to find sanctuary, but it can also be an imaginary place. Use as much or as little specificity to describe it, keeping in mind the following considerations:

- **Body:** Are you lying down, seated, or standing? Moving or still? Outdoors or inside your home? How are you clothed? Are you wearing socks or going barefoot?

- **Temperature:** What is ideal—cool, warm, or hot?

- **Food and hydration:** Is there something you eat that provides comfort that you can receive as nourishment and nurture? Do you have a beverage? What is it?

- **Activity:** Is there something you are doing, such as writing, talking, walking, gardening, cooking, cleaning, or driving?

- **Visual:** Is the lighting soft or bright? Are you watching something, reading something, or are your eyes closed?

- **Auditory:** What is the ideal sound for comfort? Is it silent or is there sound? If there's music, what is it? Do you hear talking, nature, or other background noise?

- **Connection:** Is there a pet, a particular person, or people close by? If so, who are they? Or do you want to take a break from being with others?

SECOND HUB: FEELINGS AND EMOTIONS

These prompts help connect your feelings and emotions with the things that matter to you. Choose a prompt from the list below, say it to yourself, and close your eyes for a few breaths as you allow your imagination to participate in the exercise. When you open your eyes, write about whatever has come to mind.

Notice if you feel any changes in your body, such as softening, tensing, relaxing, or pleasant feelings. Read what you've written and underline anything that feels particularly important. A real-life example is from a client who wrote, "I feel safe when I'm with people, and trust and feel a sense of optimism for what the future will hold." In this case, there was a genuine surprise for this person that the sense of clarity and optimism for the future was tied to feelings of safety. This same person wrote, "I feel joy when collaborating with others and feel like there's something to look forward to."

- I feel safe when . . .

- I feel joy when . . .

- I am powerful when . . .

- I feel loved when . . .

- I'm showing love when I . . .

- I feel understood when . . .

THIRD HUB: POWER

Following is an exploration by Judith about how we learned about power. It looks at the family dynamics of how we were introduced to power so that we can examine our beliefs and consciously reclaim how we choose to demonstrate power in our lives:

- **Who holds or held the most power in your family?** Is or was it your father, your mother, a sibling, or a grandparent? Whose approval is or was the most elusive?

- **How does or did the person hold that power?** Does or did the person use violence or threats, emotional manipulation/withdrawal, intense discipline, or was the person articulate, firm, and compassionate?

- **How do or did you react?** Do or did you fight back and rebel, emotionally withdraw and hide, or agree and comply?

- **Given these dynamics, what do you do now?** Rebel? Withdraw? Comply? Are you still in the patterns of your family or have the patterns changed?

- **Do you feel that your right to act has been compromised?** Would you like to change how you respond to power and authority? If so, how? Is there a leader whose style you admire? What are the qualities you wish to adopt as your own?

THIRD HUB: IDENTITY

Our identity was formed as we responded to the dynamics of our childhood home. To recover our true self, we must look at who we had to be back then and must determine if this is a role we still want to play. Were you the helpful child who was well behaved and cheerful or did you speak truths that nobody wanted to hear and act out in the face of your family's secrets, denials, and delusions? As children, we play these roles to survive and to belong, but as adults they may be maladaptive for living the life we want. You may believe that if only you can finally do what's required to deserve and earn the exact love and approval you crave, one or both of your parents will finally be able to give it to you. This is a holdover from the early-childhood perception that how you were treated was your fault. The reality is that it's parents' limitations that keep them from loving and understanding their children in the specific ways they need to be loved and understood.

Therapist Lindsay Gibson, author of *Adult Children of Emotionally Immature Parents*, provides an exercise that looks at the roles we played as children and the corresponding healing fantasies we believe will make us deserving of the love we crave—our beliefs in the behaviors we need to enact and the changes others need to make that would unlock their ideal love and acceptance of us. For this exercise, you must write down the answers so that you can read them back to yourself. In your journal on two separate pages or on two separate pieces of paper, complete the following sentences:

On page one, finish these sentences:

- I try hard to be _____.
- The main reason people like me is because I _____.
- Other people do not appreciate how much I _____.

- I always have to be the one who _____.
- I try to be the kind of person who _____.

On page two, finish these sentences:

- I wish other people were more _____.
- Why is it so hard for people to _____?
- For a change, I would like people to _____.
- Maybe one of these days I will find someone who will _____.
- In an ideal world with good people, other people would _____.

Page one is your role self: who you believe you need to be to deserve love. Page two is your healing fantasy: who you hope your parents (and intimate relationships) will become for you. This is a potent exercise to share with someone you love and trust; discuss their experience with seeing these needs in you and their willingness to love and support you as you grow.

FOURTH HUB: LOVED AND CONNECTED

The following prompts for this hub are for reminding ourselves that we are surrounded by love and for receiving it and inspiring expressions of sincere gratitude. Take an inventory: What do you like about yourself and what do you love about yourself? Start by completing the following statement: "[Your name], I know you love me because _____."

Like and love: We're used to focusing on everything that needs work and improvement, but what about what we appreciate? Start by journaling about the difference between liking things about yourself and loving them, that is, liking the friendship you have with yourself and loving the deeper aspects you admire that inspire self-devotion. Now write down at least three examples each: what you like, what you love. Do you like your taste in music, your ability to cook, your smile, your hands, and your style? Do you love your ability to survive difficult circumstances, your commitment to the people you love, and your ability to remain lighthearted even when things get tough? While writing, be mindful of a creeping inclination to point out things that need work: this is *not* that list, so don't write these things down. This is a love letter. When you're finished writing, place your hands on your heart, take a few slow breaths, and turn the corners of your mouth up in a gentle smile.

Look for your helpers: Make a list of at least 20 people who have supported you through your life: teachers, friends, strangers, coaches, bosses, colleagues, neighbors, artists, authors, and anyone else who has helped you, ranging from small kindnesses and acts of mercy to significant advocacy and inspiration. When you're finished writing, take the time to feel deep gratitude for their care and support, and send them loving thoughts. If you want to enhance the exercise, write them a note of appreciation, or give them a call.

FIFTH HUB: RELEASE
(Fuck-you journaling)

Sometimes genuinely awful things happen, and we can't figure out whether we're supposed to or are even allowed to be upset about them, that is, to risk being too sensitive. This is common with professional or personal experiences in which diplomacy and sugarcoating are passive-aggressive, demeaning, destructive, or diminishing. As leaders and professionals, we've been conditioned to take responsibility. This comes back to bite us when we're dealing with mistreatment, such as being passed over for advancement for unfair reasons or being laid off or fired without respect or dignity.

Unfortunately, there's an epidemic of mistreatment in the workplace. Perhaps you don't even feel angry—you feel demoralized, depressed, and your confidence has taken a hit. We won't always feel comfortable accessing anger or won't feel ready to speak it aloud. Many of the folks I've done this exercise with begin the process with reluctance about the notion that they're angry, but afterward find themselves a bit astonished (and relieved by the release) that there was so much of it. Keep in mind that full-blown anger is socially stigmatized as out-of-control, harmful, and even immature, so it's often hidden while the indicators of its existence are feelings of irritation and frustration. This is where the fuck-you journal comes in handy. It can take a few minutes to build momentum but be patient. Consider that anger and/or irritation are forms of grieving mistreatment and allow yourself this process. Don't worry about the negativity that arises; surfacing it moves it out of your body-mind and leaves it on pages that can be shredded, burned, or trashed. The following steps take you through the process of fuck-you journaling:

- It's best to do this where you feel safe and when you can rest afterward. If there are people around, make sure they can hold space if tears and emotions arise.

- Find some pages of paper that can be ripped up (some folks burn them). An empty page on your computer can work, but if you handwrite, you're more likely to feel the physical release and the words will likely become big and messy as the feelings release and express themselves.

- Imagine the person you want to confront the most. (There may be a line, but you know who's at the head of it.)

- Now start writing what you want to say to the person. It may begin politely; let the energy build.

- Don't be afraid if the emotions surge; they will pass as you continue to write. But if you begin to feel distressed and sense that stopping is a good idea, then take a break or stop.

- Use the words you've always wanted to say, even if they feel dark and nasty. Remember that everything coming up is coming out, and that releasing it means you no longer need to carry it, so make them as ugly and messy as they need to be.

- If you can, keep going until you can feel the intensity winding down.

- Take a few cleansing breaths. Allow yourself time to settle. Close your eyes and feel the release.

- Destroy or delete the pages. If you can do it safely, burn or shred them, and dispose of them in a way reminiscent of trashing and flushing waste.

- Gently massage your jaw and neck and make some noise by singing or making a sound that brings some vibration into your throat (for example, *ahhh*). Notice any change in your body.

- Drink some water and get some rest. You're amazing.

- Repeat with as many (usually separate) sessions as it takes to clear it all out.

SIXTH HUB: INSIGHT AND DREAM JOURNAL (What's your superpower?)

Insights and dreams tend to arrive and then quickly fly away, so the sixth-hub journaling practice is to plan for the arrival and capture of spontaneous insights and ideas. Again, keep a journal by your bed (or carry one with you throughout the day). You can use your phone's notes app when ideas arise, but keep in mind that using a phone in the morning abruptly shifts our brain out of the liminal, theta state.

Journal prompt: What's my superpower? Where do I have a unique vision? Are there areas you see potential where most others can't or don't? Perhaps you have a knack for making a remarkable meal out of a few measly ingredients or for recognizing capability in people or for decorating and organizing a physical space. This exercise can involve the validation of being seen by others, so ask a few people you trust what they see as your greatest strength or what type of problems they see you as being uniquely skilled at solving. It can help to give them some time; tell them this is an exercise that's part of a process. (Optional: once they tell you what they see in you, prepare some words of appreciation for them to make this an exercise in reciprocity, validation, and gratitude.)

SEVENTH HUB: INQUIRY

Seventh-hub inquiries are not questions that have immediate answers. Instead, there's grace and effortlessness, and the only work required is forming the questions and being receptive to the answers when they arrive. Instead of inquiring with respect to things you feel certain about, try venturing into the areas of your life where you feel the mystery, that is, be open to new ideas in places of certainty. Ask the question, write it down, and allow for the time required for the answer to arrive. Sometimes it takes a little while, so you may need to have patience. Below are four prompts to help get the inquiry juices flowing:

1. If you could snap your fingers and get the definitive answer to one question, which one would it be?

2. What is something you've always wondered about? How would you phrase it as a question?

3. What's the strangest question you could ever ask?

4. Is there something you often think about but don't share with other people? How would you phrase it as a question?

The exercises in this chapter are a continuation of the actualization process that's been explored throughout *The Parinama Method*—grounding ourselves physically so we can transcend to feel more fully alive.

In the next chapter, we find an idea and turn it into a physical reality. Using the awareness of all the hubs, we use the reverse order of actualization, starting at the top with the expansive space of the seventh hub, to catch inspiration and draw it down through the hubs all the way to the grounding of the first hub.

Chapter 12

FROM THE TOP DOWN—CREATING AND BUILDING

Whatever good things we build end up building us.
—*Jim Rohn*

I DISCUSS THE BOTTOM-UP approach to self-actualization throughout Part 2 and in Chapter 11, starting from a grounded first hub and extending up to the expansive seventh hub—in the service of gaining access to a richer and fuller experience of life. The top-down approach of creation covered in this chapter works in the reverse direction, beginning in the luminous seventh hub and descending through the other six hubs with ever-increasing densification in a process of becoming grounded in the physical world—we turn a dream into reality to further the fulfillment of our lived experience. This process requires navigating the paradox of creation because the work is both easy (flow state) and hard (resistance). You've experienced relatively effortless manifestation at certain times in your life, but this is manifesting's next level: conscious creation. Here, I provide a high-level overview with exercises (by no means exhaustive) that help overcome obstacles faced in the process of building and creation.

This paradox (creation is easy and hard) addresses a common misunderstanding and belief that inspired creation is and should feel completely effortless. Because of this, when we encounter difficulty, we may believe it's a sign we're on the wrong path and that we should turn back. But struggle often indicates that we need to grow and transform to become the person capable of our aspiration. It's an unavoidable part of building wonderful things: we begin the undertaking in a state that's incapable of creating the end result but become capable through the pursuit of achieving our goal. It's the work and the struggle that shape us, often sanding down the rough edges of adaptations. This chapter and the exercises it contains are inspired by Judith's work and by her "Creating on Purpose" workshop, as well as by my experience building successful organizations.

When I advise and consult, the people and companies I speak with are often working ahead of where they actually are in the process of creating and building. The following is a look at the order of operations that I call "the funnel." Similar to Chapter 11's ascending path, it doesn't always happen in exact order, but keep in mind that when a hub is skipped, there's an impact on future progress.

- *Seventh hub:* Inquiry and inspiration—getting an idea

- *Sixth hub:* Visualization—seeing in your mind's eye both the idea and the understanding that to achieve your goal, you'll need to grow beyond your current capability—what will that be

- *Fifth hub:* Communication—putting the vision into words for others to understand, as well as listening and being receptive to feedback

- *Fourth hub:* People and relationships—understanding why your project matters to people and figuring out the team you'll need and how to recruit it to make it happen

- *Third hub:* Action and focus—comprehensively clarifying what needs to be done, creating a manageable plan with goals and timelines, and driving it to execution

- *Second hub:* Inner and outer emotional awareness—tuning the project to be emotionally evocative for its target audience, being aware of and being able to manage your own emotions

- *First hub:* Completion and consistency—fulfilling your commitments, building trust through consistent action, and making the project real

Many creation stories are more about building than they are about creation—they start in the middle of the funnel by using an idea that either already exists (with some modification but no substantive advancement) or that hasn't been vetted through the essential fifth-hub process of communication and feedback. Also, the fourth-hub enrollment of other people may have happened before the essential work of the earlier stages of ideation has been done. When stages are skipped the price will be paid later, especially through an inability to articulate (or truly understand) your venture's value proposition—or in lacking a clear understanding of its value outside your insular world.

Before I discuss the stratospheric space of the upper hubs, a few words about timing and the counterbalance of containment and practical physical considerations. When I'm asked to do an advisory call as a consultant for an early-stage company, time is short: I get straight to the point with two questions:

1. What is your specific goal and purpose, and how will you measure success? This first diagnostic is the starting point before asking more detailed questions to figure out where the company's efforts will have the most impact, based on where it actually is versus where it believes itself to be. It's an efficient way for me to figure out where a company is in the funnel. Being vague is an indication that it's still in the early upper hubs and lacking a clear vision and explanation is the best tell I know; regardless of the level of investment in the activities of a more mature business, there's no skipping steps.

2. How long can you do this before you need to make money and what other limiting considerations are there? The so-called funding runway of a company or an individual's personal cash reserves must be considered part of a project's practical reality. This is first-hub stuff, mundane but essential—remember, if physical needs like food and shelter are threatened, you will be distracted. If you don't have the resources right now, become focused on creating them and setting yourself up to succeed by building skills, cash, and network. Timing is a necessary consideration for this process.

Following is an assay of the top-down process working through each descending hub, along with practical exercises targeting common obstructions. It goes step-by-step using a selection of exercises identifying pitfalls and eliminating the common blocks encountered in the transitions.

THE SEVENTH HUB—DESCENDING

Before bringing anything new into your life, the first step to take is to create physical and psychological space by inviting stillness (see Chapter 10). If you get defensive and feel especially challenged by new ways of doing things or by ideas that stretch your mental capacity, then make some room. It's especially helpful to be open to the possibility that you could be wrong about things, such as how the world works regarding money or opportunity, and the acknowledgment that your mindset—your beliefs and attachments—can be holding back your potential for creating and building.

DO NOTHING: INQUIRY AND RECEPTIVITY

Begin a process of inquiry and allow inspiration to arrive by giving it wide-open space. If you don't have an idea, you'll need to coax it forward by asking questions that have deep resonance for you. This active paradox of doing nothing and actively holding the space for inspiration can be unfamiliar and uncomfortable, because many of us live in a world of near-constant activity and distraction.

The seventh-hub processes are an overlooked and largely unknown stage of creation. You may feel that you're meant to build a company, yet you don't have a big idea. You may want to write a book but don't know what to write about, or even how to write. Perhaps you want to connect with your purpose yet feel lost not knowing what it could be. Even if it's only a single minute every day, clear some space in your thoughts, ask a specific question in earnest, and allow for revelation to arrive. Don't rush or force it; eventually, it comes.

Some new-age teachers imply that we're not comfortable with quiet, but I counter this. It's not the quietness of our inner space that we avoid; it's the loudness of the revelations that we may not feel ready to know. We avoid meditation because when the inner voice is given a microphone, it can have disruptive things to say; your inner voice will wait to reveal itself to make sure you're ready. When you ask into the void about how your life's purpose can be of greater service, how receptive you are to hearing the answer—without trying to steer the narrative into comfortable, familiar territory—will inform the quality of the answer you receive. What if this responsive inspiration indicates that there are things in your life that need to be reconsidered, such as your career, habits, or certain relationships? There's almost always something we're doing that makes us feel safe but holds us back, and just because something is difficult to know, awareness of it does not mean you need to act on it. You can also explore with *I may not be ready to act on this, but I'm ready to listen.*

Many of us are aware that we lack answers to important questions but don't consider that we first need the right question(s); most of us were educated and/or trained how to have answers, not how to ask questions. Start with finding your question—perhaps something like *What do I truly care about?* or *How do I best serve the world?* (This one is particularly strong, and if you have something more specific, use it.) Ask your question into the vastness of your faith, cosmic connection, higher power, or your own inner knowing. As the old business adage goes, if you don't ask, the answer is always *no*. It applies here. Allow for the answer to come, keep allowing for emptiness, and be patient. The answer is trying to find you and it may come in a clear revelation or it may come into focus slowly, arriving in bits and pieces. Try to capture arising insights by writing them down, even when they're in incomplete sentences (or pictures—make a sketch).

There may be crosscurrents that come up as you begin to ask your questions (see Chapter 9). This is just how the mind works, so the trick is to know these thoughts are not signs that you shouldn't proceed—see them for what they are: products of adaptations and holding patterns. Before you can move to sharpen the vision in the sixth hub, the distortion of crosscurrents needs to be addressed.

EXERCISE: WORKING WITH CROSSCURRENTS

- State your perceived limitation, for example, "I *don't* know how to do it."

- Next, flip the statement into what the person you need to become in this process would say. You don't need to be this person yet—in fact if you are, you're thinking too small. This exercise tries on a future version of yourself when you flip the limiting statement and say, "I *know* how to do it."

- This is your intention. State it clearly and imagine how it will feel. Now observe how your body responds. You'll probably be surprised.

- If you notice a crosscurrent coming from an internalized critic, do what Judith teaches: exaggerate it to reveal its maturity. If you think, *I can't do this,* say it aloud and express it with your body (maybe it's pouty, snarky, petulant): stomp your feet and exaggerate your facial expression and tone of voice to be a full expression of the crosscurrent. See it for what it is.

Perfectionism is flaw seeking and debilitating—needing to know how to do everything or having credentials before you begin this process interferes with building and creating (see Chapter 10). Seeing other people who don't adhere to limiting perfectionism (folks who proceed with a certain intrepid, idiotic brilliance) can be triggering, and the inner critic can get *loud* as the suppressed self activates, perhaps thinking: *I can't believe they're doing that* or *They're so unqualified.* The crosscurrents of a limiting belief system pay a lot of attention to people who *have some nerve building things they have no business building.* So, instead of allowing this to become a hang up, be willing to learn as you go. You may start as a novice, but the process of building will change you. You may question what value you bring as a person who wants to do something you haven't done before, but the value you bring will be uniquely yours and, in many ways, it will reveal itself over time. The key is to stick with it.

THE SIXTH HUB—DESCENDING

The answer to your seventh-hub inquiry will come, but in the beginning it may be a bit blurry and incomplete. Sometimes it starts as the first pearl in a long strand that requires your continued attention as it begins to reveal itself pearl by pearl. Starting as inspiration that only you can conceive in your mind's eye, this can be like downloading an image pixel by pixel. It will require staying with it as it becomes increasingly clear. A common trap is to expect the vision to be apparent immediately: the truth is you must stay with it as it crystallizes—and even when it's clear, it will continue to show new dimensions of itself like the ongoing rainbow revelation of the petrol on a puddle from Chapter 1. The longer you can tolerate this without involving the opinions of others, the more likely you are to connect with something remarkable. You're the first person to see this insight as it travels on its path to becoming real, and as a new idea that has no physical form, it's vulnerable, fragile, and usually won't withstand criticism and scrutiny—be very careful about who you share things with at this stage. When you realize that you need to return to school, gain special training, or want to build something (or any other manner of creation), incubating and fostering the initial growth of the vision should only happen with warm, positive, and encouraging people. Eventually, testing it with harsher elements of the larger world and incorporating feedback will be important (this comes next, in the fifth hub), but not at this stage, not yet.

Changing how you see yourself is part of the sixth-hub descending process. The doubts—crosscurrents—don't know that the ability to achieve the size and scope of your vision is what you'll grow into and become throughout the process of doing it. Creation doesn't just transform the world around you through making things—you will be transformed through the process. The fact is, you are not yet the person who can achieve your dream; you only become this person by doing it. You will need to envision the person you want and need to be to make your creation happen. Maybe you've never imagined yourself as the kind of person capable of doing something so big and brave; perhaps you have the mistaken belief that you're not the person who can do it and you may be right to a certain extent. In the fourth-hub descending, I'll discuss the recruitment of people who help make your vision possible—you won't do it alone. Your limiting beliefs will resist this new idea of who you can be and will also be particularly aware and receptive to people projecting their insecurities and fears on you. Our brains are meaning-making machines, and they will find validation for any strongly held belief, regardless of its validity. Although the nonbelievers may be easy targets for blame, it isn't their lack of belief in you that's holding you back. When you believe in yourself, those people will find it increasingly difficult to voice their criticism—and you will have a hard time taking them seriously. If people don't have the vision to see your potential it's their limitation, but when you choose to tolerate and believe them, you make it yours, too. Again, you don't need to have all the talents and capabilities required to make your vision real. You won't do this alone: if you actively engage in this process as you continue, you'll find help when you need it—in most cases you don't know who they are yet—but if you keep going, you will. You are the captain of this ship, but you don't need to know how to build one—you just need the vision to point the bow forward, to inspire, and to keep trying.

It can be a lonely process in these upper hubs—it's hard to have an idea that you believe in before there's physical evidence of its existence. Keep in mind that most people haven't gone through this, so they don't have receipts, and their so-called advice is a thinly disguised projection of their own insecurity. People try to be helpful but feel helpless when you're navigating depths they have yet to face themselves. Unless they have been successful at doing what you want to do (folks who have tried, failed, and given up can be particularly dangerous), just smile and nod and don't take what they offer seriously.

Again, be careful about sharing ideas when you're at this stage; they're gestating and highly vulnerable to outside influence. Talking about something you don't yet fully understand can confuse everyone involved, including you. In addition, people who don't have the vision, imagination, or experience with the personal transformation of creation won't be able to see your potential, and their limited perspective will be disturbing when you are incubating the delicate new belief in yourself. Even if it's well meaning, a single comment or question can deflate or destroy something before it even has the chance to form. The time to talk to everyone will come in the fifth hub, not now.

Sometimes folks get upset about people who didn't believe in them before they changed and succeeded, but it's not the responsibility or obligation of others to understand your vision. There is nobody who can truly know your full potential better than you do, and you are going through a process that few people undertake. Friends, partners, and family will try to understand, but unless they've gone through it, even their attempts to connect and relate will come up short. The temptation to enroll people to assuage insecurities of your expanding identity can get intense, but if you enroll others at this stage, they'll be sharing the captain's chair with you, so choose wisely.

Once you know how to navigate this early period you can return to the process again and again, building things with ever-increasing complexity. Use the techniques and exercises in Chapter 9 to support the ideation process, reread the section on cognitive biases, and identify and clear out limiting beliefs using the crosscurrents exercise from the seventh hub descending in this chapter.

TRACK PATTERNS

Understanding who you'll need to become is related to understanding who you've always been and to finding what has been obscured through programming and the limiting beliefs of adaptations and holding patterns (most of *The Parinama Method* addresses this). If you're feeling called to lead but don't think you've been leading yet, think of the times when you've stood up for someone, when you did the right thing—even when it was hard.

Insights that land throughout this process will illuminate the person you've always been, a person whose truer nature may have been obscured by the need for survival. At first, you may feel like you're not the right person or that your dream is too big, but with some recollection you'll be astonished by what comes up (such as grade- and high-school accomplishments and memories). Think of the times when you felt most alive, excited, and confident. The scope of this can be as wide as you please: start with high school and remember the clubs you joined, the friends you loved, the jobs you had, the classes and teachers you liked (and even some of the trouble you got into, along with its associated bravery and risks) and why. Look for any patterns and pay particular attention to emotional resonance and charge—the things that energize and excite you act like a divining rod pointing you in the right direction.

THE FIFTH HUB—DESCENDING

In the fifth hub, you'll need to convey your vision and discover words that resonate with other people. This transition can be challenging because feedback can be hard to hear, especially because you may still feel vulnerable. At this stage the focus is on communication (speaking and listening)—telling your story and listening to and watching how people react. Finding the right words takes time and involves a lot of practice with listening to how people respond, incorporating their input, and trying again until you find messaging that engages. Also, this stage is uncomfortable: it's jarring to emerge from the nascent vulnerability of the sixth hub and come face to face with the inability to explain what you're doing or what you aspire to do. The only way you get better is to practice—and I cannot overemphasize how hard this is. In fact, most folks avoid it (at great cost to the long-term success of their project). It's hard because some people will misunderstand you or think you have a bad idea while others will be encouraging and will give you inspiration that helps reveal things you'd never have considered on your own. Both are important. This process helps you to clarify your understanding of what you're doing by exposing your blind spots and growing your resilience to feedback. It's essential to remember that it's your responsibility to tell your story in a way that people can understand—a mistake is blaming the audience for not understanding you, instead of considering that it's your job to present a clear explanation. Explicit communication is your responsibility, so use analogies and concise, understandable language, and pay attention to engagement. There are considerable differences between having someone criticize you or disagree with you; not engage with you; and not understand what you're talking about. It helps to know the difference.

TELLING YOUR STORY

Your project is tied to your personal story, and as you undertake this process the importance and relevance of past life events will become increasingly clear. Your story is the only one you can tell with ultimate authority, and because authenticity rings like a bell, you build trust with folks when you tell it. Here, five steps for finding and telling your story:

Step 1: Think of the emotionally resonant events of your life that make this project important (some of the groundwork for this was done in the sixth hub). Tell this story, keep telling it, try different approaches, and notice and listen to how people respond to them. The prospect of hearing feedback can be scary, and we can unknowingly, nonverbally signal that we're not ready for it, so people hold back valuable insights. (I provide a journaling exercise below for preparing and exploring feedback.)

Step 2: Keep refining through feedback. Pay attention to what feels energizing and the words and phrases folks repeat back to you. Do you see people lose interest at certain points, and what are the clarifying questions they ask? Focus on what's enlivening and divest from what bores and/or confuses people. This story is yours, but it isn't only about you; it's about how your experience connects with others.

Step 3: Using your story, develop an elevator pitch through the framework below. Take the most potent notes from your narrative and create a pitch that intrigues and piques interest. Its purpose is not to educate, but to generate engagement. Think of it as a provocation to generate questions and increased attention.

Step 4: Build your confidence with practice: broadcast your vision to increasingly larger audiences.

Step 5: The more authentic, inspiring, and emotionally evocative your story is, the more the right people will want to get involved. This is not a popularity contest: you don't need everyone to like what you're doing. In fact, clarity will both repel and draw people in, and if you stay on the fence about your project, so will everyone else. Try to capture the believers in a way that they can be called on when your project comes to life—get it out there and enroll your allies by collecting email addresses on a list for future updates or choose a social media platform for creating an audience.

JOURNALING EXERCISE
(Preparing for and exploring feedback)

- What are the most important aspects of your project that you want others to know? Why?

- What's the affect you want to have on or the impression you want to leave with someone when you speak about your project?

- What feedback are you most afraid to hear from others? Conversely, what's the most useful response you could expect to hear?

- What specific, quantifiable action do you want others to take after they hear about your project? How can you best ask them to take that action?

ELEVATOR PITCH
(Should be under 30 seconds and should generate the intrigue needed to open the doors to a more substantive conversation)

- **This is who I am:** (title, company, name) "I'm the [title] of [project]. My name is _____." Yes, your name comes last. Example: "I'm the CEO and founder of *High-end Egyptian.* My name is Adia." Your title or position helps anchor the introduction (it's the piece of information most familiar to them). Giving your name at the end helps people use and remember it.

- **This is what I do:** Ideally, one or two sentences such as, "We're making low-cost, high-end fashion with fabrics from factories on the Nile using designs recovered from Nefertiti's tomb," will do.

- **This is who it's for** (see So what? below): "The designs flatter all body types, and professional women tell us they feel more confident in the workplace knowing they're wearing royal garments."

- **This is how I do it:** Explain the central tenet of your project in one or two sentences, with a compelling differentiator or a surprising, positive fact. Example: "We source low and no-cost fabric remnants that factories pay us to take away and we turn them into high-end clothing."

- **Wait for it.** Now stop talking. A great elevator pitch leaves the listener wanting more and should be enticing but not a complete explanation. A common error is mistaking a pitch as an opportunity to educate when the purpose is to spark intrigue.

SO WHAT?

Why does it matter? The things people find important help them in ways they find meaningful. To most people, it won't matter that you're living your dream or expressing your purpose—they want to know how you can help them live *their* dreams, how you can solve their problems. In this message-testing method, we ask, "So what?" (or more diplomatically, "Why does this matter?") until we can uncover a specific understanding of how what we do matters to people in ways they find meaningful. Being told, "I hate cold weather" is a general statement that could relate to selling mittens or buying Florida real estate. The more specific you can get about how hating cold weather affects the person's life, the more likely you are to find your value proposition. For example, if someone states, "Poor circulation in my hands in the colder months makes doing things I enjoy difficult," ask, "Can you help me understand why this matters to you?" The response could be, "I tend not to go outside in the winter, which leads to me feeling lethargic." This process can continue by asking for specific examples with "Can you tell me a little bit more about that? How does being lethargic impact you?" This is how to gather valuable insights. Look for the stories with specifics and find the shared themes that keep coming up in your discovery conversations.

This all takes time, and when you invest in the process of clarifying your vision you become more secure as you get better at weathering challenging interactions. Your ability to withstand criticism and to hear the truth in feedback is essential for long-term success—it's an ability that takes time to develop. Even if you choose not to incorporate feedback, it's vital to be aware of other perspectives. The input will only become more intense as the sphere of your influence widens, so consider this training part of the Fibonacci-spiral pattern of life (see Chapters 9 and 10), with things presenting with increasing difficulty as you continue to evolve and grow. If you're feeling crosscurrents and limiting beliefs, this stage is particularly hard: feedback can feel like criticism (and some of it will be). It's okay; this is part of the transformation process. If you keep working on your crosscurrents, you will tolerate and ultimately even enjoy this. Always try to keep in mind that there will never be a person other than you who can determine your fate. There's no one you need more than yourself, so even if people you wanted for your team aren't onboard, keep the faith: the time isn't right (yet), which means that the right people are out there and waiting for you to find them.

THE FOURTH HUB—DESCENDING

Collaboration should not come at the expense of realized leadership. A team of talented creators in a professional kitchen makes incredible meals that would be difficult to create alone, but it all happens under the singular vision of the chef. Even though it's collaboration, the chef is responsible for the overall meal and takes the hit for any failure. If a clear vision is not formed and articulated—and if boundaries and roles are not communicated—the collaborative process results in too many cooks in the kitchen. When there's a shared vision and collaboration, the roles and responsibilities need to be defined and understood.

The fourth-hub stage of creation involves enrolling other people when the time is right. Enrolling others too soon before the vision has crystallized enough or when there's a lack of personal confidence can be a crutch that interferes with the ability too stand on one's own. The too-many-cooks problem is solved through confident leadership and clear direction for everyone within a group.

Other people are essential because there are things that you don't know how to do and there are people who can help you do them. The first time I read the pages of *The Parinama Method*'s manuscript after my editor had worked on them, I felt a satisfaction like looking out a newly cleaned window. For some folks, it can be all too easy to forget the people who provided early support and inspiration and to undermine their important role. Suppose people are brought in early and contribute to creating the vision or to solidifying your confidence. Without clear expectations, it will only be a matter of time before confusion and resentment emerge. This is a caution for both the visionaries and the folks who get enrolled too early. Each person's specific contribution and focus will need to be determined relatively early on and will need to be revised periodically to avoid misunderstandings that eventually can become destructive to the project. This can feel like a buzz-kill in the moment, but it's an important investment in the long-term viability of key relationships. Keep in mind that having difficult-but-important conversations is another opportunity for growth and transformation.

Enrolling others in a project without a clear compensation plan can be unintentionally predatory when the right balance of compensation and recognition is not established. *We'll figure it out later* from the leader and *It doesn't matter, I trust you* from the enrollee are both time bombs. The trusting person will expect more than the leader intends to give, and the initial excitement will wear off as the practicalities of the work set in; when this happens, it's not the time or place to figure this stuff out. These incubating conflicts tend to erupt when projects become challenging (as they eventually do), often at the cost of derailing progress at a critical time in the growth of the venture, a time when surfacing complex dynamics can have damaging consequences to a project's success. If they're not caught early, resentment and the feeling of being taken for granted grow and are hard to resolve.

There's a period in the process of creation that is singular (even if your venture involves another early-stage creator, such as a cofounder). You'll need to know how to walk alone and to be capable of tolerating imperfections, errors, and incompleteness in creating and manifesting. Something that previously didn't exist is becoming a reality, so incompleteness and imperfection are unavoidable. When your creation does exist in the future, you'll face people's projections and resistance to new ideas, so you will need to be able to stand firm in representing your creation as you—and doing this early will prepare you. The time that feels lonely prepares you for the ever-increasing scope of bringing something to significant numbers of people, which inevitably involves some rejection. Before you can convince anyone else, you need to make the most crucial sale: your own buy-in.

EXERCISE: THE DREAM TEAM

Make a list of the people, talents, and skills you'll need before it's time to enroll them. Who are the people you'll need? You won't always get whom you want or expect to, but it's useful to consider the specific functions you'll need to fill and the people you want on your team—the dream team that can be both a practical list and a wish list of ideal contacts and advisors who are (currently) outside of your network.

If you don't know who you'll need to make your project happen, find someone who does; people like to help when they can, especially when you're clear about what you're trying to figure out. Whenever possible, find people who have done something similar and ask them about who they needed to make their venture happen (and perhaps about some of the mistakes they made that you can learn from). In this stage you'll benefit further from all the work in the fifth hub of crafting your message—telling people about your purpose and your project. There's no doubt that some of the people you talk to will suggest other people for you to meet with, such as someone they know or even someone you already know but didn't realize could be valuable for your process. Many people love to help and to demonstrate value.

There's a sales expression about professional relationships: make as many deposits as you make withdrawals, meaning that we should balance receiving support from others with contributing in ways that are fulfilling to them. The reciprocity and balance of gratitude and generosity are important for maintaining integrity in all mature relationships (see Chapter 7). It can be satisfying for mentors to hear about a positive outcome from an introduction they made or how a piece of advice made a positive impact. This makes giving in the future a more appealing proposition. Invest the time in expressing gratitude with the specifics of how and why the gift of time and connection was valuable.

THE THIRD HUB—DESCENDING

There's a lot of imperfect, gritty work that needs to be done, and the third hub is where we do it—inevitably, a relationship with perfection will be tested here. Achievement in this stage requires you to get over two ideas: that you need to know what you're doing and that your first try is going to be the one that takes. Avoid getting attached to the idea that something that takes a lot of time and effort to build is guaranteed to succeed. Although you're not guaranteed success, you are guaranteed the opportunity to learn and grow if you choose to take it.

In this stage, you'll be doing a lot of imperfect work as you iterate and figure things out; much of your effort will not be reflected in the final product (although the lessons learned will be embedded). Therefore, you need to be connected to your *why*. Adopt a relationship to work that is a quest for mastery and growth more than anything else. A side effect of the traditional salaried work model is getting programmed to believe there's a consistent, linear reward for work. The work itself is the reward in this stage, and its fruits will be inconsistent. You need to show up, and if you are a hard worker already, that's good, but be prepared to get stretched with work that doesn't provide an immediate, predictable reward. Know that the more you do it, the easier it gets as you become increasingly clear about what works and what doesn't. The tools for third-hub descending are purpose, making tasks manageable, planning, accountability, handling obstacles and distractions, and delegation, each of which I discuss below.

The third hub descending requires the confidence and self-esteem to believe in something enough to sacrifice other choices and to give the project everything you've got. It's the time for committing to focused, courageous action. Every hub in the descending path is a gate that opens to a new aspect of the process; the third hub is the one that decides if the project will happen. This is the hub in which bravery, discipline, and resilience provide the power of an iterative process that doesn't fear hard work and is where the grind of more familiar work begins. There are specific considerations: devotional discipline and the requirement to stop talking and start doing. This is the crucible, the arena, and the combustion, and it is intense and demanding. There will be unexpected pitfalls in this hub that you can only learn about by doing, and you will be both humbled and emboldened as you learn to overcome the obstacles. You burn off ego and insecurity and grow strong if you can just stay in the arena; there will be many times that you will want to leave—wanting to leave is not a problem but leaving is.

Everything in the third hub of creation is in service for purpose. *Have to* is replaced with *choose to* and *want to*. This is a critical reframing for this challenging work. The cycles you go through in the third hub may be joyless as you work to break through to increasing levels of who you need to become to make this project a physical reality, but greater joy and freedom exists on the other side. The sixth hub was the one in which you had to imagine who you needed to become; the third hub is the one in which the practical transformation happens in the work.

This is also the stage at which competition becomes a consideration. One of the many stumbling blocks of this stage is becoming consumed and fixated with negative feelings toward competitors. It's important not to fall into the trap of hating the people you compete with and so, lose the opportunity to admire and to learn from what they do well. Again, critical thinking is not to be confused with criticism: critical thinking is curiosity and criticism is an attempt to minimize (see Chapter 6). The practice of loving to win requires conscious effort because our brains evolved to hate losing (and to avoid risk) more than they love winning (see Chapter 9). You don't have to like your competitors, but there are reasons why they're contenders, and figuring out why can save you time and effort. Next, I discuss the third hub-descending tools for transformation that I list above.

PURPOSE

If you don't connect to both your personal reason for doing this (fifth-hub exploration) and to devotional discipline (third and fourth hub) before you enter the arena, you may find yourself easily weakened by the challenges you face. The earlier hubs provide the connection to meaning, and the people who skip these steps enter this warrior stage unprepared, finding themselves easily overwhelmed and outmatched by the force of resistance. They may blame outside parties for their lack of preparation, but as I discuss, the captain takes ultimate responsibility and accountability. In the third hub, perfection is the enemy of good, and moving forward with your best available effort in each moment is the practice. Expecting that the undertaking will always feel great and be easy (along with the contamination of perfectionism) creates drag, which only slows you down.

Staying connected to your purpose will carry you through the dark times. Remember why this project matters for you and write it down. Put the reminder in a place where you will either see it often or will know to look for it when you need to. Also, remember why this matters for other people; write that down, too, and put it somewhere to be consistently reminded. This part is hard, so before you need them, make the reminders of why you're creating.

When I decided to write *The Parinama Method,* I thought the manuscript's development, research, organization, and writing would take about three months—it took more than three years. At one point, I covered my refrigerator door with written notes and letters from people thanking me for making a difference in their lives. I also wrote notes as daily reminders about my goals for this project and put them where I could see them. When I looked at all the notes and letters, I was reminded that I had a larger contribution to make in the world and that I was in the process of building it.

Another way to stay connected to purpose is to put a few bullet points of your intentions and aspirations on a note in your phone that you look at every few days. They should reflect what you aspire to build, what you want it to do for the world, and how it will change lives (including your own). Then bring some of the good feelings into your body—access and activate the future state you're building.

MAKING TASKS MANAGEABLE

This hub strains under large, obtuse goals, such as *to build a company.* Tasks are like eating a meal in small bites rather than choking on one large gulp. Use the specific, measurable, attainable, relevant (to the larger goal), and time-bound (SMART) method for goal setting. A seemingly infinite number of tasks and actions will likely be necessary, so you should be clear about what gets done first. If you don't know, get some guidance from a trusted mentor to help break down the work into actionable tasks with prioritization. If you still feel overwhelmed, break your tasks into even smaller units of work that energize you. Don't try to fight with your willpower; the more you push, the more it pushes back. Work with it by creating achievable, actionable tasks that connect to a sense of satisfaction. Tasks and goals that are too big or not interesting to you are a trap in this stage; break them down into actionable steps that energize and provide a sense of accomplishment. If a task fills you with dread, it's the wrong one and needs to be reimagined. Say you're supposed to research projects comparable to yours but feel overwhelmed and unclear about how to approach the work. Make your first task simply to compile a list of articles and videos or to schedule a conversation with someone relevant and make a list of things that you find interesting and pay attention to what will give you energy and use it to create momentum.

I caution my teams about starting a day without a plan or having a plan that doesn't energize them. For example, if they have a list of calls to make to contacts, they've tried a million times without success, my guidance would be to create a new list that gets them excited about what's possible. Reposition your tasks so you feel energized by them to build momentum for when you get to the less exciting stuff.

PLANNING (And follow-through)

Make the time and do the work. Calendar reminders and commitments to show up can feel like drudgery when you're not feeling inspired or energized, but you still need to sit with your work during the scheduled time. Even if you just sit in front of your computer feeling miserable while not allowing distractions you're clearing the space, and a shift will eventually come. If you don't show up for yourself and your project, it will never happen; devotional discipline is showing up even when your best for today isn't close to your personal best.

ACCOUNTABILITY

Set benchmarks and tell them to someone who will hold you accountable; explain what they are, when they should be met, and send evidence when you meet them (or own up when you don't). This person is someone to consider as part of your fourth-hub dream team: an ideal candidate is a mentor or someone you admire or fear letting down.

HANDLING OBSTACLES AND DISTRACTIONS

The closer you get to transformation and creation, the more resistance you will experience. It's as if you're being strengthened with readiness to handle the bigger world you're creating for yourself—when you stretch your sense of what's possible, there will be growing pains. Obstacles and distractions do their best work—activating your adaptations, holding patterns, and limiting beliefs—when they hide in the shadows or when they become busyness rationalized as productivity. The best way to handle obstacles and distractions is to name them, call them out, and bring them up for conscious evaluation: *Answering a friend's call right now is a distraction* or *Cleaning my desk right now is a distraction* or *Looking at social media right now is a distraction from work.*

A common obstacle is that there will be people who agree to do something and either not follow through or not do it on time. And you'll make decisions that don't work out, invest in efforts that get no return. When obstacles arise, they can overwhelm and throw you off track. When this happens, call it out as a matter-of-fact so you can move forward: *My logo designer quit; that's an obstacle* or *I'm tired right now when I need to be energized; that's an obstacle.* Time can be lost fuming about the bad thing that's happened but naming it an obstacle better positions you to stop stewing over it, to address the reality, and resolve the issue.

DELEGATING

Perfectionism may have you believing you're supposed to be good at everything that's part of your project. But this is not possible, and even if you are great at everything, your time is a limited asset. A trap at this stage is not trusting others to do the same high-quality work as you—and believing this is a reason to do it all yourself. Learning to work with your unique capabilities and shortcomings is part of knowing and accepting yourself. It's surprisingly common for people to fixate on the talents they lack. Instead, get support from people who are strong where you're weak and double down on your strengths. The reality is that there are things you're extraordinarily good at doing, things you're okay at doing, and things you're not good at doing. To be outstanding, focus on doing the extraordinary and delegate. Also, if you beat yourself up as you struggle with your attention span (or anything else typically associated with willpower), you may be neurodivergent, so take the time to get support, create work habits that make sense for you, and give yourself a (fucking) break.

THE SECOND HUB—DESCENDING

What you build and create needs to evoke feelings and emotions in the people you intend to affect. Moving people is about connecting with them through feeling and being emotionally evocative. Marketing expert Seth Godin writes on his blog that we "[L]ike to think we make complicated decisions based on rational analysis, but most of the time, we actually make an emotional decision and then invent a rational analysis to justify it . . . if our goal is to help people make better choices, it helps to first create better feelings."

The creative process is a journey of self-development and personal transformation that involves building things that support people in ways that matter to them. Building and creation are at their best when they're responsive and iterative, just like the attunement in the early development of the second hub. An important part of the process is finding how you create emotional connection through taking something that makes sense to you (and to a relatively small group of people) and testing its resonance with increasingly larger groups. This presents a paradox: maintaining your integrity while being aware of what people want and need from you. A stumbling block at this stage can be receiving a bad reaction without knowing how to keep the response in perspective (and how to learn from it).

I've noticed a tendency across most technology-company founders I've consulted with; they are attached to their original vision and have a hard time balancing it with feedback from customers and employees. They struggle to respond to the priorities of their prospective customers (who signal the direction of the overall market) while prioritizing a specific version from their early inspiration that holds meaning for them. It's easy to understand how and why this happens, considering the delicate nature of the sixth-hub descending phase and how much work it takes to get to the second hub. Projects may begin as inspiration that emerged from facing a personal challenge, but sometimes that specific experience is not relatable to the larger market, hence, we need to be responsive and willing to incorporate other points of view.

Founders and executives can have trouble knowing when their emotions are hijacking their decision-making processes. In some cases, big decisions can be made for a company based on one piece of particularly charged feedback received while founders felt especially vulnerable. I would receive their calls throughout the day about having heard something from staff, and before the founders could even process and contextualize it, they were frantically looking to make changes. Some struggled with emotional regulation to the point that their staff was exhausted and facing burnout from weathering the ups and downs and the lack of a clear, consistent plan. When leaders don't get the support of therapy, the people around them can wind up being pulled into the role.

Emotional illiteracy is epidemic, especially for people who ignore their feelings and emotions to make third-hub super-productivity possible. There are times we need to do punishing hours of work and to push ourselves, but doing this too much leads to burnout and so, it's not a long-term strategy. It's essential to not let go of the string holding the kite, because you'll eventually need to pull back joy, rest, and nourishment. The pleasure and restoration from the second hub make a venture sustainable.

At this stage of building, it's good to know your emotional needs and to be able to ask for help; this knowledge will help determine the project's sustainability and will be a key predictor of your long-term success. Hyper-independence is an adaptation. The process of conscious creation gets disruptive as it transforms, and you will need emotional support to counter the sacrifice, the challenge, and the changes that will come. If the project you're working on will change your life, you are in it for a long haul and the grinding of the third hub will eventually lead to burnout if it isn't countered with the release and enjoyment of at least some second-hub self-gratification. For people with the tremendous drive that got them this far, this hub will be an enormous challenge, especially if there's perfectionism that still needs to be subdued. So, get yourself the good chair, invest in ergonomics for your workspace, play, pet your cat, take a walk, exercise, make time for your Parinama practice, and get a massage. As the captain, you are essential to the actualization of this project, which will only be sustainable if you take care of yourself.

MAKE IT FUN

Fun makes lighter work of challenging tasks. Laughter is a tension release, and it allows people to feel greater ease as they work hard. Many years ago, I told a high-performing team of mine that if it hit a particularly ambitious goal, I'd throw a pizza party with a clown that makes balloon animals. The team did it and I threw the party—folks on the team still bring it up in conversation over a decade later. The clown was terrifying and at the time I was secretly nervous about how this stunt would reflect on me in the office, but nevertheless, I delivered—and our fun, wild team went on to exceed goal after goal.

CELEBRATE YOUR WINS

In grind culture we move to the next challenge before taking time to celebrate a win. This is a short-term strategy. The first few times you skip the celebration it may feel productive, but the absence of joy eventually erodes the ability to remain motivated. Joy is part of surviving, sustaining, and maintaining.

THE FIRST HUB—DESCENDING

The top of the funnel is expansive and limitless, but there are practical realities for bringing something into the physical world: your time is finite and financial resources have limitations. This is the stage of the process with the least amount of magical thinking. It becomes an exercise in practicality and accounting as you reach completion and transition into ongoing execution and maintenance. If there's still the unrestricted and expansive thinking of earlier stages, the project will struggle with lack of focus. This is where specialization, delegation, and focus are crucial to your success. If you try to be good at too many things at once, you'll wind up not being good at anything.

As unsexy as it is, this is the hub of limitation. If you've skipped stages, you may be too expansive and impractical, out of touch with the market, or even out of touch with yourself. When the rubber meets the road, you'll know how well you've prepared, which can be sobering, and which requires further iteration and the effort of revisiting previous hubs.

GET REAL ABOUT MONEY AND LIMITATIONS

There are practical realities about what you can afford to do and how you can make your project financially sustainable. Not everything needs to be monetized, but the people who work for you should be compensated. If you're taking on unpaid interns, encouraging people to work for exposure and experience, and pushing for substandard compensation in exchange for equity that is currently worthless, then you're not ready. If you can't afford to pay people, you don't deserve their labor—preying on others is unacceptable. There are exceptions to this, but very few—figure out how to save money or raise funds for your project. This is especially potent if you expect to be well paid or enriched for your work. Also, fair compensation inspires a high quality of work and attention. If people are being tasked with creative work while trying to handle the anxiety of not being able to pay bills, you will not access their full potential. There's no better way to enact your respect for other people's effort than to compensate them and express your appreciation.

FULFILLING COMMITMENTS

Trust is built by consistently fulfilling commitments. What you promise must be delivered or there needs to be transparent, accountable communication. In this final hub on the descending path, the integrity of delivering on expectations is the grounded and practical complementary counterforce to more expansive upper hubs. As the project descends through the hubs, promises are made, and the vision as originally stated can change. Ignoring this and hoping that people forget the commitments and promises you made is tempting because taking responsibility will often be challenging (especially where the stakes can be particularly high), but because so few rise to this challenge, you'll be respected and admired when you do—even when the news is bad. It's a small world, and you never know when people will pop back into your life; doing right by others has many benefits.

The exercise for this is to make a list of the commitments you've made and build a plan with a timeline of how you'll either deliver or communicate expectations. If you have incomplete projects in your personal life, make a list of them and complete them. Having the distraction of things left undone is a subtle, subconscious bother that steals focus and energy.

PHYSICAL SYMBOL

Having a physical symbol of your project that you can see or hold can be grounding. A piece of jewelry, a stone, a picture, or a small token object can help to reconnect you to the larger purpose of your work. Even a transition object, as I discuss in the second hub, can be used for soothing (see Chapter 5). You can also assign a meaningful symbol to your project that can feel like a wink from creation whenever you see it; finding money or feathers or seeing a specific flower or bird or even seeing something that you aspire to have as a result of this process all work (the symbols I use are pennies and feathers).

If you don't believe in miracles or don't think this process is for you, look at an airplane in the sky, look out the window of a skyscraper, tap an app to receive a ride, groceries, or any other material pleasure. You are part of the tapestry of creation, and the more engaged you get with knowing your true nature, the more you can access your innate ability to create. Anything that energizes and inspires you acts as your compass, steering you toward your unique brilliance and creation. Keep an aliveness journal or a notes app on your phone. Every time you see something that evokes a feeling, record it. Your emotions, sense of enjoyment, and pleasure are important instruments for accessing charge, purpose, and connection.

The simultaneous grit and grace of creation can throw off even the most intrepid emblooms. Yet there's ease in the sense of following a pursuit that's uniquely your own along with the satisfying intensity in the crucible of transformation where growth occurs. By facing the trials and tribulations of your shadows and adaptations, and by expanding your dynamism and capacity as you descend through the hubs of building and creation, there's paradox encountered at nearly every turn. But as I discuss in Chapter 13, you're worthy of this pursuit—and as a miracle of creation what you are called to do matters.

Chapter 13

THIS IS IT

Life is like arriving late for a movie, having to figure out what was going
on without bothering everybody with a lot of questions, and then being
unexpectedly called away before you find out how it ends.
—Joseph Campbell

IF YOU'VE BEEN WAITING for a sign: this is it. You're a natural phenomenon that's complex, nuanced, and a miraculous expression of life. You can change your relationship with discipline and devotion from punishing to patient, persistent, and brightly burning, one in which you show up for yourself, progress, and continue to evolve. There's never been anything wrong with you, and for those who have been informed that there is, it's the greatest lie ever told. You're the creator, and it's your calling to inhabit yourself fully as a warrior, builder, lover, and destroyer, advancing and liberating your humanity and your potential. Life is both beautiful and brutal, and it's your responsibility to act first for yourself so you can have more and have more to give. Keeping your body alive, continuing to experience life, and following the mission of your embloom: this is enough to keep you busy for a lifetime.

This practice can be like a log you're riding to cross a river, seeking a more authentic experience of personal integrity by reducing the interference of adaptations, holding patterns, and limiting belief systems, but it becomes an alligator when it turns into another pursuit of perfection, purity, and judgment of yourself and others. We grow wiser and more aware through experiencing both the rough edges of sorrow and tragedy, and the amazing grace of spontaneous insights. Naturally, we're bound to question hardship, cruelty, and injustice as evidence of an imperfect system, but it's time to surrender the fantasy that you were born into a friction-free life. It's also time to surrender the fantasy that your parents were supposed to do a perfect job of preparing you for the world.

This work is not a tool to diagnose and/or figure out what's wrong with everyone around you. When we realize that we all face challenges, understanding other people's confusing behavior as their adaptations helps to build more compassion and understanding—both for them and for ourselves. Just like you, the factors that shape them are circumstances of life, not moral failings. If you're focused on everyone else's holding patterns instead of your own, you're on the alligator, not the log. The only thing close to being wrong with anybody is believing that there *is* something wrong. Again, this work is an inside job, but ultimately, it's experienced and validated through relationships and connections.

The sense of right and wrong (and of anxiety and peace) are course correctors that support action. Occasionally, we all act in harmful and hurtful ways and have harmful and painful things done to us. The trick is to not let these feelings consume and obliterate us with guilt and shame. Once fear, guilt, and shame overwhelm, they paralyze us and our ability to initiate corrective action gets blocked. If we believe our life is defined by its worst moments, we naturally defend ourselves, build walls, and start wars. You are not a scorecard of your mistakes and accomplishments. You're part of the natural world; there is both brutality and tranquility within your very being. Using the Parinama Method, we seek to restore and remain dynamic in our adaptability, to be responsible, and to be held accountable.

You are an embloom on a mission, and allowing your full expression means you let yourself have pleasure without guilt, uphold boundaries, be open to change, take responsibility for the effects of your actions, love yourself like your life depends on it, use concentration to stay present and to create, connect, and contribute. Nature and the messages that come through inspiration are always looking for people to do their creation. Opening yourself to this opens you to accessing your unique genius. There's something vital for you to do with your life—to simultaneously experience it and to create it. People don't fail because of obstacles, they fail because they give up—so, don't. Life's rhythms are both predictable and unpredictable, and riding the waves develops skill and agility.

PSYCHOLOGICAL REVERSALS

Using the Applied Kinesiology method, clinician Roger Callahan was one of the first to address inner conflicts interfering with the achievement of treatment goals. He uncovered what psychologists call "psychological reversals," unconscious resistance to the conscious desire for an outcome. For example, you want to get a master's degree but keep missing deadlines and second-guessing yourself; perhaps you subconsciously fear becoming more successful than your parents, spouse, or friends, and sense they would become distant and resentful. Or perhaps conscious efforts to appear more physically attractive get blocked by the fear of not being attractive even if you try or not wishing to receive unwanted sexual attention—feeling less visible is a comfort and protection which is often favored by the subconscious. The deep familiarity of our hubs' early programming drives much of the behavior that mystifies us. How can we want something and simultaneously get in the way of having it? As Jung wrote in *Aion, Researches into the Phenomenology of the Self*, "[U]ntil you make the unconscious conscious, it will direct you and you will call it fate."

According to Callahan, first you need to accept yourself as you are right now. Remember the tapping statements: *Even though I have [limiting belief], I deeply love and accept myself* and *Even though I feel [pain or struggle], I deeply love and accept myself* (see Chapter 5). As we look back at everything we've been through, remember that rather than seeking perfection or considering ourselves a series of problems to solve (even if we do desire to change), transformation starts with loving and accepting ourselves as we are. If loving acceptance is not yet possible, other choices are: *I know I am doing my best*; *I deserve to feel good*; and *I know deep down that I am a good and worthy person.* Peace and happiness are a combination of acceptance of the present moment and a sense of optimism about the future.

WE'RE ULTIMATELY FULFILLED THROUGH CONNECTION

We experience moments of insight and enlightenment throughout life that last for an instant, an hour, weeks, and even years. Everything about us happens in rhythms that come in cycles, phases, and waves—feast and famine. This practice is not a final destination; it's a process that's ongoing for as long as we're breathing, a method for continuous personal breakthrough and growth. There's great joy that can be experienced by changing how we relate to other people and the world at large. The Method reduces the obstructions of early subconscious programming and holding patterns and increases our capacity within the hubs. Even when these patterns have worn deep grooves in our behavior, simply knowing what they are and having the language to describe them provides some liberation. You are already everything you need to be and the potential for everything you need is already within you.

I discuss the four phases of a human life, which Indian mystics connect with 1,008 cycles of the moon, in Chapter 3. Childhood is the first cycle, the second is young adulthood, the third is middle age, and the fourth is our senior years. Erikson's psychosocial model includes phases of life that correspond to the later phases occurring after childhood (see Chapter 4). According to Erikson, young adulthood (our 20s and 30s)—the second phase—is the reconciliation of *intimacy versus isolation*, a process of building one's own family in whatever form that takes (the alternative is to live in isolation). The third stage, *generativity versus stagnation*, corresponds with middle age (approximately 40 to 65). In this stage, the primary reconciliation is one's contribution to the world and leaving it better. Activities like mentoring, upholding commitments, developing deeper relationships, and contributing to the next generation tend to lead to fulfillment. Stagnation results from isolation, self-absorption, and cynicism. The last stage, *integrity versus despair*, corresponds with the fourth phase, which is a period of wisdom and reflection. Integrity in this stage is acceptance, a lack of regret, feeling at peace, and having a sense of success. Despair in this stage is expressed as bitterness, regret, ruminating over mistakes, and feeling unproductive.

There's a Chinese proverb: The best time to plant a tree was 20 years ago. The second-best time is now. For as long as we're alive, it's never too late to begin the process of achieving greater fulfillment. It's also helpful to consider the bigger picture at any stage of life; again, Ware lists the primary deathbed regret as, "I wish I'd had the courage to live a life true to myself, not the one others expected of me [see Chapter 6]." My point is two-fold: it's never too late to focus on living a fulfilling life, and by making them conscious you have the power to affect the reflexive holding patterns that block your capacity and potential.

You'll notice that these regrets are simple: people don't regret not becoming billionaires or impressing people. In fact, it seems like those types of accomplishments are more likely to be tied to significant regret.

CONSCIOUS RECLAMATION: AN ONGOING PROCESS

You are alive and living a life. Little by little, enlightenment happens through silver linings and the so-called blessings in disguise of hardship and the amazing grace of insight and awakenings that come without effort in times of tranquility. There are moments of brilliance followed by recoil and regression—and sometimes, long periods of mundane living. This is your life: the mountaintops, the valleys, and the journey in between. A primary shift occurs when we can see and know that we are not the journey itself, but the presence within us that's having the experience. Your life is the experience, and you are what's experiencing it. Pay attention and be patient with yourself. The Parinama Method is an exploration, a discovery, and an allowing, and gives you the tools to consciously reclaim and become aware of the programming that blocks you from the truth about your capability. The truth is that within you there's immeasurable capacity for love and creation. You are an essential part of a world that needs you to listen, to be patient, to empower, to feel, and to fight for the evolution of humanity.

Your body doesn't know how to lie: it adapts, but it never lies. However, your mind has a very sophisticated ability to perceive and rationalize in the service of your survival, and so, your thoughts can be (and often are) deceptive. Nonetheless, your posture, body language, and so-called vibe constantly communicate to the world and influence how people see you and as a result, how they respond to you. Your body houses the sensation of what it feels like to be alive, and it shapes how you think about life. Through adaptations to circumstances and experiences, the body shifts as it stiffens or grows slack and resigned, often getting stuck in patterns. We often believe these patterns are who we are. Self-awareness and the ease that comes with the ongoing process of conscious reclamation releases long-held limitations, ultimately generating the charisma and magnetism of people who are both comfortable with themselves and self-aware. As your inner experience shifts, the ease and confidence that come with unblocking rigidity change how the world responds to you. Happiness is magnetic, and even when you're unhappy, your self-aware authenticity can be compelling.

The Parinama of it all is the brilliant, shifting iridescence of this life, constantly revealing new dynamics and perspectives then dissolving into something else. We are nomads traveling the seasons of our lives surrounded by an ever-changing world. There's no standing still and there's no arrival at a final conclusion or an absolute certainty that's real.

The opportunity to be in a practice that liberates your true nature and achieves access to your greater potential is here right now. It's not an end goal for the future: it's happening in this very moment. Your consciousness allows you to be an active creator of your life, to push back on interrupting forces and to reclaim your humanity by releasing holding patterns. There's something important for you to do with your experience of life and for the greater good of yourself and the world—and whatever this is, it's as unique and as identifying as your DNA. You have a mission, and if you're waiting or looking for a sign to act, *this is it*.

BIBLIOGRAPHY

Ackerman, C. E. 2021. "Theory of Positive Disintegration 101: On Becoming Your Authentic Self." PositivePsychology.com. https://positivepsychology.com/dabrowskis-positive-disintegration/

A Conversation with Maya Angelou. 2015. BillMoyers.com. August 13. Retrieved April 16, 2022. https://billmoyers.com/content /conversation-maya-angelou/

Aeschylus, and Podlecki, A. J. 2005. *Prometheus Bound.* Aris & Phillips.

Aggarwal-Schifellite, M. 2021. "Spanking Children May Impair Their Brain Development." April 13. *Harvard Gazette.* https://news.harvard.edu/gazette/story/2021/04/spanking-children-may-impair-their-brain-development

Alighieri, D. 1971. *La Vita Nuova.* De Gruyter Mouton.

Andrews, E. 2016. "What Was the Gordian Knot?" History.com. February 3. Retrieved April 19, 2022. https://www.history.com /news/what-was-the-gordian-knot

Ashton, K. 2015. *How to Fly a Horse: The Secret History of Creation, Invention, and Discovery.* Heinemann.

Ball, C. 2019. *Childhood Amnesia: Here's Why Your Child Can't Remember Being a Baby.* December 19. Parents. https://www.parents .com/kids/development/childhood-amnesia-heres-why-your-child-cant-remember-being-a-baby/

Baum, L. F. and Santore, C. 2021. *The Wizard of Oz.* Cider Mill Press.

Becker-Phelps, L. 2014. *Insecure in Love: How Anxious Attachment Can Make You Feel Jealous, Needy, and Worried and What You Can Do About It* (1st ed.) New Harbinger Publications.

Bellow, S. 2006. *The Adventures of Augie March.* Penguin Classics.

Binazir, A. 2011. *Are You a Miracle? On the Probability of Your Being Born.* August 16. HuffPost. Blog. https://www.huffpost.com/entry /probability-being-born_b_877853#:~:text=On%20my%20birthday%2C%20I%20had,about%20one%20in%20400%20trillion

Blake, W. 1994. *The Marriage of Heaven and Hell in Full Color.* Dover Publications.

Bolte Taylor, J. 2022. *Whole Brain Living: The Anatomy of Choice and the Four Characters that Drive Our Life.* Hay House UK LTD.

Borysenko, J. Z. 2005. *Healing and Spirituality: The Sacred Quest for Transformation of Body and Soul.* Hay House.

Bosker, B. 2017. "The App that Reminds You You're Going to Die." December 11. The Atlantic. https://www.theatlantic.com /magazine/archive/2018/01/when-death-pings/546587/

Boston Center for Contemplative Practice. 2019. "Imagine Ideal Parents (powerful exercise) | Dr. Daniel P Brown | TheBCCP [Video]. April 16. Accessed April 23, 2022. https://youtu.be/z2au4jtL0O4

Bowlby, J. 1983. *Attachment.* (2nd ed.) Harper Collins Publishers.

Brown, A. C. 2018. *I'm Still Here: Black Dignity in a World Made for Whiteness.* (1st ed.) Convergent Books.

Brown, B. 2018. *Dare to Lead: Brave Work. Tough Conversations. Whole Hearts.* (1st ed.) Random House.

Brown, B. 2019. *Braving the Wilderness: The Quest for True Belonging and the Courage to Stand Alone.* Random House.

Brown, D. P., and Elliott, D. S. 2016. *Attachment Disturbances in Adults: Treatment for Comprehensive Repair.* W.W. Norton & Company.

Brown, M. T., and Bussell, J. K. 2011. "Medication Adherence: Who Cares?" *Mayo Clinic Proceedings*, 86 (4), 304–14. doi.org /10.4065/mcp.2010.0575

Braidotti, R. 2013. *The Posthuman* (1st ed.) Polity.

Bronner, S. J. 2020. *Researchers Say This Is the Ideal Salary for Happiness and Well-being.* May 28. Inverse. https://www.inverse.com /innovation/this-is-the-way-to-think-about-money-to-lead-a-happier-life

Burke, A. 2018. *8 Poses for Iliopsoas Release.* July 2. Yoga International. Retrieved April 17, 2022. https://yogainternational.com /article/view/8-poses-for-iliopsoas-release

Callahan, R. J., and Trubo, R. 2013. *Tapping the Healer Within: Using Thought-Field Therapy to Instantly Conquer Your Fears, Anxieties and Emotional Distress.* Piatkus.

Cambridge University. 2021. "Scientists Reverse Age-Related Memory Loss in Mice." July 22. *Newswise.* Retrieved April 18, 2022. https://www.newswise.com/articles/scientists-reverse-age-related-memory-loss-in-mice

Cameron, J. 2016. *The Artist's Way: A Spiritual Path to Higher Creativity.* TarcherPerigee.

Campbell, J. 2004. *Pathways to Bliss: Mythology and Personal Transformation.* New World Library.

Campbell, J. 2008. *The Hero with a Thousand Faces.* (3rd ed.) New World Library.

Campbell, J. 2012. *Myths of Light: Eastern Metaphors of the Eternal.* New World Library.

Campbell, J., and Moyers, B. 1991. *The Power of Myth.* Anchor.

Campbell, J., and Roberts, R. 1987. *Tarot Revelations.* Vernal Equinox.

Campbell, J. 2013. *Thou Art That: Transforming Religious Metaphor.* New World Library.

Carey, B. 2010. "Evidence That Little Touches Do Mean So Much." February 22. *New York Times.* https://www.nytimes.com/2010 /02/23/health/23mind.html?scp=3&sq=touch&st=cse

Casey, B. J. 2011. Behavioral and Neural Correlates of Delay of Gratification 40 Years Later." *Proceedings of the National Academy of Sciences*, 108 (36): 14998–15003.

Chu, C.-N. 2007. *The Art of War for Women*. Crown Business.

Cialdini, R. 2021. *Influence: The Psychology of Persuasion*. Harper Business.

Clear, J. 2018. *Atomic Habits: An Easy & Proven Way to Build Good Habits & Break Bad Ones*. Avery.

Corporate Finance Institute. 2022. "Cognitive Bias." January 22. Retrieved April 18, 2022. https://corporatefinanceinstitute.com/resources/knowledge/trading -investing/list-top-10-types-cognitive-bias/

Cowell, A. 1992. "After 350 Years, Vatican Says Galileo Was Right: It Moves." October 31. New York Times. Retrieved April 19, 2022. https://www.nytimes .com/1992/10/31/world/after-350-years-vatican-says-galileo-was-right-it -moves

Cozolino, L. 2013. *The Social Neuroscience of Education: Optimizing Attachment and Learning in the Classroom* (illustrated edition). W. W. Norton & Company.

Cozolino, L. 2014. *Attachment-Based Teaching: Creating a Tribal Classroom*. W. W. Norton.

Cuartas, J., Weissman, D. G., Sheridan, M. A., Lengua, L., and McLaughlin, K. A. 2021. "Corporal Punishment and Elevated Neural Response to Threat in Children." April 9. *Child Development*, 92 (3) 821–32.

Cummings, E. E. (1964). *Seventy-Three Poems*. Faber.

Dana, D., and Porges, S. W. 2018. *The Polyvagal Theory in Therapy: Engaging the Rhythm of Regulation*. W.W. Norton & Company.

Darko. 2020. "19 Amazing MLM Statistics You Should Read in 2020." February 19. Jobsinmarketing.io. Retrieved April 18, 2022. https://jobsinmarketing.io /blog/mlm-statistics/

Darwin, C. 1898. *The Expression of Emotions in Man and Animals*. D. Appleton and Company.

Day, L. 1999. *Practical Intuition for Success: A Step-by-Step Program to Increase Your Wealth Today*. HarperPerennial.

deGrasse T. N. 2017. *Astrophysics for People in a Hurry* (1st ed.) W.W. Norton & Company.

Delizonna, L. 2017. "High-Performing Teams Need Psychological Safety. Here's How to Create It" August 24. *Harvard Business Review*. Accessed April 16, 2022. https://hbr.org/2017/08/high-performing-teams-need-psychological -safety-heres-how-to-create-it

Desmond, M. 2017. *Evicted: Poverty and Profit in the American City*. Crown.

Dickenson, E. 1924. *The Complete Poems of Emily Dickenson*. Pantianos Classics.

Driver, J., and van Aalst, M. 2011. *You Say More Than You Think: A 7-Day Plan for Using the New Body Language to Get What You Want*. Harmony.

Driver, J., and van Aalst, M. 2014. *You Can't Lie to Me: The Revolutionary Program to Supercharge Your Inner Lie Detector and Get to the Truth*. HarperOne.

Dwyer, C. P. 2017. *Critical Thinking Conceptual Perspectives & Practical Guidelines*. Cambridge University Press.

Dwyer, C. P. 2018. "12 Common Biases That Affect How We Make Everyday Decisions." September 7. Psychology Today. Retrieved April 18, 2022. https ://www.psychologytoday.com/us/blog/thoughts-thinking/201809/12 -common-biases-affect-how-we-make-everyday-decisions

Dzedzickis, A., Kaklauskas, A., Bucinskas, V. 2020. "Human Emotion Recognition: Review of Sensors and Methods." MDPI Sensors, 20 (3). Accessed April 16, 2022. https://www.mdpi.com/1424-8220/20/3/592

The Economist. 2021. "How Many American Children Have Cut Contact with Their Parents?" May 20. The Economist. https://www.economist.com/united -states/2021/05/20/how-many-american-children-have-cut-contact-with -their-parents

Edmondson, A. C. 2019. *The Fearless Organization: Creating Psychological Safety in the Workplace for Learning, Innovation, and Growth*. John Wiley & Sons.

Elkind, D. 2010. *The Hurried Child: Growing Up Too Fast Too Soon*. Da Capo Press.

Erikson, E. 1994. *Identity and the Life Cycle*. W. W. Norton & Company.

Estroff Marano, H. 2003. *"Our Brain's Negative Bias."* June 20. *Psychology Today*. Retrieved April 19, 2022. https://www.psychologytoday.com/us/articles /200306/our-brains-negative-bias

Fagan, D. (n.d.). "The Role of the Psoas Muscle in Common TMS Symptoms." My TMS Journey. Retrieved April 17, 2022. https://mytmsjourney.com /resources/the-role-of-the-psoas-muscle-in-common-tms-symptoms/

Fair, J. 2021. "Apex Predators in the Wild: Which Mammals Are the Most Dangerous?" Discovery Wildlife, Accessed April 14, 2022. https://www .discoverwildlife.com/animal-facts/mammals/hunting-success-rates-how -predators-compare/

Farah, S. 2015. *The Archetypes of the Anima and Animus*. Center of Applied Jungian Studies. Accessed April 16, 2022. https://appliedjung.com/the -archetypes-of-the-anima-and-animus/

Feinstein, D., and Eden, D. 2005. *The Promise of Energy Psychology: Revolutionary Tools for Dramatic Personal Change*. Jeremy P. Tarcher/The Penguin Group.

Feintzeig, Rachel. 2014. "Want to BE a CEO? Stand Tall." June 9. Wall Street Journal. https://www.wsj.com/articles/BL-ATWORKB-1831

Feldman Barrett, L. 2018. *How Emotions Are Made: The Secret Life of the Brain*. Mariner Books.

Feldman Barrett, L. 2020. "People's Words and Actions Can Actually Shape Your Brain—a Neuroscientist Explains How." November 17. ideas.ted.com. Retrieved April 18, 2022. https://ideas.ted.com/peoples-words-and-actions -can-actually-shape-your-brain-a-neuroscientist-explains-how/

Forster, E. M. 2022. *Aspects of the Novel*. Dover Publications.

Freeman, R. 2012. *The Mirror of Yoga: Awakening the Intelligence of Body and Mind*. Shambhala.

Freud, S. 1915. *The Psychopathology of Everyday Life*. Macmillan Company.

Friedman, F. 1975. *There's No Such Thing as a Free Lunch: Essays on Public Policy*. Open Court Publishing Company.

Gardner, H. 2006. *Multiple Intelligences: New Horizons*. Basic Books.

Gay, R. 2017. *Hunger: A Memoir of (My) Body* (1st ed.) Harper Collins.

Gender Spectrum. 2021. "Understanding Gender." May 25. Gender Spectrum. https://www.genderspectrum.org/articles/understanding-gender.

Gibran, K., Baer, U., and Wallis, G. 2019. *The Prophet with The Forerunner and The Madman*. Warbler Classics.

Gibson, L. 2015. *Adult Children of Emotionally Immature Parents: How to Heal from Distant, Rejecting, or Self-Involved Parents*. New Harbinger Publications.

Gilbert, E. 2016. *Big Magic: Creative Living Beyond Fear*. Penguin Publishing Group.

Gildiner, C. 2020. *Good Morning, Monster: A Therapist Shares Five Heroic Stories of Emotional Recovery*. St. Martin's Press.

Gladwell, M. 2019. *Blink: The Power of Thinking Without Thinking*. Back Bay Books.

Godin, S. 2007. *Purple Cow: Transform Your Business by Being Remarkable* (1st ed.) Penguin Books.

Godin, S. 2011. *Linchpin: Are You Indispensable?* (1st ed.) Portfolio.

Godin, S. 2018. *This Is Marketing: You Can't Be Seen Until You Learn to See*. Portfolio.

Gorman, J. 1999. *The Seven Principles for Making a Marriage Work*. Potter/ Tenspeed/Harmony.

Gottlieb, L., and Winch, G. 2020. "Jeff's Critical Parents." (Audio podcast episode). September 17. In *Dear Therapists*. Podbean. https://www.podbean .com/media/share/dir-4scvd-a9bffd9

Grant, A. 2014. *Give and Take: Why Helping Others Drives Our Success*. Penguin Books.

Grant, A. 2021. *Think Again: The Power of Knowing What You Don't Know*. Viking.

Grant, A., and Sandberg, S. 2017. *Originals: How Non-Conformists Move the World*. Penguin Books.

Gray, D. 2016. *Liminal Thinking: Create the Change You Want by Changing the Way You Think* (1st ed.) Two Waves Books.

Gover Tawwab, N. 2021. *Set Boundaries, Find Peace: A Guide to Reclaiming Yourself.* TarcherPerigee.

Hanh, T. N. 2005. *Happiness: Essential Mindfulness Practices.* Parallax Press.

Harari, Y. N. 2019. *21 Lessons for the 21st Century.* Random House.

Harlow, H. F. 1971. *Learning to Love.* Jones & Bartlett Learning.

Harlow, H. F. 1979. *Human Model: Primate Perspective.* V. H. Winston.

Hasa. 2020. "What Is the Difference between Mood and Emotion. February 11. Pediaa.Com. Retrieved April 17, 2022. https://pediaa.com/what-is-the-difference-between-mood-and-emotion/

Hay, L. 1984. *You Can Heal Your Life.* Hay House.

Hay, L. 2013. *Anger Releasing* (Audiobook). Hay House.

Heid, M. 2018. "Does Thinking Burn Calories? Here's What the Science Says." September 19. *Time.* https://time.com/5400025/does-thinking-burn-calories/

Hendricks, G. 2010. *The Big Leap: Conquer Your Hidden Fear and Take Life to the Next Level.* HarperOne.

Hendrix, H., and Hunt, H. 2019. *Getting the Love You Want: A Guide for Couples* (3rd ed.) St. Martin's Griffin.

Hinds, A. 2013. "Messages of Shame Are Organized Around Gender: A Conversation with Brené Brown about How Men and Women Experience Shame Differently." April 26. *The Atlantic.* Accessed April 16, 2022. https://www.theatlantic.com/sexes/archive/2013/04/messages-of-shame-are-organized-around-gender/275322/

Hopkins, C. 1923. *Scientific Advertising.* Cosimo Classics.

Hoffer, E. 2006. *Reflections on the Human Condition.* Hopewell Publications.

Hoffer, E. 2010. *The True Believer: Thoughts on the Nature of Mass Movements.* Harper Perennial.

Hossain Salahuddin. 2019. "The Tibetan Book of the Dead—A Way of Life." October 28. (Video, 1 of 2). https://www.youtube.com/watch?v=P5A2erZXJx8

TED Talk. 2019. "How Does Income Affect Childhood Brain Development?" Kimberly Noble. January. Retrieved April 17, 2022. https://www.ted.com/talks/kimberly_noble_how_does_income_affect_childhood_brain_development?language=en.

Huber, C., and Shiver, J. 2001. *There Is Nothing Wrong with You: Going Beyond Self-Hate.* Keep It Simple Books.

Huddleston, T. 2021. *"Mega Millions Is Up to $970 Million—There's One Way to Up the Odds of Winning, According to a Harvard Statistics Professor."* January 21. CNBC. https://www.cnbc.com/2021/01/21/how-to-up-the-odds-of-winning-a-lottery-harvard-professor.html

Huston, M. 2017. *Why Daughters of Unloving Mothers Struggle with Shame.* June 23. *Psychology Today.* https://www.psychologytoday.com/us/blog/tech-support/201706/why-daughters-unloving-mothers-struggle-shame

Isaacson, W. 2018. *Leonardo da Vinci.* Simon & Schuster.

Johnstone, K. 1987. *Impro: Improvisation and the Theatre* (1st ed.) Routledge.

Joyce, J. 1916. *Dubliners.* B.W. Huesch, Inc.

Judith, A. 1987. *Wheels of Life: A User's Guide to the Chakra System.* Llewellyn Publications.

Judith, A. 2004. *Eastern Body, Western Mind: Psychology and the Chakra System as a Path to the Self.* Ten Speed Press.

Judith, A. 2018. *Charge and the Energy Body: The Vital Key to Healing Your Life, Your Chakras, and Your Relationships.* Hay House Inc.

Judith, A., and Goodman, L. 2012. *Creating on Purpose: The Spiritual Technology of Manifesting Through the Chakras* (1st ed.) Sounds True.

Jung, C. G. 1968. *Man and His Symbols.* Dell Publishing Co.

Jung, C. G.1976. *Psychological Types.* Princeton University Press.

Jung, C. G. 1989. *Memories, Dreams, Reflections.* Vintage Books.

Jung, C. G. 2017. *Modern Man in Search of a Soul.* Martino Fine Books.

Juveniles and the death penalty. American Civil Liberties Union. (n.d.) Retrieved April 19, 2022. https://www.aclu.org/other/juveniles-and-death-penalty.

Kabat-Zinn, J. 2013. *Full Catastrophe Living: Using the Wisdom of Your Body and Mind to Face Stress, Pain, and Illness.* Bantam Books.

Kahneman, D. 1986. Fairness as a Constraint on Profit Seeking Entitlements in the Market. *American Economic Review,* 76 (4), 728–41. http://www.jstor.org/stable/1806070

Kaplan, K. 2018. "Brain Scans Reveal That Friends Really Are on the Same Wavelength. January 30. *Los Angeles Times.* https://www.latimes.com/science/sciencenow/la-sci-sn-friends-brains-same-20180130-story.html

Karp, H. 2015. *The Happiest Baby on the Block: The New Way to Calm Crying and Help Your Newborn Baby Sleep Longer* (2nd ed.) Bantam.

Karp, H., and Spencer Scott, P. 2008. *The Happiest Toddler on the Block: How to Eliminate Tantrums and Raise a Patient, Respectful, and Cooperative One- to Four-Year-Old.* Bantam.

Keleman, S. 1989. *Emotional Anatomy: The Structure of Experience.* Center Press.

Kenfield, K. 2018. "Are You Doing These 5 'Anti-Empathy' Strategies?" September 30. Kate Kenfield. Retrieved April 19, 2022. https://katekenfield.com/articles/antiempathy

Kennedy-Moore, E. 2014. *Raising Emotionally and Socially Healthy Kids* (Audiobook) The Great Courses.

King, S. 2000. *On Writing: A Memoir of the Craft* (1st ed.) Scribner.

Knapp, B. L. 1979. *Anais Nin.* Ungar.

Kohlberg, L., and Puka, B. 1994. *Kohlberg's Original Study of Moral Development.* Garland.

Koltko-Rivera, M. E. 2006. "Rediscovering the Later Version of Maslow's Hierarchy of Needs: Self-Transcendence and Opportunities for Theory, Research, and Unification." *Review of General Psychology.*

Kondo, M. 2014. *The Life-Changing Magic of Tidying Up: The Japanese Art of Decluttering and Organizing* (1st ed.) Ten Speed Press.

Konnikova, M. 2017. *The Confidence Game: Why We Fall for It . . . Every Time.* Penguin Books.

Konnikova, M. 2021. *The Biggest Bluff: How I Learned to Pay Attention, Master Myself, and Win.* Penguin Books.

Kueper, J. 2015. "Evidence for the Adverse Effect of Starvation on Bone Quality: A Review of the Literature." *International Journal of Endocrinology 2015.* 1–7. doi.org/10.1155/2015/628740

Lakhiani, V. 2020. *Code of the Extraordinary Mind: 10 Unconventional Laws to Redefine Your Life and Succeed on Your Own Terms.* Rodale Books.

Lamott, A. 1995. *Bird by Bird: Some Instructions on Writing and Life* (1st ed.) Anchor.

Levine, A., and Heller, R. S. F. 2012. *Attached: The New Science of Adult Attachment and How It Can Help You Find—and Keep—Love.* TarcherPerigee.

Levine, P. 2021. *Two Techniques That Can Help Trauma Patients Feel Safe.* July 8. NICABM. Retrieved April 18, 2022. https://www.nicabm.com/trauma-two-simple-techniques-that-can-help-trauma-patients-feel-safe/

Levine, P. A. 1997. *Waking the Tiger: Healing Trauma.* North Atlantic Books.

Levine, P. A. 2015. *Trauma and Memory: Brain and Body in a Search for the Living Past: A Practical Guide for Understanding and Working with Traumatic Memory.* North Atlantic Books.

Li, Q. 2018. *Forest Bathing: How Trees Can Help You Find Health and Happiness.* Penguin Life.

Loudenback, T., and Gould, S. 2017. "Here's How Much Money You Actually Take Home from a $75,000 Salary Depending on Where You Live." November 2. *Business Insider.* https://www.businessinsider.com/salary-after-taxes-us-cities-2017-9

Lowen, A. 1995. *Joy: The Surrender to the Body and to Life* (1st ed.) Penguin Books.

Lowen, A., and Lowen, L. 2012. *The Way to Vibrant Health: A Manual of Bioenergetic Exercises* (1st ed.) Alexander Lowen Foundation.

Lucas Films. 1983. *Star Wars: Return of the Jedi.* Disney Plus. https://www.disneyplus.com.

MacLaughlin, S. S. 2020. *Helping Young Children with Sharing.* Zero to Three. Accessed April 14, 2022. https://www.zerotothree.org/resources/1964-helping-young-children-with-sharing

MacLean, P. D. 1990. *The Triune Brain in Evolution: Role in Paleocerebral Functions.* New York: Plenum Press.

Maclear, K., and Arsenault, I. 2017. *Virginia Woolf.* Book Island.

Mardell, A. (n.d.) *An Accompaniment (Abridged) to the ABCs of LGBT+.* Publitas. https://view.publitas.com/none-122/the-gay-bcs-of-lgbt/page/12-13

Magee, R. V., and Kabat-Zinn, J. 2019. *The Inner Work of Racial Justice: Healing Ourselves and Transforming Our Communities Through Mindfulness.* TarcherPerigee.

Maslow, A. H. 2013. *A Theory of Human Motivation.* Martino Publishing.

Maté, G. 2010. *In the Realm of Hungry Ghosts: Close Encounters with Addiction.* North Atlantic Books.

McDermott, N. 2014. *How to Do a Perfect Plank.* November 10. Greatist. Retrieved April 17, 2022. https://greatist.com/fitness/perfect-plank#plank-variations

Menakem, R. 2017. *My Grandmother's Hands: Racialized Trauma and the Pathway to Mending Our Hearts and Bodies.* Central Recovery Press.

O'Neal, K. 2004. *Art of Seduction.* Gardners Books.

MacIsaac, T. 2015. "Five Scientific Discoveries Made in Dreams." November 8. Ancient Origins. https://www.ancient-origins.net/unexplained-phenomena/five-scientific-discoveries-made-dreams-004491

McKee, R., and Gerace, T. 2018. *Storynomics: Story-Driven Marketing in the Post-Advertising World.* Grand Central Publishing.

McLeod, S. 1970. *Cognitive Dissonance.* January 1. Simply Psychology. Retrieved April 18, 2022. https://www.simplypsychology.org/cognitive-dissonance.html.

McLeod, S. 1970. *Erik Erikson's Stages of Psychosocial Development.* January 1. Simply Psychology. Retrieved April 18, 2022. https://www.simplypsychology.org/Erik-Erikson.html

Miller, A. 1990. *For Your Own Good: Hidden Cruelty in Child-Rearing and the Roots of Violence.* (3rd ed.) Farrar, Straus, and Giroux.

Miller, A. 1997. *The Drama of the Gifted Child: The Search for the True Self.* (3rd ed.) Basic Books.

Millman, D. 2006. *Way of the Peaceful Warrior: A Book That Changes Lives.* H. J. Kramer.

Mischel, W. 1970. "Attention in Delay of Gratification." *Journal of Personality and Social Psychology, 16* (2): 329–37.

Mischel, W., Shoda, Y., and Rodriguez, M. L. 1989. "Delay of Gratification in Children." 26 May. *Science, 244* (4907): 933–38.

Mitchell, S. 2002. The Bhagavad Gita. Crown Publications.

Miyazaki, Y. 2018. *Shinrin Yoku: the Japanese Art of Forest Bathing.* Timber Press.

Mock, J. 2014. *Redefining Realness: My Path to Womanhood, Identity, Love & So Much More* (1st ed.) Atria Books.

Molecular Devices. (n.d.) "What Is an Action Potential?" *MolecularDevices,* Accessed April 16, 2022. https://www.moleculardevices.com/applications/patch-clamp-electrophysiology/what-action-potential#gref

Montagu, A. 1952. *Darwin: Competition & Cooperation.* H. Shuman.

Montagu, M. 1986. *Touching: The Human Significance of the Skin.* (3rd ed.) Harper & Row.

Moran, G. 2009. "Mini-MBQS-V Revised Mini-MBQS 25 Items for Video Coding." Unpublished article. https://works.bepress.com/gregmoran/49/

Morishima, Y., Schunk, D., Bruhin, A., Ruff, C. C., and Fehr, E. 2012. Linking Brain Structure and Activation in Temporoparietal Junction to Explain the Neurobiology of Human Altruism. July 12. *Neuron,* 75 (1): 73–9. doi.org/10.1016/j.neuron.2012.05.021

Morningstar, D. 2018. *Out of the Fog: Moving from Confusion to Clarity After Narcissistic Abuse.* Morningstar Media.

Morris, D. 1996. *The Human Zoo: A Zoologist's Classic Study of the Urban Animal.* Kodansha Globe.

Mowbray, D. 2019. "Greatest Scientific Discoveries that Were Made in Dreams." August 7. Mattress Online Blog. https://www.mattressonline.co.uk/blog/sleep-science/greatest-scientific-discoveries-that-were-made-in-dreams/

Murdock, J. 2020. "Humans Have More than 6,000 Thoughts Per Day, Psychologists Discover." July 15. *Newsweek.* Retrieved April 19, 2022. https://www.newsweek.com/humans-6000-thoughts-every-day-1517963

Murphy, K. 2020. *You're Not Listening: What You're Missing and Why It Matters.* Celadon Books.

Nelson, B. 2019. *The Emotion Code: How to Release Your Trapped Emotions for Abundant Health, Love, and Happiness.* St. Martin's Essentials.

Nestor, J. 2020. *Breath: The New Science of a Lost Art.* Riverhead Books. NeuroHealth Associates. 2019. *The Science of Brainwaves—The Language of the Brain.* Retrieved April 19, 2022. https://nhahealth.com/brainwaves-the-language

Netflix. 2019. *Brené Brown: The Call to Courage.* Retrieved April 18, 2022. https://www.netflix.com/title/81010166

No author is given. 2018. *Toddler Property Laws • kellymom.com.* January 1. KellyMom.com. Retrieved April 19, 2022. https://kellymom.com/fun/wisdom/property/

Nummenmaa, L., Glerean, E., Hari, R., and Hietanen, J. K. 2014. "Bodily Maps of Emotions." January 14. PNAS. doi.org/10.1073/pnas.1321664111

Orwell, G. 1972. *Down and Out in Paris and London.* Mariner Books.

Osho. (n.d.) *Buddha – Beliefs – Seeking?* Osho.com. Retrieved April 19, 2022. https://www.osho.com/osho-online-library/osho-talks/buddha-beliefs-seeking-b3466bc2-879?p=2190e605d86a97fb6cdc1e66b5a9e275

Palmer, A., and Brown, B. 2015. *The Art of Asking: How I Learned to Stop Worrying and Let People Help.* Grand Central Publishing.

Park Hong, C. 2020. *Minor Feelings: An Asian American Reckoning.* Random House Publishing Group.

Parkinson, C., Kleinbaum, A. M., and Wheatly, T. 2018. "Similar Neural Responses Predict Friendship." January 30. *Nature News.* Retrieved April 19, 2022. https://www.nature.com/articles/s41467-017-02722-7

Patterson Neubert, A. 2018. "Money Only Buys Happiness for a Certain Amount." *Perdue University News.* Accessed April 16, 2022. https://www.purdue.edu/newsroom/releases/2018/Q1/money-only-buys-happiness-for-a-certain-amount.html

Perel, E. 2017. *Mating in Captivity: Unlocking Erotic Intelligence.* HarperCollins.

Perel, E. 2018. *The State of Affairs: Rethinking Infidelity.* Harper Paperbacks.

Pert, C. 2005. *Your Body Is Your Subconscious Mind.* Sounds True.

Pert, C. B. 1999. *Molecules of Emotion: The Science Behind Mind-Body Medicine* (1st ed.) Simon & Schuster.

Piaget, J., Gabain, M., and Gabain, R. 2014. *The Language and Thought of the Child.* Routledge.

Piaget, J., and Inhelder, B. 1969. *The Psychology of the Child.* Basic Books.

Pink, D. 2009. *Drive: The Surprising Truth About What Motivates Us.* Riverhead Books.

Planned Parenthood. (n.d.) "What Are Gender Roles and Stereotypes?" Planned Parenthood. https://www.plannedparenthood.org/learn/gender-identity/sex-gender-identity/what-are-gender-roles-and-stereotypes

Porges, S. W. 2011. *The Polyvagal Theory: Neurophysiological Foundations of Emotions, Attachment, Communication, and Self-Regulation.* W.W. Norton.

Pressfield, S. 2002. *The War of Art: Break Through the Blocks and Win Your Inner Creative Battles.* Black Irish Entertainment.

Raichle, M. E., and Gusnard, D. A. 2002. "Appraising the Brain's Energy Budget." August 6. *Proceedings of the National Academy of Sciences, 99* (16), 10237–39. doi.org/10.1073/pnas.172399499

Rank, O. 2010. *The Trauma of Birth.* Martino Fine Books.

Rank, O., and Nin, A. 1989. *Art and Artist: Creative Urge and Personality Development.* W. W. Norton & Company.

Rank, O., and Robbins, F. 2016. *The Myth of the Birth of the Hero: A Psychological Interpretation of Mythology.* Palala Press.

Rifkin-Graboi, A. 2015. "Maternal Sensitivity, Infant Limbic Structure Volume and Functional Connectivity: A Preliminary Study". October 27. *Translational Psychiatry, 5* (10). doi.org/10.1038/tp.2015.133

Rogers, C. R. 1987. *On Becoming a Person*. Thomas Allen & Son.

Ruff, M. 2014. "The Legacy of Dr. Candace Pert, Beyond the Molecules of Emotion by Michael Ruff." (Video). Retrieved April 19, 2022. https://www.youtube.com/watch?v=yVzS0Radz5Q

Rushkoff, D. 2021. *Team Human* (1st ed.) W.W. Norton & Company.

Sagan, C. 2019. *Contact*. Gallery Books.

Sagan, C., deGrasse Tyson, N., & Druyan, A. 2013. *Cosmos*. Ballantine Books.

Sagar, K. 1971. *Hamlet (Shakespeare)*. Blackwell.

Sapolsky, R. M. 2004. *Why Zebras Don't Get Ulcers* (3rd ed.) Holt Paperbacks.

Sapolsky, R. M. 2018. *Behave: The Biology of Humans at Our Best and Worst*. Penguin Books.

Sarno, J. E. 1991. *Healing Back Pain: The Mind-Body Connection* (1st ed.) Warner Books.

Schlam, T. R. 2013. "Preschoolers' Delay of Gratification Predicts Their Body Mass 30 Years Late." *The Journal of Pediatrics, 162* (1): 90–93.

Sharma, S. *Peter Levine Somatic Experiencing*. April 2010. Relational Implicit. https://relationalimplicit.com/zug/transcripts/Levine-2010-04.pdf

Siegel, D. 2020. *The Developing Mind: How Relationships and the Brain Interact to Shape Who We Are*. (3rd ed.) The Guilford Press.

Sinek, S. 2021. *Start with Why: How Great Leaders Inspire Everyone to Take Action*. Segyesa.

Sinek, S., Mead, D., and Docker, P. 2017. *Find Your Why: A Practical Guide for Discovering Purpose for You and Your Team*. Portfolio.

Singer, D. G., and Revenson, T. A. 1997. *A Piaget Primer: How a Child Thinks*. (Revised ed.) International Universities Press.

Sherman, R. 2019. *Uneasy Street: The Anxieties of Affluence*. (2nd ed.) Princeton University Press.

SLT for Kids. 2022. Child 5–12 Years. Retrieved April 18, 2022. https://sltforkids.co.uk/ages-and-stages-developmental-milestones/child-5-12-years/

Small, M. F. 1999. *Our Babies, Ourselves: How Biology and Culture Shape the Way We Parent*. Anchor.

Small, M. F. 2001. *Kids: How Biology and Culture Shape the Way We Raise Our Children* (1st ed.) Doubleday.

Small, M. F. 2006. *The Culture of Our Discontent: Beyond the Medical Model of Mental Illness* (1st ed.) Joseph Henry Press.

Smith, C.U.M. 2010. "The Triune Brain in Antiquity: Plato, Aristotle, Erasistratus." January 15. *Journal of the History of the Neurosciences*. https://www.tandfonline.com/doi/abs/10.1080/09647040802601605

Smith, D. 2019. "What Everyone Gets Wrong About This Famous Steve Jobs Quote, According to Lyft's Design Boss." April 19. *Business Insider*. Retrieved April 19, 2022. https://www.businessinsider.com/steve-jobs-quote-misunderstood-katie-dill-2019-4

Spiritist Medical Association. 2018. *The Legacy of Dr. Candace Pert: Beyond the Molecules of Emotion by Michael Ruff, PhD*. November. (Video). https://www.youtube.com/watch?v=yVzS0Radz5Q

Spock, B. 2012. *Dr. Spock's Baby and Child Care, A Handbook for Parents of Developing Children from Birth to Adolescence* (9th ed.) Pocket Books.

Stanborough, R. J. 2020. "Does Everyone Dream and Other Interesting Dream Facts." May 12. Healthline. Retrieved April 18, 2022. https://www.healthline.com/health/healthy-sleep/does-everyone-dream

Stanier, M. B. 2016. *The Coaching Habit: Say Less, Ask More & Change the Way You Lead Forever*. Box of Crayons Press.

Stewart Holland, S., and Silvers, B. 2020. *I Think You're Wrong (But I'm Listening): A Guide to Grace-Filled Political Conversations*. Thomas Nelson.

Stone, A. M. 2020. "90 Seconds to Emotional Resilience." November 12. https://www.alysonmstone.com/90-seconds-to-emotional-resilience/

Strayed, C. 2012. *Tiny Beautiful Things: Advice on Love and Life from Dear Sugar*. Knopf Doubleday Publishing Group.

Strecker, M. 2018. "Less Is More in Remembrance of Stanley Keleman." *International Body Psychology Journal, 17* (2) 52–56. https://www.ibpj.org/issues/articles/Strecker%20-%20Less%20is%20More.pdf

Successful By Design. 2020. *Drive (Daniel Pink)*. (Video). March 4. https://www.youtube.com/watch?v=Ulx5d6nhqz8

Sun-Tzu. 1992. *The Art of War by Sun-Tzu*. Penguin Books.

Szalavitz, M. 2010. "Touching Empathy." March 1. *Psychology Today*. https://www.psychologytoday.com/us/blog/born-love/201003/touching-empathy

Taylor, J., and Taylor, J. 1978. *The Bible*. Printed by Fay & Davison (1813).

Taylor, R. P. 2002. *Order in Pollock's Chaos*. December 1. *Scientific American*. Retrieved April 18, 2022. https://www.scientificamerican.com/article/order-in-pollocks-chaos/

Taylor, S. R. 2018. *The Body Is Not an Apology: The Power of Radical Self-Love* (1st ed.) Berrett-Koehler Publishers.

TED. 2010. *The Riddle of Experience vs. Memory* (Video). https://www.ted.com/talks/daniel_kahneman_the_riddle_of_experience_vs_memory?language=en

The Doc. (n.d.). "7 Great Examples of Scientific Discoveries Made in Dreams." Famous Scientists. https://www.famousscientists.org/7-great-examples-of-scientific-discoveries-made-in-dreams/

Thurman, R.A.F. 1993. *The Tibetan Book of the Great Liberation: Or the Method of Realizing Nirvana through Knowing the Mind*. Random House Publishing Group.

Tolle, E. 2005. *A New Earth: Awakening to Your Life's Purpose* (1st ed.). Penguin Books.

Toms, M. 2005. *The Wisdom of Joseph Campbell in Conversation with Michael Toms* (Audiobook). Hay House.

Turner, R. (n.d.). "10 Dreams That Changed Human History." World of Lucid Dreaming. https://www.world-of-lucid-dreaming.com/10-dreams-that-changed-the-course-of-human-history.html

Van der Kolk Bessel, B. 2015. *The Body Keeps the Score: Brain, Mind, and Body in the Healing of Trauma*. Penguin Books.

Voss, C., and Raz, T. 2016. *Never Split the Difference: Negotiating as If Your Life Depended on It* (1st ed.). HarperBusiness.

Walker, P. 2013. *Complex PTSD: From Surviving to Thriving: A Guide and Map for Recovering from Childhood Trauma* (1st ed.) CreateSpace.

Walker, P. 2015. *The Tao of Fully Feeling: Harvesting Forgiveness Out of Blame*. CreateSpace.

Ware, B. 2019. *Top Five Regrets of the Dying: A Life Transformed by the Dearly Departing*. Hay House, Inc.

Watanabe, M. 1974. "The Conception of Nature in Japanese Culture." January 25. *Science*. Retrieved April 18, 2022. https://www.science.org/doi/10.1126/science.183.4122.279

WBOC. 2021. "The Chances of You Being Born Are Far Lower Than You Think." March 25. WBOC TV. https://www.wboc.com/story/43554205/the-chances-of-you-being-born-are-far-lower-than-you-think.

Whitman, W. 1855. *Leaves of Grass*. American Renaissance Books.

Wiener, M., and Mehrabian, A. 1968. *Language Within Language: Immediacy, a Channel in Verbal Communication*. Appleton-Century-Crofts.

Williamson, M. 1992. *A Return to Love: Reflections on the Principles of 'A Course in Miracles.'* HarperOne.

Winnicott, D. W. 1971. *Playing and Reality*, Routledge.

Wolynn, M. 2017. *It Didn't Start with You: How Inherited Family Trauma Shapes Who We Are and How to End the Cycle*. Penguin Life.

Zeldetz V. 2018. "A New Method for Inducing a Depression-Like Behavior in Rats." February 18. *Journal of Visualized Experiments: JoVE*. Retrieved April 16, 2022. https://pubmed.ncbi.nlm.nih.gov/29553503/

Zoë. 2021. *Social Bodies the Shaping of Internal and External Worlds*. www.ThirdspaceSomatics.com

ACKNOWLEDGMENTS

THANK YOU TO MY grandmothers Ethel and Erika. As I was writing *The Parinama Method*, I felt inspired by the bravery and sacrifices you made to make my life possible. Your presence was deeply felt, and it is your brilliance and resilience that I attempt to represent in these pages. I often celebrate the unique freedoms I enjoy—knowing that you did not have them—and any good that I do in my life I dedicate to you both.

Thank you to everyone who contributed to *The Parinama Method* project, either directly by working on it or indirectly through your encouragement and inspiration—every kind word and lesson has made a difference.

To my editor, Alison C. Lowander, thank you for guiding me in the process of becoming a writer with your skill and brilliance—acting as Sherpa, coach, and guardian angel through the year-long editorial process; *The Parinama Method* wouldn't have been possible without you. Your wisdom both shaped the book and contributed to my own transformation while writing it.

And to my designer, Sheila Parr, for providing validation with the early visuals and bringing the experience of reading the book to another level through talent and vision in layout, design, and illustrations. Your guidance and patient support gave me energy when it was sorely needed—and you taught me that great design is just as much about what you leave out as what remains. Thank you Jacquelyn Krieger for the introduction.

Also, thanks to everyone who helped create visuals, do research and do other bits of mundane work. Christiana Grant for helping compile the bibliography. Scott Hussey for the author's photo. To the early readers who generously gave their time, insight, and encouragement—a special thank you to Connie S., Judy H., Rachel Walter, Leonor Veiga, Robert S., Sam, and Kurt for taking the time to share detailed feedback—your in-depth notes and calls supported the clarity and direction for the future of *The Parinama Method*. There's a world of difference between saying "that's good" and taking the time to explain what works and how other parts could be better—thank you. To the hundreds of people who participated in interviews and shared personal experiences from their lives as individuals, colleagues, partners, children, and parents: I continue to be in awe of your openness and vulnerability that supported so much of the content within this book. And thank you to the psychologists, developmental biologists, therapists, executives, and academics who generously offered their time to discuss their work and proffered candid feedback on mine. In addition, I'm thankful to Jeannette McLaughlin for legal counsel and to Marynka Burnes and Michelle Laidlaw (rest in peace) for getting excited and laughing *with* me about wild ideas. Marynka, we met through John and Nicole Churchill over a decade ago at Samadhi, and it has been a joy and solace to work with you to elevate this mission. You are a radiant mix of vision and practical application, mixed with real-world practicality that makes important things (like a beautiful website) possible.

This book is intended to make complex material accessible, and it is through the skilled and detailed work of Haley Hampton on the proofreading that all the details were attended to so the reader can focus on the book and not the bloopers—proofreading is an often overlooked step and working with Haley showed me how getting the little details right is a big deal. Thank you to Laura Robinson for the support and knowledge in understanding the publishing industry—it means a lot to work with someone I know from elementary school (when our fourth hubs were under development).

I'm eternally grateful for all the encouragement (which may have been against their better judgment) when I started this project. Bob Stringer's ongoing mentorship and generosity were a gift beyond measure—using your good name opened so many doors for me. An early conversation with Diane Hessan—when I needed it the most—surprised and elevated my sense that I was on to something: thank you, Diane. Kurt Fisette for telling me it was time to step up; I'm not sure that this is what you expected me to do—you are the constant constructive collaborator that has been energizing my work for the last fifteen years. Dana Cordova for her wise counsel when I needed it: "Henry Ford didn't invent the car, he invented the assembly line." And thanks to all the inspirational leaders who continue to honor me with their time and encouragement, especially Connie Steward, Judy Habib, and Sam Zimmerman. I still have to pinch myself every time we connect... I'm so lucky.

A special thank you to The Boston Public Library Copley branch. I owe a debt of gratitude to the work of the hundreds of authors and creators who inspired and kept me company throughout the writing process—thank you from the bottom of my heart. It is my aspiration for this book to support others in making their own contributions.

To my friends who were patiently by my side as I processed this work through the filter of my own experience, thank you for always taking my calls and being physically present whenever possible, especially my beloved friend Amy, along with Adia (holding a special place in my heart), Imani, Moziah, and Iyla. You all brought light, laughter, and insight into my life and home as I wrestled with the manuscript. To my sister, Liz, for important early conversations about pleasure, satisfaction, and stigma that were foundational to early thinking on the topic: thank you for always being my rock during turbulent times. And my thanks to every person who lit me up through this strange and often challenging process—sometimes a single conversation or note put wind in my sails and kept me going. A special thank you to Joy GR, who introduced me to Anodea Judith's work, and the participants in Anodea's workshops who helped me learn and grow. And to the many loved ones and dear friends who inspired me in ways both large and small before and throughout the process of creating this method: Buddy, Lisa B., Georgia, Mira, Bagus, Mary S., Dafina, Lauren P., Derrick, Jonathan, Tarikh, Jose, Dasha, Chris D., Kristen T., Jaimee, Jordan, Margarita, Danielle M., Pete, Sarah G, Sara, Kimmie, Erik M., Mimi, Mohammed, Chad, David, Rebecca S., Becca, Nikki T, Matt M., Jon F., Marieme, Ben, Aileen C., Taro, Courtney, Samara, Joseph, Gaynelle, Joel, Kelsey, Sam, Kate W., Roman, Dan Brown, Kate O, Jane, Natalie P., and Les K. And a heartfelt thank you to my childhood guardian angel: Anne V.

The team at Funnel.io has been fantastic and supportive, a special thank you to Kevin and Bob, and also my group: Maggie, Brian, Tyler, Aaron, Nehal, and Marty. Spending time with fantastic people was extremely important during the last year of this process. The organization Fredrik Skantze has built is a demonstration of what is a possibility for all companies: to humanize the process of building successful software companies.

And a special thank you to you, Luke C. Skywalker Bickford, my constant companion, and spiritual advisor.

ABOUT THE AUTHOR

KATIE BICKFORD IS AN award-winning executive who has been building high-performing sales organizations both nationally and internationally for over 20 years. Three of her companies grew to become publicly listed on a major stock exchange and/or acquired for over a billion dollars. Bickford attributes her success to her passion for identifying and unlocking human potential. In addition to her own long-standing practice, she has obtained extensive training in teaching yoga, meditation, and a wide range of related studies in India, Thailand, Bali, Europe, and the United States. She holds a BS in Biology from Keene State College, NH, and currently lives in the Back Bay of Boston, MA.